PRUDERY AND PASSION

PRUDERY & PASSION

Milton Rugoff

Rupert Hart-Davis London

Granada Publishing Limited
First published in Great Britain 1972 by
Rupert Hart-Davis Ltd
3 Upper James Street London W1R 4BP

ISBN 0 246 10529 1
Printed in Great Britain by
Fletcher & Son Ltd, Norwich

Acknowledgments

I wish to express my thanks to the Institute for Sex Research, Inc., of Indiana University and especially the librarian, Mrs. Rebecca Dixon, for making available various rare books in their collection. I also wish to thank the librarians of the Rare Book Division and the American History Room of the New York Public Library, the Mercantile Library and the Library of Mechanics and Tradesmen, both in New York City, and the libraries of Westchester County, especially Greenburgh.

I am also grateful to William Targ for valuable suggestions and to my wife, Helen, for her unwearying assistance.

On the one hand Nature urges us on to this desire by associating it with the noblest, most useful and pleasant of all her acts; and on the other hand she allows us to condemn it and flee from it as from a shameless and immodest deed, to blush at it and recommend abstinence. Are we not indeed brutes to call the very act that created us, brutish?

—MONTAIGNE, in his essay on Vergil

Preface

A principal cause of the sexual revolt of our time is the moral standards of the nineteenth century, and yet readers will look in vain in our histories for any adequate treatment of this theme. Although two of the most familiar names of periods in the American past, Puritan and Victorian, have a predominantly sexual connotation, our historians have told us little or nothing about sexual behavior or attitudes in either period. They have told us how our forebears prayed and played, worked and warred, what their songs and superstitions were, their books and clothes, their triumphs and defeats. But they have been completely silent on how Americans loved, how they expressed or repressed their sexual desires, and how their attitudes toward sexuality influenced their education, books, art and speech, their dress, pastimes, and medical practice and, above all, their family life and love relationships.

The historians have been silent largely because they as much as their readers have been bound by taboos that are themselves Puritan or Victorian in origin. For almost fifty years we have been freeing ourselves from these restraints, and it is time that we examined without shame and in some depth the sexual activities and attitudes of our forebears.

To do justice to all aspects of the subject, I have approached it from three directions. Part I examines the prudery; Part II, "The Partisans of Love," presents the attitudes and the fate of those who rebelled, and Part III, "Hidden Fires," reveals the evasions and more or less furtive escapes from prohibitions and taboos.

Although I have concentrated on the period between 1789 and 1900, I have in the "Background" section and elsewhere traced nineteenth-century attitudes back to their Puritan roots and sometimes beyond. And in the Epilogue I have tried to bring the account up to date—to the revolution that is shaking us today, that threatens to jettison the sexual standards not only of the American past but of much of the Judeo-Christian tradition.

Contents

Part 3

Hidden Fires

Background

1.

GOD, THE FLESH, AND THE PURITAN WAY

IT all began in the Garden of Eden. According to the story in Genesis, Adam and Eve were created innocent and divinely happy. They were naked, but they did not care. Apparently to test them, the Lord told them about the Tree of Knowledge and then tantalizingly forbade them to eat of it. They disobeyed, and the very first thing they learned was that they were naked and that this was the most shameful of all conditions. Immediately they covered themselves with fig leaves. But it was too late. The Lord thrust them out of Eden and put a curse on them and all their progeny to the end of time.

Now, Genesis does not explain the Lord's motives in creating Adam and Eve innocent and then in tempting them and allowing them to yield to the temptation. It does not explain why the first evil they were made aware of was their nakedness. Nor does it explain why becoming aware of sexual desire became a sin—and a sin unto eternity—presumably because they were not first "married."

Despite all these mysteries surrounding the Biblical tale, everyone who has accepted the Bible literally, and notably the Puritans, believes that the chief cause of the suffering of all mankind was Adam and Eve's disobedience, the shame of their nakedness, and their desire for each other.

It is upon this primitive folk myth of a treacherous serpent and a human being fashioned out of a rib that the Christian West was for two thousand years to base its tradition of the sexual act as the original sin. Even the Freudian explanation of this story as an Oedipal myth does not dispel its barbarous quality.

The most influential fathers of the church encouraged this tradition: St. Paul distrusted women, allowing them only the function of serving man and bearing children, and St. Augustine, guilt-ridden at having indulged himself inordinately in his youth, later practiced rigorous self-denial. Pathologically revolted by the entire process of conception, St. Augustine said: "We are born between the feces and the urine." St. Jerome fled into the desert to avoid temptation—yet confessed that even while his body was half dead with fasting, "the fires of lust kept bubbling up before me." It was hardly surprising that early Roman converts to Christianity, revolted by the debauchery of the age, should have embraced the asceticism of the new religion. Later, the great Protestant reformers, Luther, Calvin, and Knox, did nothing to abate this distrust of sexuality and in some ways intensified it.

Even the sanctification of the Virgin Mary in the Middle Ages failed to offset the evil attributed to Eve. Indeed, all Protestants rejected, with a distaste as intense as the medieval adulation, this elevation of a woman. John Donne, having exchanged the erotic ardors of his youth for the holy fervors of an Anglican divine, said, "I know the fathers are frequent in comparing and paralleling Eve and Mary. But God forbid any should say that the Virgin concurred to our good so as Eve did to our ruin."

To the long, long shadow cast by the Fall, Christian zealots added the warning that no earthly love should rival man's love of God. Whereas the pagans celebrated fertility rites, venerated an Earth Mother and phallic symbols, and made a place for such gods as Dionysius, the Christians deified a chaste Christ and his virgin mother, and advocated the celibacy of the priest and monk and the chastity of the nun.

In the Christian view, any act of sexual love was, as Wayland Young says,[1] a betrayal of God. Had the average man followed this creed, European man might have died out through continence.

The church taught that man's body was perishable clay and that its functions were beastly. Self-denial and continence became virtues, and the indulgence of the masses in sexual activity, one of the few pleasures that cost nothing, was constantly denounced. Thus sexuality was transformed from an instinct and appetite into a matter of right or wrong, a sin, and, at last, a crime. By a radical distortion, an act in which the parties participated willingly and gave each other as much pleasure as they could was equated with stealing, slander, and assault, in all of which one individual mercilessly injures another.

So it was that an act of love performed by the primal man and woman left Judeo-Christian man with a withering sense of guilt.

As most Americans know, the very first text that New England children learned, from 1690 on, was the rhyme,

In Adam's fall
We sinned all.

Intended to acquaint five-year-olds with the initial letter of the alphabet, it taught them, in one sledgehammer blow, that they were damned. Guilt was stamped on their souls as soon as they could read. The letter *A*, which today stands for excellence, would forever mean for them, especially if they saw it on the breast of an adulteress, Hell.

The Puritan attitude toward the sins of sexuality was a matter of religious conviction backed up by the habit of frugality. The conviction stemmed from the Protestant revolt against the Catholic and Anglican churches as morally corrupt. The frugality, part of a credo of thrift and industry, made any indulgence seem like a waste of time and money, one that would lead to ruin.

All the fervor behind this point of view came, of course, from a religious conviction, especially since the main Puritan spokesmen on morality, at least until 1750, were the preachers. It was they who gave the Puritan opposition to any sexual freedom its intensity. Beside their lightning and thunder, their dreadful warnings and prophecies, the moral strictures of the Victorians appear to be only priggish pleas for propriety.

The Puritan code was at least a total commitment: to God and to the view of man's fate formulated by John Calvin. And it was a basic tenet of that belief that copulation outside of marriage was a sin whose wages were damnation. The sin was also a crime, punishable by man with fines, whipping, branding, banishment, and even death. If there was one sin the Puritans were thinking of when they proclaimed that man was inherently depraved and tainted by original sin, it was this one. The believer who sinned might escape detection on earth, but guilt would haunt him all the days of his life and eternal torment awaited him in the hereafter.

Whence came the harshness of this drive to suppress all sexuality outside of wedlock? Why did the Puritans struggle so frantically for a century and a half against all such indulgence? In the dim background was Hebrew law and legend with its recurrent expression of fear that man was weakened by sexual intercourse, its references to the sexual act as a "little death" and even as a form of castration.[2] The morning prayers of orthodox Jews still proclaim: "I thank Thee, Lord, for not having created me a woman." But far more important were the lesson of Adam and Eve, the Seventh Commandment, and the pitiless warnings in Leviticus. Of course, acceptance of these guides entailed the rejection of a welter of Biblical evidence of polygamy, concubinage, and other Near Eastern forms of mating that we think shameful.

What really moved the Pilgrims to such prohibitions and suppressions was their profound respect for the power of temptation and their recognition of the weakness of the flesh in both man and woman. There was little or no hypocritical effort to deny the force or pleasure of passion. Nor did they assume, as did Victorian prudes, that in any seduction the woman was only a passive victim. When that Puritan of Puritans, Cotton Mather, railed against fornication (in his *Magnalia Christi Americana*) early in the eighteenth century, he described his own lustful visions in such palpable detail and gave such dramatic accounts of how he had barely escaped the temptation offered by admiring young ladies that his books and sermons must have excited as much as edified his audience.

The men in the first waves of Pilgrims were lusty English yeomen, stubborn-minded dissenters stout enough to brave the unknown New World, while the women, as Hawthorne described them in *The Scarlet Letter,* were coarser in moral fiber, as well as in other ways, than their descendants. (Nor should we forget the adventurers, the weak-willed, and, among the indentured servants, the pardoned criminals.) The Puritans were, in short, realists who had no faith in celibacy, a virile breed only too well aware of the hungers of the body. This alone may explain both the repressiveness of the Puritan code and the fact that there were always sinners—passionate and uninhibited sinners—and enough of them to appall fainthearted reformers and enrage fanatics.

Puritans were at least in theory the enemies of such worldly pleasures and self-indulgence as had marked England's archbishops, kings, and cavaliers. And in America they remained faithful to their Calvinist vows long after Cromwell and his Roundheads had given way to the Restoration. To their preachers the senses seemed a snare and a delusion, enslaving the soul and polluting the body by means of fleeting joys. Desire was a beast that must be disciplined. And of all desires the most subversive of total devotion to God was sexuality. They polarized holy and profane love and decreed that the latter must be restricted to procreation. (This rigid restriction may well have been a carryover from early Biblical days when the survival of a people often depended on its size and especially the number of its warriors.)

So it was that the first code of law in Connecticut,[3] adopted in 1638–39 and borrowing its terms and punishments from Leviticus, decreed that if any man or woman should commit adultery, or lie with a beast, or if any man should lie with another man, he should be put to death, and that if any man was guilty of fornication with a maid, the couple should be forced to marry or should be fined or be given corporal punishment, or be subjected to all three penalties. With supreme distrust of their fellowmen the Puritans opposed anything they thought might inflame concupiscence, frowning on dancing, singing, kissing, flirting, and gay clothes, and banning shows and frivolity.

We shall see how they succeeded.

Hardly had God's order been established in New England when signs of backsliding appeared. As early as 1642, Governor William Bradford of Plymouth Plantation bewailed the fact that the strictest surveillance and punishment had not been able to "suppress the breaking out of sundrie notorious sins . . . not only incontinence between persons unmarried . . . but some married persons also. But that which is worse, even sodomy and buggery (things fearful to name) have broken forth in this land oftener than once." [4] Sermons during the next half-century increasingly deplored the waning of the Pilgrim enthusiasm and the decay of morals.[5] As the community grew and prospered, so did its vices and sins. Security encouraged relaxation, and ease permitted a little self-indulgence. Ministers fulminated against a splendid array of sins: worldliness, drunkenness, luxurious clothes, lewdness, fornication, and adultery. There was even shocked talk of a brothel in Boston. In *God's Controversy with New England* (1662), the Puritan versifier Michael Wigglesworth had the Creator amazed at the change that had taken place in the Puritans:

> If these be they, how is it that I find
> In stead of holiness Carnality,
> In stead of heavenly frames an Earthly mind,
> For burning zeal luke-warm Indifferency,
> For flaming love, key-cold Dead-heartedness,
> For temperance (in meat, and drinke, and cloathes) excess?

By 1682, Increase Mather, sovereign theocrat, goad of the less holy, seeing Massachusetts declining in manners and morals to the level of Virginia, was crying, "Be astonished at this, O ye Heavens!" [6] The decline must indeed have baffled such men. Moral crusaders are forever appalled by the realization that the God they adore made procreation dependent on sexual desire. There is for them a profound perversity in the fact that unless lads and maids itch with desire—and desire that is impure since it begins long before marriage—the race is doomed. The Increase Mathers are fanatics whose own sense of guilt or other psychic deformities makes it impossible for them to understand that desire cannot be suppressed. Despite their best efforts, the fires of sexuality burned in Boston as hotly as ever.

A very early visitor, Jasper Danckaerts, a Netherlander seeking land for a sect known as Labadists, had this to say of vaunted Boston morality in 1680: ". . . you discover little difference between this and other places. Drinking and fighting occur there not less than elsewhere, and as to truth and true godliness, you must not expect more of them than of others." Summing up in a sentence both the inroads of worldly pursuits and the waning prestige of the church, he adds: "While we were there four sons of ministers were learning the silversmith's trade." [7]

We now know that there were many sexual irregularities well before marriage. Bundling, the quaint, curiously naïve practice of allowing a couple to go to bed together in their clothes allegedly in order to keep warm and save fuel, was not uncommon in New England and especially on Cape Cod. A typical reference occurs in the church trial of a Joseph Tucker in which two witnesses testified that they had seen him and Susannah Pelton "early in the morning in bed together, covered with bedding." [8] Although preachers complained about bundling, and it was certainly a most un-Puritanical kind of liberty, it probably did little damage to morals as long as it was confined to courting couples close to marriage. But the practice appears to have spread and become so scandalous that churchmen, including Jonathan Edwards, sought to put a stop to it. As late as 1781 a preacher at Dedham, only ten miles from Boston, attributed the alarming increase in unlawful intercourse to the custom of young women "admitting young men to their beds who sought their company with intentions of marriage." And such candid verses as the following in a popular almanac in 1785 make clear that the practice was then still very much alive:

It shant be so, they rage and storm
And country girls in clusters swarm,
    And fly and buzz like angry bees,
    And vow they'll bundle when they please.
Some mothers, too, will plead their cause,
And give their daughters great applause
    And tell them, 'tis no sin nor shame,
    For we your mothers did the same.'

If I won't take my sparks to bed
A laughing stock I shall be made.

But where's the man that fire can
    Into his bosom take,
Or go through coals on his foot soles,
    And not a blister make? [9]

With its warm, cozy overtones, the tradition of bundling is a valuable corrective to stereotypes of the pervasive bleakness of the Puritan world. In the privacy of their households some rural families were obviously far from being as strict with their daughters as their preachers would have liked. When young couples in the middle of the eighteenth century began to use sofas for courting purposes, such is the force of custom that some old-fashioned parents actually insisted that bundling was more proper.

It has even been suggested that bundling and other such liberties were encouraged as a way of hastening and possibly precipitating early marriage.[10] Marriage was, in fact, the only tolerable state for either a man or a woman in the colonial period. It provided a man with a homemaker, an all-around servant, and a convenient source of sexual satisfaction. It saved a woman from the dreaded fate of spinsterhood and from dependence on relatives (except for teaching, there was no way for a single woman to support herself), and it gave her an outlet for sexual and maternal urges. If it also made her a man's property, that was after all the common lot of women.

Even more substantial is the evidence of unreserved intimacy before marriage, first in the confessions of young married couples seeking admittance to a church and, still plainer, in the number of babies born to unwed mothers or less than seven months after the marriage of their parents. The records of confessions are too scattered to permit broad generalizations, but they do give us some startling glimpses of the sexual activity of Puritan youth. During the Great Awakening from 1726 to 1744 there were many admissions of premarital incontinence, and of sixteen couples admitted to full communion in the church at Groton from 1789 to 1791, nine confessed to fornication before marriage. The records of children born very prematurely or out of wedlock are much more extensive because it was nearly impossible to keep such births secret. Few practices reveal the cruelty of the Puritan elders more harshly than their branding as bastards any baby born to a married couple well before the normal term. To avoid having the infant damned, most such couples made a shameful and degrading public confession of the sin of fornication.

Despite the severe penalties meted out to women who bore children out of wedlock, the records of every colony are liberally sprinkled with such cases. In 1883, Charles Francis Adams, distinguished member of the Adams family, declared: "The illegitimate child was more commonly met with in the last than in the present century and bastardy cases furnished a class of business with which country lawyers seem to have been as familiar as they are with liquor cases now." [11] It is not difficult to account for such a disregard of the most rigid prohibitions. Trapped in the bleak sobriety of a New England settlement, some young people found the temptation irresistible and had no way of avoiding the consequences. Copulation is notoriously the one pleasure that even the poorest can afford.

As with bundling, some country families took an unexpectedly lenient view of an unwed daughter who bore a child: Apparently all children were welcome in the effort to people and conquer the wilderness. Doubtless there was a certain amount of admiration for the intensity of passion thus revealed. In some areas the stigma of having borne a child out of wedlock did not linger, and the guilty maid had no particular difficulty in getting a husband. In a surprising number of towns the authorities closed their eyes to such births, especially if the burden of supporting the child did not fall on the community.

There were even unregenerate creatures who had two and three children without benefit of marriage. Several went so far as to defy the church authorities. A celebrated hoax, generally attributed to Benjamin Franklin, was the so-called "Speech of Polly Baker"—first published in 1747—before a New England court where she was being prosecuted for bearing her fifth child out of wedlock. Polly concluded her saucy defense by asserting that she was simply obeying the Biblical injunction to increase and multiply, and that she deserved, "instead of whipping to have a statue erected to my memory."

Although the penalty for fornication was generally a fine and a public whipping, hardly a day passed in Massachusetts without a conviction for this offense—a paltry number until we realize that it represents only the very few that were apprehended. As we know from *The Scarlet Letter,* several colonies made a woman taken in adultery wear a capital *A* on her dress forever, and a few went so far as to decree death for this act. Most records of such cases supply few or no details, but those that do give any information reveal that a persistent lover, especially one who could give a religious turn to his ardor, might have as much success in a New England town as anywhere else. The idea that devout men and women were free to mate without benefit of religious or legal marriage was, in fact, a tenet of the Brownists, a Puritan sect that influenced a number of emigrants to New England.

One of the few records of a trial for fornication that go into detail was that of a Captain Underhill. As early as 1638 he had been suspected of "incontinence" with a neighbor's wife. The report was that "the woman being young and beautiful and withal of a jovial spirit and behavior, he did daily frequent her house, and was divers times found there alone with her, the door being locked on the outside." The captain claimed that the goodwife was in trouble and under temptation and that they were praying together. Some time later he was accused by "a more godly young woman" of having "solicited her chastity under pretence of Christian love" and of having confessed to her that he had oftentimes had his will of the cooper's wife, and "all out of strength of love." Underhill finally confessed in congregation, explaining that for six months the woman had resisted

> all his solicitations (which he thought no woman could have resisted) before he could overcome her chastity, but being once overcome she was wholly at his will. And to make his peace the more sound, he went to her husband . . . and fell upon his knees before him in the presence of some of the elders . . . and confessed the wrong he had done him, and besought him to forgive him, which he did very freely, and in testimony thereof he sent the captain's wife a token.[12]

Underhill's story is a good example of the solemn absurdities to which religion-inspired suppression of sex had led. The persistent captain had the satisfaction of bedding his neighbors' wives, boasting of his conquests under the guise of confessing them, and having his philanderings condoned by the deceived husband and his own wife.

Although there was not yet a double standard in the nineteenth-century sense, women convicted of adultery were generally punished more severely than men, suffering not only fines but a public whipping. Both men and women were set in the stocks and given from ten to thirty strokes on the bared back.

Like the public confession, wherein the victim was expected to reveal shameful details of the sin, the public whippings yielded a vicarious sexual experience—a mixture of sadism and mass voyeurism cloaked in righteous disapproval. For citizens lacking other shows and entertainments a confession or a whipping was an exciting spectacle, a welcome interruption of the grim monotony of New England life. Such a scene challenges any assumption that the Puritans were a disciplined breed who had subdued the sexuality in themselves. They gathered on such occasions to watch as a woman convicted of uncontrolled desire bared her back down to the waist and was whipped by a man with a kind of erotic violence later made notorious by the Comte de Sade. Or the legs of the woman might be thrust into the bilboes, a pair of shackles on a bar that was often raised above the culprit's head, thus punishing indecency with indecency.

Unless the characterizations in *The Scarlet Letter* are completely unreliable, the adulterous passion of Hester Prynne and the Reverend Arthur Dimmesdale is witness to the ineffectuality of the Puritan prohibitions. Although Hester is evidently a woman of remarkable character and will power, and Dimmesdale is worshiped by everyone for his nobility and spirituality, both were willing to carry a love affair to the point of no return. The lovers are haunted by guilt, but Hester never voices any regret for what she has done and is ready some seven years later to flee to England with Dimmesdale and their daughter. A study in the pangs of conscience, *The Scarlet Letter* is nevertheless testimony to the force of love literally in defiance of Hell.

Despite the strictness of the Puritan code, men who emigrated to America without their wives showed a tendency to remarry without disclosing their earlier ties. The New England authorities generally punished such a man if he came to their attention, and they often tried to break up the second marriage. There was, moreover, little or no place in the New World for unmarried men: Every settler needed a wife as housekeeper, a helper with farm work, and a bearer of other future workers.

For much the same reasons men remarried soon after a wife died. Since there were usually children from the first marriage, and sometimes many of them, widowers often remarried within a month or two, and a remarkable number of men took as many as three or four wives in the course of a lifetime. We who are accustomed to wives outliving their husbands may find this surprising until we recall that many a seventeenth-century woman married at eighteen, had eight or ten children in rapid succession, and having been pregnant much of her married life, died of overwork and obscure ailments before she was forty. A widower would often marry a second woman fifteen or twenty years younger than himself, have a few children by her, and if she too broke under the burden of bringing up too many children, including those of his first wife, he did not hesitate to turn to a third woman, who might be no older than his oldest daughter. Thus, unlike widows, who usually married older men, widowers were able to enjoy a succession of ever younger mates. In the women's rights movement of the mid-nineteenth century the more radical feminists argued that it was pure hypocrisy to accept this "serial polygamy" and yet condemn as bigamy a married man or woman who took a second spouse or a lover. The system did serve to keep many women too busy bearing and rearing children and running a house to think about rights, double standards, the development of their own personalities, or the fulfillment of their emotional life.

The same circumstances made prostitution uncommon. In the early period prostitutes were scarce because girls married young, sometimes at the age of fourteen or fifteen, few women lived outside of a family, and there were none of those poor working girls who in the nineteenth century would find it much easier to sell their bodies than their labor. The customers were also scarce because bachelors were few, and most men had little opportunity, especially in a small town, for commercial vice. Concealment of such activity in the average New England community was difficult. There was, finally, a dread if not of God then of the preacher. But soon bawds were turning up in such port cities as New York and Boston, no less than eleven of them being publicly whipped in New York in 1755;[13] by the early 1800's they had become a permanent part of the population of large cities.

Although New England dominated the colonial scene—at least until 1750—other social groups, notably in New York, Philadelphia, and the South, developed quite different customs and standards. The Dutch in the New Netherlands were a bourgeois, sober-sided, clannish people whose Protestantism was neither as spiritually intense or fanatical or as concerned with theological absolutes as the Calvinism of the English settlers to the north. Since they lived in a somewhat less hostile climate and on more fertile soil, their lives were not so austere and their family relations were warmer. Although their regulation of marriage was strict, they never imposed such merciless penalties on adultery as death or even the scarlet *A*. "Improper conduct" with women was a not infrequent charge against New Amsterdamers, and in the last years of Dutch rule, "sins of sensuality" were of common occurrence. In one case, which was soon hushed up, Peter Stuyvesant wrote bitterly of the daughter of a prominent Dutch family who had become the paramour of a married man. And Stuyvesant's own half-sister had a child by her fiancé, a rich bachelor who died before they could be married. In general, early marriage and large families—but not so large as those in New England—were the rule, bachelors were looked on with disfavor, and marriages were celebrated joyously and on occasion riotously.

The taking over of New Amsterdam by the English brought little change in manners. New York society continued to sanction conviviality, including much drinking. Sabbath observance became somewhat more stringent, but one traveler, Sarah Knight, remarked in 1704 that the Sunday laws were much less strict than in Boston. After the middle of the century, complaints increased, as elsewhere in the colonies, about the indulgence in luxuries and the relaxation of moral standards. One newspaper poem commented on the coy aspects of a lady's fashionable dress:

> Cut her hair the shortest dock. . . .
> Let her hoop extending wide
> Show her garters and her pride.
> Her stockings must be pure and white
> For they are seldom out of sight.[14]

Much more significant was, as we have noted, the public whipping in 1755 of prostitutes in the city. But this kind of Puritan rigor would soon be a thing of the past. After the Revolution, New York began to assume the aspect of a metropolis, with a conservative but urbane aristocracy and with many portents of the center of wealth and commerce it was to become.

At first the Quakers who settled Pennsylvania punished such moral trespasses as fornication with public whippings, but they were never as severe as the New England Puritans or even the earliest Virginia settlers. Within a few generations they were tolerating a variety of amusements and luxuries, and a visitor in 1722 was struck by the freedom with which men kissed young women. By 1770 Philadelphians had a reputation for spending more on clothes, hairdressers, and dancing lessons than any other group of colonists.

Coming from Boston at the age of seventeen, Benjamin Franklin made his name in Philadelphia with the calculated, shopkeeper's morality of *Poor Richard's Almanack*. The guidelines he worked out for himself under the heading of Chastity were nothing if not practical: "Rarely use venery but for health or offspring, never to dullness, weakness or the injury of your own or another's peace or reputation." But he was no hypocrite, and in his *Autobiography* he confesses that he was not able to hew to this prescription: "That hard-to-be-governed passion of youth hurried me frequently into intrigues with low women that fell my way." The result was several children born out of wedlock. Even more extraordinary is the fact that Franklin, defying all the taboos of the time, and with royal aplomb, acknowledged these children and furthered the career of one of them until he reached the governorship of New Jersey. But nothing is as incongruous as the fact that this model of a prudent man should have written, in the very decade of the Great Awakening, erotica—unabashed guides to or defenses of sensuality. His most famous piece of this kind was "Advice to a Young Man on Choosing a Mistress" (1746). With an Addisonian judiciousness he recommends an older woman because she will be in no danger of having children or of being ruined, she will be more experienced and discreet, she will be indistinguishable, below the waist, from a younger woman, and she will above all be more grateful. The aim, purely and simply, is maximum pleasure with maximum safety. At about the same time, he wrote "The Speech of Polly Baker," which is sometimes considered a half-jocular justification of his own indiscretions. It may seem surprising that such pieces, or his satire on breaking wind, or indeed his relaxed relations with woman on his sojourns in Europe, came from one who had once hearkened to the preaching of Increase and Cotton Mather and looked on the latter as guide and counsellor.

But Benjamin Franklin was a very uncommon man and the changes in his standards between boyhood and maturity are hardly representative. Closer to the average were the attitudes of Sally Wister, a Quaker girl of Welsh and German descent who was sixteen years old in 1777 when some officers in the Continental Army were quartered in her home in a Philadelphia suburb. She and her friends immediately prepared for an exciting encounter. "When we were alone," she wrote in her journal, "our dress and lips were put in order for conquest, and the hope of adventures gave brightness to each before passive countenance." We get a glimpse of how far restrictions had been lifted not only from her little flirtations with the officers but her reference to a "charming collection of books" that included Fielding's realistic *Joseph Andrews*. One of the officers, a Captain Dandridge from Virginia, even proposed marriage after only a very brief acquaintance. "Had we been acquainted seven years," she wrote, "we would not have been more sociable." Once, while they were alone in the parlor, he caught her hand and showed much disappointment when she would not let him kiss her. When he bade her farewell, however, she let him press her hand to his lips.[15] Sally's was an innocent freedom, but it was a far cry from the way such a girl would have behaved with strange officers a century earlier.

The ferment of the Revolutionary period resulted in greater social freedom, however temporary. According to Nicholas Cresswell, a young, well-born Englishman who spent the turbulent years 1774–77 fortune hunting in America, there were women who made a great show of piety to screen their true nature. At tea in the home of a Mrs. Bennett in New York, the young wife of a major cited Scriptures from Genesis to Revelations in support of her stern condemnation of a neighbor who had made a misstep. Her husband being away, Cresswell escorted the major's wife to her home and at her insistence stayed on. After supper and a glass of wine he "soon found she was made of warm flesh and blood." ". . . We entered," he writes, "into a very agreeable *tête-à-tête* and then O! Matrimony, matrimony, thou coverest more female frailties than charity does sins! Nicholas, if ever thou sinned religiously in thy life, it has been this time!" He concludes: "She showed in private, the air and behavior of a professed courtesan, and in bed the lechery of a guinea pig."[16]

The differences between the sexual standards of New York and Philadelphia and those of Boston were a matter of degree; the standards of the South were of another kind. They were the result, like almost everything else in the South, of those two peculiar institutions—plantations and slavery. Between them they created a master class, each member of which ruled an independent domain. In such a society as much damage is done to masters and mistresses as to slaves. Most corrupting of all was the habit of many masters of copulating with slave women and having children by them. As we shall see, the curious position of the white mistress that resulted from this practice influenced the attitude toward women throughout America in the second half of the eighteenth century.

The white woman on the big plantations had by 1800 already become a figure of romance, a cold white goddess surrounded by her menfolk with chivalric courtesy but often forced to accept or block out the fact that her husband took his pleasure of young black women. As we shall see, she contributed to the myth that the well-bred white woman in America was too pure for the voluptuous pleasures and must be shielded from all that was not ladylike or genteel.

We shall also see that this double standard influenced all Southern society, so that even the lower classes had much freer sexual relationships than their counterparts in New England.

The decline in Calvinist domination of moral standards began much earlier than is usually assumed. The kind of holy zeal that marked the first Pilgrims was, as Increase Mather lamented, waning steadily by the end of the seventeenth century. As early as 1706 the Reverend Cotton Mather in his *The Good Old Way* lamented that the common people no longer considered the clergy "Angels of God" or provided so generously for them. We must not be misled by such hysterical outbursts as The Great Awakening of the 1740's, by later revivals, or by the morbid exhortations of a Jonathan Edwards. These occurred precisely because there had been a sharp decline in devotion and a notable relaxation of moral standards and were each followed by a backsliding that was always more acute than the one before.

New forces were constantly undermining the dedication to God and his laws as interpreted by the Mathers and other Puritan high priests: the Age of Reason with its skepticism and deism, the Revolution, exalting civil and republican government at the expense of both monarchy and the church, the pioneer settler rejecting authority of every kind, the hectic pursuit of the dollar, the arrival of immigrants with different gods, and an optimism about man's future, not in the hereafter, but in this world, this brave New World.

The result was a period—from about the 1770's to the 1810's—of tolerance, a lull between Colonial Puritanism and nineteenth-century prudery, between the decline of Jonathan Edwards and the rise of Mrs. Grundy. It was far from being a time of license or hedonism, but it did accept luxuries and expensive clothes and carriages among those who could afford them. It was marked by the opening of theaters in every city and by young women venturing to see such plays as Nicholas Rowe's *The Fair Penitent*. Mixed dancing was tolerated, young women consorted more freely with young men, and chaperonage was not yet thought necessary. Women's street dress as well as ball gowns revealed bare necks and arms, and a display of ankles, garters, or silk stockings was not deemed a sin. Men dressed their hair almost as elaborately as did women, and pantaloons were noticeably tight. Readers felt free to read such forthright novelists as Fielding and Smollett, such a bold feminist as Mary Wollstonecraft, the letters of Lord Chesterfield, and the poetry of Byron. Drinking was widespread and heavy, even among the New England clergy,[17] and gambling and carousing were not unknown in the staid halls of Yale Divinity School.

But the interlude, if it was an interlude and not simply a period of transition, was brief. Before long, the forces of suppression and intolerance, in new guises, spread across the land. They were encouraged by an ever-increasing concern with propriety, a desexualizing of woman, and moral pretenses that amounted to fantasy. By 1840 prudery had reached extremes almost without parallel in Western society.

2.

FROM COTTON MATHER TO MRS. GRUNDY

ONE of the most significant results of democracy in nineteenth-century America was the rise to moral dominance of the middle class. With each man convinced that he was as good as the next, it was almost inevitable that the standards of this class should become those of the nation at large. It was also inevitable because the church, for a century and a half the absolute dictator of behavior, had lost much of its authority. The guides to behavior were no longer the ministers but the most respectable citizens.

The virtues that respectable citizens admired, as set forth in Parson Weems' *The Life of Washington* (1806), that masterpiece of priggishness, and later glorified in Horatio Alger's immensely popular stories for boys, were diligence, enterprise, prudence, sobriety, perseverance, and, finally, clean living, meaning continence.

Although we tend to think of America and England as sharing the same standards as well as the same ancestors and language, the English social situation was quite different from the one in America. England had retained, above all, a rigid class system. At the top of the pyramid was a privileged minority, a small group of titled or landed gentry who were rich enough to ignore bourgeois moral codes and had the leisure to indulge their appetites if they were so inclined. So strong were class distinctions that the so-called Lower Orders looked on the privileges of the aristocracy as the rights due to gentlemen. Such attitudes are perfectly illustrated in Samuel Richardson's novels, particularly in *Pamela,* in which the master of the house pursues his serving-maid with complete confidence in his right to bed her without marrying her.

At the bottom of the heap were the poor, and especially the masses of city poor—far more numerous than those in America—created by the industrial revolution. Brutalized by their life in slums that were as wretched as any in Europe, the lower classes practiced every vice, that is to say, every prohibited pleasure that might yield them relief from their misery. With little hope of climbing out of the depths, and sometimes as idle, through unemployment, as the rich, many of them were as uninhibited as the rich, and almost as free to do as they pleased. And plainly they were often pleased to fornicate, become whores and whoremongers, commit incest and rape, and breed babies as casually outside of marriage as in it. *My Secret Life,* the eleven-volume journal of a wealthy Victorian libertine, illustrates the lax morality of both rich and poor. The author devotes over three thousand pages to describing how easy it was for him as a man of means to seduce girls, usually of the working class, on the average of once a week for forty years.

The only privilege the English middle class seems to have enjoyed was that of proclaiming its views openly and having them received as though they were official. It also had the satisfaction of being constantly scandalized by the behavior of both its social superiors and its social inferiors.

There was also an important historical difference between the British and the Americans: The American Puritans maintained their stranglehold on social life for a century and a half, whereas their English brethren were crushed in 1660 after ruling for only eighteen years. Cromwell's Roundheads were succeeded, moreover, by the Restoration, notorious for its profligate nobility and its licentious plays and poetry. The nobles and the poets were gradually tamed, but when a species of lusty country squires emerged in the eighteenth century, almost no Puritan moralists remained to condemn their fleshly dissipations.

By contrast, America up to mid-nineteenth century had only one class, a variegated group of men who were neither rich nor poor, neither overprivileged nor underprivileged. They were not bourgeois in the French tradition of stodgy tradesmen and shopkeepers: Many of them were self-reliant farmers, venturesome settlers, or able Yankee craftsmen, yet in manners and morals they were the product of Puritanism combined with Poor Richard's faith in doing whatever was necessary to achieve success.

It would be as misleading to suggest that there was no elite in America as that libertines were typical of upper-class England. Tory families here and there, the patrician descendants of the Dutch along the Hudson and in New York, and of course the "first families" of the South formed aristocratic clusters, but except for the plantation slave holders—who would in time be humbled—they did not assume privileges. If they did, they were likely to be challenged or mocked by the commonalty.

Men of wealth did begin to appear in America in the 1840's and 1850's, but the democratic spirit of society still made it difficult for them to take full advantage of their means. Not only was there no aristocracy to teach them the pastimes of the privileged, but most of them had little taste or training for leisure-class indulgences. When a moneyed elite did take shape in the 1870's, however, the *nouveaux riches* soon appeared and learned to ape their excesses.

Until well after the Civil War America had no sizable body of degraded poor. There were always misfits and ne'er-do-wells, but just as democracy had kept the rich from the privileges of station, so it had saved the poor from degradation. Every poor man could hope to move upward sooner or later, and in anticipation of such a rise he generally held to much the same standards as his more successful neighbors.

Thus did the middle class become the principal molder of morals. Although this class was an undefined body with no official capacity or spokesmen, it made its will felt powerfully and pervasively. It confronted offenders with an immediate threat of community disapproval as well as the possibility of permanent disgrace. A sin against religion could keep a man from heaven, but an offense against the community code could keep him from a far more immediate and valuable goal—respectability. Mrs. Grundy had taken over from Cotton Mather.

Part 1

PRUDERY: THE DENIAL OF EROS

3.

THE WORSHIP OF RESPECTABILITY

SUSAN B. ANTHONY, pioneer in the women's rights movement, recalling her childhood in the 1820's, tells us that her mother went into seclusion before the birth of every one of her children. At the same time her grandmother would prepare all the necessary garments and bring them to the house without ever uttering a word about the event they were anticipating.[1] The degree of prudery revealed by such behavior is almost beyond our comprehension. It signifies not simply a neurotic modesty and a repression of natural impulses but an effort to repudiate the sexual implications of childbirth.

This abhorrence of all things sexual was not the old Puritan dread but an abject concern for the opinions of one's peers. Reputable citizens, no longer threatened with God's damnation (except by such Calvinist throwbacks as Timothy Dwight or in backwoods revival meetings) if they defied sexual taboos, kept up the tradition of suppression on social grounds. It was the shell of the old religious prohibitions without the kernel, the manner without the substance. And just as the tide of primitive Puritanism receded earlier than is commonly supposed, so social censorship, that prurient prudery that we call Victorian, began long before Victoria came to the throne. There were signs of it in the middle of the eighteenth century, and it reached full strength in the first decades of the nineteenth century. When a farmer's wife in a London play in 1798 [2] kept fearfully saying of another farmer's wife (who never even appears onstage), "What will Mrs. Grundy say?" the question became a popular joke. But by the 1830's, Mrs. Grundy had become the moral monitor of every bourgeois on both sides of the Atlantic.

Compared to the vengeful Jehovah of the Calvinists, the God of such Unitarians of the early nineteenth century as William Ellery Channing was a benign deity. Under the influence of the new creed, benevolence, forgiveness, and hope began to displace the dark prophecies and blood-chilling judgments of the old orthodoxy. The new faith repudiated infant damnation and original sin, and it insisted that man was at heart good and full of potentialities for being better.

The optimism—or at least the exuberance—of the Romantic era, the belief of the followers of William Godwin in man's perfectibility, contributed to this spirit. But by the time the message of the more popular preachers of the new religion or of the Transcendentalists and perfectibilitarians filtered down to the average man, it had been converted into mere self-satisfaction and righteousness. One of the consequences of this was an aversion to acknowledging the ugly or the sordid, the more violent emotions and the more ungovernable cravings, notably those of sexuality. How could someone committed to the ideals of nineteenth-century gentility concede that such a frenzy of the spirit, such a wildfire of the flesh as an orgasm could be the consummation of love? There was a tendency to gloss over such primal urges, to veil, gild, prettify, idealize or sentimentalize them, or simply to push them into the cellars of the mind.

As Longfellow and a host of lesser poets, mostly ladies, along with such immensely influential British poets as Tennyson of *The Idylls of the King,* exalted pure love and spiritual values, glorified chivalric ideals, gentlemanly conduct, and the domestic sentiments, it became more and more difficult for the average person to face squarely the realities of human nature and the more turbulent desires. What preparation for the facts of life was the emasculate purity of Tennyson's Galahad and the ineffable nobility of King Arthur?

When Thomas Arnold, headmaster of Rugby and father of Matthew Arnold, was asked in 1835 what one should do with such an argument against God as the existence of evil, he solemnly declared: "We should act and speak, and try to feel as if they had no existence, and then in the most cases they do cease to exist after a time." [3] Although he meant only that one's doubts about God would go away, there is clearly the implication here that the evil itself might also be exorcised in the same way.

Such an attitude points up one of the main differences between the Victorian and the Puritan, especially in their estimate of the power of sexuality. The Puritans were realists who did not dream of denying that women as well as men experienced the strongest desires or that libidinous visions beset many men beside libertines. The Puritan recognized the Devil as a mighty opponent, dragged him out into the open and fought him tooth and nail. The Victorian treated him as a gentleman would deal with an obstreperous beggar or drunkard, turning quickly away or seeing to it that he was sent back to the dark alleys whence he came. Or if the gentleman was one of the new humanitarians, earnest, priggish, and sentimental, he would give the creature a coin and the address of a religious "rescue society."

Whether in the colonial period or in nineteenth-century America, man's sexual relationship to women was one of domination and, by and large, selfish use. Under Puritanism man used the Bible to establish the absurd doctrine that he was woman's head and master, and that, as the descendant of the original temptress, woman had a sinful nature and a weakness of the flesh. But when, as the old religion receded after the Revolution, he no longer had a pretext for dwelling on her fleshly frailties, he began to extol her domestic virtues and her moral purity. He did so to the point where he was able to treat her as a drudge or a doll. Very little of his treatment of her recognized that she was, like himself, a mixture of qualities and neither goddess nor puppet. The victim of ages of Judeo-Christian prejudices, the vast majority of women accepted whatever fate men bestowed on them.

Once the excessive idealization of American woman had begun, it proceeded apace. Changing circumstances abetted this transformation. In pioneer New England, women had been busy with early marriage, bearing children and endless tasks around the homestead or in the kitchen. They had not had the leisure, money, or opportunity for the fashions, pastimes, or liberties that would eventually provoke the virulence of the Mrs. Grundys. But by the time of the Revolution, there were signs, especially among the well-to-do in the towns and on plantations, that woman was becoming the patron of fashion, repository of gentility, keeper of manners. As more and more men, particularly in the cities, left their homes daily to work in office, shop, or factory, the wife remained behind as mistress not only of household and children but of family taste, religion, social affairs, and ethical standards—the high priestess in the domestic shrine. The degree of her idleness became an index to her social position. As Thorstein Veblen later said, prosperity required respectable women to be freed from any taint of utility.

As a mother the American woman taught her children a code of behavior that stressed propriety, piety, and purity. As a wife she was expected to honor and obey as well as love her husband, to be submissive, gentle, innocent, and tender, a haven of comfort, unquestioning in her allegiance, and a fountain of inspiration and elevated thoughts. She must above all be a model of modesty. James Fenimore Cooper wrote in his *Notions of the Americans* in 1828: "Retired within the sacred precincts of her own abode, she is preserved from the destroying taint of excessive intercourse in the world . . . and her heart is untainted by the dire temptations of strife with her fellows." [4] The ideal woman would not trouble her pretty head with serious study or business or politics. Whereas her husband was assumed to be by nature physical, she was spiritual; whereas he was aggressive, she should be diffident; whereas he was daring, she was timid. She was more imaginative and sensitive but less stable; more affectionate, but more sentimental—in short, more angel and less human.

Women as much as men supported this view. In one of the most popular post-Civil War novels, *St. Elmo,* the author, Augusta Evans Wilson, makes her heroine, a learned young lady, exclaim: "God, the Maker, tenderly anchored womanhood in the peaceful, blessed haven of home; and if man is ever insane enough to mar the divine economy, by setting women afloat on the turbulent, roaring sea of politics, they will speedily become pitiable wrecks." [5] The law also encouraged this view: Since a woman could not own property or vote, she was in many respects, as feminists pointed out, in the class of children and idiots.

And yet, as every traveler noted, American women were

adored, etherealized, and treated with elaborate, almost absurd courtesy and gallantry. That outspoken British visitor, Harriet Martineau, noted in the mid-1830's that Americans boasted of the "chivalrous" treatment of women, meaning that a man would give his seat to a woman or guard her morals by "the strictest observance of propriety in her presence," or a husband might indulge his wife with money or let her head be filled with "religious excitement"—thereby diverting her attention from morals and politics. "In short," said Miss Martineau, "indulgence is given her as a substitute for justice." [6]

Such courtesy converted woman into a figure on a pedestal, a doll in a glass case—and so thrust her out of the real world. Because this was unction applied to an entire sex and was not a tribute to a particular woman, it was only a gesture; it gave women the title of angel or goddess but not the function. "When men *respect* women, they do not attempt to make fools of them," Captain Marryat, British naval officer and popular novelist, observed after a sojourn in America in 1837–38, "but treat them as rational . . . beings, and this general adulation is cheating them with the shadow while they withhold from them the substance." [7] It permitted men to succumb to their "baser instincts" while contritely admitting that they were of coarser fiber and closer to the animals. At the risk of oversimplification it may be said that men insisted on innocence in their womenfolk in proportion to their own incapacity or unwillingness to control their passions and thoughts.

In the South, this attitude led to an almost pathological conception of the purity of white women. It created a circle of behavior in which the preservation of that purity made the white men on plantations resort to black women for sexual gratification, while this in turn forced many of the white women to behave as though they were untouchable. The fantasy of the Southern white woman's purity also left their men obsessed with the need to protect them. Guiltily aware that they themselves had robbed the black men of their women, the white men's fears focused on the black man. Assuming that the black man lusted for white women out of both frustration and a thirst for revenge, the white man soon developed dreadful punishments for any Negro accused of familiarity with a white woman.

By the early 1800's the image of woman as Eve the Temptress was almost entirely overlaid by that of woman as the Madonna, the eternal virgin. The Eve image did persist both in life and in fiction, but in life she was identified with the prostitute (or, in the South, the black woman), degraded but indispensable. In fiction, American novelists, as Leslie Fiedler has shown,[8] embodied the Madonna conception in a Fair Maiden, chaste and asexual, but they sometimes poured their sexual fantasies into another figure, usually dark and exotic, sexually potent if not corrupting. But the Dark Lady was largely a figure of dreams or fears. In life, everything conspired to make woman try to be as sexually passive as possible.

Even the changing economy contributed to the rise in prudery. As money eclipsed God in American life, respectability became more important than piety. In place of the holy intensity of the Puritan war on sexuality came the distinctly middle-class belief that sexuality was vulgar. The Puritans bore down on sensual pleasures with the wrath of God; the Victorians treated them with suppression, euphemism, and silence.

The Victorian treatment succeeded no better than the Puritan. This is not to say that mid-nineteenth-century prudery was all hypocritical or a mask for license; the great majority of men and women of the time were probably convinced that sex was deplorable and that it was proper to censor, suppress, or ignore it. It does say that genuine innocence was characteristic mainly of young ladies of stable families and that it was valued in them partly for its usefulness in capturing a desirable husband. Sin had ceased to be a purely religious matter and was becoming more and more a social and economic question. Before 1850 a recreant had to cope in the main with his conscience and the opinion of neighbors; and it was of course easier to conceal a transgression from either of these two than from God. As Locker-Lampson put it in his *London Lyrics* (1857):

> They eat, and drink, and scheme, and plod,
> They go to church on Sunday;
> And many are afraid of God,
> And more of Mrs. Grundy.

So a bourgeois concern for propriety—or rather, the dread of impropriety—combined with a stale residue of the Puritan distrust of the instincts to suppress sexuality and to require, especially of the young, a rigid purity. There is no exaggerating how many times Victorians said that dishonor, meaning seduction, was worse than death.

Later in the century even Darwinism was made to yield support for the ideal of purity. Man's natural lusts, it was asserted, were a throwback to his animal origins. Darwinism became far more palatable when one learned that it was leading to ever loftier levels of spirituality. What could be more reassuring to a man than to be told that he was in the "foremost files of time"—willy-nilly, at the highest stage in man's moral development. Purity thus became a sign of civilization.

If the moral establishment was intolerant and unrealistic in condemning any errant thought or gesture as evil, it truly overreached itself in the virtues and ideals it set up. In its demand for chastity, piety, elevated sentiments, and purity of thought it was insufferably pretentious, encouraging a canting acquiescence. It is this acquiescence, this lip service to a priggish perfection that has made "Victorian" almost a synonym for sanctimony.

What mattered was appearances. For many Americans, decorous behavior and dutiful moralizing seem to have fostered the delusion that virtue had truly triumphed. Francis J. Grund, a Viennese who migrated to America in 1827 and lived there for ten years, interpreted the American's urge to conform as a product of the domination by majority opinion. He quotes a Bostonian as admitting: "In no other place, I believe, is there such a stress laid upon 'saving appearances.' "[9] In England, so Captain Marryat claimed, vice was constantly exposed in newspapers, thus subjecting it to public indignation, whereas America, "from national vanity and a wish that all should *appear* correct . . . conceals the facts and permits the guilty parties to escape without censure. . . ." Conjugal infidelity, he asserted, was hushed up. If their communities are "so much more moral as they pretend . . ." he argued, "why is it that they . . . form societies on such an extensive scale for the prevention of a crime from which they declare themselves to be exempt."[10]

Many Americans were much more afraid of seeming guilty of an impropriety than of actually being guilty of it. If an act or performance that might be thought improper could be given a morally or socially acceptable name or setting, it might well be approved. There were those of course who saw through this hypocrisy and mocked it. A striking instance occurred in Boston, according to Harriet Martineau, when someone suggested that Italian opera should be set up in the city. Another gentleman observed that people would be afraid of the very name, whereupon a third exclaimed, "O! call it Lectures on Music, with illustrations, and everybody will come." [11]

The contradictions between the theory that woman was purer than man and the observable fact that she was sometimes not so pure produced some revealing observations. In a tract against woman's suffrage in 1869, the Reverend Horace Bushnell, a keen observer, wrote: "Women often show a strange faculty of debasement and moral abandonment, when they have once given way consentingly to wrong. Men go down by a descent—*facilis descensus*—women by a precipitation." [12] What Bushnell did not note was that the tighter the bonds, the more violently they snap.

To imply that all Americans in the nineteenth century were hypocrites or moral frauds would be far too sweeping and would crudely lump together various types, some of which were in fact the opposite of each other. The Victorians who accepted or appeared to accept rectory-parlor morality and the copybook virtues ranged all the way from earnest humanitarians to secret debauchees. At the latter extreme were those who, like the English author of that account book of erotic adventures, *My Secret Life*, gave the impression of respectability while covertly pursuing a life of lechery. More often pathetic than fiendish, such men were largely the victims of a compulsion, while the innocent girls they were said to have ruined were generally neither innocent nor ruined. Made possible in England by the privileged position of the moneyed classes, such men were uncommon in the United States and had little effect on public morality.

Another group of libertines, but even rarer, undertook, as did the Reverend Henry Ward Beecher of Plymouth Church in Brooklyn or the Reverend Isaac Kalloch of Tremont Temple in Boston, the moral and spiritual guidance of a community while they themselves gave way to erotic impulses in private. A few of the split personalities who chose to play such contradictory roles were complete frauds, but others evidently convinced themselves that the public good they did far outweighed their private misconduct. From what little we know of them they leaned heavily on the theory that one need not be a possessor of a quality or a gift in order to teach it.

Far more numerous—the mass of men, in fact—were those who simply conformed, passively and without thought. In public they complied with and gave tacit approval of the code of fine pretensions, and in private they did the best they could. No one knows how many did not quite succeed in conforming but engaged in petty, furtive trespasses or took out their frustrations on their wives. And no one knows how many who did succeed in withstanding temptation did so through fear or sheer default. Their greatest sin was that they simply accepted the domination of self-appointed guardians of morals, allowing others to tell them what feelings they should have and when they should have them. They are the faceless many, whose lives are most dependent on the age they live in. "It does not occur to them," John Stuart Mill observed, "to have any inclination except what is customary." After a while, it is easy for such persons to believe they are doing as they wish when they do whatever their peers are doing. There is nothing new in such conformity, but it seems especially harmful when it makes every sensual urge appear vicious.

There were of course those who genuinely believed that they had achieved the ideal of never harboring an impure thought or a lustful urge. But both the seventeenth-century Puritan and the modern psychoanalyst agree in effect that such a state is impossible or an illusion, the Puritan declaring that we are born damned and can never in this life be sure that we have been redeemed, while the analyst claims that sexual desire cannot be indefinitely repressed without unhealthy consequences.

The most influential group of all, the activists as we would say, were the professors of morality, the policemen of vice, the keepers of everyone else's conscience. They have usually been charged with hypocrisy, but they had no need to pursue their obsessions in secret because they were able to do so in public. The classic example probably is vice crusader Anthony Comstock. The Comstocks, as we shall see, are not to be blamed as much as the society that supported them.

One of the major ironies of nineteenth-century life is that the community respected and rewarded the vice crusader, failing utterly to see that in many instances he was motivated by pruriency, by his own thwarted hungers. In England a few realized as early as the 1820's that a mealy-mouthed bigotry was sweeping the land, as when Mary Shelley, returning from a long stay abroad, said that "the reign of Cant in England is growing wider and stronger each day." [13] But no one, not even the most perspicuous novelists, perceived that the leaders in the crusade were often driven by sexual urges as uncontrolled as those they were hunting. Under the righteous pretext of purifying the community, they pried into the most private corners of their neighbors' lives, and delivered them over to persecution and sometimes to jail. They alone could practice voyeurism and sadism in the service of God and the community.

It is worth noting that sexuality is the only appetite that modern man has tried to curb on the broadest scale and with the greatest intensity. The most widely accepted explanation of this is economic: Max Weber, R. H. Tawney, and others have shown how the moral standards of the Reformation, a seventeenth-century Puritanism, and nineteenth-century Evangelical movements served the interests of the rising bourgeoisie, encouraging submission, conformity, and the domestic virtues. The Marxists have suggested that the very origins of monogamy were economic, that when the strongest and most acquisitive men in early societies began appropriating too many of the women as well as too much property, other men began to defend a monogamous system. Certainly the condemnation of an unfaithful wife who brought an outsider's child into the line of inheritance was a matter of property. Whatever its origin, monogamy was a solution well suited to early America, where women were scarce and every settler needed a helpmate and a breeder of children.

No period of repression is without its critics and rebels. Among the doubters, a few, more outspoken in England than in America, complained bitterly—as did John Stuart Mill and Walter Bagehot—of the "tyranny of public opinion" and the "hostile and dreaded censorship" of bourgeois attitudes, but they themselves lived more or less conventionally.

Rarest of all were such militant rebels as Victoria Woodhull and Stephen Pearl Andrews. They not only assailed the moral code as a patchwork of shams and lies that frustrated natural impulses and made unhappy marriages a form of legal prostitution, but they also defied the conventions in their own lives. They were punished with every weapon of society from ostracism to jail.

4.

EXORCISING THE DEVILS OF DESIRE

It is difficult to overstate the extent and intensity of prudery in America in 1840. The most sweeping form of suppression was the denial that a "normal" woman experienced desire. This conviction was popular not alone among preachers, who might be excused for basing such a conclusion on their experiences with frigid wives, but also among doctors. In his *History of Prostitution,* a remarkably thorough report on what was called "the commerce of the sexes," Dr. William W. Sanger, a New York physician of wide experience, wrote in the 1850's:

> But it must be repeated and most decidedly, that without these or some other equally stimulating cause (such as destitution, drink or seduction and abandonment), the full force of sexual desire is seldom known to a virtuous woman. In the male sex, nature has provided a more susceptible organization than in the females, apparently with the beneficent design of repressing those evils which must result from mutual appetite equally felt by both.[1]

Incredibly, this seems to suggest that some nameless and horrid immorality will result if the two parties even in a legal union are equally passionate.

One of the most respected of English medical men, Sir William Acton, made the same point in *The Functions and Disorders of the Reproductive Organs* (1857), which went into many editions in the United States as well as in England. He declared that married couples should not indulge in coitus more often than once in every seven or ten days, and when he learned that a patient of his was having coitus two or three times a week and sometimes twice a night, he was sure it was drastically impairing the man's sexual function.[2] In scientists like Acton, as Steven Marcus has shown, the lack of correlation between what Victorians asserted about sexuality and what they observed was heightened to absurdity.

Such an American counsellor to young couples as Dr. William A. Alcott did not hesitate—in *The Young Husband* (1839) and *The Young Wife* (1837)—to condemn sexual indulgence by married couples as a "prostitution of matrimonial life." Elsewhere he declared that, by some kind of unexplained analogy with the menstrual cycle, once a month was often enough for coitus in marriage. The husband, he asserted, was to blame for overindulgence, man always being the "grand seducer," but even the most virtuous wife is "contaminated" by a licentious husband: "little by little, she falls—to rise, alas! no more."[3] This is not the last time we will find a bewildering contradiction between the Victorian conception—or fantasy—of women as "pure" and the lurking fear that such purity was only superficial and easily dissolved.

Alcott's opinions are of interest because he was a popular and staggeringly prolific writer and because he stood somewhere between the tiny group of reformers and the legion of ultraconservative moralists who controlled public opinion. Alcott, like his cousin Bronson Alcott, began as a devoted teacher of children, but a tubercular condition turned him to the study of medicine. The meager medical school requirements of the time enabled him to graduate from Yale Medical College in 1826 after he had attended for only one winter. But he soon began writing, and in the next thirty years published more than one hundred books, mainly on health and morals. The 1830's and 1840's were a time of fads in health as well as in social experiment, and Alcott was soon a prime mover in societies and on periodicals dedicated to water or fresh-air or bathing cures, to vegetarianism, Dr. Sylvester Graham's whole-wheat bread, temperance, and moderation. Unfortunately, the moderation was more often inspired by prudery than by physiology—by remnants of the Puritan belief that denial of the appetites is healthful as well as virtuous. So in *Moral Reformer,* a magazine Alcott edited in the middle 1830's, he opposed not only fermented liquor, smoking, and tight corsets but also gambling, late parties, coffee, tea, condiments, and confections. Characteristically his opposition to condiments was related to the old wives' tale that rich and spicy foods resulting from the use of lard, butter, sugar, eggs, pepper, gravies, ginger, and even salt lead not only to disease but to vice. "No man," he declared with monumental assurance, "has ever become an adulterer, a fornicator, or an idolater eating simples such as plain wheat, corn, rye, potatoes, rice, peas, beans, turnips, apples." [4]

The fetish of moderation led Alcott to declare in *The Moral Philosophy of Courtship and Marriage* that an indulgence in sexual activity before the age of twenty-five or twenty-six in a man, or twenty-one or twenty-two in a woman, depleted the vital juices.[5] He even quoted an unnamed British writer who claimed that for every year of married life before twenty-two a woman risks shortening her life by about three years.

Even phrenology, one of the crazes that swept America in the mid-nineteenth century, joined in proving that woman's natural sexuality, or what it called amativeness, was much less than man's. The leading phrenologist of the time, Orson Squire Fowler, a writer of many tracts on the human body and the emotions, testified in *Love and Parentage* (1855) that the organ of passion in woman was smaller than in man. A virgin, he noted, will spurn an invitation to sexual pleasure unless it is preceded by a show of love and affection.[6] There was no recognition of the possibility that such an initial reluctance might result from Puritanical indoctrination and fear. It would be unfair, however, to leave the impression that Fowler was prudish: he insisted that "reciprocity" was the chief requisite for satisfactory coitus, the wife in particular being urged to respond passionately.

Although there were later some writers who hazarded that enforced continence might have disturbing effects, the doctrine of "chastity in marriage" continued to find supporters. As late as the 1880's and 1890's, Alice B. Stockham, a physician who managed her own publishing company, advocated what she called "Tokology," a regimen based on the avoidance of all animal foods and on maximum continence. Any husband who required coitus except for the purposes of procreation was not only making his wife his private prostitute and killing her love of him but was endangering the health of any children she might bear him.[7] Dr. Stockham was something of a quack, but she wrote as a trained physician, and she sold, or claimed she sold, 200,000 copies of *Tokology*.

All such views were based on the assumption that normal wives were only "passive receptacles," that they merely submitted to their husbands, and did so only for the sake of having children. Brought up on such attitudes, many women were doubtless intimidated into passivity or frigidity. Such a statement as Sanger's must in itself have had an almost traumatic effect on young women who heard of it. But of course the young men who married such young women were taught to consider passivity in women a sign of decency.

The restrictive training of girls began early: Soon after puberty, it was suggested, they should be discouraged from using soft beds or soft chairs or sitting with legs crossed or astride a see-saw. Young women were advised not to drink tea, coffee, or other stimulating beverages. They were not allowed to go to the theater or to dance with boys. They were expected to learn to discipline their bodies by the use of corsets, and they were cautioned, especially in boarding schools, to sleep alone.

Up until the late 1840's young men and women mingled and went about without chaperones, and a courting couple was permitted to exchange kisses and caresses. Soon these liberties were curtailed. But up to the Civil War courtship remained essentially a matter of long conversations and long letters, of ardent vows and declarations, of walks and picnics and excursions with friends. Young women were often warned against the overamorous wooer, and occasionally a particularly prurient counsellor would advise young men against a maiden who was too compliant. Thomas Branagan did not think it improper or cruel—despite the title of his book, *The Excellency of Female Character Vindicated* (1808)—for a suitor to test a girl's virtue to see if she resisted with "becoming abhorrence." A young man was advised, in the name of morality, to play the provocateur and, if the poor girl responded, presumably to spurn her.[8]

How real the fear of sexual love could be even among relatively enlightened young people is revealed in letters written in 1838 by Theodore Weld, already famous as a militant abolitionist, and Angelina Grimké, who, along with her sister, had freed the slaves on their South Carolina plantation and joined the antislavery movement in the North. After telling Angelina that she has long had his "whole heart," Weld adds: *"Not supremely.* Grace has restrained me from that extreme. I *do* love the Lord our righteousness *better* than I love *you.* And it is *because* I love him *better* that I love you *as* I do." [9] Equally troubled but not quite such a casuist, Angelina answered: "Ought God to be *all in all* to us *on earth?* I tho't so, and am frightened to find *He is not.* . . . I laid awake thinking why it was that my heart longed and panted and reached after you as it does. Am I sinning, am I ungrateful, *am I an* IDOLATOR?" [10]

In a later letter, Weld, revealing a pathetic distaste, or fear, for what the marriage bed would require of him, declares that marriage should be consummated with a sense of duty and responsibility rather than those "innumerable, horrible, unspeakable, earthly, sensual and devilish distortions of married life." [11] This is the morbid and neurotic aftermath of the Puritan assault on sexuality—a naturally passionate woman haunted by a totally irrelevant guilt and a young man sick with disgust over his sexual duties.

About 1850, in imitation of long-standing European custom, chaperonage of young people was introduced into polite society in America. It was soon considered improper for a young woman to ride unattended in an omnibus or go unchaperoned to a play with a young man; in 1855 N. P. Willis refers to all of these practices as "newly forbidden things" that had long been considered innocent privileges. The aim of the custom was the purely practical one of preventing an unsuitable marriage or any indiscretion. Such supervision was continued through the betrothal period and right up to the wedding day. How intimidating the practice could be is illustrated in Henry James' *A London Life* in which a young woman fears that a man who does not love her will have to marry her because they have been left alone in a box at the opera.

Although the urgency of men's sexual desires was recognized —openly in the earlier decades of the century and tacitly later on—it was stigmatized as animalism, one of the baser instincts and one that must be tamed. Young men were told to subdue desire by means of exercise, cold baths, hard beds, religion, and avoiding French novels. Men of education and culture mistrusted sexuality as an appetite not subject to reason. John Stuart Mill observed that in his father "*Logos* was forever engaged in slaying *Eros*." The ideal was sublimation. It was an ideal that sometimes arose out of a high-minded notion of what man should be but more often out of a squeamish dislike or fear of what men are.

5.

FORBIDDEN GROUND

SINCE copulation, except for the purpose of procreation, was disapproved of, it is not surprising that all other sexual practices were abominated. Any sign of sexuality among the young was of course rigorously suppressed. With post-Freudian hindsight we find it difficult to understand why no one observed that sexual curiosity was common among children or concluded that a characteristic so widespread could not be as unnatural and vicious as was assumed.

The main target of parental horror was masturbation, often mistakenly called onanism, after Onan, who, in Genesis, "spilled his seed on the ground" in order not to impregnate his brother's widow. Referred to as the "solitary evil" or as "self-abuse," masturbation was almost always treated with loathing. The very intensity of the denunciation makes the attitude suspect. Only acute guilt could have led the Victorian moral establishment to declare that masturbation was not only a filthy act but one that led to every conceivable disorder from bloodshot eyes to idiocy. In its Sixth Annual Report, the Massachusetts State Lunatic Hospital at Worcester solemnly declared: ". . . above all other kinds of insanity, it stamps its victims with every abhorrent and loathsome stigma of degradation." [1] The stigma was of course in the eye of the beholder, and it made him a creator of bogeys that terrorized many a youth. It never occurred to doctors that excessive masturbation was a symptom of a condition rather than a cause, that it might be almost inevitable in a society that made any sexual contact between boys and girls seem evil. As for masturbation by women, it was considered too shocking even to be attacked. When in 1846 an audacious lecturer on hygiene, Mary Gove Nichols, insisted that the practice was widespread among women as well as men, her audiences were horrified—as much at Mrs. Nichols' temerity as at the revelation.[2] On the rare occasions when it was thereafter discussed, it joined its male counterpart as the secret vice that leads, as one doctor warned, in the classic Victorian crescendo of catastrophes, "to the grave, the madhouse, or worse yet, the brothel." [3]

Later, Dr. Edward Bliss Foote in his highly successful and outspoken books of medical and marital advice declared that girls under sixteen or eighteen years of age were not so addicted to this "pernicious habit" as boys but that after that age the rule was reversed. "The hot blood of budding man and womanhood," he wrote in *Medical Common Sense* (1864), "stimulated by exciting food, drinks, and condiments, leads the young man to the embraces of the harlot and the young woman to the vices of the secret chamber, so that the former sacrifices his moral sense, and the latter her physical bloom and health." [4]

Although the injuriousness of masturbation as ordinarily practiced was not confirmed by a shred of proof, one can see why it seemed to the typical Victorian an act of gross sensuality and self-indulgence. But it is less easy to justify the English medical authority Sir James Paget who asserted that "nocturnal emissions," the ejaculation of semen during sleep, usually as a result of erotic dreams, signified an impurity and must arouse deep feelings of guilt in men of conscience.[5] His distinguished colleague Sir William Acton suggested that such dreams resulted from continence, but thought they could be controlled, and recommended a cold water enema before retiring, cauterizing of the urethra with silver nitrate, or even tying a cord around the penis at night! Lest this be dismissed as an oddity of morbid Puritanism, an American authority on masculine hygiene, Dr. George H. Napheys, suggested that in persistent cases of this kind the victim should buy and wear a "spermatorrhoeal ring," a metal band with sharp points on its inner side that would awaken the sleeper as soon as an erection began.[6] What we have here is not simply scientists lending their names to obscurantism but actually arousing a sense of guilt where none may have existed before.

Unlike masturbation, homosexuality, or sodomy, as it was called, was not often assailed, mainly because it was not even open to discussion. It was simply in the horrid category of sexual abominations that did not lead to procreation. Those who did refer to it considered it, as we shall see later, along with other deviations such as a union between two women, unspeakably vile. Probably many women and even some men did not know that such relationships could be sexual or would have rejected the information as an obscene invention. The entire Victorian view of the love between man and woman as constantly in danger of becoming impure, but of the love between man and man or between woman and woman as manifestly of the soul, fostered many relationships that verged on homosexuality or lesbianism and a few that plunged into it.

Equally forbidden was any effort to prevent conception. Perhaps the strongest barrier to sexual relations outside of marriage had always been the possibility of pregnancy. Even the nineteenth-century moralists who condemned fornication as a sin against God relied heavily on the fact that it was a sin that might leave telltale evidence—an unwanted child. Lest their prey escape them, the moralists further insisted that any attempt to avert conception—even within marriage—was just as much of a sin, and a crime against nature to boot.

Despite this, in the early part of the nineteenth century a variety of forces—which we shall examine in a later chapter—led Englishmen and Americans to seek methods of controlling childbirth. So several English and American reformers—in America notably Robert Dale Owen and Charles Knowlton—braved all the wrath of pietists not only to justify contraception but also to describe techniques for practicing it.

By the late 1850's, prudes and preachers were beginning to cry out against the spread of unmentionable practices that not only robbed unchastity and infidelity of their deserved punishment but allowed married people to defy nature and God. In the January, 1860, issue of *The Knickerbocker,* Dr. Augustus Kinsley Gardner maintained that the moral sense of the community had reached a fearful pass, with each woman claiming the right to decide whether or not to have children. How widespread the practice had become was revealed when he wrote: "Local congestions, nervous affections and debilities are the direct and indisputable results of the *coitus imperfecti, tegumenta extaria, ablutiones gelidae, infusiones astringentes,* etcetera, so commonly employed by the community. . . ." He added that under such circumstances, "sexual congress is rendered but a species of self-abuse." [7] The charge that all preventive methods were harmful both physically and spiritually was not uncommon. Dr. John Cowan, who shored up his prudish marriage counsel with phrenology, asserted in his *The Science of a New Life* (1869) that *coitus interruptus* was beastly, *coitus reservatus* provided only an animal kind of pleasure, and that most other methods were injurious or unreliable or both. The doctor's conclusion: strict continence.[8] In a later edition, the publisher deleted the references to specific contraceptive techniques. A university joined in the war of suppression. When Burt Green Wilder, a highly respected professor of physiology and zoology at Cornell, included a chapter on birth control in the manuscript of his book, *What Young People Should Know* (1875), the university governing body compelled him to omit it.[9]

When the dry goods clerk Anthony Comstock became chief agent of the New York Society for the Suppression of Vice after the Civil War, he made contraceptive information and devices the main object of his fanatical crusades against "vice." One of the outstanding cases that Comstock prosecuted was that against Dr. Edward Bliss Foote, author of several practical, frank, and very successful books of medical advice. As early as 1858, in his *Medical Common Sense,* Dr. Foote advocated what amounted to planned parenthood and the right of wives to decide when to have children,[10] but it was through a ten-cent pamphlet, *Words in Pearl for the Married* (1876), that he ran afoul of Comstock. Using a false name, Comstock got Foote to send him the pamphlet. Foote was convicted, and he paid $3,000 in fines and $5,000 in costs.

Foote continued to protest strenuously against such interference and predicted that popular demand would force a change in the laws. But in the 1880's medical men were still proclaiming the evils attendant on contraception. When more and more of the poor complained that they could not afford an unlimited number of children, there were always preachers ready to guarantee that God would take care of all of them.

Even a doctor, Henry N. Guernsey (1889), could assert: "I have faith enough to reply, 'Our Heavenly Father never sends more mouths than he can feed.' " [11]

Hope for a change in the laws remained exceedingly faint while a man like Anthony Comstock was a power in New York and Washington, Godfrey Lowell Cabot was head of the Watch and Ward Society in Boston, or Theodore Roosevelt was climbing to the Presidency of the United States. Roosevelt, who had grown from a sickly child into a permanently boyish exponent of the strenuous outdoor life, believed that anyone who did not want children was "a criminal against the race" and that "willful sterility," as he termed it, "inevitably produces and accentuates every hideous form of vice. . . . It is itself worse, more debasing, more destructive, than ordinary vice. I rank celibate profligacy as not one whit better than polygamy." [12] The mixture of prejudices in this statement makes it easy to understand why it was not until the 1920's that birth control information could be disseminated with any degree of freedom.

In a later chapter we shall consider prostitution as an aspect of clandestine sexuality, but something must be said here about the way in which it was publicly attacked but tacitly tolerated. The theory was that men, particularly unmarried men, must have a constantly available outlet for their sexual urges and that it was better that prostitutes should serve this need than that decent women should be exposed to seduction or corruption by men driven by unsatisfied lust. Was this an admission that the average man would turn into a seducer or rapist if he could not have prostitutes? Hardly. Part of the mythology was that only the dissolute patronized prostitutes; presumably it was such men who would be loosed on the community if the whorehouses were closed down.

Such attitudes were of course not invented by the Victorians. Both St. Augustine and St. Ambrose regarded prostitution as an indispensable outlet for men's lust. With the peculiar cruelty of the righteous they declared: "Prostitutes are to a city what servers are to a palace."

The result was the double standard that sanctioned almost unlimited sexual activity in men but no such activity whatever in unmarried women. It also sanctioned brothels that were a prime source of venereal disease and crime, that corrupted police and other officials, and doomed most of the women who served in them to an early and ugly death.

All this was of course too shameful and hideous for the community to acknowledge. As for the preachers or crusaders who did speak out against the evil, their hypocrisy was almost as great as that of the others because they demanded abstinence among the unmarried and, at the same time, purity among the married. For many preachers the pleasures as well as penalties of "houses of ill fame" was a theme calculated not only to win the approval of a congregation but to hold it spellbound. It was, for example, one of the set pieces on which the great reputation of the Reverend Henry Ward Beecher rested. In "The Strange Woman," one of his lectures for young men, he would begin with a sensational, vividly detailed description of the harlot, her face, clothes, gardens—she apparently enjoyed ancient Roman luxuries—and other lures, and then would follow with equally bravura passages on all the horrors that lurked in the aftermath of her embrace. The climax began thus:

> Every year, in every town, die wretches scalded and scorched with agony. Were the sum of all the pain that comes with the last stages of vice collected, it would rend the very heavens with its outcry. . . . Ye that are listening in the garden of this strange woman . . . come hither, look upon her fourth ward [presumably the last stages of syphilis]—its vomited blood, its sores and fiery blotches, its prurient sweat, its dissolving ichor and rotten bones! Stop, young man! [18]

But as long as Americans believed that a maiden's purity or a wife's fidelity was an indispensable virtue, the only alternative to prostitution was complete abstinence by every unmarried man or maid and complete fidelity by every married man. Finally, the Victorian code failed to acknowledge how dishonest it was to allow an evil to flourish because it protected certain women from the admittedly natural passions of men.

The distrust of sensual indulgence and the etherealization of women explain the war on masturbation and contraception and the denial of sexual feelings in respectable women. But as time passes and our standards become more and more relaxed, it is harder and harder to credit the extremes to which nineteenth-century America went in expurgating speech, novels, biographies, and plays, and in the prudery of their attitudes toward clothes, medical examination, courtship, art, education, and even the most trivial aspects of daily life.

6.

THE WORD MADE CLEAN

IN the early period of Puritanism a sinner was anyone who gave less than complete devotion to God or had any doubt that he was a vessel of corruption destined for damnation. In the late eighteenth century, city life, increasing prosperity, and women with leisure fostered, in the eyes of moralists, a host of new "sins": luxurious clothes, frivolous entertainments, romantic poetry and novels, profane art, social dancing, and popular music. As early as the 1780's, Timothy Dwight, Congregationalist minister, professor of theology, and Puritan throwback, preached passionately against such worldly diversions. Becoming President of Yale in 1795 and finding many students indulging in drink, gambling, "loose living," and, under the influence of Voltaire and Paine, in deism, Dwight returned the school to Puritan fear and fervor. In books of sermons that would remain popular for decades, he inveighed against all signs of moral laxity in entertainment, art, and literature.

One of the first areas to be affected by such attacks was that of daily speech. In the desire to establish their gentility, the rising middle class, and especially the women, censored their every utterance—the first affectation of those who hope to be considered of superior breeding. All the old Anglo-Saxon four-letter sexual and excremental words, used by more robust citizens from the time of Chaucer to that of the Elizabethans, had been banished by the Puritans. Although they had been revived by bolder Englishmen during the Restoration and were even included in school dictionaries in eighteenth-century England,[1] they were now more than ever forbidden in America.

Along with these went almost all words referring to the covered parts of the body: breast, nipple, thigh, hip, navel, belly, buttock, and even leg, or to specifically male or female animals such as cock, bull, bitch, stallion, ram, buck, and boar. Moreau de St. Méry, a French émigré who lived in Philadelphia in the 1790's, asserted that American women divided their bodies into two parts: "from the top of the waist to the stomach; from there to the foot and ankles." [2] In general, a woman's body was considered increasingly indecent from the throat down: proper persons referred to the *neck* when they meant *breast,* and *breast* when they meant *abdomen.* And an extreme of prudery was achieved by women who spoke of the *bosom* of a chicken.

One of the most famous accounts of the squeamishness of American women was that of a young lady who stumbled and fell as Captain Marryat was escorting her near Niagara Falls. When he asked her if she had hurt her leg, she was obviously shocked and only with reluctance explained that in the presence of ladies a gentleman referred to a leg as a limb, even if it belonged to a table.* [3]

Another English traveler, Marianne Finch, noted the gap between manners and speech on an Ohio River steamer in the 1850's. The American woman who shared her mattress on the floor of the Ladies' Cabin was not disturbed by the glances of men passing the cabin but thought Miss Finch's references to a sister who had been "confined" and had given birth were indelicate.[4]

Mrs. Frances Trollope, who took revenge for the failure of the fantastic "Moorish bazaar" department store she opened in Cincinnati in 1829 by publishing her merciless *Domestic Manners of the Americans* (1832), told of how a well-mannered young German offended one of the principal local families by using the word *corset* in the presence of ladies.[5] She also described a conversation in which a supposedly well-read man expressed disgust at the very title of *The Rape of the Lock.* The impression given by British travelers that such priggishness was rare in Britain was something of an exaggeration. It was a

* Marryat's report that he came across an even more absurd instance of delicacy in a seminary for young ladies—the "limbs" of a pianoforte covered with frilled pantalettes—was apparently a sophisticated hoax played on him because he was so quick to criticize American behavior.

British writer, Lady Gough, who in her *Etiquette* (1863) advocated a piece of prudery staggering in its absurdity. "The perfect hostess," she warned, "will see to it that the works of male and female authors be properly separated on her bookshelves. Their proximity unless they happen to be married should not be tolerated."

Because excesses beget excesses, producing a kind of competition in which each participant tries to prove his superior refinement, quite modest as well as forthright words fell into disrepute. Banished were *pregnant, virgin, whore, seduce, rape, castration,* and *abortion;* the names of garments such as trousers, breeches, shirt, corset, and women's stockings, and the names of such animals as ass and cockroach.

Syphilis became the *social disease, masturbation* the *solitary vice, adultery* turned into *criminal conversation,* and whores were *fallen women.* The censorship of animals made *bull* into *male cow, cock* into *rooster, cockroach* into *roach,* and *ass* sometimes became *a––.* High on the scale of affectation was *enceinte* for *pregnant, statutory offense* or *criminal assault* for *rape, house of ill repute* for *brothel, linen* for *shirt, lingerie* (introduced by *Godey's Lady's Book* in 1852) for *women's underclothes, lower extremities* for *legs, be confined* for *give birth* and, sickening in their coyness, *unmentionables* and *inexpressibles* for *trousers, breeches,* and *underdrawers* and for what Civil War soldiers called *pants. Naked* was often replaced by *nude,* which, ironically, derived from a related root, and sometimes by *unclothed.* For the sexual act itself there were of course countless euphemisms, most of them such pompous circumlocutions as *sexual congress, carnal knowledge, intercourse,* and *connection.*

Perhaps the most revealing example of the semantics of prudery was evoked by a child born out of wedlock. The Puritans damned it as a *child of sin. Bastard* was still used in courts of law in the nineteenth century, but elsewhere it had degenerated, like many other words associated with sexual relations, into an insult. The accepted term, *illegitimate,* stigmatized the child gratuitously. But also very common were *love child* and *natural child,* both of which implied, with unconscious candor, that other children might well be the unwanted offspring of loveless unions.

There is no end to the making of euphemisms. The absurdity of a euphemism is of course that it conceals nothing; it simply creates the illusion, beyond all logic, that the forbidden object is no longer objectionable. After all, what word is more obscene than the dashes or asterisks that were at one time commonly used to denote an objectionable word? Indeed, the process of contamination by association sees to it that each new euphemism becomes tomorrow's naughty or undignified word. Thus when the honorable old word *woman* lost caste simply because it covered the lowborn as well as the well bred, *female* came into popular use. Early nineteenth-century fiction abounded in "females"; Cooper's *The Pioneers,* for example, is sprinkled with such sentences as, "He approached the young females" and "There is no fear of anything unpleasant occurring to a female in this new country." But even *female* eventually aroused objections, the editor of *Godey's Lady's Book,* Mrs. Hale, observing that when used as a noun, it sounded exactly like a reference to an animal. She campaigned against the name Vassar Female College until the word "female" was dropped.[6]

Then "lady" came into its own. Thus in 1842, Mrs. A. J. Graves in her *Woman in America* declared that there were many "females" who "in their ambition to be considered *ladies* use their fair hands only in playing with their ringlets, or touching the piano or guitar." [7] The extent of both the hypocrisy and snobbery in such a distinction is revealed in the title of a women's organization in the frontier town of Jacksonville, Illinois, in 1831: The Ladies' Association for Educating Females. And when Harriet Martineau asked the warden of the Nashville prison whether she might visit the women's cells, he replied: "We have no ladies here at present. We have never had but two ladies, who were convicted for stealing a steak, but . . . they were pardoned." [8] In time, even *lady* was not elegant enough for some. In her *Court Circles of the Republic* Mrs. Ellet says of Mrs. Paulding, wife of the Secretary of the Navy: "The word *lady* hardly defined her; she was a perfect gentlewoman." [9] No word associated with the sexes is immune from contamination. When applied to a woman, even *decent* had by the 1870's become slightly indecent! [10]

There were of course obstinate fellows, notably the testy, outspoken publisher of the New York *Herald,* James Gordon

Bennett, who insisted on using *legs, shirt,* and *trousers,*[11] among others, and Richard Grant White, essayist and vigorous critic of American English, who scoffed at the use of *limbs, enceinte,* and *female.*[12] But that was not the way of respectability, and few followed them.

Those living in the villages and small cities of the West were the worst offenders. Latecomers to the cultural scene and living in raw communities, they were obviously out to prove their unimpeachable gentility and cultivation.

The fumigation of everyday speech was abhorrent enough, but even more objectionable was the tampering with great creative works of the past. Such works are of course hardly sacred to the self-elected censor; he is convinced that he is morally wiser than his peers and is generously helping them save their souls. Armed with righteousness, he will not only ban or mutilate the work of famous playwrights, novelists, painters, and sculptors, but he will undertake to purify even the sacred books of society.

Thus an Englishman decided in the early nineteenth century that Shakespeare was in many passages unfit for decent-minded readers. What is not so well known is that the Bible was also subjected to a similar, if much more superficial, cleansing at about the same time. In 1833 Noah Webster, blandly moving from defining words to censoring them, issued an edition of the King James version of the Bible "with amendments." "In early stages of society," he explained, "when men are savage or half civilized, such terms are not offensive; but in the present state of refinement, the utterance of many words and passages in our version is not to be endured." [13] The implication here was not only that the holy book was set down by members of a savage race, but that the taste and judgment of the translators of the Authorized Version were not to be trusted. So Webster deleted the words *womb* and *teat,* changed *give suck* to *nurse* or *nourish, fornication* to *lewdness, whore* to *harlot* or *lewd woman, stones* (meaning testicles) to *peculiar members* or *secrets, stink* to *smell, in the belly* (referring to a fetus) to *in embryo,* and "when he went in unto his brother's wife . . . he spilled it on the ground, lest that he should give seed to his brother" to "when he went into his brother's wife . . . he frustrated the purpose." [14] One hardly knows which to deplore more—the prudery or the ineptness of the changes.

It may be said that Webster tampered only with a translation and that his alterations are superficial. But Thomas Bowdler's *Family Shakspere,* published in ten volumes in 1818 (following an edition prepared by his sister Harriet in 1807) and long popular in England and the United States, was a rigorous expurgation of the work of a poet whose every turn of phrase has been cherished beyond that of any other writer. Although Bowdler declared that nothing had been added to the text and that only those "words and expressions are omitted which cannot with propriety be read aloud in a family," [15] he cut and patched with such fear and dislike of all that is earthy, frankly passionate, and gaily ribald that his name has become a synonym for maximum prudery and minimum discernment.

Bowdler, who was educated as a physician but preferred working for such causes as those of the Society for the Suppression of Vice, firmly believed that he was purging the plays of dross. But he did in fact do damage to everything that makes the plays great: dramatic structure, characterization, poetry. Typical of his offenses against structure is his deletion of the drunken porter episode in *Macbeth.* Bowdler thought the episode was irrelevant as well as indecent, never seeing that it had been created precisely to provide indispensable relief and suspense between two crises—the murder of Duncan and the discovery of the murder. His sins against character are equally heinous; a striking example of this is his pruning of just those qualities that make Falstaff whatever he is: bawdy imagination, uninhibited candor, the wisdom of a man who lives by his wits.

Finally, there is Bowdler's utter insensitivity to all that makes great poetry, as, to take one small example, when he reduces the swelling passion of Juliet's

> Spread thy close curtain, love-performing night,
> That runaway's eyes may wink, and Romeo
> Leap to these arms untalk'd of and unseen!
> Lovers can see to do their amorous rites
> By their own beauties; or, if love be blind,
> It best agrees with night.

to one forlorn line,

Spread thy close curtain, love-performing night.

Encouraged by his success in rendering Shakespeare tame enough for maidenly minds, Bowdler busied himself in his last years erasing "irreligious" as well as "indecent" expressions from Gibbon's *Decline and Fall of the Roman Empire.*[16] Whether his decontamination of a masterly study of history is more of an offense than his mutilation of great plays is a nice question in values.

Such treatment of Shakespeare and the Bible was an object lesson in how far censorship will go when it is not checked. The evil here is truly in great part in the eye of the beholder. It is the vice crusader, not the average citizen, whose imagination is excited beyond control by what he considers an indecent novel, painting, or statue. The history of taste tells us that if the matter is simply obscene and without merit, the public will in the end find it either boring or disgusting. And it is likely that anyone who can be corrupted by a book or a painting would already have been corrupted by what he has seen or heard or imagined in his daily life. Unopposed, the watchdogs of public purity end by suppressing, as they did in the nineteenth century, everything that will conceivably offend a completely callow adolescent girl. A century ago this meant censoring not only information about the human body but also any realistic treatment of love, marriage, or even frustration.

7.

LITERATURE AND THE PRICE OF PURITY

THE effect of such purism on the arts was incalculable. From 1800 to 1875 it impoverished the work of any number of novelists, poets, biographers, playwrights, painters, and sculptors, both in the themes and qualities it shut from them and in those it thrust on them. It bitterly opposed fiction. Despite the intellectual preeminence of Boston, it was no accident that, except for Hawthorne, all nineteenth-century American novelists and story writers of note—Brown, Irving, Cooper, Poe, Melville, James, Twain, Howells, Garland, and Crane—came from other regions. Purism cheated novelists of freedom in dealing with every aspect of life. Nor can it be said that they did not know what they had lost, because any reader could find the missing qualities and themes in the Song of Solomon and in the work of, among others, Ovid, Aristophanes, Euripides, Chaucer, Rabelais, Boccaccio, Shakespeare, Donne, Congreve, Fielding, Richardson, Smollett, Sterne, Burns, and many lesser writers, or in painting and sculpture from Greek vases and Pompeiian murals through Titian and Rubens to Hogarth and Goya. It prevented them from probing character in all its depths and, most of all, from exploring fully the relationship between man and woman and the power of sexuality. Even Charlotte Brontë, who was herself considered too free in her treatment of sex, cautioned a correspondent to whom she had recommended Shakespeare and Byron: "You will know how to choose the good, and to avoid the evil; the finest passages are always the purest, the bad are invariably revolting; you will never wish to read them over twice." [1]

But the greatest damage was done in the attitudes and values that the age imposed on the creative artists themselves. The principal qualities were moral didacticism, piety, the overdrawn pathos of their sad endings, and the smug optimism of their happy endings. The didacticism was a matter of catering to a large new audience: middle-class readers who saw no value in a book unless it served a purpose. And the one purpose that all the arts of this era found it easiest to stress was that of moral improvement—propaganda for purity, chastity, religious devotion and faith, and against cynicism, worldliness and dissipation. Sometimes, following an English practice, a distinction was made, as Noel Perrin[2] has shown, between the classes for whom a book was intended: a classic would be issued in an expensive and unexpurgated edition for the few along with an inexpensive expurgated edition for the many.

The ever-increasing preponderance of women readers had an equally inhibiting effect. While American men were bending all their energies to making money—as every European traveler in the nineteenth century monotonously agreed—the women of the middle and upper class had more and more leisure and inclination to read. For the same reason an ever greater number of women became novelists and poets—"the d—d mob of scribbling women," in Hawthorne's blunt phrase. Between women readers, women authors, and the rule of middle-class mores, the literary climate was one of primness, mawkish sentiment, and religiosity.

Three of the greatest novelists of the period, Thackeray, Scott, and Dickens, felt this pressure—and submitted to it. They were British, but they had more readers in America than in England. Thackeray openly acknowledged that he had been gagged. In Chapter 64 of *Vanity Fair* (1848), a novel which sold several times as well in the United States as in England, Thackeray announced that he would have to pass over a part of Mrs. Rebecca Crawley's biography because the "moral world" has, perhaps,

> no particular objection to vice, but an insuperable repugnance to hearing vice called by its proper name . . . and a polite public will no more bear to read an authentic description of vice than a truly-refined English or American female will permit the word breeches to be pronounced in her chaste hearing. And yet, Madam, both are walking the world before our faces

> every day, without much shocking us. It is only when their naughty names are called out that your modesty has any occasion to show alarm or sense of outrage. . . .

He had deferentially submitted, Thackeray adds, to the prevailing fashion and had presented Becky's vices only in "a perfectly genteel and inoffensive manner." For those who want to peep down below, he says, the water is pretty transparent; above, everything is "proper, agreeable and decorous." It would be difficult to compose a more acute description of the world of pretense in which an aware Victorian novelist wrote.

By today's standards the heroines in Scott's novels seem idealized beyond cavil, but after reading the original version of *St. Ronan's Well,* in which Clara Mowbray yielded to Tyrrel before her mock marriage to his brother, Scott's publisher found it intolerable that the character of a well-born young lady of the nineteenth century should be so contaminated. Scott gave way, decontaminating Mrs. Mowbray.

Dickens, too, gave way. Under pressure from his friend, the novelist Bulwer, he rewrote the end of *Great Expectations* in order to reunite Pip with a repentant Estella: the novel closes with the couple walking off hand in hand into a tranquil evening mist. To Dickens it may have seemed a small concession, but it is hard to imagine a writer today asking a fellow novelist to alter the resolution of a novel to spare the sensitivities of his audience.

Byron of course defied and mocked such conventions, but he was an aristocrat who took full advantage of the privileges of his class. Not that he escaped violent censure of both his life and his art. Very soon after *Childe Harold* appeared, American preachers and teachers lashed out at Byron's skepticism and immorality and he became along with Burns and Sheridan a lesson in the wages of vice.[3] Booksellers refused to carry his books and shortly before his death, an English traveler, Isaac Candler, reported:

> We have indeed of late seen the mighty genius of Byron prostituted to the base purpose of pandering to the corrupt appetites of sensualists, but we have at the same time seen a manifestation of public feeling hostile to such degradation of intellect. To the credit of the American ladies be it recorded that since

> the character of Don Juan has become known, it has been proscribed.[4]

Mrs. Trollope noted that a Cincinnati gentleman who disparaged Byron's poetry had missed the noble passages while learning by rote those lines he wished the poet had not written.[5] But as Samuel G. Goodrich, the famous "Peter Parley," said, "Byron could no more be kept at bay than the cholera." Americans who continued to read Byron did not, it is plain, reveal their inclinations to the likes of Mr. Candler.

The most bizarre aftermath of Byron's license was Harriet Beecher Stowe's effort almost fifty years later to clear Lady Byron of the imputation that she had alienated her husband by her cold and prim demeanor. As a girl, Harriet Beecher had been captured by Byron's poetry and by his image. In 1853, as the famous Mrs. Stowe, she met the aging widow of the poet. A close friendship followed. Then, one day, Lady Byron horrified Mrs. Stowe by asserting that she had left the poet because she had become convinced that his relation with his half-sister, Augusta, was incestuous.

The secret lay burning in Mrs. Stowe's memory until in 1869, nine years after Lady Byron's death, the recollections of the Countess Guiccioli, Byron's last mistress, revived the view of Lady Byron as a cold-hearted wife. Stirred by confused impulses—an exaggerated sense of her Christian duty, disillusion with an idol of her youth, pride in being the confidante of an English noblewoman—Mrs. Stowe revealed her secret at book length in *The Vindication of Lady Byron* (1870).[6] The general response was that Mrs. Stowe was an old busybody who had without proof besmirched the name of the defenseless dead.

It is quite possible, biographers say, that Byron was guilty as charged, but Mrs. Stowe's book hurt her reputation more than it did Byron's and it did nothing to vindicate Lady Byron. It was characteristic of Victorian prurience that such a woman as Mrs. Stowe should have dared to devote a book to the details of a man's sexual irregularities. For its part, the public chose to overlook Byron's adultery with the lovely Countess Guiccioli as a foible of romantic genius and simply rejected the idea that a great English poet could be guilty of incest.

Even such an innocuous and sentimental lyricist as Thomas

Moore, who was widely read in America after his visit in 1804, was taken to task by Thomas Branagan for "voluptuous performances" that "overturn the ramparts of female innocense," [7] and Edward T. Channing in the *North American Review* described the lush, exotic *Lalla Rookh* (1817) as little more than a mixture of "musick, conceit and debauchery." [8]

The poets who were most adored by both American and British readers from the late 1840's on were of course Longfellow and Tennyson. Longfellow's *Hiawatha,* which sold 50,000 copies within five months of its publication in 1855 and at least one million copies in the next eighty years, is a Victorianized Indian romance, while Tennyson's *The Idylls of the King,* that favorite of American public schools, is Victorianized Arthurian romance; both are inextricably linked to the idealizing morality of their time.

If there was one writer to whom American novelists from 1790 to 1860 owed their view of the relations between the sexes, it was Samuel Richardson, London printer turned chronicler of the war of the sexes. Under the influence of *Pamela* (1740) and, even more, of *Clarissa* (1748), novelist after novelist saw courtship as the struggle of an innocent maiden to preserve her honor from the Male Tempter. If she succeeded, her reward would be a respectable husband here—and heaven hereafter. *Pamela,* in which a serving girl copes successfully with the son of her aristocratic master, was popular; but it was *Clarissa,* a thousand-page chronicle, in intimate letters, of the unavailing efforts of a daughter of the rich bourgeoisie to fend off Lovelace, a titled young libertine, that won the moral approval as well as the hearts of readers.

Richardson had his cake and ate it too, for Clarissa is raped, but raped after she is drugged, so that she emerges still essentially pure in heaven's eyes. And although Lovelace repents, he is punished—slain in a duel with one of Clarissa's relatives. As Leslie Fiedler observes, Clarissa is a Protestant Virgin, product of the long Puritan-bourgeois campaign to clear the image of woman from the stigma of Temptress Eve.[9] Clarissa, we may add, is all sentiment and soul, and yet, paradoxically, she dies with piety in full control of her feelings. At the same time Lovelace, representing unleashed sexuality, is portrayed as the godless aristocrat, doomed by vice.

For our purposes *Clarissa* is significant not so much for its picture of society as for its popularity—the evidence that it satisfied a want. Its characters, filtered through Richardson's moral biases, are absurdly distorted: Lovelace is too diabolic, and Clarissa is at first too innocent and later too pious and self-punishing. It is, in fine, not a transcript of life but a bourgeois morality play on the theme of lust. But Jonathan Edwards thought it so dangerous that he denounced the young people of Northampton who read it.

Although there was much that was peculiarly British about the Clarissa-Lovelace relationship, American readers, who were after all still partly Englishmen living abroad, embraced *Clarissa*. The first American edition appeared only four years after the one in England, and by 1800 a score of other editions were available.

Almost all of the earliest American novels of any consequence—William Hill Brown's *The Power of Sympathy* (1789), Suzanna Rowson's *Charlotte Temple* (1794), and Hannah Foster's *The Coquette* (1797)—betray the influence of Richardson, but their heroines tend to be too gay and flirtatious or too clinging and pathetic, their villains merely libertines, and their moralizing insufferable. Next to them, Charles Brockden Brown, America's first professional novelist, seems intensely and even wildly imaginative. Born in 1771 and coming of age in a time of revolutions, he was influenced by Mary Wollstonecraft, champion of the emancipation of women, and her husband, William Godwin, whose faith in reason led him to challenge all institutions.

Brown's first book, *Alcuin* (1798), was a dialog on the rights of women, a stilted piece of writing but evidence enough of the effect of Wollstonecraft and Godwin. This influence, along with that of Richardson, is still evident in Brown's first novels, *Wieland* (1798) and *Ormond* (1799), in which two of the leading characters, Carwin and Ormond, breathe contempt for chastity and marriage. But both men are so cold and calculating that they seem to represent the worst consequences of rationalism rather than of passion. Brown appears to use them and their outrageous creeds mainly to create melodramatic confrontations with young women bent on remaining virtuous. Although the heroines in both novels, Clara[10] and Constantia,[11] declare, like

Clarissa, that death is better than loss of honor, Brown tells us that both would have been better able to deal with threats to their virtue if they had had a stricter religious training. In Brown's last novels this faith in religion grows much stronger. In *Jane Talbot* (1801) not only is the heroine ennobled by faith, but the hero, Colden, who begins as a Godwinian radical,[12] despising revelation and scorning marriage, sees the error of his ways and embraces religion. Like Colden, Brown, respectably married and supporting a growing family, grew more orthodox with the years, in the end going so far as to repudiate his novels.

Unlike Brown, who was never very successful and is today read mainly by students, James Fenimore Cooper was not only the best-known American of his time but the creator of a tradition and a mythology. The appeal of Cooper's most popular books, the five volumes of the *Leatherstocking* tales, published between 1826 and 1841, are plain: The white hunter Natty Bumppo and his lordly Indian comrade Chingachgook and Chingachgook's son Uncas were original creations who confirmed the Romantic dream of the new race that the New World would breed. The honest, brave, and pure-minded white man and the noble, equally brave and pure redskin held out to disillusioned and world-weary Europeans the hope of a fresh start, a kind of instant return to Eden before Adam was betrayed by Eve.

Within a few decades, however, Cooper had been lumped with that growing group of American story writers—it would include Irving, Poe, and, later, Mark Twain—who, whatever their intentions, were read chiefly by boys. The Leatherstocking tales were in fact a prototype of the "Western" adventure story and eventually of such boys' dime novels as the Frank Merriwell series. Young readers relished the violence and danger in Cooper's tales, the white hero who was Nature's nobleman, a superman among hunters, and his foes, the bad Indians, so satisfyingly malevolent and fierce. They accepted the stagey speech, ignored the set tributes to Nature, and if they took any note of Deerslayer's lack of sexual interest in women, they accepted it as natural to so "manly" a man. And perhaps more of a man's man, Leslie Fiedler suggests,[13] than Cooper realized. So out of an adventure story appealing to twelve-year-olds came one of America's archetypal images of the male—rugged, man of action, guileless, distrustful of culture, chivalrous in a scout-masterish way, and debarred from love by his morals.

Natty Bumppo's sexual block is most fully revealed in *The Deerslayer*. When Judith Hutter, a mettlesome young woman, is left alone in her wilderness home after her father and sister have been killed by Indians, she offers to marry her rescuer, the young white hunter known as Deerslayer. He not only rejects her but priggishly warns her against relying on the appeal of her beauty and charms. Judith accepts Deerslayer's reproof as though it were deserved. A lovely woman who has bitten of the apple, Judith is clearly the Temptress-Eve. But if, as R. W. B. Lewis avers,[14] Deerslayer is America's first full-fledged fictional Adam, he is an Adam who is not interested in Eve, an Adam who never becomes a complete man sexually.

The only other threat to Natty's celibacy comes in the third volume, *The Pathfinder,* when the hunter, approaching forty, is attracted to Mabel Dunham, the young daughter of an old army sergeant. But Mabel recoils at the thought and reminds him that he is old enough to be her father. The mighty hunter is almost relieved when it becomes evident that Mabel loves young Jasper Warren: Indeed, when the two young lovers embrace, their feeling is obviously a revelation to Leatherstocking. So, ironically, Leatherstocking's very manliness prevents him from fulfilling his sexual role.

Although a few major American writers seem to have escaped the worst effects of prudery, they were all tainted by it. Poe decried the didacticism and moralizing that marred Longfellow's poetry, but the men and women in his own stories and poems are not only sexless but bodiless. Reflecting the view of women that he had absorbed in his youth in the South, he declared that the main purpose of women's education was to prepare them to be wives and mothers. Betraying his own sexual inadequacies, he avoided the responsibilities of a normal union by marrying his fourteen-year-old cousin, and after her death a few years later he entered into a series of intimate yet avowedly Platonic friendships with older women.

Almost all of Poe's heroes are high-born, high-minded, mysteriously tainted men in love with pure and ethereal women who are either dying of a nameless malady, are already dead, or are in some inaccessible Nevermore. There is no possibility that any of them—Ligeia, Ulalume, Berenice, Lenore, Annabel Lee—will experience the heat of desire, make love or beget children. Despite the aura of romantic evil Baudelaire thought he found in him, Poe remains a writer for young readers; we realize there is no true evil in his characters because there is no true passion. They are merely sick. We may continue to admire Poe's mastery of morbid fantasies and the macabre even though we know these were shaped by grave emotional disturbances and the desexualized image of love fostered by the age.

Hawthorne is a striking example of a man of more or less normal sexual impulses whose moral views were sharply constricted by his time, place, and lineage. The awareness of evil and the varieties of guilt that permeate his work were largely the product of a childhood and youth in an old Salem family amid the ghosts of sin-haunted ancestors. Such a sense of sin comes not from successfully repressed desires but from the constant effort to cope with supposedly shameful emotions. Although he did not marry until he was thirty-eight, once he fell in love he became an ardent suitor. And after his marriage, his letters to his wife reveal a continuing ardor. When she was away from home on a winter visit, he wrote to her, "The thought of going to bed is hateful to me; especially these polar nights, when my body shivers like my heart. Hast thou slept warm?" During a summer separation he made an even more frankly passionate avowal, writing of "our great, lonesome bed, at night—the scene of so many blissful intercourses—now so solitary." [15]

But that was within the sanctuary of a respectable marriage achieved after long years of isolation. And during those formative years it was his New England heritage that made the deepest impression on his imagination. Moral guilt is the psychological matrix of many of his stories, and sexual guilt is the subject of his most famous novel. Although the sense of sin—what he thought of as "a stain upon the soul"—yielded the themes of his best work, it was in a sense a circumscribing influence. Not able to deal with sexuality openly, he concentrated on the psychological aftermath of forbidden emotions, an aftermath that seems more real than its sources. The result is work that has the quality of legend or parable, dominated by characters who live in the shadow of past deeds. Thus, although *The Scarlet Letter* is the outstanding classical American novel on the subject of sexuality, it contains only echoes of the act of passion.

The passion must be taken on faith. This is difficult because we are never convinced that that high-minded Puritan minister, Arthur Dimmesdale, could have been capable of so rash a passion with so responsible a married woman as Hester Prynne. We can believe Hester capable of the act especially after we have seen the pride with which she wears the *A* on her dress, but how can we believe it of Dimmesdale, so faint of heart, so consumed by fears? In the light of her glowing *A,* Hester shines; Dimmesdale is dim beside her. The moral is clear: Confess your sin and you may survive; hide it and it will consume you. But either way you will pay. Who can doubt that Hawthorne accepted the Puritan view of sexual sin—not to speak of the old myth of feminine evil—when he says of Hester Prynne: "Here, there was the taint of deepest sin in the most sacred quality of human life, working such effect, that the world was only the darker for this woman's beauty, and the more lost for the infant that she had borne." Despite this submission to the morality of his time and place, *The Scarlet Letter* is a great novel because it acknowledges the supreme power of passion and dares to make a sinning woman a noble figure. Perhaps Hawthorne himself did not realize how much Hester's love had transfigured her. Even though Hawthorne was never able to reconcile the life-affirming nature of love with its potentiality for sin, he grasped the greatness of the theme and at least once made it into an enduring drama.

In other Hawthorne novels there are men who are too ineffectual or too inhibited to woo or win the women who attract them. In *The Blythedale Romance,* Miles Coverdale, having joined an experimental community resembling Brook Farm, relates the romantic history of two women in the community, the radiant, theatrical Xenobia and a disembodied creature named Priscilla, and confesses only in the last line that he was all along in love with Priscilla. A lackluster figure throughout, Coverdale achieves the distinction of being the most reticent narrator as well as the most inhibited lover in fiction.

Equally self-denying in his own way is the young hero in

Hawthorne's very first novel, a creaky little Gothic romance called *Fanshawe*. Fanshawe, an ascetic student at a New England seminary in the 1750's, strikes a sympathetic chord in Ellen Langton, an angelic maiden who lives with the college president's family. When Ellen is lured away by a mysterious stranger, Fanshawe leads the pursuit and stumbles upon the pair just as the stranger seems about to rape Ellen. Rescued, Ellen faints, whereupon Fanshawe furtively kisses her, but after she recovers he rejects her advances, telling her he is not long for this world. He returns to his studies and dies a year or two later. Even as the novel of a twenty-three-year-old, *Fanshawe* is an immature work, one that makes physical weakness an excuse for psychological impotence.

By comparison with Poe and Hawthorne, Melville seems a fairly robust and rounded human being, furnished by his early career at sea with a rich body of uncensored experience. This experience gave rise again and again to a main character who leaves home and all the old patterns of life, including courtship and marriage. He becomes a wanderer, even an outcast, without ties or memories, sometimes tasting a moment of love with some tawny dream maiden on a South Sea isle or perhaps cleaving to a male companion in a way that verges on homosexuality. Forgotten or blocked out are the prim girls or inhibited wives back home.

In Melville's first book *Typee* (1843), coyly subtitled, *A Peep at Polynesian Life,* his account of how the native maidens anoint the body of the young American sailor—who is the narrator—with aromatic oils and frolic half naked with him seems calculated to make male readers back home realize how artificial and fearfully repressed their womenfolk were. Although the main point of such passages was the innocence and naturalness of the girls, and although the youth is not described as taking any liberties with them, *The Living Age,* an English periodical much respected in America, referred to the hero as having "cohabited" with a native girl, and added: "We shall not pollute our pages by transferring to them the scenes in which this wretched profligate appears." [16] Americans in general agreed with this verdict, and before the publisher consented to issue the second printing, he insisted that all the more candid passages be cut out. And it was done.

In Melville's next book, *Omoo,* also set in the South Pacific, there is little about women except for some bitter passages on the way the white man debauches the girls of such islands as Tahiti and leaves entire populations dying of a disease that Melville does not name. There are also the Christian missionaries who take drastic steps to end the age-old sexual liberties and innocent immodesty of the islanders. To Melville nothing revealed more harshly the unnaturalness of the Protestant moral code than this substitution of a code of abstinence, sin, and guilt for the free but taboo-regulated dalliance of the natives. It contributed powerfully to Melville's alienation.

Only in *Pierre; or, The Ambiguities* (1852) does Melville make any effort to deal with American women of his own class: the result is a bizarre tale of homoerotic and incestuous impulses. In a later chapter we shall return to it and such other of Melville's books as *White Jacket, Moby Dick,* and *Billy Budd* as evidence of the errant passions that sometimes lay beneath the surface of Victorian life.

There was no need to censor the most popular American novelists of the period; they were mostly women willing and eager to satisfy the demand for sentimental romance glazed with piety and for melodramatic incidents disguised as lessons in conduct. The Richardson or Rowson treatments of the seduction theme were too bold for nineteenth-century taste and the formula was soon purified into an account of the experiences of a young woman, usually a poor but beautiful orphan, on the road to marriage. After all sorts of preposterous misunderstandings and estrangements, mainly the result of the girl's bottomless innocence or false pride or of the machinations of jealous or simply villainous characters, she wins her true love. He is generally a splendid young man who has rich parents and is plainly destined for success. Other standard ingredients are crippled or blind children who die, providing pathos; prodigals who repent, supplying a moral; rich women who are victims of fashion and dissipation, edifying the frugal; clergymen who are saintly, pleasing the pious; and Negroes who are grotesquely comical, furnishing humor.

More and more of such novels appeared during the 1830's and 1840's and swelled into a flood in the 1850's. Their popularity is hard to believe. The four or five best-known novelists of the middle of the century each wrote from twenty to forty novels, including at least one that sold from half a million to one million copies, the equivalent of a sale of many times that number today. A reading of such once immensely popular novels as *Rutledge* (1860) by Miriam Coles Harris, *Tempest and Sunshine* (1854) by Mary J. Holmes, and *St. Elmo* (1869) by Augusta Evans Wilson, or almost any of the books of Fanny Fern, Caroline Lee Hentz, Maria S. Cummins, and Mrs. E. D. E. N. Southworth, carries one into a world so simple, with heroes and heroines so good and pure, villains so self-consciously villainous, complications so artificial, and endings so perfectly just that it would be cruel to take such books seriously had they not been read so widely. They were ready-made dreams for girls in drab villages or the boardinghouses of factory towns, a mixture of sensational incidents and cheap tears for emotion-starved housewives and spinster schoolteachers. They held out a promise or a reward for all, no matter how poor, who remain virtuous. Generally limited in time to the four or five years between the heroine's adolescence and her marriage, such novels had a pretext for never coming to grips with the ultimate realities of love and marriage. As any European visitor would have agreed, only in America could the most popular fiction be devoted to the lives of adolescent girls.

Realizing that they were losing the battle against the novels, the moralists grew ever more shrill and sweeping in their charges. The Reverend Daniel Wise, considering such reading an addiction wherein one began on the upper slopes with Scott and inevitably ended in the depths with Eugène Sue and the "abominations" of Paul de Kock, cried, "Young man, beware of reading your first novel!" [17]

In his *Lectures to Young Men,* that immensely popular preacher Henry Ward Beecher discusses literature almost entirely on a scale of moral purity. With a great show of discrimination he says he prefers the frankness of Chaucer to the "witching" licentiousness of Tom Moore, and the "abominable vulgarity" of Swift to the "scoundrel-indirections" of Sterne. But he then adds: "What an incredible state of morals, in the English church, that permitted two of her eminent clergy to be the most licentious writers of the age." Shakespeare he finds gross but immeasurably purer than his age, Bulwer he detests, and Byron and Fielding he lumps with such "abominable" French writers as Sue, Balzac, George Sands (sic), and Dumas.[18]

Publishers often formed a major censorship barrier. In 1889 a Lippincott editor explained to an author that the frankness of her manuscript made it a "dangerous experiment, commercially speaking," and he shamelessly added, "I am very much afraid we shall have to go back to the conventional lies of modern fiction and leave such books . . . to other publishers." [19]

Others besides preachers and editors rejected books that were not bleached clean. Just after his engagement to Olivia Langdon in 1869, Mark Twain insisted on expurgating *Gulliver's Travels* before she read it, and he reproached himself for letting her read *Don Quixote* before he could make it fit for her. "It pains me to think of you reading that book as it stands. . . . If you haven't finished it, Livy, don't do it. You are as pure as snow, and I would have you always so—untainted, untouched even by the impure thoughts of others." [20] The mixture of values in this statement is remarkable: Clemens implies not only that he cannot trust Livy to resist corruption, but that he is corrupt and his wife must remain pure to make up for his weakness and give him the pleasure of possessing an untainted sexual partner.

The more conservative guardians of the public purity found even some of the most didactic and sermon-plated novels unfit for youthful readers. One of the more pompous of the tribe of counsellors of youth, Charles Butler, declared in 1849 that even novels purporting to trace "the progress of vice to infamy and unhappiness" introduced scenes that corrupted innocence. Holy Scriptures, he concluded, was the only reading worth the time.[21] Narrow as such critics may have been, there was, ironically, some justice in their complaints. They saw through the pretense that a last-chapter conversion in a Faustian or Byronic career or a sermon tacked onto an account of sinfulness, usually romantically vague or mysterious, made a novel a force for virtue. The title character of *St. Elmo,* a cynical and bitter man in his late thirties, has in him echoes of Byron, Lovelace, Jane Eyre's Mr. Rochester, and Poe's Roderick Usher. Even though the heroine, a paragon of piety, beauty, and literary talents declares that she abhors everything he represents, she is helplessly fascinated by him. Preachers realized that readers were also fascinated by such a character and that they made use of the highly moral ending of the tale—St. Elmo not only repudiates his entire past but becomes a minister—to excuse their interest. It was genteel trash designed to be read without a pang of guilt.

Novels, poetry, history, Shakespeare's plays, the Bible—nothing written was safe from the prudes. Even the classical myths, as remote as they were in time, space, and culture from nineteenth-century America, were scored. That they were among the loveliest products of a rare civilization and had inspired masterpieces of poetry, painting, and sculpture for two thousand years impressed such prurient souls not at all. Dr. William Sanger, discussing the decay of morals as a cause of prostitution in the 1850's, puts "immoral literature" high on the list of bad influences. "Mythology, in particular," he writes, "introduces our youth to courtesans who are described as goddesses, and goddesses who are but courtesans in disguise. Poetry and history as frequently have for their themes the ecstasies of illicit love as the innocent joys of pure affection." [22] These are poisonous fruits, he asserts, and must be culled. Elsewhere Sanger himself points out that many of New York's prostitutes were immigrant girls who had been domestic servants earning a weekly wage of $1.05 and board.[23] And yet it was the Greek myths that he feared.

In the same year that Longfellow's *Hiawatha* appeared, a thirty-six-year-old Brooklyn journalist named Walt Whitman printed, bound, and distributed a tiny edition of a book of poems called *Leaves of Grass*. But within a day or two, the first bookseller to carry the book discovered objectionable lines in it and returned all his copies to the author.[24] The following year Whitman found a publisher for an enlarged edition, but after selling a handful of copies and despite a resounding testimonial from Emerson, the publishers, frightened by charges of immorality, turned back almost the entire edition to the author. Emerson himself was acutely annoyed when his letter to Whitman turned up in the New York *Tribune*. He was even more disturbed by some of the bolder poems that were added to the second edition of *Leaves of Grass,* and during a meeting with Whitman in Boston in 1860 spent two hours pleading with the poet not to include the "Children of Adam" poems in his book.[25] More typical of the New England reaction was Whittier's gesture—picking up the book and dropping it into the fireplace.

Not content with action against his book, the bigots, as we know, had Whitman dismissed in 1865 from his clerkship in the Interior Department. But there was a cry of protest, and the poet was soon given a job in another department.[26] Then *Leaves of Grass,* partly as a result of enthusiastic praise from abroad, began to gain attention in America. Nevertheless, when a reputable Boston publisher, Osgood, took over its distribution in 1881, the Boston Society for the Suppression of Vice threatened legal action against him. Osgood immediately gave way, turning over the plates to Whitman. It was not until 1891–92 that a publisher put out an edition that remained in print. It had taken thirty-seven years and eight editions to achieve permanent publication for what is today considered one of the few masterpieces of American literature.

The history of the rejection and abuse of *Leaves of Grass* in the face of endorsement by Emerson, W. M. Rossetti, Swinburne, and others is depressing evidence of the extent to which moral values overrode all other considerations in the Victorian judgment of books. The average reader in 1855, morally intimidated to the point of helplessness, was no more ready for *Leaves of Grass* than he would have been for Joyce's *Ulysses.* Even the relatively informed and sensitive critic was psychologically crippled by the moral pressures of the age. When Edmund Clarence Stedman published his *Poets of America* in 1885, he treated Whitman as a genius with one intolerable defect—his sexuality. Stedman was understandably troubled by what he came close to identifying as the homosexual note in *Leaves of Grass.* But it was precisely because he recognized Whitman as a great and original voice, and because he was aware, with shame, of the hypocrisy of his own time, that his criticism of Whitman's candor in sexual matters is a revelation of the damaging effect of the genteel view. Stedman argues thus:

> The fault was not that he discussed matters which others timidly evade, but that he did not do it in a clear way,—that he was too anatomical and malodorous withal; furthermore, that in this department he showed a morbid interest . . . as if with a special purpose to lug it in. His pictures were sometimes so realistic, his speech so free, as to excite the hue and cry of

> indecent exposure; the display of things natural, indeed, but which we think is unnatural to exhibit on the highway, or in the reading-room and parlor.[27]

A shrewd prosecutor, he parades his understanding of the poet's motives and incidentally, an almost psychoanalytical awareness of the mutilating effect of suppression:

> On the poet's side it is urged that . . . it was necessary to celebrate the body with special unction, since, with respect to the physical basis of life, our social weakness and hypocrisy are most extreme. Not only should the generative functions be proclaimed, but, also . . . the side of our life which is hidden because it is of the earth, earthy, should be plainly recognized . . . and thus, out of rankness and coarseness, a new virility be bred, an impotent and squeamish race at last be made whole.[28]

Stedman then asserts that Nature, the great goddess by whom Whitman is supposed to be guided, herself disguises the ugly and repulsive on her surface. She, too, the critic claims, has "her sweet and sacred sophistries, and the delight of Art is to heighten her beguilement and . . . to portray what she might be in ideal combinations. Nature, I say, covers her slime, her muck, her ruins, with garments that to us are beautiful. . . . The law of suggestion, of half-concealment . . . is the surest road to truth." [29]

Having exhausted the role of sympathetic critic, Stedman blandly uses a falsified, Victorianized view of Mother Nature—which equates Whitman's sexuality with slime and muck—to assert that poetry must idealize. Idealizing may be a function of poetry, but when it becomes the main or only function, as it did in the verse of Stedman and his circle, it results in a thin, overpolished, imitative product destined to be forgotten along with other shallow fashions of an age.

These were America's novelists and poets. The prophets and sages were Emerson and Thoreau, and they were as great as America has had. But they were all light, blinding light, and very little heat. So clear of mind and soul, they yet lacked the central vitality that gives force to sympathies and enthusiasms, the passion by which a man is made whole. Perhaps two centuries of Puritans living on a stony soil had bred out or driven off the bold and enterprising types, leaving a strain that was at its best high-minded and of supreme integrity but thin-blooded, content to search out truths and let others discover how to live by them.

Emerson was well aware of his lack. "I was born cold. . . ." he wrote in his *Journals*. "I shiver in and out." And again: "The capital defect of my nature for society is the want of animal spirits. . . . Even for those whom I really love I have not animal spirits. . . ." [30] Even though he was married to a lovely woman, he added: ". . . I husband all my strength in this bachelor life I lead," and elsewhere: "Love is temporary and ends with marriage . . . which dwarfs love to green fruit." [31] Once or twice he strikes with something like frustrated fury at the lure of sensuality: "There is no greater lie than a voluptuous book like Boccaccio. For it represents the pleasures of appetite, which only at rare intervals, a few times in a lifetime, are intense, and to whose acme continence is essential, as frequent, habitual and belonging to the incontinent." [32]

And yet as the prophet of the individual and a writer in search of words that would awake the proper and complacent, he felt the need for "salt and fire" in language, for a new invigorating coarseness:

> What a pity that we cannot curse and swear in good society! Cannot the stinging dialect of the sailors be domesticated? It is the best rhetoric and . . . those forbidden words are the only good ones. . . . This profane swearing and bar-room wit has salt and fire in it. . . . One who wishes to refresh himself by contact with the bone and sinew of society must avoid what is called the respectable portion of this city. . . . Dante knows "God damn" and can be rowdy if he please, and he does please.[33]

And elsewhere he wrote: "I hate goodies. . . . We will almost sin to spite them." [34] Such outbursts were an all too infrequent kind of relief from the passages in which every sentence was a new flight into another empyrean.

Unlike Emerson, Thoreau was unaware of his crucial defect —his lack not simply of warmth and affection ("As for taking Thoreau's arm, I should as soon take the arm of an elm-tree,"

Emerson said) but of all sexual desire. He lived in the severest simplicity, gladly doing without wife or family or wine or meat, but it required not the slightest sacrifice for, as Emerson says, he had no temptations to fight against, no fleshly appetites, no passions. Thoreau generally avoids the entire subject of love and sex because it is both distasteful and of no importance to him. He was wise in this for his rare comments on them are among the few priggish and immature passages in his writings. Thus, in the *Letters,* he says of marriage: "If it is the result of pure love, there can be nothing sensual in marriage. Chastity is something positive, not negative. It is the virtue of the married especially. All lusts or base pleasures must give a place to loftier delights. . . . Virginity, too, is a budding flower and by an impure marriage the virgin is deflowered." [35] This is the vaporizing of a man who is simply ignorant of the nature of love relationships.

Thoreau himself tells us that he found young women flighty and their presence annoying. When one woman wrote to him proposing marriage (what, we wonder, could have led her to it), his response, as he describes it in a letter, was shock and repulsion. "Of course I did not write a deliberate answer. How could I deliberate upon it? I sent back as distinct a *no* as I have learned to pronounce. . . . I wished that it might burst like a hollow shot, after it had struck and buried itself." [36] The prissiness here is that of a man to whom a woman has far less interest than an ant or pigeon. He was so puzzled by what he consistently called the "impure" relationship between men and women that once in his *Journal* he speculated about it as though it were an uncommon disease. "May it consist with the health of some bodies to be impure?" [37] Priggishness intrudes even on the simple profundities of *Walden.* The chapter "Higher Laws" is full of a fetishistic abhorrence of sensual pleasures, culminating in such meaningless flourishes as "Chastity is the flowering of man."

Once, in a letter in 1852, he makes a unique, almost poignant admission: "The intercourse of the sexes, I have dreamed, is incredibly beautiful, too fair to be remembered. . . . I have had thoughts about it but they are among the most fleeting and irrecoverable in my experience." But the letter soon shifts back to the note of puzzlement and reaches an ultimate pathos with,

"What the essential difference between man and woman is, that they should be thus attracted to one another, no one has satisfactorily explained." [38] No lover since the world began has thought that this required an explanation.

Whether or not it diminishes the value of Thoreau's ideal of living barely and simply, unfettered by creature comforts, human friendship, or love, we must recognize that he was able to adopt the solitary stance as much because of his deficiencies as because of his virtues. That is why even the men who most admire and envy him have not really imitated him. They need the love of woman, and they realize that, whatever the reason—physiological, psychological, or the moral climate—Thoreau did not.

There is probably no more striking example of the conflict between nineteenth-century prudery and a natural inclination to bawdry than Mark Twain. Students have long been aware of the struggle between Samuel L. Clemens, worshiper of respectability and success, and Mark Twain, unreconstructed and sometimes savage satirist. A profound part of this split personality was his dual view of sex.

It was not that Clemens subscribed to the conventional double standard of his time, whereby men who publicly decried any freedom of behavior, especially in women, indulged in libidinous acts or thoughts in private. He believed that well-bred women were and should be pure, but he could hardly conceal his own taste for the salacious and profane, or, as he grew older, his conviction that the object of man's laws was in great part to thwart man's nature. His insistence on purity in women and in the art and books that good women were exposed to was an almost desperate effort to preserve the last sanctums of innocence in a corrupt world. This left him far more concerned with the morals of such women as his wife Livy than with the need of painters and writers for freedom of expression. He kept trying, as Leslie Fiedler has said, to cling to the lost Eden of his childhood.

That is why Clemens warned Livy against the impurities in *Gulliver's Travels* and *Don Quixote,* why *Tom Jones* disgusted him, and why he found a *Venus* by Titian, which he saw in the Uffizi, obscene.[39] That is why he idolized a sexless conception of Joan of Arc in his book on the Maid of Orleans and partly why he flayed Abelard as "a dastardly seducer" who deserved castration.[40]

The inconsistencies in his standards is nowhere better illustrated than in his obsessive thrusts at the looseness of French novels. Despite the licentiousness he had surely seen in Western mining towns and on Mississippi riverboats, he described the French as a "filthy-minded" people and was forever making such cracks as that France had neither winter nor summer nor morals. Elsewhere he defined the "two great branches of French thought" as science and adultery, and in still another place he declared that "a Frenchman's home is where another man's wife is." [41] Such attitudes may well have stemmed from his boyhood in a Missouri village where the sexual morality was a stale residue of New England Puritanism, and from his zeal, after coming East, to demonstrate to his wife's rich family in upstate New York that he could be as respectable as any of them.

Although in the satires of *Letters from Earth,* written late in life and left unpublished, he revealed an entirely different attitude, he always behaved as though women—that is, decent women—were and should be untouchable while men in general were simply untrustworthy. (As a corollary, he accepted prostitution as a necessary evil.) When a woman of this class allowed herself to be seduced, her fall, as he depicts it in Laura Hawkins in *The Gilded Age,* was total. After Laura is abandoned by her seducer—the usual wages, in Victorian novels, for such a misstep—she throws off all scruple and thereafter makes her way by bribery and blackmail.

Always, even in the cynical moments of his later years, Clemens justified obedience to customs. In 1906 he gladly joined in preparing a welcome for Maxim Gorki, already world famous as a short story writer, but when he learned that the woman accompanying the Russian was not married to him, Clemens refused to have anything to do with them. In a fragment not published until 1962, Clemens defended his behavior on the grounds that Gorki offended American custom and that custom is more sacred than the law. "Customs are not enacted," he wrote, "they grow gradually up. . . . In the fullness of their strength they can stand up straight in front of a world of argument, and yield not an inch. . . . Maybe it is right; maybe it is wrong—that has nothing to do with the matter. . . . But they have to be obeyed." [42] The conformity demanded here seems rigid even by the standards of 1906; it seems even more baffling in the light of other unpublished pieces in which he bitterly mocks such conformity. This can only be explained as the private Mark Twain trying to rationalize the priggish behavior of the public Mark Twain.

The other side of Samuel Clemens' nature was the Mark Twain of the mining camps, boom towns, and Mississippi riverboats who became known in certain circles (all male, of course) for his salacious jokes, smoking-car stories, and sundry items of plain pornography. We should not be surprised that Mark Twain told dirty jokes and stories: These have always been a stock-in-trade of humorists because they have always served as explosive relief for pent-up sexual urges, a rebellion against censors, Grundys, and preachers. Aside from jottings in the back of his notebooks, only a few of these jokes and jibes have been recorded. All of them were outrageous, calculated to shock; for example, when a judge in 1907 fined the Standard Oil Company of Indiana over $29,000,000 for accepting illegal rebates, Clemens said he was reminded of the bride who declared the next morning: "I expected it but didn't suppose it would be so big." [43] But these were all trifles as compared to such elaborate concoctions as his *1601,* a bawdy conversation among prominent Elizabethans, or the talk on masturbation, "Some Thoughts on the Science of Onanism," that he gave to a men's club in Paris. We will take these up in a later chapter along with other evidence that men in the 1870's could be quite as smutty if not quite as lusty as Elizabethans—but never in mixed company. Doubtless Mark Twain's excuse for all these was that they were jokes; and, in fact, they are robbed of their sexual significance by their wild exaggeration.

In his books, Mark Twain was coarse but never sexually candid. For all the relative realism of such works as *Huckleberry Finn,* especially in its treatment of bigotry and meanness, there is no sexuality in them. Clemens not only censored his own writings but, mistrusting his instincts, he submitted them to his wife Olivia, to William Dean Howells, and to others for further cleansing. How far they went is illustrated by Howells' warning that too much space in *Tom Sawyer* was devoted to the way Becky Thatcher looks at the "stark naked" human figures in the schoolmaster's anatomy book.[44] Of one of the illustrations made for *Huckleberry Finn,* that of "the lecherous old rascal kissing the girl at campmeeting," Clemens conceded that it was "powerful good" but insisted that the whole subject of camp meetings was too disgusting and that pictures were "sure to tell the truth about it too plainly." [45]

After all this, the gods must have laughed cruelly when the Library Committee of Concord, Massachusetts, threw out *Huckleberry Finn* as rough, coarse, and inelegant, when the Springfield *Republican* called it immoral, and Louisa May Alcott, high priestess among authors of children's books, said: "If Mr. Clemens cannot think of something better to tell our pure-minded lads and lasses, he had better stop writing for them." [46] Clemens did not join the gods in their laughter; instead he fumed and fretted, half in shame and half in anger.

But such contradictions are further complicated by the recently published *Letters from Earth.* These are reports from the archangel Satan (as he was before his fall) to his fellow archangels concerning that curious creation of God, the earth, and its "insane inhabitants." The letters contain some of the wittiest and most devastating passages ever put down about man's sexual mores and marriage laws. Although evidently written in Mark Twain's later years, when he is generally said to have become cynical about "the damned human race," these comments seem more bawdily amused and baffled than bitter.

Whereas all men, he says in Letter III, enter the world, like Adam and Eve, naked, unashamed, and pure-minded, a Christian mother's first duty is to soil her child's mind, so that he grows up to become a missionary and in turn soils the minds of innocent savages by teaching them to be ashamed of their bodies. Modesty, Mark Twain explains, has no standards because it defies nature and reason and is subject to "anybody's diseased caprice." Equally absurd is the fact that God requires man to forgive offenders seventy-and-seven times, but himself punished Adam and Eve's progeny to the end of time for a trifling offense committed long before they were born.[47]

But these observations are merely offhand thrusts leading to the scathing satire of Letter VIII.[48] There Mark Twain describes man's laws against adultery as stupid because by temperament, "which is the *real* law of God . . . many men can't help committing adultery when they get a chance." But the Bible doesn't allow adultery at all, whether a person can help it or not. He continues:

> It allows no distinction between goat and tortoise—the excitable goat . . . that has to have some adultery every day or fade or die; and the tortoise, that cold calm puritan, that takes a treat only once in two years and then goes to sleep in the midst of it and doesn't wake up for sixty days. No lady goat is safe from criminal assault, even on the Sabbath Day, when there is a gentleman goat within three miles to leeward of her and nothing in the way but a fence fourteen feet high, whereas neither the gentleman tortoise nor the lady tortoise is ever hungry enough for the solemn joys of fornication to be willing to break the Sabbath to get them. Now according to man's curious reasoning, the goat has earned punishment, the tortoise praise.

Just as nonsensical, he says, is the way the command, "Thou shalt not commit adultery," is applied equally to children in the cradle, to youths and maidens, and to men and women "of forty, of fifty, of sixty, of seventy, of eighty, of ninety, of one hundred." It is not hard on the children, it is cruelly hard on the youths, and it is "blessedly softened" on adults of forty, fifty, and sixty; yet, "with comical imbecility . . . it puts the four remaining estates under its crushing ban." Mark Twain adds:

> Poor old wrecks, they couldn't disobey if they tried. And think —because they holily refrain from adulterating each other, they get praise for it! Which is nonsense; for even the Bible knows . . . that if the oldest veteran could get his lost heyday back again for an hour he would cast that commandment to the winds and ruin the first woman he came across.

Boldly, Satan—speaking for Mark Twain of course—describes every statute in the Bible and the lawbooks as an attempt to defeat the law of God and Nature. The law of God, as plainly expressed in woman's construction, is that there shall be no limit on her sexual intercourse, while man is under inflexible bonds. "During twenty-three days in every month . . . till she dies of old age," Mark Twain writes of woman, "she is ready for action, and *competent*. As competent as the candlestick is to receive the candle. Competent every day, competent every night. Also, she *wants* that candle—yearns for it, longs for it, hankers after it, as commanded by the law of God in her heart." By contrast, man is competent only from the age of sixteen for about thirty-five years. "After fifty his performance is of poor quality . . . whereas his great-grandmother is as good as new. . . . Her candlestick is as firm as ever, whereas his candle is increasingly softened and weakened . . . until at last it can no longer stand, and is mournfully laid to rest. . . ." Woman has the unlimited privilege of adultery almost all the days of her life. But she is everywhere robbed of this by man and his statutes. Man knows, furthermore, that he will never see the day that "she can't overwork, and defeat, and put out of commission any ten masculine plants . . . put to bed with her." Man assembles these "luminous facts," Satan reports, and draws this astonishing conclusion: "The Creator intended the woman to be restricted to one man." Man constructs this conclusion into a law. And he does it without consulting woman although she has infinitely more at stake than he has, being capable of at least 150,000 "refreshments" in a lifetime where he is good for scarcely five thousand. "You have heretofore found out, by my teachings, that man is a fool; you are now aware that woman is a damned fool."

What emerges from the welter of Clemens' opinions is this: Human conventions on sex and marriage are contrary to the emotional nature of both men and women, but the conventions must be obeyed lest we have chaos. Clemens himself evidently obeyed the conventions in his attachment to his wife and in his efforts to protect her and women like her from all "corrupting" influences, including sundry masterpieces of literature and art. But he accepted the view that men had somewhat more of the animal in them; so he apparently felt free to enjoy bawdy stag parties and indulge in the rawest ribaldry.

This interpretation is strikingly borne out by Clemens' account (published by Bernard De Voto in 1940) of a visit in 1908 from Elinor Glyn, the author of *Three Weeks*. Considered shocking at the time, *Three Weeks* was the story of the brilliant wife of a coarse husband and her love affair with a gifted man married to a commonplace woman. Clemens told the novelist that her lovers were obeying the law of God, but he firmly added that we were all servants of convention and that while "the laws of Nature, that is to say the laws of God, plainly made every human being a law unto himself, we must steadfastly refuse to obey those laws, and we must steadfastly stand by the conventions . . . since the statutes furnish us peace . . . and stability, and therefore are better for us than the laws of God, which would soon plunge us into confusion . . . and anarchy." When Miss Glyn implored Clemens to publish his views, he answered that if he or any other "wise, intelligent, and experienced person should suddenly throw down the walls that protect and conceal his real opinions on almost any subject," it would be clear that he had lost his mind and should be sent to an asylum.[49]

Such are the knots into which a repressive age can tie a man who was sometimes a devastating foe of hypocrisy.

Although the novels and stories of Henry James may seem to offer a vast mass of evidence on the relationship between the sexes, they are of little use for our purposes because they never enter the realm of genuine sexuality. James avoided this theme not so much out of prudery as out of a constitutional inability to cope with it. It is tempting to attribute this to inhibitions fostered by the age, but the evidence suggests that an incident in about his seventeenth year left him physiologically and probably psychologically incapable of consummating a sexual relationship. In his later years he had at least one friendship—with the young sculptor Hendrik Andersen—that was homosexual in attitudes if not in practice. What is more significant is that he never saw his unfulfilled relationship with women as a barrier to exploring in his stories the nature of heterosexual love. Anticipating what often happens in novels today, James asserted that novelists who concentrate on physical love soon find that it leaves no place for anything else. But he went toward the other extreme, dwelling exclusively on the psychological aspects. Had he been able, he might have seen in *Anna Karenina* how indispensable both the physical and the psychological are to a full rendering of love.

Modern critics have been aware that in his hundreds of searching studies of the relationship of the sexes James only once or twice describes anything even remotely resembling physical passion. A few critics, such as Van Wyck Brooks, have seen this as a serious deficiency, and a close student of this aspect of James' work, Maxwell Geismar, has made a case for it as a crippling defect. Geismar sees James' fictions as an immense, ingenious, and, in the later works, almost mad exercise in the abstract manipulation of hypothetical characters—all based on an outsider's, a kind of voyeur's, acquaintance with the love relationship.[50] He is the first novelist, as Fiedler says, to make a peeper, and even a peeping child, the focus of a work of art.[51]

Many critics who have dealt seriously with James have accepted or rationalized this vital lack in James' approach. They make this accommodation despite the fact that James' reputation rests heavily on his psychological realism. By Victorian moral standards there was of course no special deficiency in James' treatment of love: his work has everything that could be desired in refinement and sophistication. James' notebooks reveal that the themes of illicit love that did come his way invariably seemed to him unacceptable to American readers. In 1884 James heard the story of a young Lord Stafford who, hopelessly in love with a Lady Grosvenor, became engaged to a younger woman. Then Lady Grosvenor's husband died, leaving the young man torn between love and obligation. James thought he was morally obliged to marry his fiancée but saw a more interesting story in a *vie à trois* in which the young lord married his fiancée and made the widow his mistress. But that kind of treatment, he said, was open only to "a Frenchman or a naturalist." [52]

A few years later Paul Bourget, French novelist and critic, told him of a young woman who had committed suicide because, Bourget thought, she fancied her mother had taken lovers. James was fascinated. But he felt he would have to modify the essential theme because he did not "want to depict in an American magazine, a woman carrying on adulteries under her daughter's eyes." [53] Similarly, in planning *The Wings of the Dove,* James considered describing a young heiress dying of consumption and a young man who, although engaged to an older woman, is tempted to give the heiress a taste of life and happiness. But James was repelled by "the ugliness, the nastiness . . . of the man 'having' a sick girl." James also thought that if he were writing for "a French public," he might let the young man make his fiancée his mistress while maintaining a liaison with the heiress so that he might inherit her money. This he also rejected as ugly and vulgar. In the book the dying girl learns of the relation between the man and the other woman and simply "turns her face to the wall." [54]

James dealt with sensual elements only as far as a respectable novelist should. To go much further was, in fact, perilous, as Zola found when he wrote *Nana* and *La Terre,* or as Hardy learned when *Jude the Obscure* appeared. Completely satisfactory sexual love depends on a psychological as well as a physical rapport, but it is in great part sensual and primitive—qualities that were utterly alien to Henry James' fastidious nature and psychologizing talents.

The writers who would end the stranglehold of propriety and respectability in literature were already at work overseas in the 1870's and not long after that in the United States. Such novelists as Zola and Tolstoi, followed by Maupassant and, on a popular, almost subliterary level, Ouida, began to shake off restraints—always less severe in France—in the treatment of sexuality. The extent of American interest in such writers can once again best be gauged by the attacks on them. In a typical assault, called "Profligacy in Fiction," A. K. Fiske, reviewing Zola's *Nana* and Ouida's *Moths* in the prestigious *North American Review* in 1880, described Zola as "a genius of the muck-rake" who had opened the sewers of society into the gardens of literature, a "Parisian scavenger" who painted dunghills and "the disgusting bestiality of the slums." Ouida, he said, was equally vile, doing for higher society what Zola did for the slum-dwellers. Fiske urged that the "foreign purveyors of infection" should be rejected just as the coarser English poets, dramatists, and novelists had been thrust aside in "these days of purer manners." It was not only the righteous Victorian speaking but the self-styled morally superior Anglo-Saxon. We today may find something almost obscene in the way Fiske himself used such terms as sewers, putridity, and foulness.[55] And his coupling of Zola and Ouida, a confectioner of romantic froth, reveals either a complete lack of discernment or an effort to link Zola with purveyors of pure sensationalism.

Although the narrow conservatism of the Fiskes was challenged in the next decade by such writer-critics as Howells and Garland, the latter were themselves still fettered by the taboos on sexual candor.

When it became fashionable in the 1920's to make fun of the Victorians, William Dean Howells, most influential American novelist and critic of his time, was damned as prudish and anemic, the darling, Sinclair Lewis said, of vicars and old maids. And the leftist critics of the 1930's added that he was intolerably bourgeois and smug. Endlessly, he was beaten with one sentence from his criticism: "Our novelists . . . concern themselves with the more smiling aspects of life, which are the more American. . . ." [56]

Actually Howells was sensitive and alert, capable of courageous and liberated opinions. By temperament moderate, trusting in reason and civility, he nevertheless despised sentimentality, and he led the fight for realism in fiction, for dealing with life as it was. In the social turbulence of the 1880's and 1890's he espoused socialism, vigorously defended the anarchists convicted in the Haymarket Riot, and opposed American colonialism. As a critic he championed such unorthodox young writers as Stephen Crane and Frank Norris and, even more noteworthy, the great European realists, Zola, Dostoevski, Tolstoi, Turgenev, Hardy, Ibsen, Verga, and the Flaubert of *Madame Bovary.*

It is all the more significant that almost the only area in which Howells believed it was not appropriate or wise for an American novelist to render life in realistic detail was that of sexuality. This is surely evidence enough, if any is needed, that sexual activity constituted a special category of reality, one in which readers could not be trusted with the truth. Fully aware of the problem, Howells discussed it in *Harper's* in an essay later included in *Criticism and Fiction* (1891). Written by a leading man of letters at the age of fifty, it is a damaging revelation of submission to propriety.

Howells begins by declaring that "the guilty intrigue, the betrayal, the extreme flirtation" is the exceptional occurrence and that it is as bad art to lug them into a story as it is bad taste to discuss them in mixed company. He said that in Europe novels were written for men and married women but in America largely for young girls, and that he would not want to cut himself off from such responsive if innocent creatures. No one denies that there is "vicious love" beneath the surface of our society, Howells wrote, as divorce trials show, but it is not characteristic. Any author, Howells adds, who deals with guilty love and hints at potential naughtiness can create intense effects and achieve popularity; but such effects are cheap and the superior novelist can get along without them.[57]

Howells did realize that Anglo-Saxon writers had at the same time lost the privilege of dealing with "one of the most serious and sorrowful problems of life in the spirit of Tolstoi and Flaubert" or as Defoe, Richardson, and Goldsmith had dealt with it in English. "In what fatal hour," he asks, "did the Young Girl rise and seal the lips of fiction . . . to some of the most vital interests of life?" Having asked this most crucial question, Howells blandly answered that it was not the Young Girl who did it but the improvement in the manners of the novel and in those of readers. "Gentlemen no longer swear or fall drunk . . ." he announced, as though only gentlemen mattered, "or so habitually set about the ruin of their neighbors' wives, as they once did." He does admit that readers have also grown "a little squeamish" but only because they now expect a novelist, like a physician or a priest, to assume a higher function and be bound by higher laws. The problems of passion can then be dealt with as George Eliot does in her novels and as Hawthorne does in *The Scarlet Letter* or Thackeray in *Pendennis*. Having raised the argument to this lofty level, Howells concludes it on a casually commercial note, pointing out that no American magazine would print a serial that a father could not read to his daughter.[58]

Setting aside this final resignation to the taboos of popular magazines, the entire essay, for all of its talk of the novelist as priest and of the achievement of Eliot, Hawthorne, and Thackeray, is a complaisant acceptance of the standards of adolescent girls. In practice Howells was too able a novelist to write down to so tame and immature a level. But if aiming at such readers did not emasculate his work, it did rob it of imaginative range, of the thrust into those darker and more turbulent reaches of character that distinguishes a Dostoevski, a Tolstoi, and a Hardy.

Two or three times in the course of some forty volumes of fiction, Howells did undertake themes that brought him to the edge of the forbidden zone; but he never entered it. In *The*

Leatherwood God (1916) he created a backwoods evangelist named Dylks who in the late 1820's—at the same time that Joseph Smith was readying Mormonism in western New York—stirred the folk, and especially the women, of a Midwestern settlement into acclaiming him a new savior. But unlike Smith—and many camp-meeting revivalists—Dylks does not take advantage of the frenzied women who kneel at his feet. Although a skeptic warns that he is a "stallion" who will capture some foolish woman, Dylks is exposed and flees.

In one of his late novels, *The Son of Royal Langbrith,* Howells comes even closer to the theme of illicit love, but he focuses only on its effect on the wife and son of the guilty man. In an augury of soap opera, Mrs. Langbrith, a widow for twenty years of the town's rich mill owner, has allowed the world to think that her husband was a noble character, although she knew he had a mistress and children in nearby Boston. Howells makes Langbrith unscrupulous in business as well as in love. A man who flouts the sexual taboos cannot, it is clear, be allowed a redeeming feature.

Conversely, Mrs. Langbrith is seen sympathetically because she protects her husband's reputation, although she must thus deceive everyone else. But even Howells cannot make a situation so fraught with hypocrisy lead to happiness: all the characters come to a dismal, if morally proper, end. And since Langbrith's transgressions take place long before the book begins, Howells can avoid dealing directly with immorality and concentrate only on its ugliest consequences.

Bred by his Swedenborgian father in the love of purity and a fear of fleshliness, Howells simply could not control his revulsion at any hint of promiscuity: despite the indignant protests of his reform-minded friends, he refused to support Grover Cleveland for the Presidency after he heard the story of, as he put it, "that harlot and her bastard" in Cleveland's past.[59] And after he had come east from Ohio to worship at the shrine of Boston culture, he never ceased trying to prove to the Brahmins that he was a gentleman with a reverence for sensibility and tradition. This, as well as his concern with decency, and his faith in the average unfitted him as a novelist for any but the well-observed commonplace, the moderated emotion, and the minor themes of life.

It is perhaps logical that the writer whose first novel would strike the hardest blow at sexual taboos should be only twenty-two years old when he wrote it. The young man was Stephen Crane, and his novel, *Maggie: A Girl of the Streets* (1893), to which we will return in a later chapter, was a tale of a girl's seduction and ruin that had no trace of religious or moral overtones.

We come away from such a survey of nineteenth-century literature, and especialy fiction, with a disturbing sense of the reluctance of the young heroes of novels to cope maturely with young women. We are all amused by the helplessness of the typical Victorian maiden, but it is astonishing how many young men were presented as without interest in a genuine sexual relationship with a woman. If we think of Cooper's Natty Bumppo, Poe's Roderick Usher or even his A. Gordon Pym, Melville's sailors and his Pierre, and Hawthorne's Fanshawe and Coverdale, we are struck by the absence of normal desire among them. It may be doubted that they reflected the men of the age; what they do reflect is the stifling effect of suppression, prudery, and a sense of guilt.

8.

THE THEATER AND OTHER "GATES TO DEBAUCHERY"

OF all forms of artistic entertainment, the theater was subjected to the most withering censure on the grounds of vice and immorality. It had the acute disadvantage of being associated, especially in the minds of the straitlaced, with rootless and disreputable performers, pleasure-seeking and dissipated audiences, and plays that were sometimes ribald, impious, or coarse.

So there were no playhouses in the colonies for almost a century and a half except for a few small ones in the South after 1716. A theater opened in New York in 1733 but gave no performances by a professional troupe until an English company, which had been treated as a band of vagabonds in Philadelphia, appeared in it in 1750. In 1774 the First Continental Congress, obviously for moral as well as patriotic reasons, banned "every species of extravagance and dissipation, especially all kinds of gaming, cock-fighting, exhibitions of shows, plays and other expensive diversions and entertainments." [1] In Boston, Puritan opposition was still powerful enough to ban any theater until 1794, and then the English company that played in it tried to placate the pious by omitting a performance when any religious service was scheduled.[2]

Unfortunately, some of the theaters were not exactly sanctums of decorum. When playhouses were legalized in Philadelphia in 1789 and a spacious theater, seating two thousand, was put up a few years later, the more respectable citizens still stayed away. Thereafter the theaters seem to have slipped into an association with prostitution. Moreau de St. Méry, a distinguished French emigré who lived in Philadelphia in the 1790's, described the plays he saw as generally coarse and vulgar.[3] In New York almost everyone knew that the third tier of the relatively elegant Park Theatre was a haunt of prostitutes.[4] When the manager of one theater balked at issuing passes to the harlots one night, the gallery remained almost empty.

In Boston, at a meeting called in 1791 to seek repeal of the ban on theaters, Samuel Adams, leading a minority, declared that plays were immoral and undesirable. Rural districts also disapproved, so actors in Boston took to advertising their plays as "moral lectures"; *Othello* was offered as a kind of sermon on jealousy, and farces were billed as "entertaining lectures."[5] Even after the ban was lifted, strong opposition continued, and in the 1830's the enemies of the theater made much of the fact that there were bars in the theaters and that one playhouse had an adjoining brothel.[6] The spirit of Yankee frugality reinforced the opposition. In 1845, when the eminent geologist Sir Charles Lyell asked why there was still no regular theater in Boston, he was told that many New Englanders stayed away from theaters as much because the plays were costly as because they were immoral.[7]

Preachers found it easy to appeal to the smug and narrow-minded morality of their congregations with blasts against actors and plays, and yet at the same time indulge in lurid descriptions and charges. As a young preacher in the raw little city of Indianapolis in the mid-1840's, Henry Ward Beecher, having already learned to say the things his audience wanted to hear, derided the idea that plays might be able to teach morals. "Half the victims of the gallows and of the penitentiary," he grandiloquently proclaimed, "will tell you that these schools for morals were to them the gate of debauchery, the porch of pollution, the vestibule of the very house of death."[8]

Even when the theater owners brought to America distinguished British actors and presented worthy performances of Shakespeare, Sheridan, and others, the theater remained the favorite and most vulnerable target of reformers and preachers. Concentrating on its more indefensible aspects—the third-rate company offering crude melodrama or even cruder comedy to an undiscriminating audience—the ministers scourged it far more fiercely than it deserved, considering how weak an influence it was. In his *Lectures to Young Men* (1853), the Reverend Rufus Clark claimed that it had always corrupted youth and swelled "the tide of profligacy, debauchery and ruin. . . . The theatres of our large cities," he concluded, "are the most powerful auxiliaries of the brothels . . . splendid gateways to the chambers of death." As for actors, he said that for every "respectable Garrick and Siddons" there are a thousand who lead "profligate and abandoned lives," contaminated by the vicious parts they play.[9]

Prudery poisoned the opinions even of the supposedly cultivated and well-informed. When Mrs. Trollope spoke of Shakespeare during a literary conversation with another guest in a Cincinnati home, he exclaimed: "Shakespeare, Madam, is obscene, and, thank God, *WE* are sufficiently advanced to have found it out! If we must have the abomination of stage plays, let them at least be marked by the refinement of the age in which we live." [10]

The dance, too, was assailed: it was frivolous and, even more, the costumes were scandalous. The tights worn by the first major French ballet troupe in New York, in 1827, made everyone blush, and some ladies stalked out of the theater. The pulpits of the city denounced the performance, whereupon the dancers put on Turkish trousers and went on to become the rage of the town. One of the leading French dancers, Celine Celesti, was soon earning, it was rumored, $50,000 a year.[11]

Two ballet dancers who came to Cincinnati a few years later did not fare so well. Although the young city was proud of its culture, it was evidently not ready for figurantes in flesh-colored tights, and it reacted, according to Frances Trollope, with as much horror as admiration. "No one, I believe," said Mrs. Trollope, who had seen many of the great dancers of Europe, "doubted their being admirable dancers, but every one agreed that the morals of the Western world would never recover the shock. . . . [Had] it been . . . Taglioni in her most remarkable pirouette, they could not have been more reprobated." [12] When Mrs. Trollope's book appeared, this passage shocked the reviewer of Boston's sedate *North American Review* into writing:

> The pirouette . . . is a movement, in which a woman . . . poising herself on one limb, extends the other . . . at right

> angles, and . . . spins around some eight or ten times, leaving her drapery, 'transparent' and short as it is at the best, to be carried up . . . as far as it will go. This we believe is an unexaggerated description of that scene, which Mrs. Trollope sneers at the ladies of Cincinnati for regarding with horror. Is there a father or a mother, a husband or wife, a brother or sister in Christendom . . . who would view it with anything but horror? [13]

Then, in 1840, the dazzling Fanny Elssler came to America and enchanted everyone. Pagan and sensual though she was, with her tunic caught up to expose her thigh, she swept all criticism before her. After seeing her dance, Emerson is reported to have said to Margaret Fuller, "Margaret, this is poetry," to which she responded, "Waldo, this is religion." [14]

The dancing of the people themselves has almost always seemed licentious to moralists. Proclaiming war on all the merriment that men and women engage in together, the Puritans of Plymouth colony invaded the tiny nearby settlement of Merry Mount in 1628 and arrested its leader, Thomas Morton, because once a month, as a religious rite, he led his followers, including friendly Indians, in revelry and gay Maypole dances.

During the later years of the century, dancing masters kept trying to establish themselves in Boston despite fierce opposition from the clergy. In 1684 Increase Mather poured out his wrath on "gynecandrical dancing, or that which is commonly called mixt dancing of men and women . . . together," [15] and a dance teacher named Stepney was driven out of the city shortly afterward. But in the fine houses of New York and in the South the cotillions spread, and in the 1750's a dancing master, Charles Pelham, became the rage among upper-class Bostonians, who flocked to him to learn the minuet as well as jigs and reels. Even a Puritan might find little to object to in a minuet, for it was a slow and stately step with little contact and no intimacy between man and woman.

The waltz changed all that. Invading England and the United States from Germany in about 1815, it was soon popular everywhere. What shocked the more sedate citizens was that in the waltz a couple not only embraced throughout the dance but whirled about in a posture that resembled copulation. It awakened horrified denunciation, some communities banning the dance altogether and preachers continuing to rail against it and the polka for half a century. Even at a large Philadelphia party that Harriet Martineau attended in 1835, it was expected that a clergyman among the guests would withdraw as soon as the dancing began; when he did not do so it was assumed that he was not religious.[16] A decade later, Alexander Mackay noted that many American women were exceedingly fond of dancing, but others looked on it as a heinous sin. "By none is it more denounced," he wrote, "than by the Presbyterians of the north, the terrors of Church censure hanging over those who might be inclined to offend," and he told of seeing all the Presbyterians at a party leave when dancing commenced.[17]

In the decades after the Civil War, the increasing indulgence in pleasure, following the example of such society leaders as Lady Astor, gradually freed dancing of any taint of sin.

9.

THE SHAME OF THE BODY

OF the two main uses women make of clothes, protection from the elements and attracting the other sex, there is little doubt that the latter is more important at some time on every social level and almost all the time on certain social levels. It used to be assumed that, as with Eve and the fig leaf, covering nakedness was an instinctive or natural habit. But in hot climates the aborigines often wear little or nothing, and the dress of courtesans in Renaissance Italy and Restoration England, to name only two periods, makes clear how little relationship there is between voluminous clothes and virtue or modesty.

Were there a connection between virtue and the number of garments a woman wore, American and English women in the nineteenth century would have been among the most virtuous in history. The austere fashions and somber hues we associate with the Pilgrims began to give way soon after the Mayflower arrived, and by 1634 in Massachusetts laws were needed forbidding such articles of dress as lace, silk, and thread of gold or silver. "Nakedness of arm" resulting from the fashion of short sleeves was banned, and "naked breasts" and elaborate hair styles were denounced.[1] A clear demonstration of the breakdown of laws against immodest fashions occurred in 1676 when sixteen-year-old Hannah Lyman was hailed before the magistrates for wearing "wicked apparel" and not only turned up in a silk dress worn in an "offensive" manner but, after paying her fine, went off unreconstructed.[2] Cotton Mather himself was painted in a periwig as curled and resplendent as any worn by Louis

XIV, and portraits of prominent Americans of the 1730's and 1740's by Robert Feke, John Wollaston, and William Williams show men with satin waistcoats and lace cuffs, and women in flower-trimmed bodices, shimmering satin ribbons, ruffles, and frills. By the 1760's travelers noted the luxurious clothes and low-necked gowns worn at dinners and parties in the North as well as in the South, and within the next few decades the cosmetics trade grew so great that a Massachusetts clergyman had to warn his flock that "at the Resurrection of the Just there will be no such sight met as the angels carrying painted ladies in their arms." [3] A few years later, Brissot de Warville, a young French visitor who moved about in the highest political and social circles, described seven or eight women at a dinner given by Cyrus Griffin, President of the Continental Congress, as dressed in the most pretentious style, two of them having "their bosoms very naked." His comment, "I was scandalized at this indecency among republicans," [4] reveals a naïve expectation that in a democracy everyone will dress with a classless simplicity. Some Europeans had evidently taken Franklin's gesture of wearing a coonskin cap at the French royal court a little too seriously.

During the brief period between 1795 and 1815, the United States was touched by a frankness and boldness inspired by the French Revolution. Men wore skin-tight pantaloons and displayed their thighs by cutting down the skirt of the coat to narrow tails. Women abandoned corsets and bared their arms, shoulders, and part of their breasts. All this undoubtedly accounts for such an assault as Thomas Branagan's on the "licentious" fashions of ordinary citizens early in the 1800's. "I blush with shame," he wrote, "when I survey the female fashions of modern times, which are both ludicrous and lascivious to behold." Even reputable ladies, he complained, dress more indecently than prostitutes, their appearance serving "not only to entice, but almost to force the male of ardent passions to acts of violence, as well as the arts of seduction." Let a New Yorker, he adds, "take a summer's evening walk on the Battery; and he will see displayed in magnitude what I dare not even depict in miniature." He found men's fashions just as wicked, in particular "worsted pantaloons, which sometimes fitted them like stockings, and exhibited spectacles which were sometimes on a par with female exhibitions." Even "female children" whose dress mimicked that of their elders came in for a slap. Where Moreau de St. Méry had noted in the 1790's that the garments worn by young girls tended to "compress" and conceal their breasts, Branagan remarked with the frankness of a Mrs. Grundy that 'before nature supplies them with real, they exhibit, as substitutes, in the usual form, artificial breasts." [5]

Branagan must have been placated in the decades that followed. First, men abandoned their displays. Then women's dress swung sharply away from revolutionary liberties and toward maximum concealment, and, so to speak, containment of the body. Petticoats were increased in number throughout the 1830's so that by the end of the decade women were wearing as many as seven of them, using as much as sixty yards of material. Women of fashion in colonial days had worn hoops and stays, but now corsets reinforced with whalebone and steel ribs became the general style. Doctors attributed various maladies, including permanent indentations in the liver, to the excessive pressure. In some fashionable schools girls were made to sleep in their corsets, constriction having become a sign of social superiority as well as restraint. The effect of both petticoats and corsets was to hobble women, compel them to move about with utmost decorum, and make them seem helpless and dependent. Women's fashions have of course rarely been notable for sense or logic, but seven petticoats must represent the ultimate pretense in covering up sex. It was a ludicrous contrivance to make women seem unapproachable, a cloth bulwark around the ark of sexuality.

But it was only make-believe. Along with the corsets and petticoats, women adopted "tight lacing," which emphasized the swelling shape of the bust and did so at a cost ranging from discomfort to agony. And décolleté, sometimes down to the cleavage of the breasts, remained popular almost throughout the century. Gordon Rattray Taylor has ingeniously explained this paradox as part of a campaign to desexualize the image of woman and make her appear to be only the Mother and Nourisher.[6] Preachers and reformers, however, chose to see décolleté as a sign of wantonness and included it among the more demoralizing influences.

When the burden of petticoats became intolerable, crinolines and later hoop skirts came into vogue, doing away with petticoats but still enveloping the body in a cage of cloth. The hoop introduced a somewhat piquant and capricious note since it could be tilted up on one side by pressure or a gust of wind on the other side. The exposure that resulted and the effort to prevent it conferred on the legs and even the ankles of women an aura of sinfulness. In flouting the elementary principle that the more a fruit is forbidden, the more desirable it may seem, the clothes mania reveals the usual Victorian concern with outward appearances—with a show of morality. Superficially, hoop skirts did of course hinder intimacy. A young man could not sit beside a hoop-skirted girl on a sofa, and the hoops made even an innocent kiss absurdly awkward. The first and last stanzas of a poem in an 1856 issue of *Godey's Lady's Book* put the problem nicely:

"It cannot be—it cannot be!"
The lady said right mockingly.
"Fain would I grant a parting kiss
But how can it be done in *this?*"
She pointed to her wide hooped skirt,
And he sighed deep in distress.

* * *

He walked again the lady round,
Then sank all weary on the ground.
"I'm sold," quoth he, " 'tis all no go.
Oh love, how could you treat me so?
Farewell! In foreign lands I'll range—
At least until the fashions change!" [7]

It was not until the 1870's, when hoop skirts had become so heavy that the waist could scarcely carry the weight of the skirt that dresses were deflated, the hoop being supplanted by the bustle.

The extremes to which covering the body was carried is illustrated even more absurdly in such pastimes as bathing and tennis. Women who wanted to go bathing in the 1790's hid themselves in a "bathing machine," which was then wheeled into the surf by a female attendant. But going for "a bathe" in mixed company had been a custom at the seaside resort of Newport for a number of years when Alexander Mackay visited there in 1846. A rather starched London barrister, Mackay thought that men and women boldly going into the surf together was "more in accordance with the social habits of Paris and Vienna." Americans, it seemed to him, were as free in this direction as they were prudish in other ways.[8] What the danger was is not quite clear since the bathers were as fully dressed as they would have been in their street clothes. Almost up to the end of the century a woman's bathing suit required fully twelve yards of cloth and not only made swimming impossible but in a rough surf may well have made it dangerous.

To a more hearty type of Englishman, Anthony Trollope, who visited the resort twenty-five years later, the fashion made little sense. Despite the settings of his novels, Trollope was a vigorous and forthright sort, and after conceding that the Newport style might be suitable for ladies or for men less "savage" in their instincts than he was, he wrote: "My idea of sea-bathing for my own gratification is not compatible with a full suit of clothing. I own that my tastes are vulgar and perhaps indecent; but I love to jump into the deep clear sea from off a rock, and I love to be hampered by no outward impediment as I do so."[9]

Bathing suits would not be cut back until the fad of sunbathing began to spread early in the twentieth century. Similarly, the clothes worn in tennis, which were so voluminous as to make the game an ordeal, were not substantially reduced until well into the new century.

Prudish bathing suits were merely silly, but when a woman who had a disorder of the abdominal or genital area would not let herself be freely examined, the consequences could be serious. Both British and American physicians reported the death of women from such a condition as a strangulated hernia because the patient would not locate the pain. Doctors made all intimate suggestions through a nurse or some older woman in the family. Only in a crisis was a genuine examination attempted and then only under a sheet in a darkened room. Gynecologists had of course the greatest difficulties, and they were taught to examine the patient through a hole in the bed cover. Elizabeth Blackwell chose to go to medical school—and became, in 1849, the first woman physician in America—partly because a woman friend, dreading treatment by male doctors, died of a painful disease.

A few doctors actually encouraged such pathological modesty. After admitting that the obstacles to examining women patients made successful treatment very difficult, a professor at the Jefferson Medical College of Philadelphia was quoted by *Godey's Lady's Book* in March, 1852, as saying: ". . . I am proud to say that in this country generally . . . women prefer to suffer the extremity of danger and pain rather than waive those scruples of delicacy which prevent their maladies from being fully explored. I say it is an evidence of a fine morality in our society." [10] How such obscurantism was reconciled with the doctor's obligation to cure his patients remains the greatest of mysteries.

But such a statement does make it easy to understand why drawings of the human body in textbooks used by girls were pasted over with heavy paper or why women were rigidly excluded from study in medical schools. Even a proposal to dissect women's bodies in medical schools was considered improper. But perhaps the outstanding example of prurience was the opposition to the use of ether, in part because of wild stories of the scandalous treatment to which women might be subjected while they were helpless. It needs no master of psychology to see that such an absurd fear—absurd because another woman could be present—was a case of the wish being father to the thought. For an equally bizarre reason, ether was not at first used to ease the pains of childbirth: the Bible had decreed that women should bring forth children in sorrow. There was a relaxation of this cruel dogma when even Queen Victoria took ether during the birth of one of her children.[11]

10.

TRIUMPH OF THE FIG LEAF

THROUGHOUT the nineteenth century most American painters and sculptors of promise went abroad, generally to Italy, France, or England. They went not only to get a more thorough training but also to find an atmosphere congenial to their aims and their work. Those who lingered in Italy were struck by the pervasive sensuality of life—in the markets, in the rituals of the old churches, in the paintings. Visual men all of them, they could hardly help becoming aware of the power of the nude in both sculpture and painting, from the morning freshness, male as well as female, in antique statues, to the sensual and sometimes voluptuous bodies in Renaissance paintings. What an extraordinary experience it must have been to come from a land in which up to the latter part of the nineteenth century there was not more than one museum worthy of the name to a continent scattered with collections rich in bold nudes by ancient Greeks, by Botticelli, Raphael, Dürer and Cranach, by Bellini, Titian, Rubens, and Boucher, and scores of lesser painters.

When they returned home, they usually found it no easy thing to readjust to a community—especially in New England—whose moral standards and tastes were still narrow and rigid. Many of them accepted the fact that America and Europe were two very different worlds and resigned themselves to an art that was polished and imitative or homely and sentimental. As early as the 1780's, Robert Edge Pine, a well-known British painter who had moved to Philadelphia, brought with him a plaster cast of the Medici Venus and in his enthusiasm sought to exhibit it.

Still in the grip of Quakers, Philadelphia was shocked. Pine thereafter kept the cast in a closet and showed it only to friends. As a painter Pine was mediocre and far from daring, but as a connoisseur he was a good forty years ahead of his time.

Another Philadelphia artist, William Rush, a sculptor justly admired for the vigor of his ships' figureheads and other ornamental statues in wood was commissioned in 1809 to carve a suitable work for the opening of the Schuylkill River waterworks. When he used the daughter of a friend, James Vanuxem, an esteemed merchant, as his model, there was something of a scandal even though a chaperone sat knitting beside the posing girl. The statue, "Water Nymph and Bittern," was draped, but it was denounced as indecent because "the draperies revealed the human form beneath." [1]

Sometimes the artist himself showed the inhibiting influence of a Puritanical upbringing. Despite a rich combination of talents and a sojourn in England after he graduated from Yale in 1810, Samuel F. B. Morse never got over the prejudices he acquired as the son of a strict Massachusetts Congregationalist minister, Jedidiah Morse, who had once been a student of Jonathan Edwards. Even after years of study in France and Italy, Morse, with that extreme compartmentalization that marks the thinking of so many Victorians, could admire and copy the masterpieces of European art but consider many of them indecent. It is the duty of American art, he said, to support truth and virtue, and not to imitate the sensualism and "stench of decay" of Europe's art. His assertion in an address that the goal of his art was to "elevate and refine public feeling by turning the thoughts of his countrymen from sensuality and luxury to intellectual pleasures" reveals how far morality dared to go in its invasion of art.[2]

The very first of Morse's works to attract attention, a statue (he also made a painting of it) called "The Dying Hercules," betrays the effect of this view. The anguished figures struggling to rid itself of the poisoned shirt of Nessus is a study in muscles, and yet the genitals are shown only as a knot—a castration, as it were, of the classical figures on which Morse modeled his work. It simply never occurred to Morse that if the Greek vision of this acme of manliness was so inspiring, the least he could do was not falsify it so crudely.

Even when the first museum in the United States, the Pennsylvania Academy of Fine Arts, opened in Philadelphia in 1806, its aim, as set forth by Charles Willson Peale, was to show "correct and elegant copies" of the old masters. To protect modesty, it arranged separate visiting days for ladies; and twenty-five years later the acidulous Mrs. Trollope described how an elderly woman attendant outside the Antique Statue Gallery told her that if she hurried, no one would see her go through the room. She found the gallery posted with warnings against indecent defacement of the statuary, an abuse that she attributed to the very fact that men went through the room separately. Her disgust at the thought that great art should be made to seem shameful was boundless.[3]

The triumph of hungry curiosity over prudery is illustrated by the comments, in 1833, of a prim New Englander, Laura Harris, on a seminude statue, "Medora," by Greenough. She writes: "I was horrified at the size of what Moore calls woman's loveliness, which actually took my eye so that I could not see the face." Although she had taken care to go at a time when few men would be present and there was only one old man among the spectators, Miss Harris naïvely confesses that she was "in terror lest the ladies should go off before I had gazed enough." [4]

Throughout the century an emphasis on refinement and elevated sentiments marked statements on the aims of art. Esthetic ideals were constantly yoked to moral uplift and purity, and this generally implied an avoidance of the indelicate and too clearly sexual. Even mature and independent minds were persuaded that art must present some kind of ideal form, which meant, in fact, that it should censor, prettify, and improve. The nature of sculpture, wrote Margaret Fuller, the intellectual wonder among the Transcendentalists, is "such as to allow us to leave out all that vulgarizes." It was this belief that led to a reverence for the polished and fashionable art and aims of Antonio Canova, who reached the peak of his influence between 1790 and 1820.

This doctrine had its parallel in poetry. Certainly it describes much of American verse from Longfellow and Bryant through Stedman and Stoddard. Such poets found Canova perfectly to their taste. On seeing the sculptor's draped Venus in Florence in 1828, Longfellow exclaimed: "What beauty, what elegance, what modesty!" revealing in one outburst the devastating effect of prudery on artistic judgment.[5]

If the moral intent of a work of art was not immediately evident, the title made it so. Joe Hart called one of his nudes "Venus," then "Purity," and finally "The Triumph of Chastity," a title that was really a triumph of sanctimony. To insure modesty, fig leaves and gratuitous bits of drapery were introduced in paintings and foisted on sculpture all across the land. Canova had said of the nude that the sculptor need not fear to copy God's work, but "with that veil of modesty which indeed nature did not need in the innocence of first creation, but does so now in her perverted estate." [6] So in Cincinnati a Mr. Fazzi was hired to make fig leaves for statues brought from Europe by the Ladies' Academy of Art. Even in private homes there was special concealment: Captain Marryat reported that a bust of the Apollo Belvedere in the home of Governor Everett of Massachusetts was commonly kept covered.[7]

John Vanderlyn, born in upstate New York in 1776, seems to have escaped some of the stifling influence of prudery by going abroad. But when he returned from Paris in 1812 and exhibited his fine reclining nude, "Ariadne," its reception in New York was far from cordial. And in Philadelphia, the Columbian Society adopted resolutions against what it called the painted display of indecency. Vanderlyn was undaunted: when a wealthy New Yorker asked him to choose an old masterpiece and make a copy for him, Vanderlyn painted Correggio's "Antiope." Its nudity left the would-be patron in despair: "What can I do with it?" he cried. "It is altogether indecent. I cannot hang it in my house, and my family reprobate it." Vanderlyn had now learned his lesson. When he painted a second version of "Ariadne" for another New York patron, he gave her, as Oliver Larkin says, an extra garment against the northern chill.[8]

One nude in the middle of the nineteenth century was a great success—"The Greek Slave" by Hiram Powers, a New Englander with a shrewd understanding of popular taste. But far from marking a relaxation of taboos, the popularity of the statue demonstrated a double hypocrisy. It appealed to American sympathies by showing a Greek Christian being sold into slavery by her Turkish captors during the Greek War of Independence. In the imagined plight of a beautiful Christian woman at the mercy of infidels, Powers found a pretext for a nude that no one would object to from a political or religious point of view. Coyly, Rogers let the slave's chained hand partly cover her pubic zone, and then, in one version, like a seal of purity, hung a cross from her discarded dress. The white marble—as compared with a painting—was, moreover, thought to have a cold purity that offset its nudity. A committee of Cincinnati clergymen approved of the statue, and it was freely visited by entire families wherever it was shown. In an engraving of the crowds that came to see it in a New York gallery, the figure seems curiously shameless among the overdressed spectators. A few saw through the genteel posture of the figure, its clever appeal to Christian prejudices, its lack of character, fiber, and bone. Henry James recalled the small replicas of the "Slave" as "so undressed, yet so refined, even so pensive, in sugar-white alabaster, exposed under little glass covers in such American homes as could bring themselves to think such things right." [9] That so many Americans of the time could think such a figure "right" was evidence of its utter lack of sexuality or, indeed, of sex. Of a similar piece, "America," by John Rogers, whose sentimental genre statuary groups became the rage after the Civil War, Hawthorne said, with unexpected frankness, that it belonged to the "cold allegorical sisterhood who have generally no merit in chastity, being really without sex." [10]

Twice in his career, Horatio Greenough, who had graduated from Harvard, married a Boston heiress and gone off to live handsomely as a sculptor in Florence, faced the sharp disapproval of squeamish Americans. In neither instance, curiously, was the cause a female nude. Once, when he did a group of "chanting cherubim" for J. Fenimore Cooper, it was the naked babies, borrowed from a painting by Raphael, that aroused indignation. Again, in 1841, when he brought from Italy to Washington his colossal seated figure of Washington, there were sermons on the indecency of the naked torso. Contemptuously, Greenough later wrote that he had been mortified by loud complaints of their nudity, but that those who complained about the cherubim said nothing about "all the harlot dancers who have found an El Dorado in these Atlantic cities." Then, Greenough added, "the same purblind squeamishness which gazed without alarm at the lascivious Fandango, awoke with a roar at the colossal nakedness of Washington's manly breast." [11] Aside from the fact that some may have found the spectacle of a bare-chested Washington simply ridiculous, Greenough damages his defense by the priggishness of his references to popular dancers. The most popular dancer of the day was Fanny Elssler, whom New Englanders as chaste as Emerson thought divine. But it was only an exceptional Bostonian who could avoid being a bit of a prig.

Nathaniel Hawthorne's opinions of art represent, as well as any we have, the attitudes of Americans—informed Americans—of the period. Although an heir of the Puritans, he was, as we have seen, a man of normal sexuality and he was a creative artist. More important, he had spent six years in Europe and had come to know many of the American and English artists in Italy. After several visits to the great Arts Exhibition held in Manchester in 1857, he recorded his admiration of the Dutch masters but a weariness of the "naked goddesses" in mythological paintings. His objection that they "never had any real life and warmth in the painter's imagination" seems an understandable judgment, but when he adds "—or, if so, it was the impure warmth of the unchaste women who sat or sprawled for them," [12] he introduces a moral question that is so farfetched as to seem prurient. In Italy he carried this kind of judgment a step further, complaining in both his journals and in *The Marble Faun* (1858), his novel of American and English artists in Rome, of "impious" painters of "impure" pictures of naked Venuses, Ledas, and Graces who also do Madonnas and Crucifixions. Again concerned about the models, he adds: "And who can trust the religious sentiment of Raphael, or receive any of his Virgins as heaven-descended likenesses, after seeing, for example, the Formarina of the Barberini Palace and feeling how sensual the artist must have been to paint such a brazen trollop of his own accord, and lovingly." [13] On the suspicion that the artist's models were not paragons of virtue, Hawthorne moves glibly from a moral judgment on one picture to a broad distrust of all of the artist's works.

But it is Hawthorne's view of Titian's "Magdalen" that reveals the contradiction between morality and esthetic judgment. At once scandalized and fascinated, Hawthorne describes the painting as

> . . . very coarse and sensual, with only an impudent assumption of penitence and religious sentiment, scarcely so deep as the eyelids; but it is a splendid picture, nevertheless, with those naked, life-like arms, and the hands that press the rich locks about her, and so carefully let those two voluptuous breasts be seen. She a penitent! She would shake off all pretense to it, as easily as she would shake aside that clustering hair and offer her nude front to the next comer.[14]

What a curiously erotic way to condemn carnality!

Hawthorne had, moreover, a logical objection to all nudes by artists of his time. Man is no longer a naked animal, he says; his clothes are as natural to him as his skin. Miriam, a painter in *The Marble Faun,* amplifies this in much more passionate terms:

> I am weary, even more than I am ashamed, of seeing such things. Nowadays people are as good as born in their clothes. . . . An artist therefore . . . cannot sculpture nudity with a pure heart, if only because he is compelled to steal guilty glimpses at hired models. The marble inevitably loses its chastity under such circumstances. An old Greek sculptor, no doubt, found his models in the open sunshine, and among pure and princely maidens, sufficiently draped in their own beauty. . . . But as for . . . all other nudities of today . . . I really . . . would be as glad to see as many heaps of quicklime. . . .[15]

Kenyon, a sculptor, disagrees strenuously with her, but only on the feeble grounds that he cannot imagine carving "a Venus in a hoop-petticoat." No one in the book challenges the assumption that the artist "steals guilty glimpses"—implying that the artist is a lecher and knows it—or that a "hired model" is not only a sinful woman but looks it. No one points out that the Greeks could approach the nude as something whose beauty is its own justification precisely because they didn't consider clothes as natural as skin or the naked body indecent.

Hawthorne's admiration for the Greeks and their nudes, based on his conviction that all their models were "pure and princely," seems to save him from the charge that he thought all nakedness wicked. The Medici "Venus" in Florence is, he says, "as young and fair today as she was three thousand years ago, and still to be young and fair as long as a beautiful thought shall require physical embodiment."[16] But, alas, the Medici "Venus" is, of all

Greek Aphrodite figures, one of the most stilted and unnatural. In a masterly analysis in *The Nude,* Kenneth Clark points out that it is a late, Hellenistic version of the Knidian "Aphrodite" (after Praxiteles) of the fourth century B.C. The earlier figure is a serene, unself-conscious maiden about to enter a bath, one hand held loosely in front of her pelvis, the other carrying her robe, and her whole body "open and defenseless." By contrast, the Medici "Venus" is a completely self-conscious figure with one hand covering the pubic area, the other sharply bent to shield her breasts, so that her arms surround her body like a sheath. With the bath theme gone, and what remains a contradictory study in nudity trying to hide itself, the Medici "Venus" has sacrificed the purity of the earlier figure for what Clark calls the vapid elegance of a drawing-room ornament.[17]

The Civil War brought an increased indulgence in pleasure, but moral standards remained oppressive, and many artists still found it necessary to go abroad for the sake of the tolerant atmosphere as well as for study. With the rise of the gospel of success and the tradition of the self-made man, another enemy of art and culture appears: the Philistine. Usually a man who had spent his life in passionate devotion to business, he was apt to be as inordinately proud of the American way as he was scornful of Europe's way. He was also apt to think of painting and poetry as effeminate activities, only a cut or two above idleness. If he was a robber baron, he might ransack Europe for *objets d'art* to show most conspicuously how rich he was, but the average successful man who made a pilgrimage to the Old World was, like the tourists in Mark Twain's *Innocents Abroad* and *A Tramp Abroad,* either overly reverent or overly cynical and contemptuous.

Twain himself contributed greatly to the cynicism by his devastating irreverence, sometimes salutary but at other times violently prejudiced. Notable for its ugly bite was his description in *A Tramp Abroad* (1879) of a Venus by Titian in Florence. He begins by complaining that statues in Rome and Florence that had stood for ages in "innocent nakedness" had lately been covered with fig leaves. This, he reasonably says, makes their nakedness even more conspicuous; the cold and pallid marble would still be unsuggestive even without "this sham and ostentatious symbol of modesty." Having quite disarmed us, he springs on us the assertion that where the fig leaves are truly needed is in "warm-blooded paintings." The work that has aroused his wrath, he says, is in the most popular gallery in the Uffizi:

> . . . There, against the wall, without obstructing rag or leaf, you may look your fill upon the foulest, the vilest, the obscenest picture the world possesses—Titian's Venus. It isn't that she is naked and stretched out on a bed—no, it is the attitude of one of her arms and hand. If I ventured to describe that attitude, there would be a fine howl—but there the Venus lies . . . and there she has a right to lie, for she is a work of art, and Art has its privileges. I saw young girls stealing furtive glances at her; I saw young men gaze long and absorbedly at her; I saw aged, infirm men hang upon her charms with a pathetic interest.

It is hard to decide which dominates—the prurience of the description or the piety of the condemnation. In the next paragraph he again strikes the pose of the true friend of art whose patience has been exhausted:

> There are pictures of nude women which suggest no impure thought—I am well aware of that. I am not railing at such. What I am trying to emphasize is that Titian's Venus is very far from being one of that sort. Without any question it was painted for a bagnio and it was probably refused because it was a trifle too strong. In truth, it is too strong for any place but a public Art Gallery.[18]

So Mr. Clemens in the end joined all those Americans who would not tolerate a nude that looks like a nude. Incidentally, the passage makes a monster of carnality out of a rather remote, indolent, and not particularly passionate-looking figure.

In view of such attitudes it is not surprising that painters in America in the 1870's and 1880's were still subjected to Puritanical harassment. Although Thomas Eakins was permitted to explore such more or less forbidden themes as surgical operations, there were barriers against the nude that he could not breach. He thought a nude "the most beautiful thing there is," and the only reason he painted very few such figures himself was that—paralleling Hawthorne's attitude some twenty years earlier—he considered them an unrealistic and unnatural subject for him. If we believe that clothes are more natural than skin, a nude woman is of course not a natural subject for any artist. But by a curious compartmentalizing of the mind, Western society since the Renaissance (with the exception of Puritanical groups) has allowed art students in a class or an artist in his studio to contemplate a nude woman freely while in any other place a woman would be mortified at having to disrobe before strangers.

But in 1877 Eakins found a justification for a nude when he undertook a painting of William Rush carving his allegorical figures of the Schuylkill River. It showed Rush working on a faintly draped statue with the back of his apparently nude model in the foreground and a chaperone seated nearby. Admiring the courage of Rush and his model in defying convention, Eakins also turned away from professional models and used instead a young teacher, a friend of his sister's. The posing itself did not cause as much of a scandal as had Rush's similar act seventy years before, but the painting was frowned on because the girl was a very real young lady rather than an idealized figure.[19]

Although the Pennsylvania Academy was controlled by conservative citizens who thought of Eakins as a rather radical young artist, they sanctioned his appointment as professor in 1879 and soon after made him director of the school. Unsympathetic to the practice of learning to draw by copying antique models, Eakins based his teaching on the nude. Anatomy lessons were given by leading surgeons, and the students themselves dissected bodies.

Most of Eakins students were enthusiastic and devoted, but a few women, interested only in such genteel accomplishments as china-painting and watercolor sketching, complained when they were made to study anatomy and especially the nude. Curiously disingenuous and provocative, however, were episodes in which Eakins had women students pose in the nude and brought together nude professional models of both sexes presumably for the sake of comparison. But the culminating incident came in 1886 when he removed a male model's loincloth in the women's class in order to make clear, so he said, the movements of the pelvis. A few women in the class complained to the directors, and they asked Eakins to exercise restraint or resign. Eakins resigned. All of the men and most of the women in his classes protested on his behalf, but the directors promptly told them they were free to leave.[20]

It has been suggested that Eakins' behavior was not entirely a matter of principle, that even in private he had a compulsion to shock and offend, as when he drove away women who had come to sit for a portrait by insisting that they be painted in the nude.[21] But only in Victorian America would his behavior in class have been thought grounds for dismissal. And insofar as there was a principle in Eakins' behavior and in his portraits, it was to get below the surface in an age when men wanted to cover up everything.

The result of prudery and a concern with surfaces—which is another way of saying appearances—was that the image of women as it appeared in American painting after 1875 was the fashionable figures in glittering silks and satins of John Singer Sargent, the virginal creatures in Abbot H. Thayer's allegories, or the cold, polished, imitation-Renaissance Madonnas of George de Forest Brush. Remote, scarcely of flesh and blood, very few of them were meant for love and even fewer for passion. All this while Manet was painting his "Olympia," Degas his "After the Bath," Renoir and Cézanne their "Bathers," Gauguin his Tahitian vahines, and Toulouse-Lautrec his Montmartre prostitutes.

Turning away from all the great themes of art in which the human body was central, most American artists painted women as idealized apparitions or costumed dolls. Only their fellow Anglo-Saxons, the Pre-Raphaelites joined them in denying that the body of a woman could be a supreme fusion of grace, tenderness, and sensuality. Even Henry Adams, cerebral and skeptical as he might seem, said that American artists, with the exception of Walt Whitman and a few flesh painters, "had used sex for sentiment, never for force," and that American art was as far as possible sexless. Emancipated, as it were, by his aversion for American standards, Adams declared that it was a society in which "an American Venus would never dare exist." [22]

11.

THE PATHOLOGY OF PRURIENCE: COMSTOCK AND HIS KIN

WHERE the Puritan preachers against sin had been churchmen of the stature of Increase and Cotton Mather, the nineteenth-century foes of vice were small-minded neurotics and bigots. The Puritans inveighed against sexual transgressions as only one of many sins; the nineteenth-century vice policemen were obsessed with sex and pursued it with prurient pleasure.

The pioneer of the nineteenth-century guardians of purity was the Reverend John R. McDowall. Born in Canada in 1801, the son of a poor circuit preacher, McDowall grew up with a consuming conviction that he was "a vile and polluted sinner." As a divinity student at Amherst and later at Union College, he developed such a concern for the spiritual condition of his classmates that some of them found him intolerable. For a time in the mid-1820's he distributed religious tracts and worked at establishing Sabbath schools.[1]

Then, in 1830, he came to New York. Going straight into the heart of the slums, the notorious district known as the Five Points, he organized a society for the "moral and religious improvement" of the area. Working with the poor was rewarding, but it was the prostitutes who interested him most. "But O, the harlots!" he wrote in his private journal. "How numerous! Modesty and purity forbid a minute detail. . . . I think some of these women have noble lineage. For strength of intellect, general knowledge, and elegant taste, perhaps few ladies in the city can excel a few at Five Points. Why are such women at this place?" [2] Finding the answer to such questions and, of course, "reclaiming" the women gave McDowall an excuse for becoming familiar with all their haunts and habits. His description of the thieves and pimps with whom the more degraded whores associated affords a rare glimpse of the underworld of the city. His methods of saving them was to "exhort" them—as sessions of prayer and preaching were described—and if they responded, to place them, with the help of the Female Benevolent Society, in "Magdalen Refuges." There he tried to rehabilitate them by means of religion; he could never understand why the treatment very rarely succeeded. He even made trips to Troy and western New York to collect "evidence" and was able to report that prostitutes and obscene material were as available along the canals and in the larger upstate towns as in New York City.

That he had an acute sexual problem of his own seems to be confirmed by his marriage in 1832 to a minister's widow who was twice his age and had a daughter. Since McDowall's posts as agent of one society or another never yielded more than the barest necessities, the McDowalls lived in bleak poverty. A pamphlet of his, *Magdalen Facts*,[3] setting forth the extent of prostitution in the city and elsewhere, created a furor, many preachers claiming that it was far too frank. Despite this, McDowall began in 1833 to publish *McDowall's Journal,* featuring the investigations of vice he had made on behalf of the New York Magdalen Society. Its detailed exposés of New York brothels caused a sensation. All readers were shocked, but while some were stirred into calling for a holy war on vice, others reviled McDowall for advertising such depravity.

Having shown the prevalence of prostitutes, McDowall decided to demonstrate the availability of obscene objects. In the winter of 1834 he called together about three hundred clergymen and other interested parties in a chapel in New York to show them what he had collected. He evidently put on a truly arresting display of obscene books, prints, and playing cards, lewdly decorated music boxes and snuff boxes, and other "diabolical" articles from all over the east. The clerics were fascinated. Then they caught hold of themselves; a few began to mutter that McDowall had gone much further than was necessary, and the meeting broke up amidst a welter of charges, more of them against McDowall than against the articles on display.[4]

After a time, McDowall was also charged with appropriating some of the money contributed to the paper. And a Grand Jury, urged on by the New York *Observer*, brought in a presentment against the *Journal* as a nuisance. It charged: "Under the pretext of cautioning the young of both sexes against the temptations to criminal indulgence, it presents such odious and revolting details as are offensive to taste, injurious to morals, and degrading to the character of our city." [5] Plainly revealed in the last clause is the jury's underlying concern: the reputation of the city.

Although several women of the newly formed Female Moral Reform Society declared their faith in McDowall, he had no choice but to resign as editor of the paper. The final blow was a series of hearings before the Third Presbytery of New York, culminating in 1836 in McDowall's suspension from the Presbyterian ministry. Always in poor health and worn out by the effort to defend himself, McDowall sickened and died only a few months later.

A tormented spirit, John McDowall expiated his sense of guilt by searching out the most abandoned women he could find and dwelling on their depravity. Although the ministers and newspapers that criticized him did so mainly because he exposed an evil they were content to leave hidden, they were probably justified in seeing something unwholesome in the zest with which he immersed himself in vice and the thoroughness with which he displayed it to the world. After his death a few friends called him "a martyr to the seventh commandment"; he was, if so, a martyred voyeur.

After the Revolution and during the early decades of the nineteenth century church membership declined sharply: at the beginning of the century only one in seven Americans belonged to a church. Harriet Martineau found that liberal-minded religious men in Boston in the 1830's did not take their ministers too seriously on everyday subjects.[6] If there was a drift back into the church after the middle of the century, it came not from any holy fervor but from a desire to "belong" and a fear of community disapproval. By the end of the century three in every seven Americans were members of a church. It was this body of men and women, eager to keep up appearances, that accepted the petty prohibitions and neurotic modesty that straitlaced American life in the latter half of the century.

The Pathology of Prurience: Comstock and His Kin

One of the results of the decline of church authority in everyday affairs was the appearance of lay enforcers of morality. That is why, from 1868 on, the leading guardian of morals, chief huntsman of what he called smut, was Anthony Comstock. Comstock was a pious man, firmly convinced he was doing the Lord's bidding, but where the Puritan divines had left much of the punishment of sinners to God and the hereafter, Comstock was determined to punish them in the here-and-now. In 1913, two years before his death, he said, with a bookkeeper's conception of the moral life: "In the forty-one years I have been here I have convicted persons enough to fill a passenger train of sixty-one coaches, sixty coaches containing sixty passengers each, and the sixty-first almost full. I have destroyed 160 tons of obscene literature."[7] He also repeatedly, and without shame, described his work as that of a man who had been "stationed in a swamp at the mouth of a sewer." In the topsy-turvy psychology of the censor, the pathological preoccupation with filth becomes lofty devotion to purity.

In such statements, too, the contrast with a Jonathan Edwards is striking. Both were merciless and fanatical, and, at his worst, Edwards left a permanent scar on those who came into his power. But there was a fearful grandeur about him; he was a man of vaulting imagination and immense personal influence; by his side Comstock appears petty, rigid, and dull, a clerk measuring good and evil in tons of books destroyed, in numbers of "smut pedlars" jailed.

Comstock was almost thirty years old and a special agent of the Post Office Department before he gave up work as a dry goods clerk and began to devote himself exclusively to the pursuit of obscenity. His Bible lent him righteousness, his Post Office badge gave him an arrogant authority, and his clerking a literal-minded approach. His emergence was the logical culmination of the nineteenth-century insistence on respectability, the belief that morals could and should be regulated by law and that any reputable citizen was competent to do the regulating. It was such a narrow and intolerant view that it eventually made "Comstockery" an epithet of contempt and started a rebellion against censorship and prudery that is still going on.

Anthony Comstock had the ideal background for a censor. He was a son of Connecticut Puritans; brought up on Calvinism, he prayed constantly to be saved from temptation and sin. He left school early and served earnestly in the Civil War, but he was known mainly as a soldier who attended prayer meetings as many as nine times a week and opposed smoking as well as drinking. Like so many young men after the war he went off to the big city and was working in New York when the YMCA started its first campaign against obscene books and pamphlets. It struck sympathetic chords in Anthony Comstock. Soon he made his first move in the cause of purity, leading a police captain to a seller of obscene books and seeing to it that the evil-doer was arrested.[8]

Anthony was twenty-seven, a large, heavy-legged man, and Margaret Hamilton was thirty-seven, a small, somewhat faded spinster, daughter of a Presbyterian elder, when he married her and took her to live in Brooklyn. A neighbor remembered Mrs. Comstock only as a wraith of a woman always dressed in black. Their one child died after a few months.

Historically, Anthony Comstock's emergence after the Civil War as a Victorian incarnation of the Puritan conscience was not an accident. The first obscenity case in America had been tried under common law in Pennsylvania in 1815 (the charge was that several men had exhibited a painting showing a man in "an obscene, impudent and indecent posture with a woman"),[9] but it was only in 1842, after obscene books and objects had begun to appear in quantity, that federal statutes against the importation of such matter were passed.

In New York, the glittering waves of corruption and dissipation after the war led the YMCA into pressing through the state legislature a law against lewd publications. But the law was a weak one, and in 1872, spurred by young Comstock, the YMCA set up the Committee (later Society) for the Suppression of Vice, modeled on the English society established in 1802. Announcing that there were no less than 165 pornographic books available in the United States, Comstock began systematically confiscating quantities of such notable erotica as *Only a Boy, The Lustful Turk, Fanny Hill, Kate Percival, the Belle of the Delaware, Peep Behind the Curtains of a Female Seminary, A Night in a Moorish Harem,* and *Beautiful Creole of Havana.* Comstock soon routed offending booksellers and drove four of the principal printers or issuers of pornography to flight or suicide. Emboldened, he extended his range to what he called the "classical traps," editions of Rabelais and Boccaccio, and prints of classical nudes.[10] His response to their reputation as masterpieces was that this made them just that much more dangerous.

But it was Comstock's role in the Beecher-Tilton scandal—that revelation of lechery amidst churchly respectability—that brought him national attention. Victoria Woodhull and her sister Tennessee Claflin had emerged from a background of living by the sale of quack panaceas and clairvoyant readings to edit a weekly journal devoted to every freethinker cause from women's rights to free love. Retaliating against attacks from the camps of respectability, they published in 1872 a sensational story charging that the immensely popular Reverend Henry Ward Beecher of Brooklyn's Plymouth Church had indulged in scandalous intimacies with a devout parishioner. Comstock immediately arrested the sisters more because of their attack on a revered minister than any immorality in the article itself. The sisters were kept in jail for four weeks without a trial. Because they were charming and feminine as well as articulate, they won a measure of sympathy and made Comstock seem like a bigot ready to crush freedom of the press to protect a pillar of church society. The sisters were released; eventually, the Beecher-Tilton trial substantiated many of their charges.

But it was Anthony Comstock, not Victoria Woodhull, who represented the moral spirit of the age. The following year he went to Washington and did so much to secure the passage of a stronger anti-obscenity bill, including a clause against contraceptives, that it became known as the Comstock Laws. And Comstock himself was rewarded with an appointment as a Special Agent (later Inspector) of the Post Office Department.

He went about his work animated by the conviction that he was saving innocent youth from sin, ruin, and death. His book, *Traps for the Young* (1883), saw the world as full of snares set by Satan, with "literature" the most dangerous of them. Many of the half-dime novels of the period were seasoned, he charged, with scenes of murder, seduction, gambling, illegitimate births, and even, in one instance, a sequence in which an abandoned white woman lives in a cave with a Negro.[11] But his assertion that such tales influenced any but the most unstable seems to have been based on little more than random stories of ruined youths who repented and "confessed" that their downfall began with these outlandish tales.

With strong laws and the Post Office Department behind him, Comstock was now censorship incarnate, making dramatic and sometimes violent arrests and prosecuting relentlessly. He was fearless and incorruptible: at one time or another he was badly slashed across the face, caned on the head, sent crashing down stairs by a kick, but almost always he captured his quarry and sent him to jail. Many attempts were made to bribe him. But he was not only honest—he loved his work. After all, it granted him the godlike power to punish sinners and, beyond that, honor from like-minded citizens.

The privilege of unlimited prurience Comstock took for granted; he doubtless spent as much time with smut as any man in history. But he was a fanatic, not a hypocrite: he believed utterly in his mission and felt justified in using any trick to enforce his views.

Sometimes his methods brought criticism. Even one of his most dramatic triumphs, the arrest of Madame Restell, queen of abortionists, who lived in a Fifth Avenue "palace," was somewhat marred by those who found his methods less than admirable. He trapped Madame Restell by pretending to be a family man who could not afford another child; as soon as she gave him instruments and medicines, he arrested her. Her servants found her the following day with her throat cut. Not exactly a merciful man, Comstock's only comment was: "A bloody enough ending to a bloody life." [12] Several newspapers censured Comstock for his role as *agent provocateur,* but he was proud of his skill.

Comstock had by this time acquired a reputation as an enemy of freethinkers and defenders of freedom of the press, one who saw no difference between treatises on contraception, women's rights or marriage reform and out-and-out pornography or obscene pictures. He reinforced this reputation by his bitter persecution of two leading freethinkers, Ezra Hervey Heywood and DeRobigné Bennett. Heywood attracted the Comstock lightning by sending a book of his, *Cupid's Yokes,* through the mails. It was a familiar kind of reform tract on love and marriage but it referred to Comstock as a monomaniac whom Congress and the fanaticism of the YMCA had empowered to suppress free inquiry. Later, in a lurid chapter of his book, Comstock told readers how he had caught Heywood as the reformer and his wife were leading a free-love convention in Boston in 1877. Describing the audience of 240 men and boys, Comstock writes: "I could see lust in every face. After a while, the wife of the president (the person I was after) took the stand and delivered the foulest address I ever heard. She seemed lost to all shame. . . . It was too vile; I had to go out." Evidently Comstock recovered quickly, for he plunged back into the "mob of free-lusters," nabbed Heywood backstage, and forcibly propelled him into a carriage and off to jail. "Thus, reader," Comstock concludes, "the devil's trapper was trapped." [13]

Heywood was promptly convicted and jailed. But 6,000 persons petitioned President Hayes to pardon Heywood. To Comstock's dismay, Hayes freed the reformer. Comstock bided his time and four years later arrested Heywood again, this time for distributing *Cupid's Yokes,* two of Whitman's poems, "To a Common Prostitute" and "A Woman Waits for Me," and a satirical piece entitled "The Comstock Syringe." A Grand Jury declared *Cupid's Yokes* and the Whitman poems "too grossly obscene and lewd to be placed on the record of the court." But the judge threw out these two counts, and the jury finally voted Heywood not guilty.[14]

Comstock was more successful in his pursuit of Bennett. The publisher had boldly challenged the vice raider by putting out a pamphlet called *Anthony Comstock, His Career of Cruelty and Crime* and, far more important, by getting 70,000 signatures, led by that of Robert Ingersoll, on a petition to repeal the Comstock Laws. Comstock hurried down to Washington and singlehandedly defeated the repeal effort. A few months later he arrested Bennett for sending *Cupid's Yokes* through the mails. Bennett was convicted and sentenced to thirteen months at hard labor; aging and in poor health, he served his term and died not long after his release.

Although such triumphs were hailed by many clergymen and the YMCA, in the long run they made Comstock a symbol of bigotry and arrogant interference with freedom of taste and opinion. By 1888, *Life,* the American counterpart of *Punch,* was constantly caricaturing Comstock, showing in one sequence on art censorship a Comstock version of "Aphrodite Rising from the Sea" with Aphrodite fully clothed and of "Paris Judging the Three Graces" with the graces behind shoulder-high screens. But Comstock was undisturbed by such criticism from the devotees of what he called "the artistic and classical traps." [15]

Having driven out the dealers in dirty pictures, Comstock descended on the famous Fifth Avenue art gallery of Herman Knoedler and confiscated 117 photographs of the works of living French artists. "Fifth Avenue has no more rights in this respect," Comstock announced, "than Centre Street or the Bowery." [16] Here Comstock not only equated recognized painters with makers of lewd postcards but assumed that he was striking a blow for democracy. Comstock had, in fact, no respect for art of any worth, detecting in artists the enemies of all the pieties to which he adhered. Like most censors, in the face of genuine art, he fell back on mindless police action. When assailed by the Society of American Artists and such men as Augustus Saint-Gaudens and William Chase, Comstock would concede that the female form was beautiful and that a nude in art was not necessarily obscene, but further probing of his beliefs always disclosed that he thought a woman should never be seen unclothed and that the nude in art should be "kept in its proper place and out of the reach of the rabble," [17] that is, in galleries that the public did not visit. The reference to rabble makes quite clear that, like most censors, he thought of himself as an enlightened guide to the ignorant masses.

Such phrases as the "Gay Nineties" and the "Mauve Decade" have created the impression that the closing decade of the century was a time of gaiety and dissipation. But these names derive mainly from the activities of small segments of the population: the so-called Four Hundred of fashionable society and some of the wastrel offspring of the "robber barons," a few Bohemians, and a demimonde of gamblers, sporting men, and loose women.

The main body of the middle class still clung firmly to the shibboleths of respectability and propriety. Piety, like holy zeal, having become old-fashioned, all that was left to the church was morality, the outward shell of spirituality. Thus although Comstock was more and more a target of contempt among the sophisticated, he continued to have the support of the genteel. He also had behind him every politician who was against sin. Who would dare to fight Comstock when, after the New York post office banned Tolstoi's *Kreutzer Sonata* in 1890, Teddy Roosevelt, dynamic Police Commissioner on his way to the Presidency, referred to the Russian writer as "a sexual and moral pervert." [18]

Buoyed up by such allies, Comstock in 1906 blundered into a foolish skirmish with the Art Students League and got somewhat the worst of it. He moved against the school when he discovered that one of its pamphlets contained studies of nudes. Unable to find a man to arrest, he took into custody a nineteen-year-old girl, a bookkeeper in the League's office. In court she became almost hysterical, and the students of the League as well as some newspapers made the most of the absurdity of it all. Even though the League was compelled to destroy the pamphlet, Comstock's Dickensian figure, massive and corpulent, and his truant-officer face lined with old-fashioned side whiskers was made more familiar than ever in dozens of cartoons.

Comstock was now in his sixties, but he was still vigorous, still able to gloat over a haul of pornographic prints or of contraceptive articles and exhibit them gleefully to his assistants. So when the New York Public Library removed *Man and Superman* from the open shelves, and its author, G. B. Shaw, assuming that this was Comstock's doing, proclaimed from London, "Comstockery is the world's standing joke at the expense of the United States," Comstock retaliated with, "George Bernard Shaw? Who is he?" Then he added, "I had nothing to do with removing this Irish smutdealer's books from the Public Library shelves, but I will take a hand in the matter now."

Comstock never failed to keep such a promise. Learning that Arnold Daly was about to produce *Mrs. Warren's Profession,* he wrote to Daly warning him of the obscenity laws. An astute promoter, Daly answered that the play was "a strong sermon and a great lesson"—which of course it is—invited Comstock to a rehearsal and then made public the letters. The result was such a crowd at the opening performance that the police had to be called out. Reveling in the publicity, Shaw observed that while he had been striving all his life to awaken the public conscience, Comstock had been examining and destroying ninety-three tons of indecent postcards.[19]

Even though a court held that there was nothing actionable in *Mrs. Warren's Profession*, the judges felt impelled to add that there was so little in it to attract anyone that it was safe to predict that its life would be brief. To Comstock, who never saw or read the play, must ironically go much of the credit for having launched it on a career that promises—the learned judges notwithstanding—to go on for a long, long time.

While the community as well as Comstock thought the discussion of prostitution in the play was shocking, streetwalkers on Broadway not far from the theater went smoothly about their business. In 1906 it was still more shameful to talk publicly about an indecent activity than to indulge in it. Like all censors, he did not fight prostitution and licentiousness as much as books and pictures about them. He would of course have rejected as Satanic the assertion that the reformers who had fought for a freer expression of sexual feeling, especially on the part of women, were infinitely closer to coping with sin than he was.

Anthony Comstock had the delusion that he knew what was best for his fellow citizens not only in the arts but in the most intimate relations of the sexes, in religious views (he assailed Robert Ingersoll in the coarsest terms), and in the education of children.

But perhaps his central delusion was that books or paintings or plays can corrupt someone who would otherwise remain chaste and pure. Like many who possess only a distant acquaintance with the arts he had an almost superstitious notion of the power of art. Those who have a close acquaintance with works of art know that the individual gets from them mainly what he brings to them. They know that books and paintings have rarely made a sensualist—much less a libertine—out of anyone who was by nature restrained or never tempted, just as a volume of sermons never made a virtuous woman out of a wanton. (Curiously, no one claims that books or paintings make gamblers, gluttons, embezzlers, or drug addicts.) If the vice crusader puts such store in the power of words and pictures, it can only be because his own subconscious fears are so strong that he must suppress any hint of sexuality anywhere.

It is in a way a misreading of the nature and function of the arts to think of them in terms of their influence on men's opinions. They do not create an age—they embody it. They do not instill passions or fears—they simply crystallize and project them. Boccaccio is a fourteenth-century Florentine, Titian is a Renaissance Italian, and Congreve and Wycherley are peculiarly Restoration Englishmen. It does not diminish them in the least to say that they are the product of their time, for they are among its greatest products—its genius.

If there was any danger in the books or magazines of mid-nineteenth-century America, it was more likely to be in meretricious and trashy works and in sentimental paintings, in the women's novels with their insipid virtues, etherealized heroines, sterile piety and Gothic villains. Approved, popular, and coming in an irresistible torrent, they saturated their readers with priggish standards and mawkish attitudes.

As contradictory as any of Comstock's beliefs was the conviction that he and his assistants could wallow in obscenity and emerge unstained while others could not be trusted for a moment among such temptations. As a man of little background, less achievement, and no distinction of mind or taste, he had almost no qualifications for judging the moral nature of arts or men. The suspicion therefore persists that he was simply a frustrated man who had found a rare way to satisfy at one and the same time his sexual needs, his religious scruples, and his hankering for influence and fame. His rewards in these directions were at first so considerable that they may well explain why he gave up more substantial remuneration, serving without salary as a postal inspector until his last years and repeatedly turning down handsome bribes. He made amply clear that he preferred freedom of action to pay.

Owing mainly to Comstock, the center of censorship activity lingered in New York until late in the century. It then shifted to Boston and it is still there, like the odor in an old house after it has been abandoned. The shift took place because as New York grew increasingly cosmopolitan, Boston became more and more parochial. Passing into its cultural twilight, it submitted to the control of a few mustily prudish descendants of wealthy Brahmin families. Chief among these was Godfrey

Lowell Cabot. It was mainly Cabot, as the power behind the Boston Watch and Ward Society, that made Boston within thirty years after Emerson's death as famous for banning books as for creating them.

Cabot was barely thirty when in 1891 he began to contribute to the society. A puny child, he had compensated by becoming an assertive youth with a compulsion to win in every kind of competition, a characteristic he would never outgrow. His parents were Unitarians, but enough of his Puritan heritage came down to him to convince him that self-indulgence was sinful, that emotions were somehow indecent and that it was the duty of a Lowell and a Cabot to see to it that others were equally diligent, thrifty, abstemious, and pure.

As a boy Godfrey Cabot was not popular with girls, but the most profoundly disturbing experience was the realization that the house which backed up to the Cabot place was a brothel.[20] Across the back fence he watched the prostitutes, and when they made obscene gestures and proposals and then laughed at him, he was not only shocked but enraged. He wished that God would punish them and that he himself could drive them away. When he grew up, he did not wait for God to punish them but spent the better part of an extraordinarily long life (he died at the age of one hundred and one) driving whores away.

A classical education at Harvard and a trip to Europe helped furnish Cabot's mind but did nothing to broaden it. He did a great deal of reading, but much of it was of second- or tenth-rate authors and he soon decided that if a novel or a play did not teach a moral lesson, it was trash and the author was a "scalawag."

Cabot went into the business of manufacturing carbon black and through astuteness, industry, and economy eventually built his inheritance into one of the largest fortunes in America. He was almost thirty years old before he married—partly because he had been turned down by three young women—but he made a faithful, if dominating husband. A strict father, he disapproved of whiskey, wine, beer, and tobacco, but he loved dancing and tennis, partly because they had helped him build up his body. The clues we have to his sexual life reveal that his own passions were so strong that his wife once confided to her sister-in-law that her greatest desire had been for a bedroom or just a bed of her own where she could escape from her husband's sexual demands.[21]

Cabot's letters to his wife when he was away on business tell her constantly of his desire for her and of his "naughty dreams" about her. He repeatedly discloses sexual urges so strange that it would be unkind to discuss them here did they not have such an obvious bearing on his fanatical insistence on sexual purity in others. At least twice he wrote that he wanted to drink her urine until he was filled with it, and once he wished that she were a giantess who would devour him alive, drawing him over her "slime-thick tongue" until he experienced the ecstasy of being lodged in her "dear belly." He put such passages in German, a rare act of furtiveness on his part and evidence that he knew how shocking they were.[22]

Even his son-in-law, who admired and liked him, declared that Cabot's sexual code was disgusting in its assumption that a married woman who enjoyed sex was wicked and that a man and wife should never see each other naked. In the son-in-law's view, Cabot practiced "legalized rape," was apparently sexually starved, and suffered from a severe mother complex. "If there had never been a Freud," he told Cabot's biographer, "you'd have had to invent one to explain Godfrey Cabot."[23]

Cabot was fearless and tenacious in his pursuit of those who flouted the moral laws that he took for granted. When a corrupt district attorney refused to take seriously Cabot's request that he prosecute a doctor who treated unmarried patients with "nervous" complaints by seducing them, Cabot spent almost ten years and $100,000 in getting the attorney removed and disbarred. He was aroused not so much by the attorney's record of corrupt practices as by his lax attitude toward fornication.

But Godfrey Lowell Cabot was the last of a breed; he was a complete anachronism long before he died in 1962. Dedicated to upholding an outworn code, he was not wrong or unjust but simply irrelevant.

To their opponents and victims, censors do not seem truly intent on suppressing allegedly obscene works since they constantly disregard the fact that censorship publicizes a work and may even make it popular. Censors have kept alive more than one work that would soon have been forgotten. Historically, suppression has often failed, and failed spectacularly. Banned books, poems, and plays seem better able than many classics to withstand changes in taste, and they are sometimes most widely read when most roundly condemned. Certain works of Sappho, Catullus, Petronius, Apuleius, Ovid, Terence, Plautus, Rabelais, Chaucer, Boccaccio, Margaret of Navarre, Casanova, Herrick, Donne, Cowley, Pepys, Congreve, Wycherley, the Earl of Rochester, Prior, Defoe, Swift, Voltaire, Burns, and Byron as well as *The Arabian Nights* and English popular ballads owe some or most of their continuing life to the fact that they have been labeled erotica, salacious, or unfit for young or proper-minded readers.

After a while, too, most censors become fanatics. Anyone who spends most of his time seeking the obscene passage, the lewd scene or the too naked nude will surely manage to find it where no one else has. He will discover it, as Comstock did, as readily in a *Cupid's Yokes* or a poem by Whitman as in *The Lustful Turk* or *The Lascivious London Beauty*. It is his business to find it, and anyone who disagrees with him is likely to be branded a defender of lewdness and pornography.

Censors never face the implications of the fact that censorship arouses curiosity in the censored work. The eagerness to know what is in a banned book or a banned play has almost always been so widespread that it must be accounted as deep-seated as the motives of the censor himself. It may well be that in America both sides are equally the product of Puritanical suppression, one seeking the erotic on the pretext that it must be suppressed, and the other seeking it out of a curiosity born of frustration.

Comstock was an extreme case of prudery, but he differed only in degree from average Americans of his time. They simply would not concede that although sexuality led to procreation, Nature had never decreed that it must lead to such an end. They refused to recognize that as long as the sex act was a rapturous delight, men and women would seek a way to enjoy it without necessarily begetting a child. They would not admit that continence and certainly celibacy were as contrary as contraception to the Biblical injunction to multiply and replenish the earth. Most hypocritical was the regularity and relish with which many married couples engaged in the sex act despite a dread of having a child each time.

The prudes agreed that women were purer than men—despite the Biblical story of Eve—and yet they would not trust women to read most novels or unexpurgated classics lest such works corrupt them. They refused to admit that they tolerated a double standard not because men were more libidinous than women but because a woman who transgressed might have to pay the penalty of having a child. If women were purer, it was ultimately because they feared to be otherwise.

It is even arguable that the whole principle of censorship is misconceived, that if it is at all effective it unfits the innocent to cope with the supposed danger. In this view the best way to combat corruption is to help the young recognize it for what it is. An acquaintance with the face of wickedness strips it of the attraction of novelty and the glamour of the forbidden. Those who have not been kept in ignorance will not be seduced out of curiosity or helplessness. Most observers agree that the young people of today, protected by far less censorship than ever before, seem not especially interested in or excited by the erotic books, plays, and films available everywhere. It is mainly the older people who are shocked—or titillated.

Spiritually, prudery and censorship are doctrines of denial. They see all passion as suspect, all sexuality as shameful; according to them the paths of love and desire bristle with the mines of lust. If a Comstock has any influence at all, it is to magnify the power of the obscene by teaching a fear of it.

In Anthony Comstock nineteenth-century prudery got what it deserved—a snooper with privileged status, a morals policeman serving an outworn Puritanism with machinelike efficiency and mechanical values. Comstock was a culmination—at once the high point and the beginning of the end. He raised prudery to a science and at the same time reduced it to absurdity. At the beginning of his career he was a leader in a powerful movement; at the end he was a diehard in a rearguard action.

Part 2

THE PARTISANS OF LOVE

12.

THE CHILDREN OF REASON

After almost two hundred years of the iron clamps of Puritanism, nineteenth-century prudery, however extreme, did not seem to the average American unnatural or oppressive. It required less of a commitment and was satisfied by lip service. Even when various changes in American life, such as the gradual release after 1850 of both middle-class and upper-class women from the harder household tasks, made certain restraints pointless, few protested, and their protests were considered brazen and immoral. Others—more than is generally thought—evaded the prohibitions, doing behind locked doors what was firmly denounced in public. In this second part we shall consider those who openly protested or rebelled; we leave to Part 3 those who took the path of evasion or secret transgression.

The first significant protest was not against sexual restraints as such but against woman's inferior position and her lack of freedom, especially in love and marriage. It came at the close of the eighteenth century, in the late afternoon of the Age of Reason, when a few men were still questioning old beliefs and bigotries, and the revolutions in America and France were still raising hopes that gross social injustices could and would be corrected.

First the pamphleteers and philosophers had called for change on the basis of reason and right, and then there had come action —violent action. The writings of Rousseau, Paine, Voltaire, Beccaria, Montesquieu, and others had given intellectual and spiritual impetus to the revolutions in America and France, revolutions not only against kings but against the temporal power of the church. There is no need to claim that books started these revolutions. It is enough that they articulated a mood, gave voice to latent resentments, supplied a rationale for wishes and dreams.

No one writer did for marital and sexual relations what Rousseau or Voltaire or Paine had done for political and religious liberties. But one Englishwoman, Mary Wollstonecraft, tried—speaking out in strong and sometimes bitter terms. She had a right to be bitter. Her father was so cruel that the story of her life up to the age of twenty rivals that of Oliver Twist for wretchedness and degradation. Edward Wollstonecraft had inherited a small fortune, but he was a wastrel. He married a submissive Irish girl, reduced her to a household slave, and drank himself into bestial rages. Though he beat the children, the mother insisted that they obey him unquestioningly.[1]

Perhaps because of her mother's weakness, Mary, the eldest daughter, became the protector of her weaker sisters and of a pair of shiftless brothers. She developed a capacity for sacrifice and an extraordinary strength of character. But at twenty she fled, taking a job as companion to a rich old lady who spent much time at fashionable Bath. To the poor, self-reliant girl most of the women at the watering place seemed insipid and self-indulgent, subject to the caprices and vices of their men. Thereafter for a few years she ran a school for girls, and when that failed she hired out as a governess in the household of Lord and Lady Kinsborough. Both as schoolteacher and governess she experienced to the full the obstacles facing a woman seeking to support herself in that time.[2] But life had bred a vein of iron in her. "Independence I have long considered as the grand blessing of life . . ." she said, "and independence I will ever secure . . . though I were to live on a barren heath." [3]

All the while she had been reading widely, and now, guided by a leading London publisher-bookseller, Joseph Johnson, she began to write and publish. Soon she was accepted into the cosmopolitan circle of writers, artists, and scholars that gathered in Johnson's drawing room. It was a time of intellectual ferment and political turbulence: the American colonies had won their independence, France was on the verge of revolution, and glittering catchwords—liberty, equality, fraternity, rights of man—kept exploding like rockets on every side. Having miraculously escaped from genteel servitude into the most brilliant London society, Mary Wollstonecraft found herself stirred and unsettled by revolutionary theories and sympathies. One result was a book, a hasty, violent answer to Burke's *Reflections on the French Revolution.* A second result was her major work, *A Vindication of the Rights of Woman,* published in 1791.

Aside from its obvious roots in her own experience and in the revolutionary spirit of the time, *A Vindication* was directed against the popular educational theories of Jean-Jacques Rousseau. The author of *Émile* had assumed that women should be educated to please men, and he appeared to subscribe to the old doctrine that a woman must be either a goddess or a slave. Mary Wollstonecraft asserted that they must be neither.

It was mainly the title of Mary Wollstonecraft's book that challenged conservative citizens. The book itself contains little that is original or startling—Mary Astell's books and pamphlets at the beginning of the eighteenth century had said almost as much—and its manner is often annoyingly rhetorical. Only those who had not read the book were convinced that it was "revolutionary," "atheistical," and an attack on morals. Horace Walpole, elegant and eccentric, called the author a "hyena in petticoats," and that highly moral adviser to young women, Hannah More, wrote: "Rights, indeed. I am sure that I have always had more rights than were good for me." [4]

Mary Wollstonecraft was that paradox, an earnest rationalist moved by burning indignation. With all the confidence of a child of reason, she asserted that men and women were equal and were differentiated only by the training they were given. The old attitude that it was allowable for a woman to be idle, extravagant, and helpless as long as she was chaste was degrading. Such a code made women weak and vain. Men and women should, she pleaded, be given the same kind of education, preferably together, and women should be prepared for employment that would make them independent. Rejecting both adoration and contempt, she demanded respect for women. They must at the very least have control over their own persons. Lasting happiness in the relations of men and women, she insisted, must be based on reason, not on emotions. If this seems like the frosty wisdom of a woman on the verge of spinsterhood —she was thirty-two years old—it is misleading, for she also declares that wives ought to be able to express their desires as freely as men.[5]

She shocked genteel readers in such passages as well as in references to women who legally prostituted their bodies in unhappy marriages.[6] She preached at and scolded her readers and was so impatient with sentimental women that she sometimes seems completely lacking in all tender feeling. In the light of this, the remaining five or six years of her life are astonishing. For in that brief period she had love affairs with two men, and bore each a child out of wedlock.

A lonely woman despite her fame, Mary went to Paris by herself. She arrived late in 1792, just as the revolutionary extremists were denouncing the moderates, and the tumult and menace of the city depressed her. It was at this point that she met Gilbert Imlay, American timber speculator, virile, intelligent, and author of a book on the topography of the American frontier. Although he let her know that he preferred casual amours, she fell in love with him, uncontrollably.[7] By autumn of 1793 she was living with Imlay in his Paris apartment. Since she had always believed in marriage, it was surely the revolutionary spirit of the time and place as much as her desperate need for love that led her into such a liaison.

Soon, however, business was calling Imlay away for months at a time—even after he knew that Mary was bearing his child. Mary Wollstonecraft's daughter, named Fanny Imlay, was born in April, 1794. By then Mary must have known that Imlay was not going to marry her. For her it had been a sublime passion, a total commitment; for him it had been only another affair. When she finally returned with her daughter to London in 1794 and her plight became known, she was twice barely prevented from committing suicide.

Plainly for the sake of her child, she resigned herself to living on. She became friendly with William Godwin, panjandrum of rationalists and the author of *Political Justice,* prolix exposition of anarchist and Communist principles. Godwin was a pedantic, forty-year-old bachelor who liked the company of women but did not believe in marriage. But somehow he was moved by Mary's situation. To him she seemed a woman who had practiced the principles of free love from the loftiest motives but had been betrayed. He proved surprisingly sympathetic, and Mary in her exhaustion of body and spirit welcomed his attentions. But what began as a recoil from her affair with Imlay quickly ripened into genuine desire. By September she was writing to Godwin: ". . . let me assure you that you are not only in my heart, but my veins this morning. I turn from you half abashed—yet you haunt me, and some look, word or touch thrills through my whole frame. . . . When the heart and reason accord there is no flying from voluptuous sensations, I find, do what a woman can." [8] She did not fly, and in a short while she found herself pregnant again. But Godwin, fortunately not an Imlay, married her. Although by mutual agreement he maintained separate lodgings where he generally worked and slept, their relationship was amicable and serene. At thirty-eight Mary Wollstonecraft had at last found security and love. She gave birth to their child Mary in September, 1797. She died a few days later of puerperal fever resulting from her unwillingness to have a doctor, rather than a midwife, attend her in childbed.

In all this and in the rest of the Wollstonecraft-Godwin family story moralists found an array of object lessons. Godwin, left with two daughters, took another wife, an ill-tempered woman who had little sympathy for her husband's daughter Mary or his step-daughter Fanny Imlay. The love child, gentle, melancholy Fanny, discovering when she came of age that she was unwanted and nameless, took her life, dying unmourned. Mary Godwin, sensitive, gifted, disliking her stepmother, took a lover and had a child by him. The lover, Shelley, was married and had children of his own; he was a poet, said to be an atheist and somewhat mad. They would not be free to wed until Shelley's first wife, Harriet, had drowned herself. Adding to these fire-storms of love, Mary Godwin's half-sister, Claire Clairmont, daughter of Godwin's second wife, accompanied Mary and Shelley when they eloped, and in Italy she wooed Lord Byron until she too bore a child out of wedlock.

There is little doubt that in the *Vindication* Mary Wollstonecraft underestimated—as she herself later realized—the power of the emotions in the relations of the sexes. Her faith in educating women for intellectual as well as economic independence was not misplaced; it simply was not the whole answer.

She herself had acquired both an education and financial freedom, and yet her heart had betrayed her; and the fact that women bear children had provided the punishment for her mistake. Regardless of her education and her principles, she had loved well but not wisely.

Yet Mary Wollstonecraft's basic prescription was sound. Education and training for work did not of course free woman from her biology, but they did open up to her other forms of fulfillment besides marriage and children. As for Mary Wollstonecraft's intellectual and moral courage, it had been immense.

It was these qualities that caused the *Vindication* to be widely read in America, while the young republic was still receptive to revolutionary views. Two separate editions appeared in the States in 1792, and a Boston periodical, *Lady's Magazine,* printed a ten-page summary of the book.[9] Although some strait-laced feminists such as Emma Willard claimed that Mary Wollstonecraft's behavior had hurt the feminist cause, Mary's life, as well as her book, remained a source of inspiration for the bolder leaders of the women's rights movement for several generations. When Sarah Grimke, courageous Southern abolitionist, saw a copy of the *Vindication* on the center table in the home of another pioneer feminist, Lucretia Mott, almost fifty years later, she said, "I admire thy independence." [10]

If Mary Wollstonecraft was devoted to reason, Godwin was obsessed with it. A nonconformist clergyman when he came to London in 1782, he was soon converted to Voltaire's faith in reason and Rousseau's conviction that mankind is naturally benevolent but has been warped by the restraints put upon it by government and laws. Combining the two schools of thought, Godwin argued in his *An Enquiry Concerning the Principles of Political Justice* (1793) that all governments and such institutions as marriage and property were evil. Marriage as Godwin saw it was a romantic delusion requiring irrevocable promises not justified by reason. Worst of all, it was a selfish property arrangement in which a man monopolized one woman. The fear that freedom from the restrictions of marriage would lead to libertinism were unwarranted; man would learn to control his appetite as well as he controlled other appetites such as eating.

Later, after two marriages and several children, Godwin modified such views drastically. In his memoir of Mary Wollstonecraft and in later essays he conceded many virtues to marriage. But *Political Justice* forever exposed him to such a scurrilous attack as appeared in an American periodical, the *Columbian Sentinel,* in 1801. One stanza read:

> When Godwin can prove that thieving is just,
> That virtue is pleasure, and pleasure is lust,
> That marriage is folly, and wh-r-ng is wise,
> And Wollstonecraft pure in philosophy's eyes.

Some of Godwin's conclusions in *Political Justice* demonstrated the thin line between academic logic and nonsense. In deifying reason Godwin reduced it to absurdity. He never suspected that only his own want of feeling led him to think that emotions were pernicious. Paradoxically, his conviction that reason would lead to a perfect society was based on the most sentimental and wishful thinking.

As soon as the fervors of the revolutionary period subsided and the rise of Napoleon brought disenchantment to reformers everywhere, the speciousness in much of Godwin's thought became evident. A residue of his attitudes, and especially his opposition to rigid institutions such as the church and marriage, continued to influence philosophic anarchists, including Josiah Warren, Stephen Pearl Andrews, Ezra Heywood, and Benjamin Tucker, to name only Americans.

But the most striking example of the Godwin-Wollstonecraft influence in America is found in the work of Charles Brockden Brown. Brown's first book, *Alcuin* (1798), was a dialogue between a poor schoolteacher and a widow, Mrs. Carter, who acts as a hostess for her brother, a man of letters. Both parties borrow most of their ideas from *A Vindication:* the widow deplores the subjection of wives to husbands and the failure to allow women to develop their talents; the teacher upholds the equality of the sexes but still thinks women are more natural as mothers than as politicians, judges, or soldiers.[11] *Alcuin* is a thin and mannered effort that does no credit to Brown or his English preceptors.

Brown was also immensely impressed by Godwin's novel *Caleb Williams* (1794), and in his earliest novels, *Wieland* and *Ormond,* he introduced a few characters who hold the most radical views on love and marriage and behave accordingly. But these characters—Carwin, Ludloe, Ormond—are such cruel and outrageous extremists that they seem more like lessons in the dangers of fanatic rationalism. Brown soon abandoned the theme altogether and later regretted the liberalism of his youth. In his last novel, *Jane Talbot,* he referred to Godwin as practicing "the art of the grand deceiver; the fatal art of carrying the worst poison under the name . . . of wholesome food; of disguising all that is impious, or blasphemous or licentious, under the guise and sanctions of virtue." [12] In this change of heart Brown reflects the general reaction against the revolutionary 1790's as well as the fact that he himself had acquired a wife and children.

An indirect channel of Godwin's influence was the high-minded, febrile genius who became his son-in-law. Shelley was barely seventeen when he read Godwin's *Political Justice.* But he was fully prepared for its most radical pronouncements, his prodigious reading having included almost all the revolutionary social thinkers of his time. All of this rebelliousness, crusading fervor, and utopian hope he poured into his first long poem, *Queen Mab* (1813). In lofty allegory and libertarian rhetoric he charged kings, priests, and defenders of property with all of mankind's woes. But reason, he prophesied, would prevail, leading man into a state of bliss. In that new Eden marriage would be unnecessary because each soul would be free to disclose

> The growing longings of its dawning love,
> Unchecked by dull and selfish chastity,
> That virtue of the cheaply virtuous,
> Who pride themselves in senselessness and frost.

In the elaborate notes to the poem he described chastity as a "monkish and evangelical superstition," and he asserted that a "system could not well have been devised more studiously hostile to human happiness than marriage." [13]

Realizing what a web of heresies *Queen Mab* was, Shelley had only 250 copies printed, never sold any of them, and gave away only seventy copies after carefully removing the title page and printer's name from each. It was ironical enough that Shelley should have espoused so many Godwinian attitudes in *Queen Mab* long after Godwin himself had abandoned them or modified them drastically. But it was even more ironical that within a few years Shelley himself repudiated the poem with the most damaging kind of comment. It might therefore seem only fair to dismiss *Queen Mab* as an adolescent outburst against authority, a handful of wishful dreams. But it was not without consequence. Perhaps because of Shelley's later fame as a poet, *Queen Mab* remained—along with the works of Paine and Voltaire—one of the books that American and English freethinkers took to heart. It appealed particularly to young men in the first throes of revolt against the injustices of society, touching their rejection of outworn dogmas with visionary fire. All the passion that Godwin lacked Shelley had.

It was not lovers of poetry but social reformers in both England and America who kept *Queen Mab* alive. Despite the opposition of Shelley himself, who thought the poem a crude and immature work that would do more harm than good to the "sacred cause of freedom," a radical publisher issued a pirated edition in 1821.[14] He was promptly jailed on complaint of the Society for the Suppression of Vice. It was a pair of reformers, Frances Wright and Robert Dale Owen, who in 1831 published in New York the first more or less authorized edition. They also ran an abridged version of the poem and many of Shelley's criticisms of marriage in their weekly, *The Free Enquirer*.

The identification of *Queen Mab* with extremist views led respectable critics of literature, lapped in Victorian complacency, to view it with abhorrence. Thus Andrews Norton, retired Professor of Sacred Literature at Harvard, declared in 1837 that the poem struck at the roots of human decency.[15] Those Americans who came to Shelley's defense, such as Orestes Brownson, whose restless quest for an ideal creed carried him from Presbyterianism through Socialism to Catholicism, tended to apologize for the poet's ideas on marriage and reform before praising him for his wide human sympathies. In time the attention of readers shifted from Shelley's morals and private life to his great lyric gift and rapturous voice. Only a few radicals from Marx to Upton Sinclair continued to acknowledge him as one of their ideological ancestors.

13.

THE FREE ENQUIRERS

THE Utopian spirit that gripped little bands of men and women here and there in America in the first half of the nineteenth century was fed from many sources. The Age of Reason had led men to believe that by education and taking thought they could eliminate injustice, superstition, and other evils. By 1840 there was also a scattering of idealists who were disgusted by what they called the Mammonism of the age, the selfish pursuit of gain; they dreamed of a return to a primitive communism. And it was a part of the Romantic faith that man could best achieve such an ideal society in virgin America. There, it was thought, he could make a completely fresh start, create a classless society in which each individual could develop himself to the fullest. Especially in frontier regions it seemed that only a minimum of government would be necessary and that free land together with a natural abundance would make it possible to achieve a return to Arcadia. The Declaration of Independence had made this official, declaring that the individual existed before government and was endowed with certain natural rights. There were, unfortunately, contradictions in such hopes and dreams: in some of the utopian communities the attempt to allow maximum freedom of expression and behavior resulted in disorder and chaos. It was easy enough, for example, to challenge marriage and monogamy, but the problem was, as it always is in a revolution, to find a better way.

All these winds of doctrine helped shape the unorthodox career of Frances Wright. She was born in 1795 into a distinguished Scottish family. Although her father was a successful tradesman, he was sufficiently infected by the radical ideas of the time to subsidize a cheap edition of Paine's *Rights of Man.* Even as a young girl Fanny protested against the social and economic injustice she saw around her. Soon, too, she was swept by Byronism and began to see herself as an exiled spirit destined, if not doomed, to defy society and its stifling conventions. By the time she was nineteen she had rejected all revealed religion and looked with suspicion even on Voltaire's deism.

At the same time she developed a consuming interest in America as the land in which would be created a new, free life. Almost as soon as she reached her majority, she made a long visit to the United States and on her return to England published *Views of Society and Manners in America* (1821), a paean, quite uncritical, to America's freedom and promise. It brought her a measure of fame and the friendship of a hero of American independence, General Lafayette. Although still the invincible idealist, the general was now an old man reduced to futile political intrigues. The emotional intensity of Fanny's idealism filled her report of her first meeting with him.[1] Soon she became a part of Lafayette's family circle and political cabals, and when the general made a visit to America in 1824, Fanny and her sister Camilla accompanied him.[2]

Throughout her second stay in America she was disturbed by one hideous flaw in the American system—Negro slavery. But her experience with freedmen in the South persuaded her that slaves must first be educated and prepared for freedom. It was at this moment that the Scottish philanthropist and reformer, Robert Owen, famous for the model mill village he had developed in New Lanark, arrived in America to spread word of a new social order. He announced that he had bought the buildings and site of the most successful cooperative religious community in America, New Harmony, belonging to the German sect known as Rappites, along with thirty thousand cultivated acres on the Wabash River in Indiana. So great was the nation's interest in such experiments that Owen was invited to lecture before the House of Representatives. In his address, Owen, a small, rather ugly man in his early fifties, called for an entirely new social system made up of self-sufficient communities engaged mainly in agriculture.[3] He believed that, given the proper training and environment, man was infinitely improvable. As shrewd as he had been in business, so gullible and impractical was he as a social reformer.

Fanny Wright was immediately fired with a plan for establishing such a community on a Southern plantation where slaves could work out their purchase price and acquire the industrial training to fit them for a free life. After months of search, Fanny and her sister established their experimental farm, called Nashoba, on a 640-acre tract near the fur-trading station at Memphis, Tennessee. Although the sisters kept it going for almost four years, their utopia was a failure from the outset—an assemblage of eight or ten indolent Negroes and three or four physically and spiritually unprepared whites living in raw, comfortless buildings on unsuitable land.

Her health failing, Fanny herself soon went to New Harmony for a rest. Like a few of its sister utopias, such as Brook Farm, New Harmony had a core of intellectual radicals, and Fanny was at once caught up in the exciting exchange of opinions, often heretical, on every institution from the church to marriage. Especially interesting was the experimental school set up by William Phiquepal D'Arusmont, a French educator in the Pestalozzi tradition.[4] D'Arusmont was a vain and irascible man but an excellent teacher. There is no evidence that Fanny was particularly attracted by him or dreamed that she would one day marry him.

The man whom she became most friendly with and who would become her closest associate was young Robert Dale Owen, eldest son of Robert Owen. Robert Dale, born in Scotland like Fanny, was a small, unprepossessing youth of twenty-four but rather charming and soft-spoken, radiating intelligence and as rabid an idealist as Fanny. Six years younger than Fanny, he saw her as a woman of the world with a remarkable background and yet a kindred spirit. Fifty years later he recalled her in the most vivid terms:

> A tall commanding figure, somewhat slender and graceful, though the shoulders were a little too high, a face the outline of which in profile, though delicately chiselled, was masculine rather than feminine . . . the forehead broad but not high, the short chestnut hair curling naturally all over the classic

> head, the large blue eyes not soft but clear and earnest. Her vigorous character, rare cultivation and hopeful enthusiasm gradually gave her great influence over me. . . .[5]

Even before Fanny ended her visit to New Harmony, the colony had begun to fail. Robert Owen was far more interested in theory than in practice, and his followers were far better at talking than working. Having spent more than $200,000 on the experiment, Owen withdrew his financial support early in 1827 and ended its cooperative character. Fanny, dreaming of turning Nashoba into another New Harmony, now persuaded Robert Dale Owen to join her. He was dismayed by the desolation he found at Nashoba, and he and Fanny decided to go to Europe to recruit new associates.

Hardly had they departed when one of two white men left at Nashoba, a young Scotsman, James Richardson, revealing an unsuspected streak of cruelty and willfulness, began whipping troublesome slaves. He also announced that he had the previous night begun to live with Josephine, the comely daughter of a free colored woman, Mam'selle Lolotte, who had been hired as a teacher. Richardson and Camilla Wright also let it be known that the free union of the sexes, with or without marriage, white and black together, would be tolerated. No woman slave, moreover, was to have a lock on her door, because the men must learn to respect women's rights. With incredible temerity Richardson published an account of the new Nashoba program in Lundy's *Genius of Universal Emancipation,* a Baltimore abolitionist journal. The response of readers may be judged from a letter in the next issue:

> Philadelphia, Aug. 8, 1827
>
> Mr. Lundy: No one possessed of moral or religious feelings, can read without horror the publication . . . of the proceedings of . . . Frances Wright's Establishment, at a place called Nashoba. . . . Is it possible that an accomplished Englishwoman (for such C. W. is known to be) could publicly declare to the slaves that the proper basis of sexual intercourse was the unconstrained and unrestrained choice of both parties?—that a lock to a chamber door, requested by a female slave, was refused . . . ? Is it possible that one of the trustees could shamelessly announce that he and one of the colored females "last night began to live to-

> gether," and this flagitiousness, announced to the community on Sunday evening, be solemnly entered on the records? What is all this but the creation of one great brothel . . . ?
>
> MENTOR[6]

Invited by Lundy to reply, Richardson answered:

> Mentor applies to us the epithet "libidinous." As applied to me I object not to its meaning. I possess the feeling which it designates in common with every other complete adult animal. But the woman has never lived whom I have wronged in its gratification. Neither am I conscious of so extravagant a propensity to change, as Mentor seems to think must result from an abrogation of the legal tie. Does Mentor actually believe that when such a propensity does exist, the legal tie ever prevents its indulgence? Mentor thinks we are instituting a brothel. I have seen a brothel, and I never knew a place so unlike it as Nashoba.

He added, for good measure, that the absurd taboos fostered by the Christian religion were the chief cause of sexual immorality.

Nashoba and Fanny Wright never lived down that article. A few months later Richardson left the colony and Josephine soon followed him. Although Fanny on her return from Europe early in 1828 found the colony in a wretched state, she gave the local newspaper a grandiose statement of Nashoba's principles. Perhaps its most interesting passages were those that declared conventional marriage laws of no force in Nashoba. "No woman can forfeit her individual rights or independent existence," it went on, "and no man assert over her any rights or power whatsoever beyond what he may exercise over her free and voluntary affection." It concludes: "Let us not attach ideas of purity to monastic chastity, impossible to man or woman without consequences fraught with evil. . . . Let us enquire—not if a mother be a wife, or a father a husband, but if parents can supply, to the creatures they have brought into being, all things requisite to make existence a blessing." [7] It was a high-minded plea, but rash. Although Nashoba was in its last days as an experimental community, Miss Wright's statement gave critics a pretext for referring to the settlement as "Fanny Wright's Free Love Colony." The malice and absurdity of such a label was evident to anyone who knew anything about Nashoba.

Deciding that men and women needed first to be prepared by education for life in an ideal society, Miss Wright now concentrated on lecturing and newspaper publishing. She lectured in Cincinnati, Philadelphia, New York, and other cities, drawing large crowds everywhere. In Cincinnati, Mrs. Trollope was struck by the excitement caused by her arrival. "But all expectations," she reported, "fell far short of the splendor, the brilliance, the overwhelming eloquence of this extraordinary orator. . . ." [8] In some cities vigorous attempts were made to keep the public from attending her lectures. Many of her audiences doubtless listened to her with a guilty fascination. A few adored her. Years later, Walt Whitman, recalling being taken by his father to Fanny Wright's lectures, wrote: "She has always been to me one of the sweetest of sweet memories, we all loved her; fell down before her; her very appearance seemed to enthrall us . . . she was beautiful in bodily shape and gifts of soul." [9]

The press was at first tolerant and even amused, but when Miss Wright settled in New York and began publishing a radical weekly, *The Free Enquirer,* the newspapers and the clergy became increasingly hostile. *The Free Enquirer,* edited by both Fanny and Robert Dale Owen, criticized the established religions, advocated equal rights for women, and above all, a free nonsectarian education, at boarding schools, for all children from the age of two years. Soon critics began referring to Miss Wright as the "Priestess of Beelzebub," the "Angel of Infidelity," and a "voluptuous preacher of licentiousness." [10]

Then, while Fanny and her sister were on a visit to Paris, Camilla, whose health had been failing, died. Fanny was plunged into a despondency that must have been partly the result of her realization that at thirty-five she was alone and without roots or personal ties. In the following months, Phiquepal D'Arusmont came to her aid. Like Mary Wollstonecraft with William Godwin, Fanny drifted into an intimacy with the fifty-two-year-old bachelor, and, like the Godwins, the couple soon found that they would have a child. Again like the Godwins, they bowed to circumstances and married. Several New York newspapers referred to the event as an object lesson for any woman who entertained unconventional attitudes toward marriage, and the record does suggest that Fanny never recovered her old élan and aggressive independence. For a few years her restless spirit was becalmed by domestic pains and pleasures; finally she and her husband sailed to America in 1834 to attend to her property.

In an effort to resume where she had left off, Fanny began a series of lectures on the history of civilization and especially such evils as the subjugation of women, but it met with chilling indifference. Although she withdrew from public notice, her name tended to come up whenever radical views of the condition of women were discussed. When Margaret Fuller's *Woman in the Nineteenth Century* appeared in 1845, the review of it in Bennett's *Herald* made a slighting reference to Frances Wright's attacks on marriage. Mme. D'Arusmont burst from her semi-retirement with a violent denial that she had ever advocated free and easy union.[11] She had attacked, she declared with all her old passion, a system that deprived woman of her independence and self-respect; and she had rejected any bond that held parents together as though in chains. The results of the present system were evident, she added, in the streets, brothels, and court records.

Gradually D'Arusmont took over the care and education of their daughter and drifted away from his wife. When she came into a large inheritance in 1846, D'Arusmont, by then a suspicious old man, claimed that she wasted her money, and he asserted control, as was his legal right, over all her property.[12] No novelist would dare contrive a more refined irony than that, as Fanny Wright in her last book, *England the Civilizer,* spoke in apocalyptic terms of the coming of a perfect state in which altruism would reign and all women would be free of subjection to men, her husband was taking away all she possessed. The irony is multiplied by the fact that D'Arusmont, like Fanny, had lived by high ideals. The most charitable comment is that he was by then an old man who had been too long dependent on his wife.

On the advice of her lawyer, Fanny divorced D'Arusmont, and she had begun proceedings to regain her property when she died from a fall in front of her Cincinnati home.

Measured in tangible reforms, memorable writings, or direct followers, not to speak of personal affairs, Frances Wright's life was hardly a success. Her death went almost unnoticed. She was essentially a woman with ideals too advanced for her time and in some respects perhaps for any time. Almost all her virtues seem to have been flawed or at some point too susceptible to extravagance. Robert Dale Owen's analysis of her faults, recorded when he was seventy, seems most acute if one allows for the condescension of conservative old age looking back on the excesses of radical youth:

> . . . a mind which had not been submitted to early discipline, courage untempered by prudence, philanthropy which had little commonsense in it . . . an enthusiasm eager but fitful, lacking the guiding check of sound judgment. An inordinate estimate of her own mental powers, an obstinate adherence to opinions once adopted. . . . With ideas on many subjects, social and religious, even more extravagant and immature than my own.[13]

All this is true: in principle she was—like Mary Wollstonecraft, it might be said—too literal a rationalist, and in practice too impulsive and romantic. Both her theories and her experiments, relying too heavily on reason and logic, failed to take into consideration the vagaries, ardors, and dark desires of human nature. And yet she was a pioneer, a venturer into uncharted areas of human relations, more than half a century ahead of her time. She groped and blundered but she went. Her temerity made it that much easier for more temperate reformers such as Elizabeth Cady Stanton—who acknowledged her influence and spoke of her as a "rational and beautiful" [14] writer—to push on. Her idealism, her enthusiasm, her altruism, and her courage left something in the air that would stimulate kindred spirits long after she was gone.

14.

LOVE WITHOUT FEAR

AFTER the decline of Puritanism, the prime deterrent to uninhibited sexual activity was the fear of pregnancy. Various taboos still restrained unmarried couples from the sexual act, but pregnancy was the major threat that hung over all coition, especially outside of wedlock. Because of the Biblical injunction to multiply and replenish the earth—which no one appeared to question—any attempt to prevent conception was bound to seem wrong in every way. Withdrawal by the man before orgasm, termed *coitus interruptus,* had always been known, but few had the will to practice it regularly and still fewer found it agreeable. Contraceptive devices had been used as far back as ancient Egypt, but Christianity had made them unthinkable for all God-fearing citizens.

Of course there were always scapegraces, men who could not resist temptation, or would not even if they could. In the eighteenth century, Englishmen who went awenching, Boswell tells us, sometimes protected themselves with a sheath that was made of sheep-gut and was called a condum after the British doctor who is supposed to have invented it. And Casanova, certainly an authority, tells of using "English overcoats" made of "very fine, transparent skin." But such devices were used largely to ward off venereal diseases. It was mainly Frenchwomen, those masters of the sexual arts, who began in the seventeenth century to successfully separate copulation for pleasure from copulation for child-getting, using such devices as a sponge inserted in the vagina.

In a revelation that no American would have dared to make,

Moreau de St. Méry, French émigré who lived in Philadelphia in the 1790's, reported that when some of his fellow Frenchmen introduced the use of vaginal syringes, Americans were at first shocked, but some apothecaries soon began to stock such appliances.[1]

After the Reverend Thomas Malthus had frightened Europe in 1798 with his gloomy prophecy that population would outstrip the means of subsistence, English social reformers, bent on helping the poor reduce the size of their families, tried to introduce a few contraceptive practices into England. As early as 1795, Jeremy Bentham, political economist who claimed to be concerned only with the greatest good for the greatest number, told of learning from a friend who had traveled in France of the use of a "spunge" in preventing conception.[2] This important piece of information probably also came across the channel from France by way of prostitutes.

Far more effective in spreading both the theory and the practice were Francis Place and Richard Carlile. Place, born of poor parents in 1771, became a tailor out of bitter necessity and a reformer out of fierce conviction. He proposed various checks to conception not only to slow the population growth but to relieve the poor family man who could scarcely feed himself and his wife, not to speak of eight or ten children. Although Place himself was hardly a model of self-control, fathering fifteen children, he declared in his *Illustrations and Proofs of the Principles of Population* (1822): "If . . . it were once clearly understood, that it was not disreputable for married persons to avail themselves of such precautionary measures as would, without being injurious to health, or destructive of female delicacy, prevent conception, a sufficient check might at once be given to the increase of population beyond the means of subsistence. . . ."[3]

Like Place, Richard Carlile was one of a group of early nineteenth-century reformers, mostly unsung, bred in poverty, and guided by the ideals of the Enlightenment, who devoted their lives to militant struggle against all privileged classes and hidebound institutions. As a pamphleteer and bookseller, he defied every effort to suppress or censor him and as a result spent nearly a third of his life in prison.

Deciding in 1822 that he must recommend "preventive

checks" to population, Carlile was troubled by the possibility that he would be encouraging immorality among the unmarried. For advice he turned to Place, who was on one of his sojourns in Dorchester jail. He wrote:

> No one shall persuade me but that healthy girls, after they pass the period of puberty, have an almost constant desire for copulation. . . . If the means to prevent conception were publicly taught, would it not lead to a general gratification of this common desire, and to a breaking up of all individual attachments? A female who has once indulged her passions before marriage is, I should think, more prone to infidelity than she who comes chaste and inviolate to the marriage bed.[4]

Place answered that there was no chastity among the poor—and not much in the class just above them—because poverty prevented young men from marrying and led girls into prostitution. Carlile was convinced. He came to believe that no subject which was either natural or useful was obscene. In response to many letters begging, he said, for information, he published *Every Woman's Book; or, What Is Love?* With engaging candor he declared that love was so delightful a passion that no one who indulged in it should have to fear the consequences. The main threat, among both the married and unmarried, was unwanted children. Carlile recommended the sponge as a preventive. He conceded that it might at first shock a woman, but once used, "all prejudice flies and gratification must be the consequence."[5] The response to Carlile's book even among working-class radicals was bitter. Place and Carlile were called foul and beastly men motivated by lust. Such charges helped the sale of the book, and Carlile claimed that ten thousand copies were sold within two years.

The man who introduced these theories and practices into America was Robert Dale Owen. Since he started what would eventually become the birth control movement in America, the revolutionary implications of his efforts cannot be overstated. As the eldest son of Robert Owen, Robert Dale Owen virtually inherited such attitudes. Although the elder Owen did not at first press his unorthodox views of marriage, he was known to be a disciple of Godwin and Mary Wollstonecraft. And in 1823 a labor journal printed a letter claiming that Owen, fearing that the success of the model community of New Lanark would contribute to overpopulation, had brought back from France various devices to check conception.[6] Owen later denied the stories. But in the colony at New Harmony there was only a minimum marriage ceremony, and divorce would have required scarcely more than a declaration of intention.

In time, the elder Owen grew more and more uncompromising in his pronouncements. In a celebrated debate in Cincinnati in 1829 with a famous preacher, the Reverend Alexander Campbell, Owen denounced all religions and at the same time delivered his most forthright condemnation of marriage: "The invention of unnatural marriages has been the sole origin of all sexual crimes. They have rendered prostitution unavoidable. They have erected spurious chastity and destroyed all knowledge of pure chastity. For real chastity consists, in connexion with affection, and prostitution, in connexion without affection."[7] Incidentally, in the heart of the land where Owen hoped to establish a new paradise, the crowds much preferred Campbell's backward-looking fundamentalism to Owen's bright visions.

Robert Dale was only twenty-four when he accompanied his father to America to set up an ideal community at New Harmony. There he edited the community journal, the *New Harmony Gazette*. Again and again he probed conventional views of propriety, chastity, and constancy. Like Shelley, he saw the prevailing idea of chastity as a vestige of monkish asceticism, an unnatural attitude leading to repression or concealment. As for constancy, that might be a virtue in a society where every marriage was perfect, but in a world where man still made errors, it often led to vice and unhappiness.

Finding New Harmony too narrow a field for her talents, Frances Wright had gone on to New York. Robert Dale Owen soon followed her, and together they began publishing *The Free Enquirer*. Many forces were making America's portal city a center of exciting movements. Frances and young Owen plunged into the middle of these with a weekly committed to the noble proposition that reason and education could solve every social problem. Since Frances was more effective as a speaker than a writer, Robert Dale became responsible for most of the editorial contributions.

Owen's overearnest efforts to enlighten his readers repeatedly embroiled him in controversy. There was, for example, his article on the Haitian alternative to marriage—"placement." Practiced by the great majority of Haitians, a placement union allowed a woman to keep her own name and property, and it could be ended almost overnight. Although placement might seem to encourage promiscuity, such a union, according to Owen, lasted far longer and was much more harmonious than a conventional marriage. It also led to much less license and prostitution because the partners were never tied to mates they no longer loved.[8] Although he intended only to show the value of unions free of coercion, his foes chose to assume that he was advocating placement, and he was again and again forced to deny the charge.

The relationship between Robert Dale Owen and Frances Wright was one of great intimacy, but he later denied that it was anything more. The intimacy ended forever when Fanny married D'Arusmont. The two reformers moved further and further apart until in his recollections, written in 1870, he characterized her without charity or affection.

Of all the ideas that Robert Dale Owen advanced, none was more misunderstood than that on the rights of women. He had let it be known that he thought Carlile's *Every Woman's Book* a courageous work calculated to benefit mankind.[9] Although he added that he had refused to publish the book in America because of prejudices that were "honestly entertained" against it, he was attacked in an anonymous pamphlet with the horrendous title of *Robert Dale Owen Unmasked by His Own Pen: Showing his Unqualified Approbation of a Most Obscenely Indelicate Work . . . Recommending the Promiscuous Intercourse of Sexual Prostitution*. This and another vicious assault finally drew Owen into defending himself: his answer was a seventy-two page, thirty-five-cent pamphlet entitled *Moral Physiology; or, a Brief and Plain Treatise on the Population Question* (1830).

Owen began by declaring that he would speak plainly and he could not help it if "pseudo-civilized man," an "animal ashamed of his own body," took it ill.[10] As for conceptions of propriety, he pointed out that they differed from place to place: thus in Central Africa women might bathe in public whereas men might not; and in Eastern lands a woman dared not uncover her face, while in Ethiopia it was considered indecent to uncover the feet. Harshly Owen warned all libertines and debauchees that the book was not for them: ". . . accustomed as you are to confound liberty with license, and pleasure with debauchery. . . ." But he reserved his most scathing comments for prudes and hypocrites, beautiful outside but "full of all uncleanliness," who affect to blush if the ankle is mentioned in conversation but will read indecencies enough in private, who "look demure by daylight, and make appointments only in the dark." [11]

As his own moral credentials he revealed that he had practiced the strictest temperance, abstaining from drink, from prostitutes, and, latterly, from animal food. He was even "girlishly sensitive to coarse and ribald jests in which you men think it is witty to indulge." Owen made clear at once that he disagreed strongly with those who, like the Shakers, believe the "instinct of reproduction" should serve only to beget children. He saw it as a beneficent force and charged that suppressing it gave rise to peevishness or unnatural practices, including the "solitary vice." Clearly anticipating the Freudians, he asserted that among those who stifle the instinct, as Shaker writings show, it occupies more of their "secret thoughts." The aim should therefore be to control the urge rather than to stifle it.[12] Such control would prevent the misery resulting from overlarge families, and it would save the health of many mothers. Finally it would prevent the suffering of a girl who is seduced and abandoned—while the seducer goes free. To those who might say that it would encourage profligacy Owen replied that this means that the vaunted chastity of their women is based only on fear and ignorance.[13]

The answer to the problem is, said Owen, to prevent conception. In the first three American editions Owen suggests three methods.[14] The first, complete withdrawal, is, he said, always effective, can be practiced by anyone with a little will power and entails only a slight loss of pleasure. The second, a damp sponge with a ribbon attached to it is not reliable and cannot be recommended until more is known about it. The third, a fine skin covering called a "baudruche," is efficacious but unclean, and the sheath can be used only once and was very costly.

By the fourth edition, published in May, 1831, the second and third methods are relegated to a footnote and the skin covering is rejected because it was inconvenient and is used to prevent syphilis in "degrading intercourse" with prostitutes. Signaling Owen's increasing conservatism, the footnote is entirely omitted in later editions, leaving withdrawal as the only method that is recommended.[15]

Although a few distinguished men praised the booklet, it met with much abuse. Far more important were the book's sales: there were nine editions in five years and about 25,000 copies were sold in the next fifty years in the United States and even more in Britain. Owen's book is bold yet temperate, passionate yet reasonable. In asserting that repression is unhealthy and does not produce an inner purity, it was singularly enlightened. As the first book of its kind, it could have come only from someone born and educated outside the American Puritan tradition.

Shortly after the book appeared, Owen married a nineteen-year-old girl who was, like him, a believer in birth control and a vegetarian. They were united in a strictly civil ceremony which entailed no wifely obligations except love. Owen gradually turned to politics, serving in the Indiana state legislature and as a Democratic Congressman from Indiana. As a politician, Owen moved steadily away from his youthful radicalism. Once he helped to secure a minor liberalization in Indiana's divorce laws; but on other issues, such as slavery, he was distinctly conservative.

Spiritualism, the last refuge of the disappointed reformers of the period, became the passion of his later years, and his books on the subject made him the leading supporter of the movement in the United States. By the time of his death in 1877, Owen's *Moral Physiology* had become only a dimly remembered episode of his intellectually prodigal youth. But he never repudiated it, and credit must go to it for preparing the way for another pioneering work, Charles Knowlton's *Fruits of Philosophy; or, the Private Companion of Young Married People* (1832).

The author of this very small but important book was a small-town Massachusetts doctor. As a youth, Knowlton developed such fears of what was called *gonorrhea dormientum,* or wet dreams, that he became a hypochondriac. He was instantly cured by marriage at the age of twenty.[16] There is little doubt that his decision to become a doctor himself and his effort to reduce the fears that ringed the sexual act stemmed from his adolescent problems. He began studying medicine with several physicians and was so fascinated by the human body that he dug up a corpse and kept it in his room until he had completely dissected it. It was this insistence on reliable fact that made Knowlton the best student at Dartmouth Medical School.

Knowlton was a kindly man and a good doctor. Noting that many married couples were too poor to support a large family and that constant child-bearing impaired the health of mothers, he prepared and lent his patients a manuscript giving contraceptive advice. This was printed, at first anonymously, as *Fruits of Philosophy,* a title calculated to give a lofty tone to the work.

Knowlton begins by saying that man should be permitted to gratify—temperately of course—his desires and that such gratification is healthful and enjoyable. He should also be taught to avoid any disagreeable consequences of such freedom. To those who fear that this will encourage illicit intercourse he answers that any woman who can be seduced could be seduced without the information in his book. The social and economic arguments he uses in favor of contraception are borrowed mainly from Owen and Carlile: checking population expansion, saving overburdened families and the health of mothers, reducing the evils, such as prostitution, resulting from delayed marriages, and decreasing abortion and infanticide.[17] He then gives a description of the reproductive organs that is detailed, frank, and not too inaccurate. The only error that had any bearing on contraceptive advice was the belief that women are not as likely to conceive in the week before as in the week after menstruation.[18] It would be another twenty years before such misleading theories of a "safest" period would be corrected.

Knowlton's main contribution is his discussion of contraceptive methods. Of withdrawal he observes that each couple must decide for themselves whether or not it is satisfactory. He describes the use of a sponge, suggesting that it be moistened with a chemical that can prevent insemination. His chief recommendation is syringing within five or ten minutes after the act, using a solution of sulphate of zinc, alum, pearl-ash, vinegar, or any salt that acts chemically on the semen. We know now that five or ten minutes after coitus is probably too late and that sulphate of zinc may act too slowly. But outside of a few statements such as that the loss of an ounce of semen is equivalent to the loss of forty ounces of blood, *Fruits of Philosophy* is a reliable book.

Perhaps that is why the opposition to it was in some quarters so violent. The authorities in various towns moved against the book after a lawyer charged that it provided a "*complete recipe* how the trade of strumpet may be carried on without its inconveniences or dangers."[19] At Taunton, Massachusetts, Knowlton was let off with a fine of $50 and costs, but at Cambridge, on the complaint of a physician, he was given three months at hard labor. Considering that he was a respectable physician, the severity of this punishment indicates how powerful the Puritan tradition still was in New England.

The publicity simply increased the interest in the book. It was more successful than Owen's *Moral Physiology,* selling about 10,000 copies within seven years. In England it sold 42,000 copies up to 1876, but after it became a central issue in the celebrated trial of the leading Victorian advocates of family limitation, Charles Bradlaugh and Annie Besant, no fewer than 180,000 copies were sold in three months—a stunning example of the public hunger for information of this kind.[20]

Charles Knowlton went on to become a successful doctor and an honored member of his profession. He took no further part in spreading contraceptive information; nevertheless, after his book and Owen's were revived by the Bradlaugh-Besant trial, they helped start the birth control movement—as it would be named long afterward by Margaret Sanger. They are, moreover, credited with playing a considerable role in the decline in the birth rate in England and western Europe beginning in the 1880's.

But the Owen and Knowlton books were only a reconnaissance. The real struggle with the forces of suppression would not be joined for another half century. In the 1830's the opposition was confident that contraception would not make headway among decent women.

At least one other physiological discovery helped break down the reluctance of some women to take active steps to prevent conception. It had generally been supposed that women, like animals, were most fertile before and after menstruation. Then, in 1849, a London professor named Oldham discovered that quite the reverse was true, that women were usually most fertile in what had been considered the safest interval—the two weeks midway between menstrual periods.[21] This was a revolutionary discovery because it enabled a woman to practice contraception almost without lifting a finger.

Upper-class and middle-class women were the first to use such information because they had learned to like their leisure and did not relish the responsibilities of a large family. Working-class families were slow to follow the lead of their richer sisters because of lack of information, and taboos bolstered by ignorance and inertia. In time, other factors spurred interest in contraception: the desire to give every child a better education, the decreasing effect of "churchyard luck," that is, infant mortality, and the problems of bringing up a large family in a city tenement.

By the 1850's contraceptive information was spreading and preventive devices were being widely advertised. Dr. William Alcott in *The Physiology of Marriage* declared that the method suggested by Knowlton was in vogue in many parts of the country. It comes as no surprise to read in *The Nation* in 1867 that a large family was more and more considered a sign of recklessness. And in the same year the Reverend John Todd revealed in his *Serpents in Doves' Nests* that the serpent had penetrated that last stronghold of innocence, New England. He described parents who boasted that they had only one or two children, and he added: "There is scarcely a young lady in New England . . . whose marriage can be announced in the paper, without her being insulted within a week—by receiving through the mail a printed circular, offering information and instrumentalities, and all needed facilities by which the laws of heaven in regard to the increase of the human family may be thwarted." [22]

Since such a circular would be illegal today, we may well be astonished that it was sent through the mails in New England over one hundred years ago. What shall we say then to a fully illustrated public advertisement for contraceptives? Such an ad appeared in Dr. H. A. Allbutt's *The Wife's Handbook,* published in England in 1886. Under the thin disguise of "Malthusian Appliances" it shows a syringe which is described as a "Vertical and Reverse Current Vaginal Tube" to be used with an injection of sufficient strength "to destroy the life properties of the spermatic fluid without injury to the person." A second illustration offers an "Improved Check Pessary," made of "soft medicated rubber, to be worn by the female (during coition) as a protection against conception." The syringe was three shillings sixpence and the pessary was two shillings threepence.[23]

Among the writers most influential in breaking down or at least shaking the opposition to birth control and divorce was Dr. Edward Bliss Foote. Much of his effectiveness he owed to the fact that he was a journalist for a few years and became a fluent writer and forceful controversialist. Belatedly attracted to medicine, he worked in a physician's office and then took the brief course at Penn Medical University in the 1850's. Still a journalist, he established his own publishing house and issued his first book, *Medical Common Sense* (1858), even before he took his degree.[24] Its amazing sale, over 200,000 copies, led him to incorporate it in his comprehensive *Plain Home Talk about the Human System* (1872), which sold half a million copies and was for many years a standard personal hygiene guide.

The key to Foote's success was his frank approach and his air of authority. The latter rested largely on his conviction that the human body is strongly electrical and that the relationship between men and women depends on the electrical attraction of opposites. Phrenology, he believed, could help determine the compatibility of a couple.[25] Armed with his pet theories, Foote took strong positions, many of them challenging the moral pieties, a few reinforcing them. His medical science was often adulterated by the mumbo-jumbo of phrenology, electrical magnetism, and assorted health fads, but he was at least true to his profession in not allowing moral issues to influence what he believed to be good or bad for health. He asserted that celibacy was incompatible with virtue, that indifference to sex was a disease, and that a woman could and should take full part in the sex act.[26] Among Foote's minor heresies was his criticism of the excessive delicacy that kept ailing women from allowing physicians to examine them. He also ridiculed the tradition that a virgin should have an unbroken hymen and that girls should never take the initiative in courting.

Instead of growing more conservative with success and wealth, Foote became more radical, espousing many free-thought doctrines. Along with his son, Edward Bond Foote, who graduated with honors from the College of Physicians and Surgeons in New York City in 1876, he published *The Health Monthly,* advocating birth control, pure foods, vivisection, and a multitude of minor social as well as health reforms.[27]

The improvement of the race remained an overriding concern of both father and son. Influenced by Darwin, Huxley, Tyndall, and Spencer, they were convinced that unfit parents were a menace to the future of the breed. It was of the utmost importance, they said, that propagation be put on a scientific basis in order to insure the survival of the fittest. For such reasons Foote offered—in what amounted to advertisements—to supply no less than four kinds of preventives to conception. One was a "Membranous Envelope" made from a fish bladder and said to be stronger than the rubber used in the "ordinary French Male Safe or Condum" but so sensitive that it would not diminish the pleasurable "electric" of coition. A second device, not quite so efficacious, was a rubber "Apex Envelope," which covered only the glans penis. A third, which Foote called an Electro-Magnetic Preventive Machine, was, he admitted, expensive—it cost fifteen dollars—but he guaranteed its effectiveness. The most advanced device was the one he called "The Womb Veil"; it was a thin rubber tissue that a woman adjusted over the mouth of the womb before copulation. This, an early version of the diaphragm, would in no way interfere with "the full enjoyment of the conjugal embrace." He offered to send any of these devices by mail.[28]

But the battle for the unrestricted circulation of information on contraceptives was hardly to be won thus easily. Foote, as we said in an earlier chapter, was tricked into mailing his pamphlet to Comstock and was fined $3,500 in addition to $5,000 in legal costs. Unchastened, Foote issued another pamphlet, *A Step Backward,* which assailed the Comstock law as imposing a "Romish asceticism of the fourth century" on free America. The law as administered by Anthony Comstock was truly a step backward;[29] Foote never again enjoyed the freedom he had had in 1859.

Foote's son continued the struggle to improve the breed. Advocating what was already being called eugenics, he wrote learnedly and with a wealth of arguments,[30] but he could not discuss any of the control devices recommended by his father twenty-seven years before or by Charles Knowlton some fifty years earlier. In his efforts to help men and women exercise some control of their destiny as parents, the younger Foote was, like his father, one of Comstock's victims. But Comstock's day was drawing to a close, and when Edward Bond Foote died in 1912, Margaret Sanger and Marie Stopes were in the offing, preparing to complete the task that Robert Dale Owen had started almost a hundred years before.

15.

WOMEN MILITANT

WHEN the first voices against the inferior position of women in America were raised in the late eighteenth century, they made only mild requests for more education, legal rights, or simply respect. Any demand for a freer expression of sexuality, no matter how reasonable, would have brought, as it still did fifty years later, withering charges of indecency and immorality.

In this and other respects America lagged behind England, where, as we have seen, Mary Wollstonecraft, Godwin, Shelley, Place, and Carlile, beginning in the 1790's, tried to mount a frontal attack on hypocrisy and obscurantism. Even in America the first blows on behalf of a greater equality of the sexes were struck by three reformers who had come from Scotland: Frances Wright and the two Owens.

In some ways, of course, the position of women in America made change seem less urgent. Despite the heritage of Puritanism—felt mainly in New England—the help that women could give in work and homemaking, particularly in rural areas, made them valuable. Moreover, as the more prosperous families in towns and cities assumed the role taken in Europe by the hereditary nobility, a woman's fine clothes and good manners were more and more often considered evidence of the success and prosperity of her family.

But even a mild expression of dissatisfaction by a woman was rare before 1830. When John Adams was in Philadelphia in 1777 helping to lay the constitutional groundwork for the new republic, his wife, Abigail, then thirty-three, wrote to him: "Do not put such unlimited power in the hands of husbands. Remember, all men would be tyrants if they could. If particular care and attention are not paid to the ladies, we are determined to foment a rebellion, and will not hold our selves bound to obey the laws in which we have no voice or representation." Her plea, it should be noted, was on behalf of married women only. Somewhat sharper was a statement by Judith Sargent Murray, whose father, a prosperous merchant, served in the Constitutional Convention in Massachusetts in 1788. She questioned the idea that men were superior to women. Is it reasonable, she asked, that a "candidate for immortality, for the joys of heaven, an intelligent being, who is to spend an eternity contemplating the works of the Deity, should . . . be so degraded as to be allowed no other ideas than those which are suggested by the mechanism of a pudding, or the sewing of the seams of a garment?" [1]

Although Tom Paine—perhaps because of his bachelor status—made few references to the subject, those few were harshly critical of the attitudes of men, noting that men ruled women with an absolute sway and construed "the slightest appearances into guilt." Women were surrounded, he said, by "judges who are at once tyrants, as well as their seducers." [2]

But until the late 1840's, the convictions of the very few who spoke up for women were weakened by reservations nourished by Biblical dogma. Hannah Mather Crocker, granddaughter of Cotton Mather and the wife of a minister, was courageous enough to write the first tract in America dealing with women's rights, *Observations on the Real Rights of Women, with Their Appropriate Duties, Agreeable to Scripture, Reason and Common Sense* (1818). Women, she wrote, should be educated and must be allowed to share rights equally with men, especially in the home, but all arrangements must comport with Scripture. Even though Christianity has done much to redeem woman, we cannot forget the evil that Eve wrought in Eden. Mrs. Crocker, who bore ten children before she wrote her book, conceded that Mary Wollstonecraft had said much that was honest and inspiring but added that women must not think of putting such ideas into practice. It was much better to be guided by that other Englishwoman, popular, pious, conservative Hannah More.

Some of the bonds imposed by the old religion were broken

by the Unitarians, whose spokesman was the high-minded and eloquent Boston preacher, William Ellery Channing. Channing declared that the Calvinist view of man as inherently evil defamed both the human race and God. He preached instead a faith in man's essential goodness. It was a natural step from there to the belief—shared, paradoxically, with such irreligious men as Godwin and Shelley—that man was infinitely perfectible and a free soul. But if we consider the Owens and Frances Wright as essentially utopianists, it was not until late in the 1830's that America heard pleas on behalf of women that were not influenced by the Bible. One of the first to speak was Margaret Fuller.

Because there was such sharp disagreement about Margaret Fuller among her contemporaries, she emerges for us as a compound of contradictions: a monster of intellectualism who was a creature of emotions; a sexless woman who yearned for love; a product of Puritan New England who flowered only after she fled to Italy; one of the most articulate women of her time, whose best-known book is vaporous and unfocused.

But in the light of her childhood and education many of these contrasts seem not at all so puzzling. Her father, a Massachusetts lawyer and Congressman, was an opinionated and domineering man. He was disappointed that Margaret, the first born of his nine children, was not a boy, but he nevertheless centered all his hopes on her. He subjected her to the most rigorous classical education, starting her on Latin grammar and the Roman virtues at the age of six. The forcing process worked: Margaret read Vergil and Horace at seven and Shakespeare at eight. But she was so overstimulated and emotionally starved that she was racked by nightmares—sometimes clearly sexual—and somnambulism.

Once out of school, she began to shine in the intellectual life of Cambridge; for what she lacked in beauty and grace she made up in wit, learning, and a magnetism that fascinated even those who did not like her. And many did not like her, finding her egotism intolerable. It was hardly surprising that a woman who could later say to Emerson, "I now know all the people worth knowing in America, and I find no intellect comparable to my own," should discourage young men. It did not matter in the least that the boast was not unjustified.

It was at this point that a score of the best or at least most interesting minds in the Boston–Concord area began to come together under the name of the Transcendentalist Club to talk informally about such subjects as Truth, Individuality, Inspiration, and Law. Building on the Unitarian belief in the inalienable worth of man, as well as German idealism, Oriental mysticism, Rousseau, Swedenborg, Fourier's social theories, and the spirit of the English Romantics—they urged a reliance on inner inspiration and self-cultivation.[3] Although there were as many conceptions of Transcendentalism as there were members of the group, they all shared a passion for free discussion and a discontent with the dogmas of the old order. For a while they made Boston and Concord the intellectual capital of America.

The chief medium by which they communicated their ideas was talk. And of this medium, by happy coincidence, Margaret Fuller was master. She was, moreover, that rare variety of talker who could get others to talk. Fully appreciating her own talents, she gathered a select group of Boston women for a series of "Conversations," and held these quite regularly from 1839 to 1843. It was not only a natural vocation for her but an attempt to introduce women to the life of the mind, to free them from a sense of intellectual inferiority. Despite the shallowness of many of the ideas aired in this imitation of a French salon (Miss Fuller was an ardent admirer of Mmes. Récamier and de Staël), the Conversations were a demonstration of intellectual independence that helped clear the way for the leaders of the feminist movement.

According to all reports, Margaret conducted the meetings with a glowing intensity, but in the end they proved more satisfying to her mind than to her heart.[4] Indeed, the sublimated energies that she poured into both public and private conversations must explain the sharp responses she evoked. Those energies were multiplied by the fact that she was in part compensating for her physical shortcomings: stringy hair, a nasal voice, a neck abnormally long and pliant ("swanlike" to her friends; "like a bird of prey" to her critics), and a trick of opening and closing her eyes incessantly.[5]

Miss Fuller had another emotional outlet not uncommon among young women of the period—passionate attachments, obviously sexual but rarely recognized as such, to other women. But as she passed into her thirties, she realized increasingly that only in marriage would "regions of her being that else had lain in cold obstruction . . . burst forth into leaf and bloom and song." With rare self-knowledge she admitted: "I have no child, and the woman in me has so craved this experience that it has seemed the want of it must paralyze me." [6]

Perhaps because she was not identified with any one religious or philosophic attitude, she was chosen by the Transcendentalists in 1840 to edit a new quarterly, the *Dial*. As editor, she allowed some contributors such as Bronson Alcott to float off into the upper regions of speculation and mysticism. She herself was not a disciplined or distinguished writer (". . . my voice excites me," she admitted, "my pen never"),[7] but one of her contributions, "The Great Lawsuit: Man vs. Men, Woman vs. Women," became the core of her *Woman in the Nineteenth Century*.

Although this small book is much too diffuse for modern taste, it was, in the words of one of her biographers, Katherine Anthony, "the first considered statement of feminism in this country." It did not go beyond Mary Wollstonecraft's *Vindication*, but it placed even greater emphasis on personal fulfillment. Woman, it said, must put off subserviency and must be permitted to unfold whatever powers she had. In a passage that was often used in ridiculing the book, she averred that women should be allowed to fill any post, exclaiming, "Let them be sea-captains, if you will." [8] Give woman hope and a standard within herself and all the details of the relationship of the sexes would fall into place.

Miss Fuller deplored the narrow morality that looked on such women of genius as Mary Wollstonecraft and George Sand as outlaws; and she dealt frankly with prostitution, idleness in women, and the double standard. Accepting the theory that prostitutes were forced into their calling only by want, she said the solution of this evil was educating women for work that would support them. Although Margaret Fuller was—as Mary Wollstonecraft had been—thirty-three years old and unmarried when she wrote her book, she spoke out boldly, even as her predecessor had, on the sexual passion in women:

> As to marriage, it has been inculcated in women, for centuries, that men have not only stronger passions than they, but of a sort that it would be shameful for them to share or even understand; that, therefore, they must "confide in their husbands," that is, submit implicitly to their will; that the least appearance of coldness or withdrawal, from whatever cause, in the wife is wicked, because liable to turn their husband's thoughts to illicit indulgence; for a man is so constituted that he must indulge his passions or die! [9]

If this passage was based on intuition rather than experience, it was all the more remarkable; and it was such passages that caused *Women in the Nineteenth Century* to be both praised and damned.

When Horace Greeley invited Margaret to become a regular contributor to the *Tribune*, she saw an opportunity to descend from the pedestal on which she found herself and to enter the mainstream of life. She succeeded, leaving behind much of the sentimental mysticism that had beclouded her writing, and establishing herself as a sharp and original critic. She served especially to awaken her readers to an appreciation of various European masters, including some, such as Goethe, Balzac, George Sand, and Eugène Sue, who were considered immoral influences.

Whether she had been released from the straitlacing of Boston or was simply desperate for affection, she now fell feverishly in love with James Nathan. Nathan was a slightly effeminate German Jew who captivated her with what she saw as a romantic Eastern soul. After a few months of clandestine meetings and letters, Nathan, a shallow character, taken aback by the intensity of this unorthodox Puritan sybil, fled to Europe.[10] Margaret must have realized that impulse had led her into an almost tragic mistake, but she nevertheless decided that she would find in Europe the emotional freedom, the tradition of beauty, the personal fulfillment she craved. So she arranged to go abroad as a correspondent for the *Tribune*.

She reached Europe on the eve of the revolutions of 1848, and in Rome she found all that she sought: the rich tradition, a revolutionary ferment, including heroes such as Mazzini and Garibaldi, and, most of all, a lover. The lover was a penniless noble, Count Ossoli, ten years her junior, and without intellectual interests of any kind—simply a young Italian who would release her at last from her New England repressions. Within a few months she was pregnant. They married—as belatedly as Mary Wollstonecraft and Godwin and as Frances Wright and D'Arusmont—but did so secretly because they had no money and because Ossoli's conservative Catholic family would have been horrified.[11]

To the private drama of Margaret Fuller's child-bearing was soon added the public drama of the defense of Rome by the revolutionaries, with Ossoli fighting in the ranks and Margaret working day and night in a military hospital. After the tragic defeat of the defenders Margaret turned with relief to devoting herself to her child and her husband. But the period of rest and peace was brief. Within a year the lack of money drove them to set out for America, resigned to facing malicious gossip and unkind rumors. But Margaret was saved from this ordeal when the vessel in which they sailed was wrecked within clear view of Fire Island on July 19, 1850.

Margaret Fuller's story continued, even after her death, to furnish insights into the morality of the age. A two-volume memorial prepared by her friends, Emerson, Channing, Clarke, and Hodge, made her seem all good and noble—part goddess and part prophetess. Her enemies, however, continued to circulate spiteful stories, climaxed in 1884 when a note by Hawthorne—written following a visit to Rome some eight years after Margaret's death—was published by his son. Quoting a Mr. Mozier, who knew Margaret casually during her stay in Rome, Hawthorne reported that Ossoli was a handsome, ignorant, and almost illiterate young man who had been only a household servant when Margaret Fuller met him. Mozier guessed that Margaret's interest in Ossoli had been purely sensual, and Hawthorne added that this was entirely credible because she had had a "strong and coarse nature" which had been only superficially refined. Hawthorne went on:

> She was a great humbug—of course with much talent and moral reality, or else she could never have been so great a humbug. . . . Thus there appears to have been a total collapse in poor Margaret, morally and intellectually; and, tragic as her catastrophe was, Providence was, after all, kind in putting her on board that fated ship. . . . It was such an awful joke, that she

> should have resolved . . . to make herself the greatest, wisest, best woman of the age. And to that end she set to work on her strong, heavy, unpliable, and in many respects defective and evil nature, and adorned it with a mosaic of admirable qualities . . . putting in here a splendid talent and there a moral excellence. . . . But . . . there was something within her that she could not possibly come at, to recreate or refine it; and, by and by, this rude, old potency bestirred itself, and undid all her labor in the twinkling of an eye. On the whole, I do not know but I like her the better for it; because she proved herself a very woman after all, and fell as the weakest of her sisters might."[12]

Biographers point out that this view was based on the testimony of a thoroughly unreliable informant. But Hawthorne chose to accept it in order to write his brilliantly malign judgment. He sees her desperate, lifelong effort to adjust to unnatural restraints as a joke and a trick, and her later surrender to natural desires as a moral collapse. His condemnation of Margaret Fuller, like his damnation of Hester Prynne, is based largely on her having given herself to a man she loved without pausing for permission from society or approval from Nathaniel Hawthorne. In all this she only proved that she was "a very woman after all."

What Hawthorne—and those friends of Margaret's who thought she had lost her way—found intolerable was that she wanted something more than the noble sentiments of the Transcendentalists, the altitudinous affirmations of Emerson, the withdrawal of Thoreau, the divided allegiances of Hawthorne. Far from suffering a moral collapse or having been defeated by a "defective and evil nature," she had at last found a place in which the entire suppressed side of her nature could bloom. There was nothing furtive in her acknowledgment of her discovery; shortly after arriving in Rome, she said of Europe: "It was no false instinct that said I might here find an atmosphere to develop me in ways I need. Had I only come ten years earlier! Now my life must be a failure, so much strength has been wasted on abstractions, which only came because I grew not in the right soil."

Margaret Fuller's lack of solid accomplishment, her inadequacies as a writer, and the unfulfilled promise of her conversation account for the persistent tendency to neglect her. But her failings in no way detract from the intuitive soundness of her conclusions about the aridity of the New England environment, the innermost needs of women, and the importance of the affections. It was largely New England that kept her from living life fully, if not from seeing it whole. But she never completely resigned herself and at least set foot in the Promised Land before she died.

It was not religion alone that blunted the thrust of the early feminists. There was also the conviction that a woman's most important roles were as wife and mother. Looked at biologically, this was an understandable conviction, but in a time when it was assumed that these were a woman's only acceptable roles, and indeed her only capabilities, it severely limited the scope of feminism. Thus, although Lucretia Coffin Mott was the first leader of the feminist movement and labored mightily in the cause, she fought not so much for the rights of women as for the rights of wives.

A religious Quaker with a deep sense of obligation to the unfortunate, she and her husband became active abolitionists early in the 1830's, but she soon learned that a woman could support a cause but not lead in it. A slender and attractive woman, she bore six children and enjoyed family life. This and the fact that her husband, a quiet, conscientious man, shared her opinions and reform activities made it easy for her to insist that a wife should have the same rights as her husband.[13] No Frances Wright seeking to change the whole social system, Lucretia Mott was a practical reformer who believed that getting domestic rights for women was enough for a first step. When the issue of sexual freedom was raised, she considered it a passing fever.

Lucretia Mott was, in other words, an appropriate leader for the feminist movement in the 1840's and 1850's when women were loath to speak out lest they be labeled shameless and unfeminine. She was not only womanly in manner and calmly reasonable in speech, but she obviously loved her husband, children, and home. Although she did go so far as to assert that women were a depressed group through "a corrupt custom and a perverted application of the Scriptures," she accepted the differences in the functions of the sexes and never agreed with those of her associates who assumed that women were morally superior to men.

Dressed always in Quaker gray, there was something of sober colonial America about Lucretia Mott. Elizabeth C. Stanton, twenty-two years younger than Mrs. Mott and coming of age in the 1830's, reflected far more of the self-confidence of the young republic. She was plump and motherly in appearance but tremendously buoyant and articulate. Most of all she was outspoken and aggressive in what she saw as a conflict between the sexes; and if she did not see it as a full-fledged war, that was only because it was so one-sided, with men doing all the dominating and women doing all the submitting.

In an age when most American women not only submitted but thought their lot enviable, it is not easy to explain why a girl of a prominent and conservative upstate New York family should have fought so stubbornly against one of the firmest postulates of society—the primacy of the male. We have a few clues of course, the chief one being Elizabeth Cady's relationship to her father. Like Margaret Fuller's father, Daniel Cady was a well-known lawyer and a Congressman, and like Timothy Fuller he regretted that his daughter was not a son who would carry on his name. But where Fuller subjected his daughter to a stern regimen of study, Judge Cady subjected his daughter to his regret and disappointment. Cady had centered his hopes on the one boy among his six children and when the young man died after graduating from Union College, the father was inconsolable. When eleven-year-old Elizabeth crept into his arms as he sat beside the casket in a darkened room, he said only: "Oh my daughter, would that you were a boy!" The girl, resolving that she would become as learned and courageous as her brother had been, devoted herself to mastering Greek and mathematics and to riding and jumping a horse with a boy's boldness. But then her father regretted all the more that she was a girl. Nor did either of them ever change. As late as 1855, when Mrs. Stanton was forty years old and had nearly grown children of her own, she reported to her most intimate associate Susan B. Anthony: ". . . I passed through a terrible scourging when last at my father's. I cannot tell you how deep the iron entered my soul. I never felt more deeply the degradation of my sex. To think that all in me of which my father would have felt a proper pride had I been a man, is deeply mortifying to him because I am a woman." [14]

Another influence was her relative, Gerrit Smith, a wealthy supporter of abolitionists whose home was a station on the "underground railway." At his home, Elizabeth met another well-known abolitionist, Henry Stanton, when she was twenty-four and he was thirty-four. She married him—with the word "obey" carefully omitted from the ceremony. Since Stanton was a delegate to the first World's Antislavery Convention, the couple went to England on their wedding journey in 1840. The visit became a momentous experience for the bride when she saw the men in charge of the convention reject women delegates from all over the world. There, too, she met and was stirred by Lucretia Mott; the older woman opened up to her a new world of thought and action.

For a time Henry Stanton practiced law in Boston and the Stantons came to know such celebrated men as William Lloyd Garrison, Whittier, Theodore Parker, Emerson, Alcott, Charles Sumner, and the Brook Farm coterie. Then in 1846 they moved to Seneca Falls, near Syracuse, in west-central New York.[15] They already had several children, but Elizabeth soon experienced a sense of frustration both in her private life and in her outside activities. Although Seneca was hardly more than a country town, it was in the "burned-over district," which was swept in the late 1830's and 1840's by millennial religious and reform movements. Farmers, faced by a harsh struggle for existence, especially after the opening of the Erie Canal introduced competition from agriculture farther west, sought panaceas. So Seneca Falls had a large group of Second Adventists or Millerites, sizable temperance and antislavery societies, Unitarian disciples of William Ellery Channing, followers of Sylvester Graham's vegetarianism, and sundry families who moved away to join the utopian communities springing up all across the land.[16] Among the other unsettling influences were the newly built factories that enabled a woman to earn a living outside the home.

Finally, in July of 1848, not by accident the year of the revolutions in Europe, Elizabeth Cady Stanton poured out her accumulated discontent in a long talk with Lucretia Mott. The two women, supported by several others, decided to call a "Woman's Rights Convention," and on July 19 more than a hundred delegates assembled in the Wesleyan Chapel in Seneca Falls. The convention, the first of its kind, was remarkable enough, but its Declaration of Sentiments was a truly revolutionary document. Among its ten resolutions were these: Woman is man's equal and must be recognized as such; the transgressions of both should be punished with equal severity; and it is the duty of women to secure "their sacred right to the elective franchise." The last resolution, the most audacious, was offered and pressed through by Mrs. Stanton. But it should be noted that the resolution concerning virtue and sin demanded equal repression for men rather than equal freedom for women. Nevertheless the entire Declaration met such criticism and ridicule from the average citizen as well as from press and pulpit that most of the women who had signed the document withdrew their support and some even joined the foe. But the fire had been lit: Similar conventions began to be held in state after state.

Now there began for Elizabeth Cady Stanton a life of lectures, protests, appeals, and letters to followers everywhere. For many years she spent much of her time in speaking tours that carried her from Maine to California. An effective speaker, she was aided by vigor, a tolerance of ridicule, and a sense of humor rare among the more zealous reformers.

Her message was that this had been a man's world and that man had made the evil laws and created the traditions that had degraded womankind. When in 1860 Wendell Phillips sharply rejected attempts to link woman's rights with the antislavery struggle, Mrs. Stanton wrote to Susan B. Anthony: "Woman's degradation is in man's idea of his sexual rights. Our religion, laws, customs, are all founded on the belief that woman was made for man." [17] In time she went on to claim that women, as a sex, were superior to men. Man, she believed, was tough, crude, and "nomadic," whereas woman was gentle, helpful, home-loving, refined, and pure. With the proper exercise and training, women could match men in all things. In particular, women must be able to achieve financial independence. "When women can support themselves," she wrote in 1851 in Amelia Bloomer's temperance journal, *Lily*, "have their entry to all the trades and professions, with a house of their own over their heads and a bank account, they will own their bodies and be dictators in the social realm." [18]

Mrs. Stanton saw the whole question of woman's rights as turning on the marriage relationship. And what she had seen of that relationship led her to characterize it as a bad bargain for women. It was rooted in men's "selfishness and sensuality," and it rendered women legally subservient so that men might have sexual freedom. To make women's subjection complete, man had fostered the theory that his passions were stronger than hers and that she must surrender even her body to his control. This, she said, was a distortion based on a falsehood.[19] In a revealing comment, made in a casual entry in her diary in 1883 concerning *Leaves of Grass*, Mrs. Stanton wrote:

> Walt Whitman seems to understand everything in nature but woman. In "There is a Woman Waiting for Me," he speaks as if the female must be forced to the creative act, apparently ignorant of the great natural fact that a healthy woman has as much passion as a man, that she needs nothing stronger than the law of attraction to draw her to the male.[20]

Thus the highly respected Seneca Falls matron on the poet notorious for his sensuality.

With much the same kind of frankness she wrote—in a letter in 1853 to Elizabeth Gerrit Smith—of Madame de Staël's free expression of feelings: "How I do love that woman! It is seldom we see affectional natures so harmoniously developed as in her. In the midst of all her triumphs, she sighed for love. How we mortals cheat ourselves out of our birthright; how few ever taste the blessedness of loving, nobly, generously, passionately." [21]

The sexual domination by husbands, Mrs. Stanton maintained, led to a multitude of evils, from the double standard to prostitution and infanticide. Boldly accepting the consequences of this view, Mrs. Stanton favored easy divorce. In the first flush of feminist fervor she even appears to have been ready to oppose all legal control of marriage. ". . . remove law and a false public sentiment," she wrote to Miss Anthony in 1853, "and woman will no more live as wife with a cruel, bestial drunkard than a servant, in this free country, will stay with a pettish, unjust mistress." If legislators insist on laws, "let them fine a woman $50 for every child she conceives by a drunkard. . . . Man in his lust has regulated long enough this whole question of sexual intercourse." [22] If having complete control over her own body meant that women must have some way of preventing conception, Mrs. Stanton was ready for that, too. In 1880, referring to a woman doctor, she wrote to a correspondent: "I never saw her, but she made it a specialty to teach women how to avoid a too general perpetuation of the race, which I consider a commendable kind of knowledge to hand down to our overburdened mothers." [23]

Her rage against the arrogance of man cannot be exaggerated. "I am at the boiling point!" she wrote to Miss Anthony in 1852 concerning the barring of women from participating in anti-slavery conventions. "If I do not find some day the use of my tongue on this question, I shall die of an intellectual depression, a woman's rights convulsion!" [24] Even stronger evidence of the mutiny that lurked in the bones of this proper-seeming Victorian matron occurs in a letter in 1871 to Martha C. Wright:

> When I think of all the wrongs that have been heaped upon womankind, I am ashamed that I am not forever in a condition of chronic wrath, stark mad, skin and bone, my eyes a fountain of tears, my lips overflowing with curses, and my hand against every man and brother! Ah, how I do repent me of the male faces I have washed, the mittens I have knit, the trousers mended, the cut fingers and broken toes I have bound up! [25]

Despite the fact that Mrs. Stanton had seven children and a sympathetic and solicitous husband, such passages together with the ready way she left her family for lecture tours lead one to wonder how happy she was in her own marriage. Did she harbor suppressed regrets at her own sexual inhibitions, or was she simply an outspoken woman who had a score to settle with men and an acute sense of mission—a conviction that she was leading a historic movement to victory and that her family could and must take care of itself?

If men, especially of the clergy, were provoked by Mrs. Stanton's attitude toward marriage and divorce, they would have been shocked had they been fully aware of her views of the church and the clergy. Her alienation from the church stemmed from girlhood memories of Scotch Presbyterian services filled with visions of death and woe. A six weeks' revival conducted by the celebrated Reverend Charles Grandison Finney had reduced her to a state of nervous terror.[26] She recovered but never returned to the church, and although she retained a belief in God—a beneficent God—and in immortality, she considered the church in America "a terrible engine of oppression," especially in its relation to women.[27] And her diary and letters are sprinkled with admiring allusions to skeptics such as Paine, Gibbon, Renan, and Ingersoll.

But it was the Bible with its treatment of woman as a mere afterthought in the creation, as the original temptress, cursed with bearing children, that aroused her bitterest reactions. These led her in her last years to prepare *The Woman's Bible* (1895–98), a commentary on those texts (about one-tenth of the whole) that bear directly on women. In this singular work, Mrs. Stanton, abetted by a group of scholarly women, denied the Scriptures divine authority and dismissed as mere allegories such episodes as the creation of woman or the story of Eve.[28] The books of the Old Testament she saw as the history of an "ignorant, underdeveloped people" and she declared that any humane person must "shudder at their cruelty and blush at their obscenity." [29] She found the New Testament hardly more acceptable in its estimate of women, pointing out that the apostles set forth the inferior position of woman even more emphatically than did the prophets and the patriarchs.[30] She even assailed the doctrine of the higher nobility of the virgin birth as a slur on all the natural motherhood of the world and as having encouraged the monasteries and nunneries that had "disgraced manhood and womanhood for a thousand years." [31]

Here and elsewhere her critical attitude toward the church and the Bible yielded her some unique insights into the hold exercised by Christianity. In *The Woman's Bible* she asked why there was a Heavenly Father and no Heavenly Mother, and in a curious anticipation of the Freudian approach, she wrote to her daughter Harriot in 1880 that "the love of Jesus among women in general, all grows out of sexual attraction. The Virgin Mary appeals in the same way to her male worshipers." [32] Although Mrs. Stanton offered no evidence to support such large generalizations, they make clear that she was far ahead of her time in more ways than one. Had she not concentrated so intensely on woman's rights and especially women's suffrage, she would have undoubtedly made her mark as an astute critic of society in general.

Mrs. Stanton's impatience with orthodoxy repeatedly betrayed her into eccentric enthusiasms. At one time or another she found much to admire in spiritualism, phrenology, and Annie Besant's theosophy. The same impulse had led her into the campaign, begun in 1851, for adoption of the Bloomer costume. The famous English-born actress Fanny Kemble liked to wear modish pantaloons on excursions and the women of the Oneida Community donned a kind of pantaloons when they were at work, but the first to wear the whole costume regularly was Elizabeth Gerrit Smith, daughter of Mrs. Stanton's relative, Gerrit Smith, the abolitionist. The dress—full Turkish-style pantaloons gathered at the ankles, with an overskirt falling to just below the knees—caused a stir and was promptly adopted by Mrs. Amelia Bloomer, who edited a temperance journal and had a penchant for publicity.

Mrs. Stanton had always thought that women's clothes were unhealthy because of the tight waists and the weight and because they prevented women from competing in many of men's occupations. Far from considering "Bloomers" a shameless or scandalous style, she believed it would reduce the attention paid to the feminine features of the body and help everyone lead "far purer and higher lives." Her husband skeptically observed that men would be delighted to learn whether the ladies they knew had plump or scrawny legs.[33] Prudish disapproval was fanned by the fact that the costume was quickly adopted in several "utopias" notorious for allowing free love relationships. Unhappily, the costume was unbecoming to all but the most shapely women: it made Mrs. Stanton look ridiculously dumpy and Miss Anthony absurdly scrawny. They and the other women who adopted the mode were admired by a few but stared at and ridiculed by the many. After about two years of such torment, most of the group gladly abandoned the costume. But the episode hurt the cause, stamping feminists in the public mind as eccentric, unfeminine, unattractive, and fair game for jeers and gibes.

If Elizabeth Cady Stanton's assault on the Bible's view of

woman seems daring, it should be remembered that it came well after Darwin had knocked a few great props from under the authority of the Old Testament. Darwinism was a major blow, however unintentional, to the myth of Eden and of Adam and Eve. When a church pastoral letter in Boston attacked Sarah Grimke's antislavery efforts as unchristian and added that "the power of Woman is her dependence, flowing from the consciousness of that weakness which God has given for her protection," Miss Grimke challenged the divine origin of Scriptures. Even if Eve led man to the fall, she argued, man showed no superiority in his readiness to follow her and in spending the next six thousand years in condemning her. "All I ask our brethren," she cried, "is that they will take their feet from off our necks and permit us to stand upright." [34]

It would be a mistake to think that feminists in general followed Elizabeth Cady Stanton in coupling demands for their property, working and voting rights with a plea for the control of their own bodies. The fact is that a number of the women who were bold in entering men's professions or in claiming property rights were conservative or even antiliberal in other respects. Or they were eager to achieve distinction only in a given field.

Perhaps the most famous of these was Elizabeth Blackwell, the first woman in the United States to become a doctor. She is particularly significant because, unlike pioneer women educators or ministers, she pushed into a field where such activities as studying the human body alongside men students or serving in hospitals with men doctors challenged sexual prudery directly. Yet, as aggressive as she was in gaining admission to a medical college—she tried twenty-nine schools before Geneva College (later Hobart) reluctantly accepted her—and in getting hospital training, so indifferent was she when it came to claiming other rights for women.[35] It is even probable that she chose medicine because many Americans had come to believe that it would be desirable to let women treat women patients.

Dr. Blackwell never married, appears to have had no intimate relationships with men, deprecated the behavior of militant feminists, and was not especially interested in woman's suffrage. She held to such views despite the fact that she came of a relatively enlightened family, with a sister, Emily, who also became a doctor, a brother who married a feminist leader, Lucy Stone, and another brother who married the first recognized woman minister in America, the Reverend Antoinette Brown. Even her extensive work in hospitals in America and Europe had little effect on her rather prudish attitude toward the relations between men and women. Her early experience in the syphilis ward of a Philadelphia hospital persuaded her only that she must wage war on "licentiousness." Her advice on the training of youth was equally moralistic. According to a recent biographer, she thought that "self-abuse" was evil and that boys should remain as "pure" as girls until they married. Thinking of herself as a "Christian physiologist," she believed in the betterment of the race through the Christian ideal of morality, and she accepted marriage as divine.

When she learned, after she moved to London in 1869, of the campaign to legalize prostitution in order to stem venereal disease through the compulsory examination of prostitutes, she opposed the movement on the grounds that any law that did not firmly suppress vice would only educate the community in evil.[36] Time and experience did not leaven her view: late in the 1870's she was still determined to promote the "organization of chastity" against the "organized forces which are now employed in the *direct promotion* of immorality." [37]

Convinced that work was more satisfying for a woman than love, marriage, and children, Elizabeth Blackwell wrote:

> How good work is—work that has a soul in it! I cannot conceive that anything can supply its wants to a woman. In all human relations the woman has to yield, to modify her individuality—the strong personality of even the best husband and children compels some sacrifice of self . . . but true work is perfect freedom, and full satisfaction.

Today, when a woman may do rewarding work and still have a satisfactory marriage, we may attribute such a statement to incomplete experience. But this ignores the fact that combining a worthwhile career and marriage was almost impossible for a woman in that day, and that Elizabeth Blackwell's work was worthwhile work indeed.

Although some of the early feminists favored more liberty for women in every respect, there is no pronounced correlation between feminism and belief in sexual freedom. Victoria Woodhull would advocate and practice both, but she was notoriously uninhibited; Mrs. Stanton thought women should have every privilege that men had, but her home life was a model of respectability.

Still another combination was exemplified by Lucy Stone. She was a militant feminist who married and had children but still maintained an almost Puritanical attitude toward sexuality. Considering her background, this was not altogether surprising. Her father, a Massachusetts farmer, was an orthodox Congregationalist who believed that daughters were less than a blessing and that, as the Bible decreed, woman must be completely submissive to man. Lucy, a strong-minded but tensely controlled girl, simply could not believe that the world was divided into a master sex and a servant sex, and she early determined that no man would ever master her.[38]

Such was her determination to enjoy every advantage granted to men that she worked and saved for years until she could get into Oberlin, the only college open to women. Although by that time she was twenty-five years old, an abolitionist, and an advocate of women's rights, she accepted all of Oberlin's moral taboos.[39] Typical of Lucy's views are those she expressed in a correspondence on self-control that she conducted in her senior year with two of her brothers and the wife of a third. The exchange was inspired in part by the fact that those intensely religious abolitionists, Theodore Weld and his wife, Angelina Grimké, were spacing the birth of their children by exercising self-restraint. Assuming the privileges of a spinster, she wrote to Sarah, wife of her brother, the Reverend William Stone, that unless sexual intercourse in marriage took place only for propagation, it was fornication and adultery, and that even propagation should be widely spaced.

Sarah and the Reverend Stone firmly rejected the adultery idea and declared that married couples should sleep together freely and accept the consequences. A second brother, Frank, whose wife had just borne him another child, dismissed the spacing of births as nonsense. Have children as fast as you can, he advised, and if you can't take care of them, trust in Providence. Just as people eat regular meals each day, not to live but because they are hungry, "so then I suppose individuals do not cohabit for the sake of children only but because they want to." The third brother, Luther, piously answered that every organ God gave man should be used "with reference to His glory" but that the generative organs should serve only for propagation. Nine-tenths of "all the invalids and men of half minds have become what they are by their own or their father's indulgence in the beastlike use of the generative organs." But he added—using capitals for emphasis—that it was as great a sin not to use these organs at all as to use them too much.[40]

Aside from the fact that such a frank correspondence took place, what is interesting about it is the sharp rejection of any limitation on intercourse by two of the brothers, and the assertion by the third—clearly a rebuke to Lucy—that it was a great sin not to use the organs at all. Lucy continued to reject all suitors, and she would surely never have married if a handsome, prosperous man seven years her junior, Henry Blackwell, brother of Dr. Elizabeth and Dr. Emily, had not won her by promising that, like Robert Dale Owen and his wife, they would make their wedding contract a model of the union of absolute equals. Although Lucy loved her husband and bore him two children, she has been remembered mainly because she refused to take his name.

Marriage did not change her prudish views: she supported Anthony Comstock, warned readers against Sarah Bernhardt because the actress had borne four children out of wedlock, and referred to President Cleveland as a "male prostitute" because he had had a child as a result of an affair in his youth.[41]

The attitudes of Elizabeth Blackwell, Lucy Stone, and other more straitlaced feminists lent a contradictory aspect to the movement. Militant though they might be in the struggle for social and economic equality, they were Victorian prudes in matters of sexuality. It was doubtless they who created the impression that feminists were a sexless breed.

Whatever sexual liberties women have achieved have come not from feminist efforts but from the general relaxation in sexual morality and the availability of contraceptives. Concentrating more and more on political and economic equality, the feminists won voting rights for women and an acceptance in professional and executive positions, but, except for a few revolutionaries such as the Fourierists, they did nothing to free women from the responsibility for homemaking and bringing up children.

Nineteenth-century moralists noted with satisfaction that such radical champions of freedom for women as Mary Wollstonecraft, Frances Wright, and Margaret Fuller all seemed to abandon their fanatical devotion to the cause of women when they plunged into desperate love affairs or when they married just as they were about to have children. Such critics interpreted this pattern as nature taking its revenge on unnatural women, and, at the same time, as the wages of sinful doctrines.

There was just enough superficial truth in this interpretation to obscure the far more salient point that such women had concentrated their passions on a social reform as long as they were able and then sought a sexual life of their own before it was too late. In those early days feminism required, at least temporarily, a militancy, a fanaticism, and a rage against men that most men thought unfeminine and certainly far from the soft and clinging creature that was the ideal of the age. It was easy for men who had always enjoyed a measure of sexual freedom and sexual domination—both in and out of marriage—to mock the efforts of women to fulfill themselves. It would still be many a year before women would be able to realize themselves in all the ways that they might desire.

16.

SPIRITUAL BRIDES AND EARTHLY LOVERS

ONE of the strangest developments in the young Republic was the proliferation of fanatical and visionary religious sects in central New York State and nearby New England. Most of these sects were small and short-lived, but they reveal how feverish was the hope for panaceas and miraculous solutions. Every force seemed to encourage highly emotional commitments to a new social system and a new spiritual order: The religious and political freedom released by the Revolution and by the disintegration of the Congregational Establishment, the loneliness and hardness of life on farms and in frontier settlements, and, beginning in the 1820's, the cycle of prosperity and depression that led to speculation, bitter disappointments, and dreams of quick remedies.

As revivalism and the millennial spirit gripped the country, every region had its own prophet promising the Second Coming or the New Jerusalem. Central New York was seared by so many revivals that it came to be known as the "burnt-over district"; it alone gave rise to the Shakers, the Mormons, the Millerites, the Fox Sisters' Spiritualism, and the Oneida Perfectionists. These sects were usually founded and led by a single dominant, sometimes Messianic personality who saw himself—or herself—as appointed to lead men to a better life here and to salvation hereafter. Whatever his promises, the leader generally made the community independent and prosperous and also kept everyone too busy to complain.

A remarkable number of the leaders of these sects also found conventional marriage and sexual relationships unsatisfactory and sought to replace them with systems ranging from celibacy to polygamy and "spiritual wifery." Sometimes the new code was dictated by circumstances, but just as often it reflected only the passions or predilections of the leader. It is little wonder that some of these codes were outlandish and a few bizarre.

As odd as any was that of the Shakers, but it merits attention because the group included at its peak, in 1860, eighteen very prosperous colonies from New York to Kentucky and Ohio, and because it outlasted almost all of the other communal societies of the time: Perfectionists, Fourierist phalansteries, Owenite associations, the celibate brethren at Ephrata, Rappites, Ebenezers and Jansenists, the Separatist Zoarites of Ohio, Etienne Cabot's Icarians, and the Transcendentalists of Brook Farm and Fruitlands. Only the Mormons, who started much later, lasted longer in their original form. Most of the others collapsed within two years. And some that flourished for a time had little influence on society because they withdrew from it, shunning outsiders and being shunned in turn.

The founder of the Shaker communities in America was a poor, illiterate Englishwoman, Ann Lee, daughter of a Manchester blacksmith. In 1758 she joined the "Shaking Quakers," a group of fanatic dissenters given to trances and to visions of the second coming of Christ. Ann Lee married a blacksmith and bore him four children in rapid succession, each one dying soon after birth. The birth of the last child left her lingering between life and death. When she recovered she decided that childbirth agonies had been a punishment for her "concupiscence," and she went through a crisis of guilt. She emerged with the conviction that she had a divine mission to teach man that the "cohabitation of the sexes" was the source of all evil.[1] Her denunciations of "lust" were marked by all the signs of religio-sexual hysteria and were so violent that those whom she assailed beat and stoned her and finally had her jailed.

Jail made Ann Lee seem a martyr and a saint. She experienced revelations, and on her release she announced that the spirit of Christ had entered into her and that she must find a home in the New World for those who had begun to believe in her.[2] With a tiny band of followers, mostly relatives, she sailed for America in 1774. For a while she was stranded in New York, and her husband deserted her there, apparently preferring the fleshpots of the world to the promises of Shakerism. The group finally settled on a wilderness tract near Albany, New York, and established a community dedicated, spiritually, to the renunciation of the "lusts of the flesh," and, practically, to communal ownership, industry, thrift, and hospitality. Their simplicity, the intensity of their ritual meetings, the tales of "Mother" Ann's "gift of healing," and their eventual success in both agriculture and handicrafts brought them a small but steady stream of converts.

One question almost invariably asked by outsiders was how man would replenish the earth if everyone was converted to celibacy. The Shakers realistically answered that there would always be many unconverted who would continue to marry and procreate. If any members found the restraints intolerable, they were free to leave—and many did so. The denial of sexuality was as much of an obsession among some of the other Shakers as it was with Ann Lee. James Whittaker, who became leader of the sect after Mother Ann's death in 1784, said: "Blessed are all those who are not defiled by women." He thanked the Lord that he had never had "carnal knowledge of any woman."[3] Ann Lee had at least spoken from bitter experience; Whittaker spoke only from a neurotic prejudice.

Although Mother Ann denied that the Shakers condemned marriage completely, any married couple who wanted to join the group was expected to confess all their "lustful gratifications" and thereafter be to each other as brother and sister. It hardly requires a psychoanalyst to see in this perverse code the effect of Ann Lee's cruel experience in child-bearing and marriage. Her assertion that a "marriage of the flesh is a covenant with death" was an effort to spiritualize her own pathological fears, to make a virtue of her compulsion to banish sexuality and procreation.

The ritual "dance" of Shaker worship was a sight that visitors traveled long distances to see. In most sessions the ranks of men and women in their uniformly plain garments moved alternately forward and backward with a leaping step or trot, accompanied at times by bowing, clapping of hands, singing, and crying out. But there were also sessions, sometimes at feasts on the hills, in which the worshipers capered and shouted as the spirit moved them, and young women might take to spinning like dervishes for fifteen minutes at a time. Reports that nightly sessions lasted until two o'clock in the morning and reached a peak in which the chamber was a bedlam of convulsive movement and sound suggest that the ritual was, at least for the younger participants, a release of sexual energies. Writing on sexuality, David Goodman Croly bluntly declared in 1872 that the bed-time Shaker dancing "neutralized the desire for coition."

Visitors were impressed by the discipline and productivity of the Shaker way and by what some believed was contentment but what others thought was resignation. Denying any indulgence of the body, they considered disease a sin against God. This and their concept of the womanhood of God anticipates, among other groups, Christian Science, which was also begun by a woman whose experiences in marriage and motherhood were less than happy.

But most visitors found Shaker life unbearably dull and narrow, noting that members were required to rise and retire at the same time, dine together in monastic silence, and avoid tea and coffee as well as tobacco and strong drinks. Men and women were forbidden to talk to one another in private, and all were enjoined to report any transgression immediately.[4] George Ripley, prime mover at Brook Farm, thought Shakerism a "detestable, miserly, barren aristocracy, without a grain of humanity about it." Even allowing for Dickens' acerb view of almost all things American, his description of the Shaker village at Lebanon in 1842 is withering. To him it was a "gloomy silent commonwealth." With pity for the children, who he hoped would run away, he concluded: "I do abhor and . . . detest that bad spirit . . . which would strip life of its healthful graces, rob youth of its innocent pleasures . . . and make existence but a narrow path towards the grave. . . . I recognize the worst among the enemies of Heaven and Earth, who turn the water at the marriage feasts of this poor world, not into wine but gall."[5]

It is difficult for us to understand how such a denial of love and birth, especially in a mixed community, could prove attractive. But it did. It drew what might be called Puritan monks, who rejected the world and saw celibacy and labor as a loftier, more spiritual way of life. It drew unmarried women who feared the limbo of spinsterhood, or men and women who were unhappy in marriage but dreaded the shame of divorce, and others who wanted security. It also accepted foundlings. However, after the Civil War, as the market for handicrafts fell off, and spinsters could find jobs, and divorce was no longer unthinkable, the Shakers declined. Their membership, which had gone up from 1,000 in 1800 to 6,000 in 1860, was down again to 1,000 by 1900. Today, all that remains of Ann Lee's crusade against sexual love is a tradition of furniture-making and of household objects prized by collectors for their plainness.

The only other celibate sect of any consequence, the Rappites, was also admired for its economy and deplored for its sexual denial. Much as Americans might envy the overflowing granaries, sturdy buildings, and well-fed cattle of the Rappites, they were repelled by the suppression of marriage and family. Temperance and prudery were in the nineteenth-century American grain but monkish celibacy was not. Visitors sensed that these immigrants were ready to satisfy every liberty for the sake of freedom from want.

Organized in an obscure German village by George Rapp, a dissenting Lutheran linen weaver who was subject to visions, the Rappites were driven by persecution to America. Mostly simple artisans and farmers, the group settled near Pittsburgh in 1804 and then established New Harmony on the banks of the Wabash in Indiana in 1815. A domineering, patriarchal figure, Father Rapp committed his followers to a primitive communism consisting chiefly of toil. Although he allowed such diversions as music and painting, one of the first rules he laid down was celibacy. Unsympathetic observers claimed that his underlying reason for imposing celibacy was to prevent lovemaking and child-bearing from interfering with work. It succeeded. By the time Robert Owen came from Scotland in 1824 and bought out the Rappite establishment, it had 30,000 rich acres and a large group of substantial buildings. After selling New Harmony, Father Rapp reestablished the colony in a Pennsylvania village that he named Economy. Although a few married couples defied Father Rapp's ban by continuing to have children and he later allowed married couples the meager privilege of living together one year in seven—thus insuring that no family would have more than one child too young to work—the ban was the object of many jests. Byron found space for it in *Don Juan,* writing,

> When Rapp the Harmonist embargo'd Marriage
> In his harmonious settlement which flourishes
> Strangely enough as yet without miscarriage,
> Because it breeds no more mouths than it nourishes,
> Without those sad expenses which disparage what
> Nature most encourages. . . .

There was one mutiny: in 1831 a certain Bernhard Muller, who claimed to be a Count Maximilian de Leon, fomented a revolt aimed at restoring love, marriage, and other pleasures. He was defeated by a vote of 500 to 250, confounding those cynics who claim that the crowd always prefers pleasure to discipline. Muller and his 250 followers seceded, but, sad to say, this Bacchus cheated and deserted his minions. Father Rapp's rich but loveless principality continued to thrive until his death in 1847 and then was slowly robbed of its unique character by accumulating property and material success.

Only a few minorities in America have been more harshly reviled and persecuted than the Mormons. But, considering their claims to special revelations, their material success and their defiance of Christian marital and sexual codes, it is a wonder that intolerant Victorian America did not wipe them out to the last man. From the time of its origins in the bizarre figure of Joseph Smith, Mormonism was the object of violent prejudices.

After Smith's death Mormonism developed, especially in its increasing respectability, in ways very different from any Smith could have foreseen. But one can hardly blame Americans from 1850 to 1890 if all they chose to remember was Joseph Smith as an ignorant youth who spent his days gazing into "peepstones," hunting buried treasure, and telling fantastic tales, of which the most fantastic was the story of being led by an angel, Moroni, to the buried golden plates called The Book of Mormon. They sensed that he was what Kimball Young, a prominent modern sociologist who is a grandson of Brigham Young, called a parapath, one who believes his own fantasies, especially if, as happens with many pretenders to magic and founders of religions, others accept the fantasies as fact. They knew that he had an appetite for women: He had said to a friend, "Whenever I see a pretty woman, I have to pray for grace," and as soon as he founded his religion he had had a revelation ordering him to espouse as many "spiritual brides" as possible. They had heard such stories as that told by eighteen-year-old Martha Brotherton, one of a family of English converts. In 1842, Brigham Young, who would succeed Smith two years later, took Martha aside and in his blunt way said: "Brother Joseph has had a revelation from God that it is lawful and right for a man to have two wives. . . . If you will accept of me I will take you straight to the celestial kingdom, and if you will have me in this world, I will have you in that which is to come, and Brother Joseph will marry us here today, and you can go home this evening, and your parents will not know anything about it." When the girl begged for time, Young called in Smith, who is said to have declared: "If you will accept of Brigham . . . God shall bless you . . . and if you do not like it in a month or two, come to me and I will make you free again; and if he turns you off, I will take you on." But she revealed her experience to her parents, and they carried her off and published the story. Young called the tale a base falsehood, and Smith preached against liars, hypocrites, and adulterers.[6]

Shortly before Smith's death, several married women with whom he had been familiar were sealed to him as plural wives. Benjamin Johnson, a devoted follower, wrote in his journal that by 1842, "men and women of previous respectability were now in free love disgracefully and insanely mixed up. . . ." and that in April, 1843, Smith disclosed to him the principle of plural marriage. When Smith asked if he could secure Johnson's sister Almera as a wife, Johnson answered: "Brother Joseph, this is all new to me. It may all be true. You know, but I do not. To my education, it is all wrong, but I am going, with the help of the Lord, to do just what you say. But I promise if you do this just to degrade my sister I will kill you." Johnson broached the plan to his sister and reported: "Soon after that the Prophet was at my house again, where he occupied my sister Almera's room and bed. . . ." Smith then urged Johnson to take as his second wife an orphan girl living in the Johnson household. "This seemed like hurrying up my blessings pretty fast," Johnson admitted, "but the spirit of it came upon me and from that hour I thought of her as my wife that the Lord had given me."[7]

While the Mormons were still denying that they took plural wives, they were attacked largely because they were an independent, prosperous society-within-a-society and because they not only claimed their own revelations and bible but mixed church and state, allowing their elders despotic power. But after Smith was slain and Brigham Young publicly announced in 1852 the doctrine of polygamy, all the wrath of their enemies was concentrated on this one practice. Even those "Gentiles" who had looked tolerantly on the religious heresies of the Mormons were apparently provoked by this flouting of the American moral structure. For almost forty years after that, until federal law forced the Latter-day Saints to set aside the practice—but not the principle—of polygamy, the Mormons were subjected to ridicule and savage harassment. It must be said that there was a cruel strain in the Mormons themselves, one that showed itself not only in retaliatory massacres of Gentiles but in the barbarous doctrine of blood atonement of sins that Brigham Young formulated.[8]

Our interest here is not in taking sides on the morality or immorality of Mormon polygamy but in determining what polygamy meant sexually and why it aroused such hostility in many Americans. Its foes charged, as we know, that polygamy was inspired by lust, that it corrupted men and debased women and somehow threatened the commonwealth. The Mormons and their few defenders pointed out that no one was forced to join the church or to stay in it, that most husbands and many wives who practiced polygamy were content with the system, that Mormon families were often models of respectability, and that polygamy came closer than Gentile practices to doing away with prostitution, abortion, and foundlings.

The more extreme charges against polygamy were grossly exaggerated. It is estimated that no more than 25 percent of most Mormon communities practiced polygamy, so that it was never a prevailing arrangement. The more prosperous men often kept their wives in separate households, with the result that each family resembled a monogamous unit, except that it saw even less of the father.

Smith, adapting current theories of "spiritual wifery," developed the doctrine of celestial marriage. According to Smith, a man married a woman for eternity as well as time, and it was therefore a virtue for him to guarantee as many women as possible a life in the hereafter. Jules Remy, noted French biologist, reported in the mid-1850's that a wife of a leading Mormon, a well-educated and beautiful woman, observed that the Lord had encouraged Abraham, Isaac, and other patriarchs to take many wives. This was the "polygamous law of God." She had said:

> Behold the . . . consequences of the adoption of the laws of Rome which forbid marriage to priests and nuns, and do not allow others to marry more than one wife. This law compels a number of women to pass their lives in *single blessedness,* without husband, without children . . . or still more, it condemns them to a life of poverty and loneliness, in which they are exposed to temptations, to culpable connections, to the necessity of selling themselves. Man, on the other hand, rich in means, is tempted to squander them in secret with his mistress . . . while the law of God would have given her to him as an honorable bride. All this engenders murder, infanticide, suicide, remorse, despair, wretchedness, premature death. . . .[9]

It is today difficult to understand how such a woman could cite the practice of a few Old Testament patriarchs as a guide to marriage. But the "Principle" was drummed into Mormons from childhood on. A remarkable number of plural wives asserted that they expected to achieve eternal glory through their marital status. Of course we cannot know to what extent such declarations were efforts to justify a subconscious urge or to participate in a group practice.

Curiously, polygamy did not lead to licentiousness or sensuality mainly because its practitioners were, after all, middle-class Christian Americans, in many instances the product of New England Puritanism. It is incredible enough that they adopted plural marriage, a practice universally associated with Moslem harems and with debauchery. Actually Mormon polygamy soon became as formalized, as limited by taboos and as respectable within its own terms as monogamy. Adultery and promiscuity were denounced as severely as elsewhere in the United States and Mormons boasted that there was less license under polygamy than under the double standard and prostitution of the outside world. A Mormon, they argued, was as strictly constrained to marry a woman he desired as was any Gentile in a parallel situation. He certainly faced greater financial responsibilities. And divorce was at least as difficult as it was in the non-Mormon world. One of Kimball Young's informants later recalled: "The morals were strict in polygamy days. A man could have many wives but a woman's virtue was highly regarded and a man was taught continence." [10] This, of course, recalls the monogamist who pointed to the purity surrounding his womenfolk while he himself accepted a double standard for men.

The Mormon church opposed the use of contraceptives or any indulgence in coitus except for procreation, and every woman was expected to bear as many children as possible. Evidently these principles were generally accepted, for Mormon women were proud of the size of their families and a remarkable number of men had as many as twenty or thirty children by their wives. Thus to plural wives coitus meant not so much sexual gratification as having another baby. Given the Puritanism of the church bishops and the unromantic approach of most polygamous husbands, it is unlikely that a plural wife enjoyed much sexual gratification or often reached an orgasm.[11] But for a man polygamy meant variety of stimulation and the possibility of finding a woman who would give him special pleasure. It also allowed him to take a succession of younger wives, affording him repeated renewals of desire.

A Mormon woman had no such outlets for sexual passion. If she brought to plural marriage the monogamous ideal of romantic love and the expectation that a woman should be queen in her own home, she was bound to be disappointed, for the Latter-day Saints frowned on elaborate courtship and romance. At best, declarations of unwavering love from a man who already had a wife or two would have seemed rather insincere. The latest wife was generally visited by her husband at intervals that depended upon the number of his wives. How well a man served two, three, or four wives we do not know, but it can hardly be assumed that he did as well by all of them as he could have done by only one. If a woman was not satisfied, there was little chance of finding a lover in a community where men who wanted more than one woman could easily have more.

Polygamy was a man-favoring system in a man-dominated society. Women were second-class citizens in every respect. In the very first official justification of plural marriage, Orson Pratt wrote that each wife should obey her husband "with meekness and patience in all things." The daughter of the second wife of Isaac Lambert once complained: "Mother figures you are supposed to spend your life taking care of a man, and he is God." [12] And Brigham Young declared, as though talking of children, that his wives must either "live their religion, or they may leave, for I will not have them about me." It was such attitudes that made even the relatively liberal reformers in the women's rights movement join in the hue and cry against the Mormons.

Generalizations about marital relations under Mormon polygamy are unsafe because attitudes ranged from wholehearted acceptance to bitter opposition. Aside from the sexual privileges, the more wives a man had, the higher would be his standing in the church and in the community. He could also enjoy true patriarchal power, punishing any wife who displeased him by favoring his other wives. In practice, most men did find it best to be, or at least appear to be, impartial.

Many of the women who adjusted most easily to the system believed that they would be divinely rewarded. Joseph Wright's second wife, whose father had had three wives, said: "Nothing in my father's household made me dislike polygamy. I always believed . . . it was a true Principle, and through it and it alone could we obtain the greatest blessings and live as fully as we should." [13] In some instances wives would cooperate with a husband in the selection of other wives and make the newcomers welcome. A few took a realistic view, one husband reporting that his wife had said, "If you're going to get married, I want you to do it while I am still young. I don't want you to wait until I'm old and good for nothing and then bring in a young wife."

More common was an attitude of acquiescence, sometimes mixed with resignation, sometimes with hope. When the church put pressure on her husband to take another wife, Elizabeth Street wrote in her journal: [14]

> I was quite willing. We all went to Conference . . . and Sister Stella Hoskins was sealed to him. . . . Eliza R. Snow asked me if I was willing. I said "yes." Then she asked me if I thought I could live in that Principle. I answered . . . that my mother and sister lived in it and I thought I could do as much.[15]

A second wife might also face such displacement. When Daisy Yates became the second wife of dashing Edmund Barclay, federal pressure was already forcing the Saints to conceal plural marriages, so Daisy was only slightly disappointed when her new husband took her back to her parents' home while he returned to his first wife. But she soon realized that his visits would remain infrequent because he was paying court to another young lady and was going to Europe on a church mission. Daisy concludes:

> So, within six months of my wedding day he had married again and was off to Europe. I had not seen the third wife but I did wonder wherein I lacked that so soon he would take another wife. Then I remembered the doctrine of the trinity as taught by the Church—that if one wanted to attain the very pinnacle of glory in the next world there must be at least three wives . . . and so I was reconciled.[16]

Many Mormon husbands consulted their wives before taking a new wife, but sometimes the act came as a complete shock. After sixteen years of monogamous marriage Jonathan Baker one day told his wife to lay out his "temple clothes" because he was going to marry Eliza Bowen. "It was a blow to Ma," the daughter records, "and naturally she resented it and never got over it." [17] Almost as poignant is the confession of Herbert Winslow's first wife, Mary, after she had lived for a year in the same house with two later wives: "I said I couldn't stand it, I was going to lose my mind. I couldn't stand to see him fondle over the others. . . . No, he never slighted me, but I just couldn't stand it." [18]

It is a relief to learn that some women rose up in wrath at this humiliating male hocus-pocus. When one elder told his wife that he had a divine revelation directing him to marry a certain girl, his wife announced the following morning that she too had received a revelation—"to shoot any woman who became his plural wife." Sometimes the resentment lasted a lifetime. Roger Knight's wife Jane bitterly opposed his marriage to their hired girl Annie Strong. A friend of the family recalled: "I think I have never seen more unadulterated hatred than she shows when speaking of this woman. She tells how she herself had refused to visit her husband on his death bed though her children told her that he had been calling for her all day. . . . She boasts that 'I haven't spoken to Annie for thirty years and don't expect to speak to her for thirty more if I live that long.' "[19]

Such testimony makes clear how polygamy used the religious emotions to gain acceptance for unorthodox marital and sexual relations, but it hardly confirms the charge that it resulted in license. There was, if anything, more immorality in the prurient curiosity of other Americans and what their imaginations conjured up. An entire literature, much of it sensational and some of it pornographic, sprang up around what was thought to go on in Mormon "harems." The frontispieces of paperback fiction, for example, showed leering elders bathing half-naked women in the "Endowment House" in Salt Lake City.[20] Other Americans were apparently vicariously stimulated by stories of how aging Mormons traded their nubile daughters, or how a sixty-year-old elder took as his sixth wife a seventeen-year-old convert fresh from England. Certainly envy of Mormon sexual freedom accounts for some of the ferocity with which "Gentiles" sought to suppress the entire Mormon way of life.

Mormon polygamy is important in the record of sexual morality in America because it was accepted by a large number of men and women and because the system worked. Most Americans were completely astonished when thousands of Mormon wives signed petitions vigorously protesting the outlawing of polygamy in 1890. Even though Mormons thought of themselves as highly moral, polygamy presented a revolutionary and shocking challenge to the whole monogamous tradition. It went completely against eighteen hundred years of Christian practice, not to speak of Judaic and Roman custom, allowing a man to sleep with as many women as he chose, either for procreation or, as far as anyone knew, pleasure. It exploded the conviction that monogamy was sacred, inevitable, or the most natural relationship. It challenged the notion that a man could love only one woman at a time. The most common reaction of other Americans was exasperation and vicious opposition.

One of the strangest of the sexual codes that developed in the religious communal experiments of the 1830's and 1840's was that of "spiritual wives." It is impossible to say how much influence it had on Americans at large, but it attracted an extraordinary amount of attention and it revealed how readily certain Americans welcomed extreme sexual and marital liberties when a sect or prophet found spiritual or religious justification for it.

The theory was that a spiritual affinity existed between certain men and women and that they consequently might unite without the sanction of the law or the blessing of the church. The theory was an old one among extreme religious dissenters.[21] In the 1530's Johann Bockholdt, better known as John of Leyden, fanatical leader of an Anabaptist sect, established himself in Leyden as king of the new "Zion," and, on the basis of visions, encouraged spiritual mating and polygamy. In the next century, a Brownist, Francis Johnson, justified bundling with other men's wives. This is significant because the Mayflower Pilgrims were Brownists, and seventeenth-century New England courts repeatedly recorded cases of otherwise law-abiding citizens who married without benefit of clergy.

There was also the influence of Emanuel Swedenborg, eighteenth-century Swedish scientist turned religious mystic. Swedenborg's ideas filtered into America during the early part of the nineteenth century through such channels as Andrew Jackson Davis, a Swedenborg medium who became the first leader of the Spiritualist movement in America. Drawing on Swedenborg's accounts of communications with angels and spirits, the Swedenborgians declared that in heaven there was no formal marriage or giving in marriage. Beyond that, they held, true "conjugial love"—as Swedenborg termed it—was of heavenly inspiration and needed no other sanction. For young men, Swedenborg believed, a mistress was better than a wandering lust.[22] As one contemporary observed, Swedenborg was a rich bachelor whose sexual philosophy might well appeal to bachelors. And in their book on marriage, Dr. Thomas L. Nichols and Mary Gove Nichols pointed out that some Swedenborgians went about having brief amours, explaining that they were only seeking their true conjugal partners.

Even against this background, the experiment in sexual mating without marriage carried on by John Humphrey Noyes at Oneida was the boldest and most successful defiance of the most sacred Puritan taboos. It was particularly astonishing because Noyes was a product of high New England culture and maintained throughout his life a faith in basic Christianity and the Bible. Nothing in his background or youth explains the assurance with which, in his early twenties, he dismissed the commandment that no one should love more than one mate. He came of an old New England family, and his father was a successful businessman and Congressman. Young Noyes was sent to Dartmouth and was studying law in a lawyer's office when revivals began once again to ignite the Vermont countryside. The youth underwent such a "conversion" that he immediately went off to Andover and later to Yale to study for the ministry.

At Yale, Noyes began to reject the doctrine of man as a miserable sinner, turning to the radical belief that a state of sinless perfection was attainable in this life. Soon a coterie of "Perfectionists" formed a "Free Church" in New Haven. In his final year at Yale, Noyes, considered a brilliant student, was granted his license to preach. With ever increasing exaltation, he pressed his beliefs, declaring to shocked audiences that he himself was free of sin. He meant that he was pure of heart even though not perfect in external things, but early in 1834 the ministers' association revoked his license and asked him to leave New Haven. In a kind of "dark night of the soul" he made a visit to New York and wandered through the slums and dives of the city for three weeks, drinking and visiting brothels. He claimed later that it was a testing of God's power to protect him from intemperance, but it was long used as evidence of his instability.

Sexual incidents marked his progress. After he and the young Reverend Simon Lovett preached zealously to a Perfectionist group in Brimfield, two young ladies, stimulated into proving that spiritual love could triumph over carnal love, visited

Lovett's room at midnight. Rumor later had it that the flesh triumphed over the spirit. Although Noyes had already left Brimfield, he defended the young women, and he was thereafter always associated with the "Brimfield scandal." [23]

Far more significant was the letter he wrote to a friend, David Harrison, in 1837, when a girl Noyes had fallen in love with married another youth. Perhaps as compensation, he poured out a series of revolutionary convictions about sex:

> When the will of God is done on earth, as it is in heaven, *there will be no marriage*. The marriage supper of the Lamb is a feast at which *every dish is free* to every guest. . . . In a holy community, there is no more reason why sexual intercourse should be restrained by law, than why eating and drinking should be—and there is little occasion for shame in the one case as in the other. . . . I call a certain woman my wife—she is yours, she is Christ's, and in him she is the bride of all saints. She is dear in the hand of a stranger, and according to my promise to her I rejoice.[24]

This letter with its sexual dynamite wrapped in Biblical tissue fell into the hands of Theophilus Gates, anarchist and enemy of all religious institutions. Gates promptly published Noyes' letter in *The Battle-Axe,* a journal devoted to his own revolutionary theories of marital relations. Noyes protested the publication of the letter, but even when criticism mounted on every side, he wrote: "The doctrine of that letter is God's truth. . . ." He hastily added that he himself was known for the blamelessness of his conduct, but the association with Gates put an indelible stamp of sexual extremism and promiscuity on the "*Battle-Axe* letter."

Noyes now paid court to one of his admirers, Harriet Holton, daughter of a leading Vermont family, and soon won her. She agreed that both should remain free to love all men and women with as much warmth as though they were not married.[25] Their marriage went smoothly in all but one respect: four of the five children Harriet bore in the next six years were stillborn. Characteristically Noyes refused to respond with the usual pious resignation. He promised his wife never again to subject her to such fruitless suffering. He began an analysis of the entire sexual function, and after experimenting with various methods he hit upon his "great discovery," which he called "male continence." [26]

As he described the method in *Bible Communism* (1848) and again in *Male Continence* (1872), it was based on the boldest and most careful study of the sex act made up to that time. He asked men of sexual experience if "the sweetest and noblest period of intercourse . . . is not that first moment of simple presence and spiritual effusion, before the muscular exercise begins." Based on this, male continence required that coitus be held at that first step. The act could thus be greatly prolonged; it would last until the male organ subsided. "If you say this is impossible," he wrote, "I answer that I *know* it is possible—nay, that it is easy." He added that it was even possible to start the "reciprocal motion" and yet stop before reaching the "crisis." [27]

To the charge that he was utilizing "withdrawal" as recommended by Robert Dale Owen, he answered almost indignantly that withdrawal was "male incontinence plus evasion," a wasteful expenditure of the seed and therefore unnatural. His method was also superior to contraception, he said, because it simply stopped short of the act of propagation. It was not *coitus interruptus,* students of sex would later say, but *coitus reservatus.* Noyes also sharply distinguished himself from "free love" advocates. He called such love licentious and constantly sought to reconcile his approach with religious principles and Biblical mores. Whether this was only a rationalization of his own appetites is beside the point: he was convinced that his method was not only satisfying and healthy but also godly.

Noyes began by drawing a line between the "amative" function and the propagative, even pointing out that the procreative organs, the testicles and the uterus, were not brought into play in coitus. To the charge that male continence encouraged licentiousness, Noyes answered that, on the contrary, it taught maximum self-control; and he always insisted that it had more in common with Shaker celibacy than any other practice. To the assertion that it was a "difficult and injurious interruption of a natural act," he retorted that it did not differ in essence from the lover who stops after kissing or caressing his beloved. It also avoided "the horrors and the fears of involuntary propagation." [28]

Whereas customary intercourse ended, according to Noyes,

in "exhaustion and disgust"—a revealing conclusion—Noyes claimed that his method made possible the "highest bliss of sexual fellowship for any length of time." Enthusiastically he described coitus as potentially a mode of intimate conversation between the sexes that would in time be cultivated as one of the fine arts. Since "male continence" precluded conception, it would become an "honored method of innocent and useful communism" in which each could marry all.

To a circle of followers consisting mainly of his family, Noyes began in 1840 to add disciples from outside. Among the first of these were the Cragins. They belonged to what might be called the spiritual avant-garde of the period, young people who lived in a continuous state of overwrought anticipation of the birth of a new world of the spirit.

George Cragin was born in 1808, near Boston, of parents who brought him up to believe that drinking wine, smoking, dancing, reading novels, or missing a divine service were deadly sins. When his father's business failed, George, a good-looking nineteen-year-old went to New York, and was soon "converted" by the noted revivalist Charles Grandison Finney.[29] In time he married Mary Johnson, a bright, amiable young woman from Portland, Maine. Her parents, Presbyterians of the strictest rite, had moved to New York, and Mary gave Bible instruction to slum children. For five or six years George acted as agent of the Female Moral Reform Society, distributing tracts, clothes, and alms among the derelict. They lived, as a later visitor, William Hepworth Dixon, editor of London's *The Athenaeum,* described it, in a "revival world, among men and women who embraced the wildest doctrines of the New Measure and the Free Church . . . always on the watch for new lights, for personal intimations, for the coming of they knew not what." [30] By her husband's own account, Mary was intensely "exercised on the subject of perfect holiness," and he himself constantly underwent "soul-tidal fluctuations."

When in 1839 several friends of the Cragins turned to Perfectionism, Mary studied Noyes' manifestos and soon exultantly announced her conversion. Destined always to be swayed by stronger spirits, George was swept along by Mary's enthusiasm. But he was also swept out of his job because of his new beliefs. Running out of money, the Cragins accepted an invitation to spend the summer with the Reverend Abram C. Smith, a Perfectionist who lived near Kingston, about seventy-five miles up the Hudson from New York City.

An itinerant Methodist parson, always in debt and casting about for ways of making a living, Smith was a willful man. He prided himself as a "zealot among the zealous, a free man among the free." [31] Dixon says of him, "Cold, hard, enduring . . . hot for the fray, he breathed the very spirit of revival fury." [32] When the Cragins and their child arrived, they found Smith living in a lonely farmhouse with his second wife and four children. His wife, tall and pretty, was, Smith later claimed, all smiles and tears in church but a dark curse at home. Cragin began to work the farm while Smith undertook the "spiritual instruction" of Mary Cragin, mostly in private. Smith announced that they must hold all things in common, no doubt including Mary Cragin. George Cragin alone failed to see which way the wind was blowing. The bickering between Smith and his wife soon reached a climax, and Smith ordered her out of the house. The neighbors, rough woodsmen, aroused by Mrs. Smith's story, threatened to tar and feather Smith. At this point, John Humphrey Noyes himself paid Smith a visit. He persuaded Smith to appease his neighbors by returning with him to Vermont for a few weeks, but he also criticized poor George Cragin for his "legalistic" attitude toward his wife.

Two weeks later Smith returned and immediately regained his hold over Mrs. Cragin, claiming that Noyes approved of his behavior. Mary Cragin's submission, like that of the devout Mrs. Elizabeth Tilton to the Reverend Henry Ward Beecher, is a classic instance of holy fervor converted to erotic ends. Given complete freedom to arouse the religious emotions, it is evidently not difficult to tap the sexual passions at the same time. Cragin even allowed Mary to accompany Smith to conferences with Perfectionists in New York and Pennsylvania. But when he learned that his wife and Smith had lived together in New York for a week, he at last challenged her. She broke down, confessed everything, and begged him to keep Smith from her lest she fall into his power again. When Smith returned, confident that he had acquired a right to Mrs. Cragin, a fierce, day-long argument ensued. Smith tried preaching and praying interspersed with "singing, amens, and hallelujahs," but finally he gave up and left the house. He even appealed to Noyes, but Noyes told him that he was no better than a rogue.[33]

Noyes invited the Cragins to stay with him in Vermont for the winter, and they accepted humbly. They came and never went away, eventually becoming leading members of the association. No one can say how normal or typically American the Cragins were, but they and a number of their families among the Perfectionists challenge the common assumption that the followers of Noyes were eccentrics or were disappointed in love or were in flight from life.

There were now about forty persons—including nine children—in the Noyes group, and they began to live communally. An important step toward the marriage of each to all, or what Noyes called "complex marriage," was the development of male continence since it served to prevent conception. In his *History of American Socialisms* (1870) Noyes justified complex marriage thus:

> All experience testifies (the theory of the novels to the contrary notwithstanding) that sexual love is not naturally restricted to pairs. Second marriages are contrary to the one-love theory, and yet are often the happiest marriages. Men and women find universally (however the fact may be concealed) that their susceptibility to love is not burnt out by one honeymoon, or satisfied by one lover. On the contrary, the secret history of the human heart will bear out the assertion that it is capable of loving any number of times and any number of persons, and that the more it loves the more it can love. This is the law of nature, thrust out of sight and condemned by common consent, and yet secretly known to all.[34]

He argued that there should be no exclusiveness in the ownership of women—a phrase that betrayed his patriarchal bent—any more than in property. With the amplitude of a Whitman, he proclaimed: "The new commandment is that we love one another, not by pairs . . . but en masse." [35]

Noyes and Mary Cragin established the first such liaison in the community, and soon the air crackled with sexual excitement as new alliances were formed and old ones were breached. Life in the community became, it is said, "one continuous courtship." Because male continence required training in self-control, young men were initiated by women who were beyond the menopause. In time, the system created an "ascending fellowship" in which the older members of the community were paired off with the younger ones.[36]

Rumors of these practices reached the outside world, generally in exaggerated form, but the townspeople took no action until several local girls of good family were drawn into the group. Almost at once a county Grand Jury investigated and charged Noyes with adultery. At first Noyes scoffed, but when indignation meetings were held in Putney and mob violence threatened, the colony decided to move out. A few months later the migrators joined a band of Perfectionists on a sawmill farm at Oneida, New York. Later a branch was also established at Wallingford, Connecticut.

The period that followed was a lean one for the Perfectionist faithful. Then, in 1854, a convert, Sewell Newhouse, who manufactured steel traps prized by hunters, turned over his secret manufacturing process to the community. The trap business boomed, and by the end of the Civil War the Oneida "trap shop" was employing hundreds of workmen, including many from outside. The establishment became an imposing cluster of buildings surrounded by spacious lawns, and groups of visitors, including family parties, wandered through the buildings and grounds. Many of the visitors were surprised and perhaps disappointed to come upon no evidence of lewdness or license. Thomas Wentworth Higginson, erstwhile liberal clergyman, confessed in the *Woman's Journal* that he had looked in vain for visible signs of "either the suffering or the sin." The community, he reported, "makes an impression utterly unlike that left by the pallid joylessness of the Shakers, or the stupid sensualism . . . in the few Mormon households I have seen." He found it baffling that their religion had kept them from the degradation to which their practices should have led. "Nevertheless," he hastily concluded, "I should count it a calamity for a boy to be brought up at Oneida."[37]

Encouraged by his success in loosening the bonds of old-fashioned matrimony, Noyes in 1869 turned his attention to controlling propagation. At fifty-eight, still probing the entire mating process, he boldly called for an end to random procreation. Fortified by Darwin's and Galton's theories of evolution and natural selection—but well before Galton coined the term "eugenics"—Noyes declared that scientific control of breeding, which he called "stirpiculture," must be applied to man as it was to domestic animals. As always, he no sooner reached a conclusion than he put it into practice. After twenty years of avoiding conception, the community, Noyes announced, was ready for planned progeny. Apparently without hesitation fifty-three young women solemnly signed a resolution to allow Mr. Noyes, as "God's true representative," to mate them as he saw fit. They offered themselves, in the astonishing words of the document, as "living sacrifices to God and true Communism." But even more incredible was the actual performance; in the next ten years fifty-eight children were born to the women, and of these no less than nine were sired by Noyes himself. All of this was offered, among other things, as evidence that male continence had previously been practiced successfully and that virility had nevertheless not been impaired.[38]

Throughout the growth of the Oneida Community there had been recurrent protests against it, but it was not until 1873 that the opposition became an organized movement. Meetings of ministers denounced the community as "harlotry" and "the hideous thing that . . . in dens and midnight hells revels in debauchery." Committees investigated, but they found only those revered Victorian virtues: thrift, industry, and prosperity. Unimpressed, a leader of the crusade, Professor John W. Mears of Hamilton College, called Oneida a "Utopia of obscenity" with "the nastiness of the Epicurean sty." Some newspapers joined the attack; others were simply fascinated by Noyes and his achievements. One of the keenest analyses observed that the community had been a success not because of its religion or its communism but because of its leader and its prosperity.[39]

But the true source of Noyes' downfall proved to be internal disaffection. It came mainly from younger men who had been allowed to go off to such colleges as Yale's Sheffield Scientific School and had come back infected with doubt and skepticism. They rejected Noyes' Biblical theology; they resented the practice of allowing older men a choice of the younger women; and they chafed against "male continence." Some women in the stirpiculture program complained that they were like white mice in a laboratory. Noyes' son Theodore, a scientist, cast serious doubt on the social significance of experiments that were both so radical and so isolated from society.

To appease his critics, Noyes resigned as president of the community and recommended that "complex marriage" be abandoned. But the pressure from outside continued, and finally one night in 1879 Noyes stole away from Oneida and retired to a house overlooking Niagara Falls. Surrounded by a few faithful friends, he lived on until 1886.

Without Noyes, the community was rent by dissension. Gradually it returned to all the orthodox institutions, couples marrying conventionally and communal ownership of property giving way to a joint stock company and an arid commercialism. Years later Oneida Community would reemerge as the center of a tableware industry of international scope but without a trace of the religious, social, or sexual values that John Humphrey Noyes had so audaciously evolved.

It is possible to dismiss Noyes as an eccentric who had enough strength of personality, plausibility, sexually attractive doctrines, and good fortune in business to create an experimental society and keep it going until a younger generation simply rejected him. But that is too easy; he could not have succeeded so well for over thirty years if hundreds of individuals, couples, and families had not been able to live contentedly and in some instances happily in this new social framework. Noyes' system demonstrated rather more convincingly than Mormon polygamy and without the pervasive male domination of Mormonism that monogamy was not inevitable and that "free love" worked under certain circumstances.

John Humphrey Noyes had a unique independence of mind and his analyses of certain of mankind's social as well as sexual problems were fresh and shrewd. Unfortunately, his solutions to such problems, unlike those of a genuinely disinterested scientist, were made to serve his own ends. All his major theories, "male continence," "complex marriage," and "stirpiculture," somehow yielded the maximum sexual privileges to one man—John Humphrey Noyes. He introduced his last experiment, stirpiculture, while he was in his sixties, when it gave him an opportunity to enjoy the most desirable of the younger women in the community. It was most revealing of his godlike notion of himself that in advocating stirpiculture, he declared:

It is very probable that the feudal custom which gave barons the first privilege of every marriage among their retainers, base and oppressive though it was, actually improved the blood of the lower classes. We see that Providence allows a very superior man to be also very attractive to women, and very licentious. Perhaps with all the immediate evil they do to morals, they do some good to the blood of after generations. Who can say how much the present race of men in Connecticut owe to the numberless adulteries and fornications of Pierrepont [*sic*] Edwards? Corrupt as he was, he must have distributed a good deal of the good blood of his noble father, Jonathan Edwards; and so we may hope the human race got a secret profit out of him.[40]

17.

THE EXTREMISTS

WE come now to the true extremists, those who believed in loving freely but did not attempt to justify their attitudes on religious or any grounds except individual rights. They were a tiny band, harassed and embattled but full of evangelical—their enemies called it diabolical—zeal. They were convinced that they had on their side not only reason but the secret desires of much of mankind.

Their doctrinal and spiritual ancestors included not only Mary Wollstonecraft, Robert Owen, and Frances Wright but also the French socialist Charles Fourier and Goethe of the "elective affinities." Fourier, championed in America mainly by Albert Brisbane, briefly by Horace Greeley, and passionately by Dr. M. Edgeworth Lazarus, propounded what was called his "natural optimism." Its basic thesis was that man could achieve happiness and full development only when society allowed him the freedom to express his desires and passions. Vice, Fourier said, springs from unnatural restraints imposed by society on man's appetites and impulses. More than forty phalansteries, as he called the ideal social unit for putting his ideas into practice, were formed in America in the 1840's and early 1850's. Although all of them soon failed, Fourierism exerted a pervasive influence on almost every social reformer and visionary of the age.

The typically Romantic and mysterious idea of natural affinities had been popularized by Goethe in 1809 in his novel *Elective Affinities,* as the German title *Wahlverwandtschaften* is usually translated. Inspired by a Swedish chemist's description of how some chemicals invariably tend to unite with certain other chemicals, Goethe wrote of a happily married man—a rich landowner—and his wife, each of whom is inexorably drawn to someone else of the opposite sex even though the attraction spells ruin for all.[1] The theory continued to be popular well into the century, with Victoria Woodhull, a leading proponent of free love, writing an introduction to a translation of Goethe's novel in 1872.

Many of those most influenced by all these theories were, it should be said, inveterate dissenters, incorrigible eccentrics, or unorthodox souls who flitted from reform to reform, clutching at every scheme for solving the problems of mankind. Yet almost all of them, even the maddest, were dedicated to the releasing of the "amative" instinct from excessive restraints, to freeing the individual from institutions. Almost all of them defended, in a rather oversimplified way, the right of all men to do as they pleased as long as they did no harm to others. If a few of them advocated an individuality bordering on anarchy, it was surely as a recoil from the stifling bigotry of the age.

Once a man has broken with the majority and experienced the exhilaration of release from reactionary ideas and institutions, he is often susceptible to all manner of libertarian causes. Thus we find the same men and women cropping up among the rebels against religion ("infidels"), against government and law ("anarchists"), against marriage ("free lovers"), against the lordship of the male ("women's rights" groups), and against private property and the oppression of the workingman ("Communists"). Under such banners as "Free Thought" and "Individual Sovereignty" one comes again and again on the names of Frances Wright, the Owens, Fourier, Josiah Warren, Stephen Pearl Andrews, Victoria Woodhull, Benjamin Tucker, Ezra Hervey Heywood, and De Robigné Bennett. From time to time they labored side by side with such other reformers as Elizabeth Cady Stanton, John Humphrey Noyes, Dr. Thomas L. Nichols and Mary S. Gove Nichols, and Dr. M. Edgeworth Lazarus. They all had in common the charge by preachers and other moralists that they were licentious, dangerous, and damned.

Insofar as such reformers tended to reject institutions and authority, they surely owed something to the influence of Josiah Warren, called the first American exponent of anarchism.

Warren's background, like that of Noyes, hardly explains his views: He belonged to an old Boston family of the Puritan breed. As a young man, Warren had successfully sold a cheap lamp that burned lard. A lecture by Robert Owen in 1825 had brought him and his family into the New Harmony settlement.[2] Lax as were the rules of the settlement, they were still too strict for Warren: He was as much irked by the laws of Owenism as by those of any other system. Aside from his faith in individual sovereignty, he was convinced that a just economic arrangement was the key to a good society. So he went to Cincinnati and opened what he called a "Time Store," in which the price of each article was based mainly on the cost of producing and distributing it. Warren's dream was to get back to that stage of society in which everything depended on each man's own labor.

When this venture languished, he tried similar experiments in Ohio and Indiana, and then, in 1850, intent on applying his principles on a broader scale, he came to New York. He drew to his side Stephen Pearl Andrews, an eccentric genius with extraordinary intellectual powers and radical theories, and the two men bought up a tract in the pine barrens at Brentwood, Long Island, and set up a utopian community called Modern Times. As Dr. Thomas L. Nichols, a health reformer who with his wife spent a year at the colony, observed, the air was pure, the water was delicious—Nichols was a water-cure enthusiast—there were neither churches nor magistrates, and Warren sold all goods at cost in the community store. Nichols wrote:

> Every one did what was right in his own eyes. The women wore bloomers or donned the entire male costume. As the sovereignty of the individual was opposed to all artificial, social, or legal restraints, marriage was abolished, and families arranged themselves according to the laws of attraction. . . . The right of the law either to unite or separate was denied, and free love was placed in the same category with all other freedoms. A man might have one wife, or ten, or more if he could take upon himself the proper cost or burden; and the same freedom was asserted to women.[3]

Moncure Daniel Conway, a liberal young clergyman who visited the settlement, was favorably impressed by it. But, Conway added, it was not considered polite to ask who was the father of a newborn child or who was the wife or husband of this or that individual. A husband or wife signified their union by wearing a red thread around one finger; the absence of the thread signaled that the "marriage" was over. And it was said that the Saturday night dances in the community hall ended at a different time each week with the understanding that whatever couples were dancing together would spend the weekend together. Dishonesty, disorder, and taxes were unknown.[4]

But cranks and irresponsible extremists slipped into this Eden: a nudist who sent his children out naked in all weathers, a woman who wore outlandish men's clothes, and a man and three women who carred on boisterously until they had to be encouraged to depart. The press seized on such stories and pictured Modern Times as an unholy fraternity of bohemians, nudists, and free lovers.[5]

Because of this, Warren in later years warned his fellow free inquirers that any reform cause was endangered when it came to be associated with free love or its disciples. He opposed promiscuity strenuously, and although he did suggest that every marriage contract be subjected to reconsideration every two years, he would not repudiate monogamy. In a letter he wrote to a friend in 1873, a year before he died, he declared that after a lifetime of pondering the question, he had concluded that if marriage was suddenly abolished without being replaced by some regulating arrangement, our social condition would be worse than it was now. He added that he honored the widespread protests against the "enslavement" of women, men, and children under prevailing institutions but could take no part in demolishing them since that work was "already being done faster than remedies follow." [6] His own behavior bore out this moderate view. He was described as a kind and simple man, faithful to his wife and devoted to his children.

The love doctrines of Fourier were introduced to Americans mainly by a wealthy young physician-writer, Dr. M. Edgeworth Lazarus. Lazarus was the author of about ten books that mixed visionary aspects of Fourierism with occult speculation and a rather precious approach to the pleasures of life. In his *Love vs. Marriage* (1852) Lazarus reviewed all the evils that reformers attributed to "civilized" marriage and all the blessings that would flow from a harmonic order and "passional liberty." Conventional marriage, he dramatically delared, is the grave of spontaneity and the tomb of love. The most delightful love relationship is in time rendered odious by the meanness and monotony of what Fourier had described as the exclusive, isolated household. In the Fourierist phalanx, Lazarus contended, woman would be free to engage in any occupation or art, and any children she bore would be cared for in a "unitary nursery." Men and women could form any kind of love relationship, from "exclusive constancy" to simultaneous connections with several persons of the opposite sex. The family unit, he concluded, would in time become a myth, regarded by children of the harmonic future as an amusing horror in a class with the story of Bluebeard.[7]

In every way more formidable, and the intellectual giant of the movement for free inquiry and free love, was Stephen Pearl Andrews. The son of an unorthodox Massachusetts Baptist minister, Andrews went to Amherst and then studied law in New Orleans. He moved to Houston in 1839 and soon became prominent in Texas politics. Because of his vigorous abolitionist activities his house was mobbed, and he, his wife, and infant son had to flee. He settled in New York in 1847 and in time became known in free-thought circles for his prodigious learning. At the time he joined Josiah Warren in establishing Modern Times he had a command of thirty-two languages, held a medical degree, and had introduced Pitman shorthand, called phonography, into America. He was already developing his theories of a world language, a world government, and a system of universal knowledge.[8]

Andrews first attracted public attention in a three-sided exchange with Horace Greeley and Henry James, Sr., in the *Tribune* in 1851–53; it was briefly resumed twenty years later by Andrews and James in *Woodhull and Claflin's Weekly* and was published in book form by Andrews. Probably the fullest exploration of marriage, divorce, and free love of the age, it was especially interesting as a confrontation between conventional and radical attitudes. The debate began with a *Tribune* review of Lazarus' *Love vs. Marriage* in which James, a religious philosopher who had turned from Calvin to Swedenborg and Fourier, deplored the book, asserting that liberalized divorce laws would provide all the freedom man required. This mild concession brought an assault on James in a religious journal, *The Observer*. James replied that he did not believe in laws to enforce marriage vows but conceded that divorce should not be granted unless support of the children of a union was guaranteed. Andrews entered the debate with a letter asking James whether "freedom of laws" included the acceptance of polygamy and whether a guarantee of support for the children did not cancel the proposed freedom of divorce.[9]

Greeley now joined the discussion and in the course of various letters brought to bear every tradition of religious and moral orthodoxy. Marriage, he declared, was the best system yet devised, and poor marriages resulted from haste or unworthy motives. Marriage should be indissoluble except for adultery; if divorce was free, every innocent maiden would be pursued by every libertine and an "unimaginable profligacy" would ensue. Any union not pledged for perpetuity is no different, he said, from "brutal connections of undisguised lewdness." Invoking religion, he argued that the seventh commandment is a part of natural as well as moral law, and that all sexual relations that do not serve to perpetuate the race are sinful. We must, he declared, restrain the seducer, adulterer, and gambler just as we do the thief, lunatic, or murderer.[10]

Pressing his Transcendental view, James declared that if conjugal ties were freed from "outward force" they would "instantly become transfigured by their inward divine and irresistible loveliness." But man is subject to nature, society, and God, and if he indulges his appetites capriciously, he will pay a penalty. When James again took up the subject twenty years later—at the age of sixty-one—he had become far less tolerant. Free lovers, he wrote, are enemies of society who make instinct as supreme in human nature as it is in animal nature. There is nothing evil in the indulgence of the natural appetites and passions, but making such indulgence the end of action converts men into brutes.[11]

Whatever Andrews' biases may have been, he had, unlike Greeley, thought through the subject with complete independence of public opinion and clichés, and he had a set of coherent principles. Greeley, Andrews said, is a man of facts, not principles; his thought rises no higher than the question of supplying man with food, clothes, and shelter. James is just the opposite: he tends toward metaphysical subtleties until he is completely off the solid earth. He dreams of a "harmonic world" to be created hereafter, but he hates actual reformers. Where Greeley needs legal training, James should have spent some time in a workshop. Greeley vibrates unsteadily between ultra-Radicalism and bigoted Orthodoxy. James is of the seers and prophets, with an inspiration that breaks into "impalpable mist." [12]

To Greeley's claim that fidelity to marriage is indispensable to purity, Andrews replied that the present system was a "house of bondage and the slaughter-house of the female sex." He questioned the value of the family in the raising of children, and he argued that if women could live in a large "unitary household" with a central nursery they could be relieved of drudgery, follow a calling of their choice, and enjoy a "well-ordered variety in the love relations." Andrews repeatedly attacked Greeley's acceptance of all "accredited" freedoms while rejecting those that were "morally wrong." Who shall decide what is wrong, Andrews asked, and pointed out that the seventh commandment was a Christian tenet observed only by a small fraction of mankind.

As for James' belief that man's animal nature would manifest itself if not restrained and that free love would convert men into brutes and devils, Andrews dismissed this as nonsense that revealed a complete lack of faith in man's nature. No free lover, Andrews concluded, expects to be exempt from responsibility for his appetites; he wants freedom *"only so long as he does not encroach on the equal freedom of all other individuals."* [13]

As Josiah Warren said of all free-love extremists, Andrews was ready to destroy marriage without replacing it with any kind of regulation. He had only a wishful dream, and he never faced the possibility that the dream might lead to chaos. He was sure only that the new way could not be any worse than the old, that it certainly would not be as hypocritical or as cruelly unfair to women. Next to Andrews' candor and freedom from cant, Greeley's utterances appear loaded with stale pieties and sanctimonious platitudes, while James emerges as an incoherent mixture of Transcendentalism and Tennyson.

Among those who sojourned at Modern Times, as we noted, were the physiologists Dr. Thomas L. Nichols and Mary S. Gove Nichols. Modern Times was actually only one of half a dozen panaceas that they tried. Confronted by the rank growth of humanitarian and reform movements of the 1840's and 1850's, they were like children hurrying enthusiastically from stall to stall at a fair.

Both of them were born in New Hampshire, she in 1810 and he in 1815, and their later attitudes were in part a rebellion against the remnants of Puritan narrowness and pessimism around them in their youth. In his autobiographical *Forty Years of American Life* (1863), Nichols says of his New England ancestors that they were a cold, hard race who "conscientiously suppressed their natural affections until they starved them out" and lost the power of loving.[14] An exception did occur in Mary Nichols' background: Her father was a reader of Paine and other freethinkers. But Mary's own disillusion with conventional marriage stemmed from the fact that a girlhood marked by idealistic hopes had ended in an unhappy marriage. She spent nine wretched years with her husband, Hiram Gove, before she dared to divorce him. She had meanwhile developed a consuming interest in physiology and health reforms and had begun to lecture widely and boldly on these subjects. An intensely curious and energetic woman, she experimented with vegetarianism, spiritualism (she claimed a medium's gift), mesmerism, phrenology, and Swedenborgianism, wrote articles on health, and turned out fiction for *Godey's Lady's Book*.

In those same years, young Thomas Nichols had entered on medical study at Dartmouth but had turned to journalism and started a small newspaper in Buffalo, New York. During the next ten years he too espoused vegetarianism and water-cure, edited various health journals, and finally took his medical degree. It is hardly surprising that when he and Mrs. Gove met, both felt that they had found a perfect spiritual affinity at last.

Together they set out in 1848 to improve mankind. They began by publishing the *Water-Cure Journal and Herald of Reform* and establishing the American Hydropathic Institute in Port Chester, north of New York City. The institute, designed for young women, was devoted to the art of healing and to creating the nucleus of a new society. Before long the institute was assailed as a center from which "free love luminaries sent forth their rays." [15] Then a letter in the New York *Tribune* declared that the school had been deserted by its entire student body because the girls had been taught "filthy doctrines" concerning their sex functions and privileges. Nichols promptly denied the charge.

But the writings of Dr. and Mrs. Nichols were hardly calculated to reassure the average American moralist. Dr. Nichols' *Women, in All Ages and Nations* (1849) begins as a scholarly survey but ends by asserting that people must "cease from the sin of living together in unions not made holy by love." [16] But this was only a prelude to the sweeping radicalism of *Marriage* (1854), a collaboration between Nichols and his wife. Apparently emboldened by their combined authority and their six years' experience of "as blessed a union as . . . ever existed upon this earth," they flayed bigots, especially the kind that wanted to put down Mormon polygamy with fire and sword and jail the Oneida Perfectionists.[17] As for morality, the Nicholses pointed out that this differed from nation to nation and from city to city, so that each individual must be a law unto himself. They called attention to the misery of the unhappily married, and to the wife who was a tool, subject to her husband's "morbid passions." Respectability required that such suffering be hushed up. They blamed the isolated family unit for fostering prostitution and the raising of unwanted children amidst discord.[18] The answer, they suggested, was the freedom of the affections opened up by Fourier. Some loves are annual, while a few are perennial, they said; some individuals are born for constancy, some for variety; and any love is more likely to endure if it is free. Morality consists, they concluded, in man's "fullest and most harmonious exercise of all his natural faculties and the complete gratification of all his natural desires." [19]

Routed from Port Chester, Dr. and Mrs. Nichols repaired to the harmonious anarchy of Modern Times to experience individual sovereignty in practice. They found it quite agreeable and after leaving it began to look for a place to set up their own little isle of bliss. They found it in Yellow Springs, Ohio, complete with a mineral water health resort and a reputation for progressivism derived from nearby newly established Antioch College. But hardly had they launched their experiment, called Memnonia, when the president of Antioch, Horace Mann, began to organize opposition to them. With something like Calvinist hyperbole, he called their theories "the superfoetation of diabolism upon polygamy." He even expressed a fear—revealing little faith in student virtue—that his charges would "rush into licentiousness." But when Mrs. Nichols in her role as medium began to convert respectable townspeople as well as students and professors to spiritualism, Mann, apparently intimidated by so versatile a foe, retreated.[20]

So, combining a water-cure with training for the true harmonic society to come, Memnonia was started in 1856. Its members, about twenty of them, each paying $150 for the first year, were mostly Easterners or Englishmen who had suffered a disappointment in love or marriage. Since there could be no "property in persons," no one was restricted to a single partner. Women "ruled their bodies" and would consent to bearing children only when the "highest duty to humanity" demanded it. Considering free love the sum of spiritual affinities, Mrs. Nichols insisted that there be a ninety-day period of total abstinence before sexual union. Memnonians were, moreover, subjected to vegetarianism, water as the only beverage, fasts, penances, daily confessions, and spiritualist seances at the unearthly hour of seven thirty A.M. Aside from free love, the colonists led a most ascetic life; thus, while the outside world thought Mrs. Nichols a libertine, her fellow utopians considered her a despot.[21]

Increasingly influenced by spiritualist communications, Mrs. Nichols began to turn to Catholicism after a message from Ignatius Loyola himself convinced her that the Catholic Church, with its water baptism and its immaculate conception, had the same ideals as she had. Within a few months, Mrs. Nichols, her husband and five relatives and friends were baptized into the church by Archbishop Purcell. Evidently a realist, the cleric wrote to a bishop in Detroit:

> What do you think . . . of my receiving into the Church the Mother Abbess of the Free Lovers? . . . I have already received a family of that droll way of perfecting human nature into the Church. . . . You know they hold that, under the old dispensation, a woman had not the possession of herself, her individuality. And that one of her sacred rights is that of choosing the father of her child. Surely God can have, or make, his elect

everywhere. And His holy grace is never more triumphant than when he subdues such souls.[22]

Thus, after their long search for a way to achieve individual sovereignty and freedom of the passions, the Nicholses surrendered all sovereignty to the closed system of the church. For a time they lectured at convents, and then in 1861, fiercely opposing Lincoln and Northern "military despots," they fled to England. In England they ran a water-cure institute and moved about in health reform societies.[23] The free-love fervor and utopian dreams of their American years were never mentioned. And Nichols' *Human Physiology* (1872) is so swollen with paeans to purity and to continence and diatribes against free love that it cannot be explained except as a Catholic convert's recantation of the sinful writings of his other days.[24]

Next to Victoria Woodhull, such figures as the Nicholses, Andrews, and Warren appear to be respectable, sober-sided citizens. She was of a completely different breed, disreputable in background, undisciplined, and emancipated by temperament as much as by conviction. Indeed, as a Victorian she is nearly incredible. The sexual freedom of her private life may be considered merely bohemian, but her attacks on loveless marriage, hypocrisy, and the double standard anticipate enlightened modern opinion. An untrained rebel, there is no doubt that she borrowed almost all her intellectual capital from a few associates and that she espoused crackbrained causes as well as sound ones. It is also true that, brought up to live by her wits, she threw scruples to the winds whenever it suited her. But on a few subjects her voice was among the bravest in a time of conformity and cant.

Victoria Woodhull's early life was so sordid that it is a minor miracle that she emerged with so buoyant a view of love and life. Born in 1838 of a shady, sometime river gambler, "Buck" Claflin, by a German tavern-keeper's daughter, she had grown into girlhood as one of ten neglected children in a hillside shack in Ohio. The Claflins were a queer lot, spiritualists even before spiritualism swept the country, the mother going into trances at revivals and using hypnotism on her children. Daughter Victoria was talking to spirits by the time she was four; she would never forget that one of them promised her wealth and fortune, and she was soon distinguished from the other Claflins by her softness of speech and manner. In their teens, Victoria and a younger sister Tennessee were already wandering the Midwest as faith-healers, selling a "Magnetic Life Elixir" at two dollars a bottle. Later, there was a cancer cure that killed at least one patient; when it brought a charge of manslaughter against Tennie, she dropped out of sight.[25] Always open to any doctrine that would justify whatever she wanted to do, Victoria Woodhull tapped both mystical and logical sources, drawing fervor from the spiritualists and reasoned arguments from women's rights crusaders.

At sixteen, Victoria married Dr. Canning Woodhull, something of a rake but mild and harmless. He preferred drinking to medical practice and lived on a small income from his family. Having borne Woodhull two children, Victoria matured into a beautiful and mettlesome woman. Tennessee remained gay and coarsely sensual, and by the time she was twenty-one her name had come up in cases of adultery and blackmail. Finally Woodhull sank into alcoholism, and Victoria left him. She now took up with a handsome Civil War veteran, Colonel James Blood. Blood had a family and a good position in St. Louis, but he was also a man of liberated opinions and ways. Spiritualist, philosophical anarchist, state socialist, Blood supplied Victoria with an intellectual framework for her natural urge to free love and the free life. With him she roved the countryside as a clairvoyant. He found her wonderfully apt, and it was doubtless he who soon directed her great vitality into crusading channels.

At thirty, pert, vibrant, wearing bold, ankle-length skirts and nobby Alpine hats, Victoria and Tennessee turned up in New York—sent, Victoria said, by her spirit-world mentor, the orator Demosthenes. Soon they had "Commodore" Vanderbilt, old, ailing and an easy prey for "healers," infatuated with their arts and charms, especially their "laying-on of hands" and Tennie's shameless intimacies. Only his relatives, it is said, prevented the doting commodore from marrying Tennie. Outrageously deciding to invade the male holy of holies, they persuaded Vanderbilt to establish them as Wall Street brokers. He not only set them up in a plush office, but with a few tips helped the "Bewitching Brokers" make a small fortune.[26]

Soon the sisters established themselves in a glittering Murray Hill mansion. Their ménage included Colonel Blood, Canning Woodhull, who had been taken back out of pity, numerous Claflins, and a crew of servants. All advanced thinkers were made welcome, and soon another visionary, tall, pale, great-bearded Stephen Pearl Andrews, now almost sixty years old, joined the household while his wife was out of town. Andrews was fascinated by the quiet way Victoria and Blood practiced the love relationship he had long preached. The total reform of society having become his passion, he had developed a system of world government called Pantarchy with himself as the "Pantarch." The huge book to which he confided his system, *Primary Synopsis of Universology* (1871), was utterly opaque, and he now seized upon Victoria as the ideal spokesman for his ideas. She in turn was deeply impressed by his learning and his vision.

Having come so far, Victoria now became boundless in her ambitions. In April, 1870, she issued her "First Pronunciamento," disclosing that, having breached the business world, she would invade politics. She announced that she would run for President in 1872. The sisters' hunger for attention became insatiable. They inveigled Vanderbilt into helping them establish a weekly newspaper. The first issue of *Woodhull & Claflin's Weekly,* a sixteen-page, tabloid-sized paper, appeared on May 14, 1870. It carried the motto "Upward and Onward" which later became, "Progress! Free Thought! Untrammeled Lives!" The paper blasted everything from prostitution to financial fraud and crusaded boldly for birth control, public housing, spiritualism, a universal language named "Alwato," and, of course, Woodhull for President. It was the first publication in the United States to print the *Communist Manifesto.* After the first few issues it became—like a mirror of Victoria herself—a catchall of utopian manifestos, muckraking, quackery, free love propaganda, and self-advertisement. It was made to look respectable by book reviews, sports news, a financial report, and even a fashion column.[27] Andrews and Blood undoubtedly did most of the writing, but Victoria had plainly assimilated their views and could express them, when she wished, in her own way.

Thrusting into the struggle for women's rights, Mrs. Woodhull went to Washington during the third annual convention of the National Woman's Suffrage Association in January, 1871, and to the astonishment of everyone, especially the suffragists, became the first woman to appear before the Judiciary Committee of the House of Representatives. The Woodhull—as she was already called—a trim, very attractive woman with a musical voice and natural magnetism, created a great stir with a long and learned memorial on women's rights. Disregarding her scandalous background and her more extravagant views, Susan B. Anthony, Elizabeth Cady Stanton, and Isabella Beecher Hooker, the tough-minded leaders of the more radical feminists, welcomed her enthusiastically. The following day she addressed the women's rights convention in Washington and captured it, too.

Her triumph made headlines across the nation. When members of the more conservative American Women's Suffrage Association called the National's acceptance of Mrs. Woodhull irresponsible, Mrs. Stanton replied: "We have had enough women sacrificed to this sentimental, hypocritical prating about purity. . . . We have crucified the Mary Wollstonecrafts, the Fanny Wrights, the George Sands, the Fanny Kembles of all ages. . . . If Victoria Woodhull must be crucified, let men drive the spikes and plait the crown of thorns." [28] Made drunk by such talk, Mrs. Woodhull started a suffrage anniversary meeting in New York a few months later by calling for treason, secession, and the overthrow of "this bogus Republic" if the government did not at once grant women their rights.

The Woodhull was thus engaged when her mother, more violent and irresponsible than ever, went into court charging that Colonel Blood was mistreating her. Nothing came of the charge, but it caused the entire bizarre household on Thirty-eighth Street to be exposed to merciless, hot-eyed publicity. The Cleveland *Leader* cried that Mrs. Woodhull's career "as a trance-physician in Cincinnati, her brazen immodesty as a stock speculator on Wall Street, and the open, shameless effrontery with which she had paraded her name . . . for the Presidency . . . has proclaimed her as a vain . . . unsexed woman." Suffragists in general disavowed her, sensing that she was not interested in any movement but her own. Conspicuous among those who began to harry her were two of the Beecher clan, Catharine

Beecher, Henry Ward Beecher's rather severe eldest sister, and the celebrated Harriet Beecher Stowe. Despite the reputation of *Uncle Tom's Cabin* Harriet Stowe's social opinions were essentially conservative, and she now wrote a romantic novel, *My Wife and I,* in which Audacia Dangyereyes, a brazen, insouciant "new woman" was held up to ridicule. Many readers, including The Woodhull, thought Audacia was modeled on Victoria Woodhull.

Unfortunately for the Beechers, Victoria now heard from a leading feminist a detailed account of how the famous Reverend Beecher had seduced Elizabeth Tilton, devout wife of his friend, the well-known editor and poet, Theodore Tilton. After years of being troubled by her conscience, Mrs. Tilton, an emotional young woman, had confessed her transgression to her husband but begged him to keep the story secret. After several confrontations between Beecher and the Tiltons, an uneasy truce had been established.

Victoria Woodhull was now ready to document her charges of male hypocrisy. On May 22, 1871, both the New York *World* and the *Times* printed the following open letter from her:

> Sir,
>
> Because I am a woman, and because I conscientiously hold opinions somewhat different from the self-elected orthodoxy . . . and because I think it . . . my absolute right . . . to advocate them with my whole strength, self-elected orthodoxy . . . endeavors to cover my life with ridicule and dishonor. . . . I do not intend to be . . . offered up as a victim to society by those who cover over the foulness of their lives and the feculence of their thoughts with a hypocritical mantle of fair professions. . . . I advocate free love in its highest, purest sense as the only cure for immorality . . . by which men corrupt and disfigure God's most holy institution of sexual relation. My judges preach against "free love" openly, and practise it secretly. . . . For example, I know of one man, a public teacher of eminence, who lives in concubinage with the wife of another public teacher of almost equal eminence. All three concur in denouncing offenses against morality. . . . I shall make it my business to analyze some of these lives, and will take my chances in the matter of libel suits.[29]

Wonderfully ironic was the spectacle of Henry Ward Beecher threatened with exposure not by a pillar of morality but by a believer in free love urging him to admit his adherence to her doctrine.

Hastily Tilton and Beecher came together and decided that Tilton should try to placate Mrs. Woodhull. Once he had met Victoria, Tilton, a quixotic, impressionable man, found the assignment delightful. Soon he was describing her in a periodical as the Joan of Arc of the women's rights movement, and not long after that he wrote a "campaign biography" of her full of glowing references to her "mad and magnificent energies." They went rowing on the Harlem River and bathing at Coney Island, and there is little doubt that he not only admired her theories but put them into practice with her. On one occasion, as she was leaving Chicago for New York, the Woodhull revealed to a reporter something he was surely itching to hear: that Tilton had been her "devoted lover for half a year" and had "slept every night for three months" in her arms. But in New York she just as casually denied the story.

When Harriet Beecher Stowe and Catharine Beecher persisted in criticizing Mrs. Woodhull, Victoria summoned Beecher himself to an interview. He came—middle-aged yet still magnetic—but he refused, he later claimed, to support her activities. Mrs. Woodhull's version of the interview was that he agreed with her on such subjects as divorce and free love but admitted, with tears, that he was too much of a moral coward to proclaim the fact. Beecher visited her repeatedly, and she later told a friend that they had not spent all their time talking about the weather. But Beecher could not keep his sisters from criticizing Mrs. Woodhull.

Whenever the voices raised against her became too much for her, Victoria Woodhull grew more aggressive. Now she scheduled a lecture boldly entitled, "Free Love, Marriage, Divorce and Prostitution." The lecture started mildly enough but soon became a passionate assault on rigid marriage and divorce laws. The climax came when someone shouted, "Are you a free lover?" She cried, "Yes! I am a free lover! I have an inalienable, constitutional and natural right to love whom I may, to love as long or as short a period as I can, to change that love every day if I please!" She added that, before long, women would withhold their bodies from the "demoralizing influence of sexual relations that are not . . . maintained by love." She scorned promiscuity because it was not founded on love. "Rather let me leave my doors and windows open," she said, "intent on living so nobly that the best cannot fail to be drawn to me by an irresistible attraction." [30]

The lecture stirred harsh criticism. Victoria's brokerage profits declined, and the family was forced to move to a modest boardinghouse. And early in 1872, Thomas Nast, famous for his savage cartoons in *Harper's Weekly,* did a cartoon captioned, "Get thee behind me, (Mrs.) Satan." It showed Victoria Woodhull as a fascinating but malevolent figure in black, with horns, bat wings, and a placard reading, "Be Saved by Free Love." It disturbed and aroused the Woodhull.

Although fringe groups calling themselves the Equal Rights Party now nominated Mrs. Woodhull for the Presidency, Victoria was actually sinking in a sea of troubles. Blunt Susan B. Anthony and other women's rights leaders were beginning to turn their backs on her; Vanderbilt having withdrawn support, the *Weekly* suspended publication; and Tilton, angered by attacks on his suffragist friends, fell out with her. Beset by critics, she struck back: at a meeting of Spiritualists in Boston, she told the whole Beecher-Tilton story, pouring it out, her shocked hearers later said, "in a rhapsody of indignant eloquence." [31] When the exposé was ignored by the newspapers, she resurrected the *Weekly* and devoted an entire issue to the case, declaring that she intended it to fall "like a bombshell into the moralistic social camp."

It did. More than 100,000 copies of the issue were sold, some at ten dollars for a second-hand copy. But the following day Anthony Comstock had the sisters arrested for sending an obscene publication through the mail and, as a district attorney added, for an "abominable . . . charge against one of the purest and best citizens." Actually there was nothing obscene in the article, nothing, as the sisters' lawyer pointed out, that could not be found in Deuteronomy 22. Beecher and his congregation, especially the stockholders in Plymouth Church, turned their backs on the whole affair. Each day the sisters cell in Ludlow Street jail was filled with their sympathizers, mainly radicals and reformers. A month passed before they were released for lack of a case. Twice again they were arrested and twice bailed out. When they were brought to trial after eight months, the judge dismissed the charge. The persecution infuriated Victoria. Whenever she was free, she went about lecturing, holding audiences spellbound with her indignation. When a speaker at a convention of Spiritualists in Chicago asserted that she had prostituted herself with men and then threatened to expose them, she cried: "A man questioning my virtue! . . . I hurl the intention back in your face, sir . . . and declare that I never had sexual intercourse with any man of whom I am ashamed to stand side by side before the world. . . . Nor am I ashamed of any desire that has been gratified, nor of any passion alluded to. Every one of them are a part of my own soul's life, for which, thank God, I am not accountable to you. . . . And this sexual intercourse business may as well be discussed now, and discussed until you are so familiar with your sexual organs that a reference to them will no longer make the blush mount to your face any more than a reference to any other part of your body. . . ." With the kind of grasp of sexual problems that would not be displayed again in a public discussion for another half-century, she pointed out that nothing was so "destructive as that intercourse carried on habitually without regard to perfect and reciprocal consummation. . . ." When sexual science is introduced into the schools, she added, "as assuredly it will be, sexual ills that now beset the young will vanish." [32] The convention voted overwhelmingly to reelect her to the presidency.

Although the Equal Rights Party soon disintegrated and Grant rode smoothly back into office, the Woodhull became a national figure—the Scarlet Woman who wore her color with pride. Wherever she went, she stirred up excitement, evoking every reaction from the ribald jibe to the passionate defense. And always there were the lurid rumors. We would hardly know how much there was in such rumors were it not for a remarkably candid memoir by Benjamin R. Tucker. More than fifty years later, while living in France after a career as a publisher of libertarian periodicals, Tucker gave Mrs. Woodhull's first biographer his recollections of his love affair with Victoria when she was thirty-five and he was nineteen.

Of an old New England family, Tucker was a studious youth with an acute susceptibility to extremist doctrines ranging from anarchism to free love. Already active at nineteen in reform movements in Boston, he met Victoria and was at once attracted to her. Intimacy between them began when he had occasion to visit her at the Parker House. She greeted him warmly and as soon as Colonel Blood left the room, she locked the door and, Tucker writes,

> In a quiet, earnest, charming manner, she marched straight to the chair in which I was seated, leaned over and kissed me, remarking then: "I've been wanting to do this so long!" Then, with a grace all her own, she gently swung herself around and placed herself upon my knee, I behaving always like a puzzled brute. In that attitude we talked for some minutes.

She rose just before Colonel Blood came back. When Tucker returned in the morning she was alone, and after some conversation she said: "Do you know I should dearly love to sleep with you?" Young Tucker had begun to confess his lack of experience when Blood came in again. Declaring that the "magnetism" they generated was too much for him, Blood finally left them alone. "Within an hour," Tucker recalls, "my 'ruin' was complete, and I, nevertheless, a proud and happy youth."

Tucker returned to Boston but soon abandoned his studies at Massachusetts Institute of Technology, rejoined Victoria in New York, and for the next five or six months spent all his days with her. He fell in with the bohemian disorder of their lives, balking only when Victoria suggested that he might like to sleep with Tennie. But he was truly disillusioned by the fact that Victoria did no reading or writing and by the "disgraceful" means she sometimes used to gain her ends. In one of the few characterizations that seems to have done justice to all of Victoria Woodhull, he concluded: "She would have been glorious if she hadn't been infamous." [33]

Meanwhile, the fuse that Mrs. Woodhull had lit two years before under the Beecher-Tilton affair had never stopped burning. Beecher had made every effort to smother it. But Tilton, unable to contain his torment, finally brought the case to court. The sensational trial, lasting through much of 1875, resulted in a split jury and left the case without any official resolution. Although Victoria Woodhull had been largely responsible for this ventilation of the hypocrisy of one of America's foremost spiritual and moral leaders, she would be associated in the public mind not with a brave blow on behalf of principle but with besmirching a pillar of virtue.

But by that time, Victoria, worn out by harassment, suffering from anemia, constantly short of money, began to retreat into mystical interpretations of the body as the "temple of God." Perhaps as a result of some ailment, she dwelt on the symbolic significance of menstruation, and went into rhapsodies on purity and the sanctity of love and marriage. Readers of the *Weekly*, baffled, began to cancel their subscriptions. Colonel Blood lost his attraction for her, and, at her mother's urging, she divorced him. Sadly he moved out and drifted from job to job. Stephen Andrews left the magic circle. And then in 1876 the paper folded. Much as in the lives of Mary Wollstonecraft and Fanny Wright as they approached forty, the fire in Victoria Woodhull's blood cooled; rebelliousness seemed to peter out.

Then, providentially, old Vanderbilt died, and his heirs, quarreling over his will, appear to have paid Victoria and Tennessee to dissuade them from testifying at the trial. No one knows exactly what happened, but the sisters and their entourage suddenly departed for Europe, traveling in style.[34]

When Victoria arrived in London the possibility of a totally new life, like another incarnation, suddenly presented itself to her. She was weary of attacks and ostracism, and eager for rest, a conventional husband, and a home. She achieved all of these when John Biddulph Martin of an old English banking family fell in love with her. Martin was a diffident, earnest Englishman who was convinced that his Victoria was a pure, misunderstood spirit, and he spent much of his life defending her from charges that she had had an immoral past. Henry James in his short novel, *The Siege of London,* probably basing the relationship between the American adventuress Nancy Headway and the rich Englishman Sir Arthur Demesne on the Woodhull-Martin liaison, saw the couple, in Jamesian fashion, as an attraction between opposites—the overcivilized, rather fatuous European of fine old lineage and the vulgar but vital American. But Mrs. Headway shares none of Mrs. Woodhull's social radicalism; she is merely a woman who has been scandalously free with love. Despite James' gift for subtilizing character, Nancy is much more obvious than Victoria and far less challenging.

It was, however, six years before Victoria convinced Martin's family that she had become a model of respectability. She did so by repudiating free love and all other radical doctrines, blaming Stephen Pearl Andrews and Colonel Blood for every heresy ever attributed to her. After her husband died in the 1890's, Victoria moved to the great old house on the estate he had left her in Worcestershire, and for the remaining twenty-seven years of her life she did everything possible to live down her past—that is, all that had made her unique and significant. As "mistress of the manor" she played at being Lady Bountiful, busying herself with countless causes, mostly eccentric, and extolling the genteel virtues. And whenever some newspaper dredged up her past, she charged that it was all lies and blackmail. In the end she was little more than another quaint old lady. Ironically, the obituaries, ignoring all her efforts at proving her conformity, recalled her as a pioneer suffragist, muckracker, and social reformer.

To some of her foes Victoria Woodhull in her prime was a lamia, glitteringly equipped by the devil to corrupt the innocent; to other detractors she was simply a purveyor of vice for publicity and profit. To her admirers she was a brave crusader, a free spirit, liberator of enslaved women and other stifled souls.

Her enemies were quite wrong, but her friends were hardly right. Circumstances had kept her outside the pale; forced to find her own way, she came to despise the hypocrisy of men and to pity the frustration and emotional immaturity of women. It was thus almost by instinct alone that she came to take so bold a stand against loveless intercourse, whether in marriage or prostitution, to advocate frank sex education in the schools, and to practice and preach free sexual relations. Bomber of the "moralistic camps," shocker of the bourgeoisie, she was in some directions almost a century ahead of her time.

But instincts are not pure, and Victoria was almost as much the victim as the beneficiary of her passions and her appetites. Crucial flaws in character led her, whenever the pressures mounted, into conscienceless acts. And eventually she denied all that she had advocated—good along with bad—for the sake of peace and security. While the passing years tamed her, much of what she had fought for had been widely accepted by the time she died in 1928. It was Elizabeth Cady Stanton who said:

"Victoria Woodhull has done a work for woman that none of us could have done."

After Victoria Woodhull—she was in the public eye scarcely seven years—later advocates of free love such as Ezra Hervey Heywood and De Robigné Bennett seem earthbound, with a brave but uninspiring interest in the cause. They espoused it vigorously enough but rather as a matter of principle than as a personal craving, rather as one of the natural rights of man than as a fire in the blood.

Like so many such reformers in this period, Heywood was a small-town New Englander of religious background. He studied for the Congregational ministry but was soon caught up in the abolitionist and women's rights movements. Fanatically determined to change men's minds, he set up a press in his own home. There, aided by his wife, who matched him in radical ardor, he turned out a vast volume of propaganda, most of it bold and plainspoken but also dry and humorless. The most famous of his pamphlets—it sold over 50,000 copies—was *Cupid's Yokes: or, The Binding Forces of Conjugal Life* (1876). Since man invented marriage, he argued, man has the right to alter or abolish it. Nature is, furthermore, a safer guide than the crude social codes of the ignorant past. Young men and women, Heywood declared, are forced to choose between two evils: abstinence and the legalized prostitution of marriage. Some men and women resort to clandestine intimacies and a few to social defiance. A system that produces so many hypocrites among men as well as martyrs among women must be based on coercion and will be abolished when a free people finally confront it.[35]

His theories on improving the species must have seemed even more shocking: he asserted that it was important for superior individuals to have children even if they were not married. Nor should anyone have a child by a marital partner when there was another person by whom he or she could have a better child. (He failed, of course, to say how the choice would be made.) It was a pity that such noble men as Plato, Jesus, and Newton, or any superior woman, he concluded, should have remained childless only because they never married.[36]

Any of these doctrines was sufficient to annoy Anthony Comstock. But what probably provoked the YMCA agent to one of his most relentless persecutions was Heywood's reference to him as a religious monomaniac.[37] Although *Cupid's Yokes* was an unadorned statement of the familiar arguments of freethinkers, and sold, unlike any pornographic book, for a mere fifteen cents a copy, Comstock said it was "too foul for description." In 1877 he managed, as described earlier, to arrest Heywood. The judge at the trial that followed declared that if Heywood's ideas prevailed, Massachusetts would become a vast house of prostitution. Heywood was convicted and given a $100 fine and two years at hard labor in Dedham jail. After he had served six months, six thousand persons at an indignation meeting in Faneuil Hall denounced the judge and petitioned President Hayes to pardon the reformers; Hayes did so. Four years later Comstock arrested Heywood again, this time charging him with distributing not only *Cupid's Yokes* but several poems by Whitman and a satire on Comstock himself. A grand jury found Heywood not guilty. And in 1883, when he was arrested for a third time, a defense committee organized by his neighbors prevented the charge from being pressed.

Meanwhile, Heywood, totally committed to reform, established The Mountain Home, a kind of summer hotel for reformers and spiritualists. And in 1873 he joined in organizing the New England Free Love League and thereafter solemnly dated all his letters "Y. L.," Year of Love, instead of "A.D." [38]

Although an insuppressible agitator, especially for sexual reform, Heywood personally practiced self-discipline. He opposed excessive sensuality in marriage and even such practices as withdrawal and contraception, describing the latter as a "cheat." A man of stubborn will when it came to principles, he was in private life, like Warren, a kindly person, close to his wife and children. Indeed his personal life confirms our surmise that he was—again like Warren and several other reformers of the time—such an extremist because he was radical in theory rather than in practice.

A far more subtle and persuasive partisan of love, member of no cult or utopian group, was David Goodman Croly, a New York newspaper editor. The influence of Darwin, sometimes in oversimplified form, is evident in much of Croly's work. During the Civil War he collaborated on a booklet so daring that it was published anonymously: it advocated intermarriage between whites and blacks as a way of improving the species. And his most substantial book, *The Truth About Love* (1872) was subtitled *A Proposed Sexual Morality Based upon the Doctrine of Evolution and Recent Discoveries in Medical Science.* At the outset, Croly warned that he would not refer to "the will of God" or "the design of Nature" since no one knew what those were. He asserted that the Christian view of the human body as bestial was "in the light of modern science wholly untrue."[39] In a striking anticipation of psychoanalytic theory Croly declared that excessive restrictions on young people forced the sexual instincts to find release in other directions. Taking Ophelia as an example, Croly, using almost Freudian terms, wrote:

> In her madness the poor girl becomes obscene, for in her disordered mind all the cryptic thoughts, the filthied impulses of awful, unknown progenitors come again to the surface. . . . any system of education which seeks to repress the potency of this feeling does but transfer its forces into other domains of the nervous sphere; and hence arise these fitful emotions, these hysteria, these dilignia, these religious aberrations that mar so many lonely lives. There is a sexual force that must be expended—if not by physical contact, then in abnormal explosions.[40]

Croly recommended letting young people express these drives through the free mixing of the sexes, dancing, embracing, kissing, reading novels, and even bundling. These did not stimulate desire as much as they appeased it, he wrote. The horde of prostitutes was not recruited from those who read love stories and mingled easily with men but from the ranks of domestics and factory girls who could not repress their instinctive desires. Although Croly deplored bawdy houses, he observed that prostitution appeared to be indispensable; and he wryly suggested that more harm would come from closing all brothels for six months than from closing all churches.

Croly had his prejudices, but he carried them lightly, recognizing that not all men and women had the same needs. We must allow, he said, for individual irregularities and diversity, barring only those who disturb society. But he rejected the idea of free love. The Lothario and the Lais are dangerous because they seek only to please themselves; the free lover wants to enjoy himself without considering offspring or any responsibility to the race. In his closing pages Croly gave voice to some daring hopes. Just as it had taken over the education of youth, so the state should regulate birth in order to improve the species. Priests and bachelors were the real enemies of the race, and old maids were immoral because they did not use their sexual organs to gratify men or their genital organs to have children. He concluded, like Noyes, with the hope that women would come to accept the act of satisfying a man sexually as a social function comparable to having a pleasing conversation.[41]

Compared to the fanatic prudes to his right and the libertarian faddists to his left, Croly was a refreshing figure, trying to shake readers loose from a Puritanical-genteel view of love. His own life was apparently quite orthodox: he married Jane Cunningham, sometimes described as the first American newspaperwoman, and had five children by her. She shared many of his views and some of his iconoclastic efforts.

But there were others who did practice what they preached. Although foreign visitors rarely got more than a superficial or fragmentary impression of sexual behavior, Hepworth Dixon, the British editor, was such a well-informed observer that we must take into account his repeated assertions that free love was widely practiced after the Civil War. He insisted that an emancipated woman who took a lover would not be excluded from society, partly because there was no infallible church to damn her and partly because a certain class in society "distinguished in some degree by art and culture" would be on her side. Free love, he observed, had its poets, lecturers, and preachers, its newspapers and colonies. Among the many poets devoted to the cause he named Lizzie Doten, Fanny Hyzer, T. N. Harris, and G. S. Burleigh, but his quotation from a presumably typical effort, called "Free Love," reads more like a Cavalier lyric than a declaration of genuine sexual independence.[42]

Because of their stubborn dedication to an extremist cause and their consequent sympathy for all radical causes, men like Heywood, Bennett, and, later, Moses Harman became a kind of corps of professional reformers at the far end of the libertarian spectrum. Their extremism constantly thrust them into intimate association with cranks and misfits, with all the eccentric movements and fads from spiritualism to phrenology. Free love thus became synonymous not only with libertinism and rampant sexuality but with queer and fanatic cults.

Isolated in their extremism, such reformers were hardly aware that social changes, especially after the turn of the century, were weakening the restrictions against which they had rebelled. With the old Puritanism gone, women everywhere thrusting into man's realms, divorce gradually becoming easier, and bohemianism creating enclaves of liberty such as Greenwich Village, rebellious individuals found it easier to practice—discreetly of course—greater freedom in sexual relations than to preach it. At the end of World War I, conventional marriage was still the American way, but few any longer thought of it as sacrosanct or eternal.

There was no counterpart in America in the 1880's for the sensualism and perverse eroticism of such men as Swinburne, Symonds, Wilde, and Beardsley in England and of Baudelaire, Rimbaud, Verlaine, and Huysman in France. In England these tendencies were fostered by a strain of effeteness in the upper class, and in France by a tradition of bohemianism, by a rejection, especially among artists, of common bourgeois values. But in the 1890's even the United States began to be affected, mainly in New York, by the *fin de siècle* spirit. It showed itself first in a critic of the arts, James Gibbons Huneker, who in turn exerted a powerful influence on members of the avant-garde that came of age between 1915 and 1925.

It will seem surprising that a sensualist, passionately devoted to the arts, should emerge from the family of a Philadelphia housepainter until one learns that Huneker's father, of German descent, loved music, conviviality, and frank talk and that his mother was a volatile Celtic intellectual. By the time Huneker was twenty he was an accomplished pianist and a music critic, and he had discovered Swinburne, Baudelaire, Gautier, and Flaubert. After a stay in Paris in 1878 he came back a true cosmopolite, an unabashed bohemian with an immense appetite for beer, good food, nightlong talk, a bawdy joke, and responsive women. As a leading critic of all the arts, he was pursued by young women aspiring to be singers or painters, and he was not unwilling to further their careers by what he called "approved horizontal methods." Asserting, only half in jest, that a man needed seven wives, each to satisfy a different need, he was married three times, divorced twice, and had a variety of mistresses. Although he conducted these affairs modestly enough, he openly mocked those who condemned such activities, asserting that if every merchant and lawyer had his life exposed after his death there would be a rustling of many old bones of scandal as well as of skirts.[43]

But it was in his attacks on censorship—in a prose full of fireworks of language and wit—that Huneker proved himself the most emancipated and mordant critic of his time. When the Boston Art Commission in 1896 rejected MacMonnies' "Bacchante with Infant Faun," Huneker (anticipating Theodore Dreiser's similar protest by eighteen months) exclaimed:

> The burghers of bean-fed Boston should wear fig leaves on their imaginations. . . . Considering that the State of Massachusetts shows such a lively list of births outside of wedlock . . . the obscene-minded old men of Boston might have accepted MacMonnies' lovely Bacchante. . . . The rotten puritanism of a city that is notoriously immoral . . . is very disheartening.[44]

A year later, when Anthony Comstock confiscated D'Annunzio's mildly sensual *The Triumph of Death,* Huneker's scorn was boundless:

> It is a subject of national laughter to think of this morbid-minded fellow nosing among the masterpieces and setting up a cry of obscenity in a city where the foulest newspapers in the world print prose and pictures of unmentionable kinds. . . . We allow a man . . . who has grown gray in the pursuit of the nasty to dictate to us our reading matter.

No latter-day critic of Comstock would be more penetrating. And Huneker was just as merciless with namby-pamby writers. Wearied, in 1903, by a long season of tame plays and novels, he laid bare the utter flabbiness of the genteel tradition:

> Love, unless it be treated as a joke or a social gumdrop, is sternly waved away. . . . When we do get a few modern masterpieces (from abroad) they are mutilated, lines excised,

> sentiments expunged, and meanings suppressed. . . . In America, the sentiment of the etiolated, the brainless, the prudish, the hypocrite is the censor. . . . Why is there absent the tragic note in America? [45]

He went on to point out that novelists wrote mostly about characters in their teens and avoided sin, crime, and poverty, "slurring over with sick music of false rhetoric all the cruel facts of life."

Stimulated by Huneker's example as well as by his contributions to such short-lived but daringly sophisticated magazines as *M'lle New York*, Mencken, Dreiser, George Jean Nathan, James Branch Cabell, Heywood Broun, Carl Van Vechten, and others took up the battle against the emasculated, the callow, the priggish, and the parochial in our culture. Embracing the fleshly as well as the esthetic pleasures, Huneker exercised an influence on styles of life no less than on styles of art. Almost alone in his time, he anticipated the Greenwich Village radicals and the debunking school of social criticism that sprang up during World War I. Himself a fusion of German and Irish, a friend of New York's Jewish intelligentsia, champion of French poets and painters, German composers, Irish playwrights, and Russian novelists, he was a vital force in undermining Protestant Anglo-Saxon dominion over American taste and morality.

Part 3

HIDDEN FIRES

18.

THE DOUBLE STANDARD

No account of nineteenth-century sexuality would be complete without some scrutiny of private or clandestine behavior, some attempt to describe what went on behind the façade of propriety and self-restraint. Although much easier than it would have been half a century ago, it will always be difficult to find out much about sexual activity in such a period as the nineteenth century. Still, there is far more information available than is generally supposed, much of it significant and part of it surprising. Some of this information was recorded but not published, as in diaries and letters; some of it was published, but in obscure places, as in books on anatomy and medicine; and some of it was published widely, as in newspaper accounts of scandals, but has not been studied or interpreted. These sources do not reveal the behavior in every home, but they do give us enough glimpses to undermine whatever remains of traditional conceptions of nineteenth-century morality. And where the information covers a broad public reaction, such as the response to a spectacular scandal, it tells us much about the contradictory urges that lurked beneath the genteel surface of the Victorian personality.

Whatever evidence we have about the sexual relations of married couples of the period suggests that some men took full advantage of the belief that they had appetites that must be satisfied. Many preachers as well as books on physiology and marriage disclose, more or less unwittingly, what went on behind closed doors by the way they exhort husbands not to abuse their wives sexually. Counsellors admonish young couples against what they call prostitution within matrimony. They warn against the husband who "contaminates" his wife with his licentious habits.[1] This implied of course that women were naturally pure but also vulnerable. Various theories were offered to reconcile the fiction that women were morally superior with the fact that they could be seduced. The *Ladies Magazine* declared in 1828: "When the female descends the scale of moral excellence . . . it cannot with certainty be foretold where she will stop. Depravity in the sex is of a deeper and darker cast, as the strongest acids are obtained from the sweetest base." [2] Even as this contradicts the cant about women's natural purity, it warns against a natural weakness in her. Poor woman: she had to remain an angel of chastity while harboring a devil of depravity. David Goodman Croly saw the increasing nomadism of American families as freeing women from the moral bonds. "Once free from the espionage of Mrs. Grundy," he wrote in *The Truth about Love,* "a woman will indulge in fancies and expectations which would be very shocking to her friends . . . although these persons are fully cognizant of such effects in themselves." [3]

With a few notable exceptions, books on health and hygiene warned that coitus during menstruation was beastly and that during pregnancy it would do all kinds of harm to the unborn child. Most of them also declared that too much sexual activity permanently impaired man's sexual powers and health. The advocates of free love and the critics of the subjection of women in marriage delighted to tell of husbands whose sexual exactions were too great for the wives to tolerate. Lucy Stone told of a woman who was driven to Shakerism because her husband "gave her no peace during menstruation, pregnancy or nursing." Similarly, Victoria Woodhull spoke of a New York clergyman who brought on the death of his wife by his "lecherous excesses" and constant demands for sexual satisfaction. Similar testimony came from the daughter of Mrs. Godfrey Lowell Cabot who, as we have seen, quoted her mother as saying that she dreamed constantly of having a room or a bed of her own to which she could escape from her husband, Boston's leading crusader against vice. Even allowing for the exaggeration in these stories and something less than passion in the wives, it is clear that the marriage certificate seemed to some men a license to indulge in maximum sexual activity without regard for their wives.

The most fraudulent aspect of the nineteenth-century social system, the double standard in morals, was based on the dogma that women did not spontaneously experience desire whereas men had passions that must be satisfied. Thus man had his cake and ate it too: he was able, if he wished, to find sexual release before marriage or outside of marriage, and yet when he came to marry he could have virgins to choose from. A man's extra-curricular sexual activity had of course to be surreptitious, usually with women outside his own class and often with prostitutes. Wealth, however, brought privileges. If a man could afford it, he might keep a mistress, as Ormond kept Helen Cleves in Brown's *Ormond,* or he might make a trip abroad, where women were freer with love.

The practice among affluent young men of going to Europe presumably to complete their studies began early in the century. The youth would make a tour of the continent and then stay for a course of lectures at a German or French university. This was, for example, the path followed by Sam Ward, Jr., son of a well-known New York banker. After graduating in 1833 from Columbia College, he awarded himself a *lehrjahr* in Europe. He managed to stretch the one year into four, and although he did get himself a degree from the University of Tübingen, his true study was the night life of Paris, drinking sessions at Heidelberg, and the management of French mistresses.[4] He returned to New York with a silken mustache, blond Van Dyke, velvet coat, and a shirt with ruffles. His first marriage was to a girl of his own class, a daughter of the Astors. But when she died in childbirth, he turned to Medora Grymes, a languorous New Orleans belle, daughter of a one-time Creole beauty. When Ward lost his family fortune, Medora left him. She went to France, and rumor had it that she fell in with a wealthy Russian debauchee and became part of an international coterie of wastrels on the Riviera. She plainly scorned the double standard, but she was, after all, Creole, and just the kind of free-living creature American parents did not want their daughters to become.

Ward settled in Washington and in time became known as

"King of the Lobbyists," celebrated for his matchless dinner parties and the eminence of his guests. Sam Ward was hardly typical—his friends Henry Wadsworth Longfellow and Charles Sumner went abroad and came back as proper as ever—but he does demonstrate that a man could enjoy a good deal of liberty, sexual and otherwise, without much damage to his reputation.

Henry Wikoff's experiences illustrate how much a young man who left American taboos behind could learn of French and Italian sexual liberties. The ward of a wealthy Philadelphian, Wikoff went abroad in 1834 and was so enchanted by European society and its diversions that he eventually spent most of his time abroad. Exploiting certain small talents, he became the intimate of famous dancers and actors.

Wikoff's *The Reminiscences of an Idler,* written many years later, is remarkably frank in its approval of the boldness with which Frenchwomen of all classes lived with men. He had known that it was common for a married man of the upper class to take a mistress and for such a man's wife to take a lover, but he had not realized that the middle and lower classes were "not a whit more prudish." An unmarried woman who supported herself could, without loss of respectability, establish a temporary liaison with a man, and, similarly, a workingwoman would not hesitate to move into a room with a workingman in a so-called *mariage de St. Jacques*—which might last only as long as their lease. As for students in the Latin Quarter, everyone knew that they consoled themselves with grisettes and often shared lodgings with them.[5]

Wikoff concluded that although this behavior may have constituted libertinage, it did not lead to depravity. By contrast, when an English girl lost her chastity, her family often drove her into the streets and a life of prostitution. Elsewhere, describing the "universal jollity" of Sundays in France, Wikoff observed that "the rigid notions of our Puritan fathers would have been regarded, not merely as fanaticism, but downright insanity."[6]

Men like Ward and Wikoff became more common as the century progressed. James Gordon Bennett, Jr., the spoiled son of the founder of the New York *Herald,* was at an early age carried off to Europe by his mother and was brought up by governesses. When he returned to New York in the 1860's, he was a cosmopolite, with experience in spending money, drinking, and sex. He became part of a postwar circle of young people devoted to novel forms of dissipation, scorning middle-class standards of conduct, and quite unconcerned about their immortal souls. Bennett's behavior reached a climax of boorishness on New Year's Day, 1877. After long confining his wenching to actresses and purchasable women he became engaged to a Miss Caroline May. Following a round of New Year's Day tippling, he staggered into the crowded drawing room of Miss May's home, downed a few more drinks, and then did something as addlebrained as it was offensive: he unbuttoned and urinated in the fireplace. Miss May broke off the engagement—which must have been what Bennett subconsciously wanted. Had Bennett been guilty of mayhem or a railroad swindle, fashionable society would probably have closed its eyes to the offense, but he had flouted good manners; so he was ostracized.[7] As furious as a child punished for a tantrum, Bennett left for Paris and remained an expatriate until his death more than forty years later.

Mainly because prominent figures like Ward and Bennett are among the few for whom we have intimate details, our examples so far have been men of wealth. An average young American who indulged in the pleasures of the flesh during a stay in Paris or Rome was unlikely to leave any record of it. But in at least one instance biographers have pieced together enough evidence to yield a classic example of the frustrated young American of little means who found release abroad. He was Horatio Alger, Jr., author of novels famous for teaching boys the way from rags to riches.

The victim of his father, a clergyman who ruled him with righteous tyranny, and of a submissive mother, Horatio grew up an inhibited youth. Something of a weakling, with sallow complexion and quavering voice, he tended to lapse into indecision and then give way to impulse. When his landlady in a Cambridge boardinghouse near Harvard came to her door scantily clad, he at once moved out of the house and confided pathetically to his diary: "I might have seen her bare but I did not look. . . ."

Alger dutifully attended Harvard Divinity School for three years. Then, a few months before graduation, coming into a $2,000 legacy and stirred by literary ambitions, he went off to

Europe. Repressed and fearful, he found both London and Paris dull—until he met Elise Monselet, a singer in an obscure Paris café. Aroused no doubt by his tremulous virginity, she seduced him. So astonished and pleased was he by the experience that he moved into her lodgings. Before long, he allowed Charlotte Evans, an aggressive, sensual English girl, to fasten herself on him and extend his sexual experience even further. But *la vie bohème* was really too much for Alger; after a brief attempt to keep up with the life of the cafés and the demands of his voracious mistress, he abruptly deserted the fleshpots of Europe. But the predatory Miss Evans followed him aboard the boat, and when it docked in New York, Horatio escaped from her only by literally running away.[8]

Horatio's father immediately repossessed him and soon had him ordained a Unitarian minister. But Horatio slipped the leash again and went off to New York in search of literary material. He found it in the Newsboys' Lodging House, a shelter for homeless working boys, and for many years spent most of his time there. He never married, but he had at least one other sexual experience worth noting. He fell passionately in love with a suburban housewife, Mrs. Una Garth, and began to woo her even in the presence of her husband. After her husband, refusing to take Alger seriously, left on a business trip, it is thought that she became Alger's lover. When business took Garth and his wife to Paris, Alger followed them. Realizing that Alger had lost control of himself, Mrs. Garth turned him away.[9] Alger suffered an acute breakdown. After a long illness he returned to New York and to the stories that would teach youth the virtues that lead to success.

The contrast between the furtive, sex-ridden nature of Alger's life and the triumph of bourgeois virtues in his fiction is complete. It is the perfect embodiment of schizoid morality. Where the Reverend Beecher guiltily knew that he was not practicing what he preached, Alger simply did not realize how utterly one side of his life belied the other.

For those who could not go abroad or afford a mistress, meaning all but a handful of men, there was that old source of gratification—prostitutes. Just as Victorian repressiveness created the duality of prudery and pornography, it created the duality of woman as virgin or prostitute. Refusing to face the facts of sexuality, man insisted that woman be either superhuman in her purity or, if she serviced his sexuality, be considered subhuman in her degradation. There was no acknowledgment that the prostitute was begotten and supported by man, that she was at best his servant and at worst his victim. To a young Victorian an experience with a whore could be an unsettling revelation of forbidden pleasures. But regardless of what he felt about it, it locked him into the prevailing hypocrisy. The attitude toward prostitution was particularly shameful because it was supposed to protect respectable women from molestation by unsatisfied men, yet at the same time it doomed the whores to their condition.

Moreau de St. Méry, French émigré who came to America in the 1790's, wrote in his journal that prostitution was rife in New York, and John Lambert asserted early in the 1800's that prostitutes amounted to one-thirtieth of the population of Boston.[10] Convincing support is given to St. Méry's statement by Philip Hone, merchant, man-about-town, and Mayor of New York in 1825; he recalled an incident in 1793 in which a young man named Henry Bedlow was accused of raping the stepdaughter of a ship's pilot in a brothel kept by a "Mother" Carey on Beekman Street. When Bedlow was acquitted, friends of the pilot tore apart Mother Carey's place and other nearby brothels and drove the inmates naked into the streets.[11]

The first public revelation that prostitution was widespread came, as we have seen, when the Reverend McDowall began issuing his sensational reports on vice in New York, both city and state. *McDowall's Journal* carried the names of so many houses of prostitution that it came to be known in less reverent circles as the Whorehouse Directory. It also told of the uninhibited South Seas maidens who came aboard United States warships when they anchored in Otaheite (Tahiti) harbor, as well as the sexual forays of American sailors in such notorious ports as Matanzas, Malaga, Messina, and Owahoo (Hawaii).[12] McDowall's revelations, including an exhibit for clergymen of obscene books, prints, and other articles, fascinated everyone but brought almost as many attacks on McDowall for publicizing wickedness as on the wickedness itself. Finally, a Grand Jury brought in a presentment against the *Journal* as injurious to morals and degrading to the character of the city. It was perfectly Victorian: the vice was ignored while the exposer was charged with the effects of the evil itself.

Only a nonreligious reformer, Robert Dale Owen, took the McDowall information seriously. Using the Magdalen Society's figure of 20,000 prostitutes in the city, Owen estimated that if each prostitute received only three visitors a day, the women were used 10,000,000 times annually; thus, half of all the adult males in the city visited a prostitute three times a week. Later estimates make the estimate of 20,000 seem wildly exaggerated. Still, the picture is of all manner of men seeking sexual satisfaction from women willing to give it whenever desired.

Little or nothing was done about the evil. During the war years prostitution increased so rapidly that by 1866 Bishop Simpson of the Methodist Episcopal Church asserted that there were as many prostitutes in New York as Methodists. Superintendent of Police John A. Kennedy called this a fearful exaggeration but then blandly admitted that there were 621 houses of prostitution, 96 houses of assignation, and 75 "concert saloons" of ill repute.[13] He also conceded that he had no way of knowing how many other available women roamed the streets or haunted the bars. What every aware person did know was that in New York a man with money could enjoy any vice at any time.

The vileness of the dives frequented by the brutalized poor in the ever-increasing slums of the city was not half so surprising as the elegance of the bordellos patronized by the affluent. Famous was a row of houses on upper Greene Street. Even more luxurious was the Seven Sisters, a "parlor house" that occupied no less than seven august brownstones in a row on West Twenty-fifth Street. With patrician ceremony the madam left engraved invitations for men registering at the best hotels. And the patrons not infrequently came in formal clothes. Not so large but even more exclusive was Josephine Wood's house on Clinton Place, west of Broadway. It welcomed only aristocrats, and every visitor had to identify himself to the satisfaction of the butler. The parlors where patrons waited were furnished with crystal chandeliers, deep velvet carpets, paintings, gilt-framed mirrors, and sofas upholstered in satin and brocade. The girls wore evening dresses and were models of decorum. Only champagne was served, and it was said that a girl could earn as much as $200 on a busy night. Josie Woods, of dark complexion and still beautiful, was herself a finished hostess. A familiar figure at Saratoga as well as in New York, she was known for her rich clothes, her diamonds, and her splendid carriages and horses.[14]

Equally notorious were some of the larger concert saloons. Perhaps the most curious was John Allen's dance hall and "fast" house on Water Street. Allen was a tough, wiry little man who made his girls wear short, low-necked scarlet dresses and sometimes spurred them on with blows and curses. The chief duty of the girls was to persuade the customers to buy drinks after each dance. Allen is particularly interesting because he had been a student at Union Theological Seminary, came of a well-to-do upstate family, and had several brothers in the clergy. He left religious tracts on the tables in his dance hall, put a Bible in the rooms to which the girls took their customers, and sometimes preached a sermon to his employees. One night when a group of evangelists descended on his place (they found him drunk) and conducted a prayer meeting, Allen was so impressed by the publicity that he let the clergymen continue to hold meetings in his hall. After a few months the hall was closed, and it was announced that Allen himself would lead revival meetings. Then a newspaperman uncovered the facts: The clergymen had rented both Allen's place and his cooperation.[15] The only lesson that could be derived from this was that clergymen would stoop fairly low to make converts.

But even more revealing than elegant bordellos or sanctimonious proprietors of dance saloons were the so-called houses of assignation. Many of these were located in the best neighborhoods, including Fifth Avenue. They guaranteed privacy, the man entering by one door, the woman by another. The busiest time, according to Dr. Sanger, who investigated the "commerce of the sexes" in the 1850's, was during the promenade hours on Broadway, approximately from noon to five o'clock. The men were often, Dr. Sanger reported, from the most respected walks of life, and the women "from our fashionable society." He suggested that in the preceding fifteen years a looseness in morals had been induced by easy money, theories of "free love," foreign influences, and such fashions as the "low-necked dress and the lascivious waltz."[16]

At the other extreme from the fashionable bordellos were loathsome dens where the services often included drugging and robbing the customer. In so-called panel-houses the owner of the establishment could reach into the room through panels in the wall and remove valuables from the clothes of the patron who was busy with the prostitute. Drinking and gambling were allowed in most houses.

Prostitutes who did not work in brothels generally sought their customers on the streets or in dance halls and bars. The upper tier in theaters was long one of their favorite haunts. Perhaps the boldest method of advertising used by enterprising harlots was the Personals columns of newspapers. There was no censorship of such notices, and the Personals in Bennett's *Herald* in particular became known as a kind of guide to prostitutes. Bennett was finally prosecuted and convicted under the obscenity laws.

Girls became inmates of the better houses because it was a relatively easy way to make money, or because they had been seduced and abandoned and could not support themselves in any other way, or simply—as only a few would admit—because they liked the life. Still others were recruited by men who went into the manufacturing towns and lured factory girls to the city with love, money and promises; the pitiful pay of working girls often made this an easy task. Once in the city the girls were soon taught how to sell themselves. Immigrant girls were sometimes recruited on the boats coming from Europe or were tricked into taking jobs as servants in brothels and then inveigled or forced into serving as prostitutes.

These were the sociological reasons. The psychological reasons were probably what they are today: a disturbed home life and a loveless childhood, hatred for the father, self-contempt, and a desire to punish the parents by abasing herself. One of the more subtle of modern psychological explanations of the prostitute's course seems to apply particularly to the Victorian prostitute—to wit, when a girl is taught that only degraded women enjoy sex, she may be able to have a sexual experience only when it is degrading to her.

Washington had its share of brothels, but it also developed, especially during the Civil War, its own variation of the trade in sex: the female lobbyist. These women arrived in Washington for the Congressional sessions, generally rented a fine house with a servant, carriage, and coachman, and entertained generously. Some of them gave parties that brought together susceptible Congressmen and sundry attractive, unattached young women. At the end of the Congressional session, their work done, the women packed their bags and vanished.[17]

Nor were other sections of the country any purer. Not a few women who followed in the wake of the young men who went west after the Civil War ended up as whores—"nymphs du prairie"—especially in such a railhead town as Dodge City, Kansas, or in the sedate row of brothels just off the main street of Denver. Dr. George H. Napheys declared in 1869 that there were 12,000 known prostitutes in Philadelphia and 7,000 in Cincinnati, and that Chicago had proportionately twice as many as New York and more than any European capital.[18] Dr. Edward B. Foote said there were at least 100,000 prostitutes in the United States during the war, and he hazarded that there were an even greater number of mistresses.[19] Hepworth Dixon, the British editor, capped these estimates by asserting that New York and a few other American cities were among the most corrupt in the world. Wrote Dixon:

> Men who know New York far worse than myself, assure me that in depth and darkness of iniquity, neither Paris in its private haunts, nor London in its open streets, can hold a candle to it. Paris may be subtler, London may be grosser, in its vices; but for largeness of depravity, for domineering insolence of sin, for rowdy callousness to censure, they tell me Atlantic City finds no rival on earth.[20]

Strong as Dixon's statement is, he does not appear to have been exaggerating greatly. George Ellington, a popular writer on New York life, tells in his *Women of New York* (1869) of the "grossest immoralities" and "Bacchanalian orgies" in parks on the outskirts of the city.[21]

The risk of making love outside of marriage was borne principally by women. And it was double-barreled: first there was the danger of pregnancy, and then, in many cases, of having to end the pregnancy by abortion. If the extent of prostitution at this time seems surprising, the prevalence of illegal abortion will seem astonishing.

We have seen how the question of controlling birth was broached in the 1830's by Owen and Knowlton. But the uses to which contraception and abortion were put are different. A woman who wanted to avoid conception had several alternatives: she could abstain from coitus or resort to *coitus interruptus* or to the substitutes for coitus. A woman who had become pregnant outside of marriage had almost no alternatives: because of the double standard, she was usually faced with ruin unless she could abort the pregnancy.

So abortion flourished. Up to 1830 it was not a statutory crime, but even after that, and especially after the middle of the century, abortionists carried on their practice with outrageous boldness. Some observers lumped abortion among the unmarried with that of wives who wanted to limit their families. Although both practices flouted the old religious prohibitions, the first defied purely sexual taboos while the second was a revolt of wives—especially of affluent women who liked their leisure and wanted to retain their physical appeal—against the obligation to bear children. The Reverend David Macrae, a Scottish visitor, declared that it was impossible to travel in the United States without noting the "frightful prevalence" of the practice of getting medical aid to avoid maternity. Newspapers, he wrote, "swarmed" with advertisements for abortion medicines and for books on this "diabolical art." A medical man, he reported, enumerated thirty practitioners of this "species of murder" in one large city, and in every city establishments with such names as "Invalids' Retreat" offered this service.[22] But other observers assumed that abortionists were patronized mainly by women pregnant outside of marriage. A French traveler, Auguste Carlier, reported in his book *Marriage in the United States* that a respected professor in a medical school declared in 1859 that every physician was often asked by respectable-looking "fathers and mothers of unborn children . . . to destroy the fruit of illicit pleasure."[23]

The crudeness of the advertisements for abortions or abortive medicines is amazing. Who could possibly mistake the meaning of "Sure cure for Ladies in trouble. No injurious medicines or instruments used. Consultation and free advice," or the advertisement that offered "Portuguese Female Pills" that "must not be used during pregnancy for they are certain to produce miscarriage"? [24]

The most striking evidence of the prevalence of abortion, however, was the fame of its leading practitioner, Madame Restell. Every book on New York life that dipped below the surface treated her Fifth Avenue mansion as a kind of landmark, a shrine of shame, dreadful but fascinating. The accounts of her activities competed in lurid details: the heavily veiled women arriving at the side door, the money that Madame—she was English born—was reputed to have paid to escape arrest, and finally, her end—vindication of God and morality—in which, trapped by Comstock, she cut her throat. Every large city had its counterparts of Madame Restell. An abortionist whom Comstock arrested in Boston was a deacon and a member of the YMCA. In smaller cities and towns midwives sometimes undertook such tasks.

There were two other alternatives, both unhappy, for an unmarried woman who became pregnant. She might bear the child and then abandon it; it would then generally end in a foundling home. Or she could do away with the infant. Although infanticide seems to have been more widespread among the poor of London, it is mentioned by every writer on moral problems in America.

It would be misleading to give the impression that these practices were common; but they were evidently familiar enough to worldly persons to make vaunted Victorian purity seem only another pretense of the Gilded Age.

The increase in the divorce rate after the middle of the century may not have been directly related to the double standard, but it was another sign of underground resistance to the old restrictions. Almost every nineteenth-century reformer in the field of women's rights and marriage problems declared that for a couple to live together when they no longer loved each other was legalized prostitution. They argued that it embittered the couple, led to discord, and made an unhappy home for children. Conservatives, led by the clergy and supported by the Bible and tradition, claimed that liberalizing the divorce laws would encourage promiscuity, destroy the family, and lead to the wide-scale neglect of children. But unhappily married couples tended more and more to see the justice in the attitude of the reformers.

Where the French statesman Alexis de Tocqueville declared in his celebrated books on America in the early 1830's that marriage ties were nowhere as much respected as in America—he had come from a France marked by the lax morality that had followed the Revolution—his countryman Carlier reported in 1860 that divorce was widespread in the United States and more common than in France. A writer in the *New Englander* in 1868 declared that divorce laws were so lax that they enabled a man to practice polygamy by having several wives in succession instead of simultaneously.

A national investigation by Carroll D. Wright in 1888 of 328,716 divorces between 1867 and 1886 showed that the divorce rate had increased almost three times as rapidly as the population.[25] The rise was almost as large in some rural areas as it was in the cities, and it was generally greater in the western territories. Sixty percent of the divorces were granted on the grounds of adultery, with desertion, cruelty, acts of crime, and drunkenness accounting for the other decrees. The main factors behind the rise were said to be increasing tendency of families to keep moving, the spread of luxury and a consequent aversion to drudgery and housework, and the growing independence of women. Although there are no figures on separations, observers agreed that they were numerous, especially among the poor. In fact, one writer called desertion the divorce of the poor.

The strongest force against the relaxation of the divorce laws was the social disapproval that, under the double standard, faced the woman. So lawyers appeared who enabled couples to get a divorce with a minimum of publicity and almost no scandal. Observers reported that "divorce mills" operated in many large cities. The Reverend Macrae found that in Chicago, which he described as notorious for its fast life and immorality, divorce was common. Macrae told of one advertisement by a Chicago law firm that claimed that it had obtained three hundred divorces and that it made no charge if it did not secure a decree.[26]

Among the upper class and the socially ambitious middle class a stigma still marked divorce until late in the century. Recalling the attitude of fashionable society toward divorce in 1870, Mrs. John King Van Renssalaer wrote some fifty years later:

> That domestic troubles should ever end in a divorce court was unthinkable; so families remained intact whatever happened, and the most outrageous conduct by husbands and fathers was accorded no further publicity than the whisper of gossip . . . the much deplored, frequently assailed morals of current Society are no bit worse than they were in the prim and prudish half century ago. In that day the woman who obtained a divorce was a Pariah.[27]

It would be hard to find a clearer statement of the cruelty of the Victorian code. Confirmation of this comes from a penetrating novelist, Edith Wharton, who belonged to this class herself. In her novel of life in the upper crust in the 1870's, *The Age of Innocence,* Ellen Mingott, a young woman of New York society, deserts her husband, a Polish count, because she finds him "a brute." She returns to America and is accepted back into society but is threatened with ostracism if she divorces the count. Although she despises hypocrisy, she yields to the tribal code.

But this rigid opposition began to break down in the 1890's. Exercising the privilege of wealth, the second and third generation of the parvenus and robber barons made divorce seem, if not fashionable, at least not an eternal disgrace. There was apparently little shock in 1895 when William Kissam Vanderbilt, grandson of the Commodore, a man enamored mainly of luxurious yachts, divorced his wife Alva, a leader of society.

Beginning in the 1870's the tendency of the *nouveaux riches* to marry off their daughters to the fortune-hunting sons of Europe's frayed nobility made it increasingly difficult for the *haut monde* to maintain the fiction of the sanctity of marriage. Jay Gould's younger daughter Anna, a spoiled and unattractive girl, acquired an insolent, posturing French count who squandered no less than $5,000,000 of her inheritance before she divorced him and married his cousin, a marquis. Unlike Edith Wharton's Ellen Mingott some thirty years earlier, Anna Gould had little or no concern for the opinions of her tribe or clan. Always aping its financial betters, the middle class would take only another decade or two to achieve the same attitude toward divorce.

Other forces besides the example of the arrogant new rich combined after 1850 to break down the old taboos and the single code of conduct: immigrants from many different traditions, the poor living by their own code in the slums, the best youth of New England going off to greener fields, and the rise of New York, Chicago, and San Francisco as magnetic centers of American life. Finally there was the political corruption beginning in the days of President Grant in Washington and "Boss" Tweed in New York. Such corruption, especially on the local level, fed on commercial vice. By the time of the "Gay Nineties"—gay of course only for those who had the means—most of the larger cities were "wide open," with prostitution, gambling, and drinking flourishing on every level. Such enclaves of pleasure as New York's Tenderloin and Haymarket were known across the nation, and their restaurants, bars, and concert saloons were imitated everywhere. New Yorkers, an increasingly cosmopolitan and tolerant breed, appeared to be undisturbed by the reputation of such districts, if not proud of it.

Then, in February, 1892, the Reverend Charles Parkhurst, a dignified, bewhiskered, highly respected clergyman, shattered the pattern of Sunday sermon clichés with a thunderous attack on the city administration as "a lying, perjured, rum-soaked and libidinous lot." Every effort "to make men respectable, honest, temperate and sexually clean," he charged, "is a direct blow between the eyes of the Mayor and his whole gang of drunken and lecherous subordinates." Brothels, gambling houses, and saloons, he said, were "protected" by police in return for carefully graded and regular payments.

The mayor, rich, well-born Hugh Grant, the puppet of Richard Croker, the most rapacious Tammany boss after Tweed, challenged Dr. Parkhurst to prove his charges. Summoned before a Grand Jury, the clergyman declared that he had based his allegations on newspaper accounts that no one had contradicted. The Grand Jury rebuked him sharply, and he appeared to be discredited.

But Dr. Parkhurst was angered and aroused. Backed by a group of righteous men of wealth, he hired a detective to take him and a young associate into the worst dens in the city. Disguised in shabby clothes, the trio spent three weeks visiting brothels, Chinese opium dens, saloons, and every other kind of dive. Whores solicited them from the stoops of houses, and pimps came around to collect the earnings of the girls. At a place with the gruesomely humorous name of Paresis Hall, the investigators saw a police precinct captain enter, look around, speak to the owner, and leave.

Fortified with sworn affidavits, Dr. Parkhurst returned to his pulpit and eloquently recounted his perilous descent into the abyss; he concluded that anyone who denied that vice was protected by city officials was a fool or a knave. For two years thereafter, assisted by private detectives and a corps of volunteers, the Reverend Parkhurst waged his campaign of exposure in pulpit, newspapers, and courtrooms. Significantly, some of the bitterest opposition to him came from leaders in social and financial circles. Their attitude was: Reform hurts business.[28]

Finally the Republican-controlled state legislature, happy to embarrass the Democratic city administration, appointed an investigating committee under Senator Lexow. The Lexow investigation became a national sensation, exposing not only politicians, police, and criminals, but many prominent citizens. Curiously, some of the purveyors of forbidden pleasure did not oppose the investigation; as business people they had found it more and more difficult to operate profitably in the face of police blackmail and "shakedowns." Chiefly to appease critics, the police made spectacular raids on brothels. But as soon as the prostitutes were arraigned in court they were bailed out by local politicians and allowed to return to work.

In the end it was not so much the evidence of vice itself as the police graft that outraged the citizenry. When the most popular police officer in the city, Captain Max Schmittberger, broke down and revealed in detail how protection money was collected and passed upward through the hierarchy, it became clear that heads must roll. Boss Croker slipped off to Europe, and in 1894 a Fusion Party made up of reform groups elected a mayor, William L. Strong, who gave the city an honest and efficient administration.

But success, as it always does, ended the reform movement. Three years later Croker returned to New York, and Tammany elected its candidate for mayor under the brazen campaign slogan of "To Hell with Reform." So the century closed with reform repudiated, and vice, if not triumphant, at least flourishing. And it was little different in cities and towns everywhere across the land. The lid had been on too long. More and more, under the cover of gentility and the tokens of decorum, there was decadence and corruption.

19.

DEVIATIONS AND DIVERSIONS

JEWS and Christians have always denounced as wicked all sexual acts besides copulation between man and woman. Such acts made Sodom the arch-symbol of depravity. Underlying this code was the religious conviction that sexuality should serve only to beget children. But all libidinous urges, including those that Christians and Jews think wicked and abnormal, are sexual, not religious, in origin. That is why laws have never succeeded in stamping them out. When a civilization, such as that of ancient Greece, has no such prejudices or taboos, the love of men for boys, or of women for other women, comes into the open. But when a society, such as that of early America, forbids such relationships, they are disguised or go underground. It is difficult to document this statement, but whatever glimpses we do get of these practices in an earlier America suggest that forbidding them did little or nothing to end them.

By the nineteenth century the strict restraints on sexual activity were beginning to stimulate a variety of open evasions. Among the more innocuous of these were risqué entertainments such as the *tableaux vivants* or *poses plastiques*—the use of French warns us that they are daring—that became popular in the 1840's. These performances, in which lightly draped girls gave the illusion of nudity, were first given at Palmo's Opera House in New York but were soon being imitated in taverns at every price from sixpence to a dollar. The most refined performance was given at the Broadway Odeon, a fashionable café, which offered tableaux ranging from "Eve in the Garden of

Eden" to "Esther in the Persian Bath." The police raided the café on the Sabbath, but the owners paid a fine and the tableaux continued to flourish with less and less drapery until some places were showing completely naked girls behind gauze.[1] The police finally put a limit on the boldness of the shows and by 1848 the New York *Sunday Messenger* was asking what had happened to

> Those nice *tableaux vivants*
> Of beautiful young ladies, *sans*
> Both petticoats and pants,
> Who, scorning fashion's shifts and whims,
> Did nightly crowds delight,
> By showing up their handsome limbs
> At fifty cents a sight.[2]

Fashionable society also turned in the 1840's to Italian opera, which was free to deal with illicit love because the public paid no attention to it and because members of the audience who did not understand Italian often did not know what was going on.

Although these outlets were still denounced by preachers, they were hardly grave evasions of the sexual code. Infinitely more abhorrent in Victorian eyes were those who turned to their own sex for gratification. Women in particular, forced to deny their sexual urges, formed fervent attachments to other women. They were encouraged in this by the view of man as sensual and animal and woman as pure and chaste. It was assumed that woman's relationship with a man was always in danger of becoming physical, while an association with another woman would remain spiritual.

Intense friendships between women were of course accepted without question. What happened when two women found that a friendship could become sexual we do not know. No outsider was likely to recognize the relationship for what it was. It is therefore not surprising that the earliest clear identification of such a relationship came from a Frenchman, Moreau de St. Méry. A West Indian lawyer who had played a role in the French Revolution, St. Méry became a bookseller in the 1790's among the émigrés in Philadelphia. A worldly man, he recognized the true nature of the liaisons he saw among certain women, declaring in his journal: "I am going to say something that is almost unbelievable. These women, without real love and without passions, give themselves up at an early age to the enjoyment of themselves; and they are not at all strangers to being willing to seek unnatural pleasures with persons of their own sex."[3] An extraordinary glimpse, it reveals how little historians have told us of the private lives of some of our forebears.

We do know of several prominent women whose associations with other women were at times ardent and loverlike. Sentimental friendships marked by gushing declarations of affection were fashionable, but they sometimes seem to have been more than merely sentimental. As we saw, the masculine qualities in Margaret Fuller drew her to women who had the kind of feminine charms she herself lacked. She was, moreover, fascinated by instances in history and literature of intimate relationships—some of them known to have been sexual—between members of the same sex. She wrote:

> It is so true that a woman may be in love with a woman, and a man with a man. . . . It is regulated by the same laws as that of love between persons of different sexes, and it is purely intellectual and spiritual, unprofaned by any mixture of lower instincts. . . . Why did Socrates love Alcibiades? Why did Kaiser so love Schneider? How natural is the love of Wallenstein for Max, that of Madame de Staël for Récamier, mine for ——! I loved —— for a time with as much passion as I was then strong enough to feel. . . . She loved me, for I well remember her suffering when she first could feel my faults. . . .[4]

The women's rights movement seems to have fostered passionate attachments among its members. Whether they came into the movement because of an attraction to other women or whether the movement released pent-up feelings, a number of leading feminists developed a more than sisterly relationship to each other. Clearly sexual was the interest of Susan B. Anthony, long-time leader of the movement, in her young protegés, and, as Andrew Sinclair has shown, especially in Anna Dickinson. Miss Anthony was a severe-looking spinster—source of many caricatures of the typical suffragist—while Anna Dickinson was, at the height of her fame during and after the Civil War, a vibrant young woman, the "Joan of Arc" of the war. But in her letters to her young friend, Miss Anthony, far from being cold and austere, revealed herself pathetically full of girlish yearnings. Her letters are sprinkled with such endearments as "Dicky darling Anna" and "Dear Chick a dee dee," and she is constantly wanting to give Anna "one awful long squeeze." She tries to make her promise "not to *marry a man,*" and she holds out the attractions of her flat in New York: "*I have plain quarters . . . double bed*—and big enough and good enough to take you *in*— So come and see me." And again: "I do so long for the scolding and pinched ears and everything I know awaits me. . . . What worlds of experience since I last snuggled the wee child in my long arms." Even many years later, when Anna had aged, Susan Anthony could still write to her that she had had many "Anna girls" and "nieces," as they called themselves, but none like her first Anna.[5]

Similarly, in the late 1840's at Oberlin College, Antoinette Brown, the first woman divinity student, fell passionately in love with an older student, Lucy Stone, an active abolitionist and feminist. Her letters to Miss Stone mix religious fervor with undisguised longing. After she had become a minister in a small town in New York, she begged Lucy, her "dearest little cow boy," to visit her, and added, "I love you Lucy any way, and if you would only come and take a nap with me here on my bed my head would get rested a great deal faster for it is aching now."[6] This was written by a woman already known for her self-reliance and independence.

It is doubtful that these attachments, however intense, led to sexual consummation. Such religious women suffered from a double set of inhibiting beliefs: first, that women had to rise above the animal nature of men, and, second, that any "unnatural" sexual activity was a deadly sin.

Although countless cloyingly sentimental attachments are described in the fiction of the period, in only one instance that I know of does the association seem plainly sexual. In Brown's *Ormond,* the narrator, Sophia Westwyn, abandoned as a child by a profligate mother, is brought up by the Dudleys and learns to love their daughter Constantia. Years later, as Sophia is about to marry an American in Italy, she hears that Constantia has been left destitute. After only a week of marriage, Sophia rushes back to the United States and seeks out Constantia. The next three days were spent, Sophia writes,

> . . . in a state of dizziness and intoxication. . . . The appetite for sleep and food were . . . lost within the impetuosities of a master passion. To look and to talk to each other afforded enchanting occupation for every moment. I would not part from her side, but ate and slept, walked and mused and read, with my arm locked in hers, and with her breath fanning my cheek.[7]

The best explanation for Brown's boldness here, as elsewhere in *Ormond,* is that he was still writing under the liberating influence of Godwin.

Only here and there, late in the century, do we get a guarded acknowledgment of such practices. Not only is the "deadly habit of self-abuse" common among girls, wrote Henry N. Guernsey, a doctor with forty years' experience, but "it is true that some young ladies, the sweetest and fairest of our race, play with one another in an immodest and indecent way, teaching immorality to the pure and innocent." [8] How prudish this statement was can be best appreciated by comparing it with, say, the theory of infant sexuality being prepared at about the same time by a Viennese doctor named Sigmund Freud.

The emotionalism born of frustration also affected some men, especially those of an impressionable nature. Although the double standard allowed them certain sexual liberties, the untouchable purity of "good" women and the sordidness of prostitutes doubtless encouraged some youths to fix their affections on other men. The attitude that such affection was unmanly and effeminate may have discouraged conscious homosexuality—although men separated from women ignore this—but among the educated the open expression of love of man for man was not uncommon. Thus James Thome, a young music teacher at Oberlin who had become a passionate disciple of abolitionist Theodore Weld, wrote to his idol in 1838:

> Pardon my frankness when I say that I have never been able, hitherto, to satisfy myself that you reciprocated *even a little* of that affection which I . . . cherished for you, but which I have been restrained from expressing lest it might appear to

> your masculine, Roman nature girlish and sickly . . . and often when the gushings of my soul have prompted me to throw my arms around your neck and kiss you, I have violently quelled these impulses and affected a *manly* bearing. . . .

Then, ingenuously identifying the role he would like to play, he adds: ". . . your stern voice startles me from my maiden dreams." But soon Weld married and so did Thome.[9]

Even more explicit—as recent biographies have disclosed—were the letters Henry James in his late fifties wrote to a young American sculptor, Hendrik Andersen. Frustrated by long absences and only fleeting meetings, James revealed a pathetic yearning for the younger artist. When Andersen's brother died, James wrote:

> The sense that I can't help you, see you, talk to you, touch you, hold you close and long, or do anything to make you rest on me and feel my participation—this torments me, dearest boy, makes me ache for you. . . . I wish I could go to Rome and put my hands on you (oh, how lovingly I should lay them!) but that, alas, is odiously impossible. . . .[10]

No hint of such an intense relationship appears in any of James' endless probing of emotional ties.

One of the more curious aspects of the sensational trial of the Reverend Henry Ward Beecher on the charge of seducing Theodore Tilton's wife was the fervent expressions of love that were constantly being exchanged by members of the circle. Early in their relationship, young Tilton wrote to Beecher: ". . . my gratitude cannot be written in words but must be expressed only in love." The two men sometimes kissed on meeting each other, and at a reconciliation after the scandal had begun, Beecher clasped Tilton's face and kissed him on the mouth. It was such behavior that caused that acerb-tongued, old-fashioned New Yorker, George Templeton Strong, to write in his diary:

> Plymouth Church is a nest of "psychological phenomena," *vulgo vocato* lunatics, and its chief Brahmin is as moonstruck as his devotees. Verily they are a peculiar people. They all call each other by their first names and perpetually kiss one another. The Rev. Beecher seduces Mrs. Tilton and then kisses her husband, and he seems to acquiesce in the osculation. . . . They all

> seem, on their showing, to have been afflicted with moral and mental insanity.[11]

Americans in general did not of course go so far in emotionalism as did Beecher and the Tiltons. But the Brooklyn group in their combination of religion, sentiment, and sexuality represented post-Civil War America far more than did that staid lawyer and pillar of society, Mr. Strong.

Except in Whitman's work, there seems to have been no open acknowledgment in the nineteenth-century-American writing of the homosexual impulse. The nearest approach to it occurs in Melville's novels. From his experiences at sea Melville was plainly aware of the attachments between men that spring up in the womanless society of a whaling ship or a man-o'-war. An almost classic instance of this is Billy Budd, the fair-haired, trusting, virginal youth who fascinates both the satanic Master-at-Arms Claggart and the noble Captain Vere. Claggart gets a deep, sadistic pleasure out of hurting Billy; and Vere must finally exorcise the youth by allowing him to be destroyed.

A much more open example, and one unrelated to the special loneliness of sailors, is the boyhood relationship in *Pierre* between Pierre and his cousin Glen. It was a love, we are told, that fell short by only "one degree, of the sweetest sentiments entertained between the sexes," a relationship full of jealousies, "occasional fillips and spicinesses," and letters from Glen throughout which he addresses his cousin as "beloved Pierre." Had Melville seen the attachment as not even one degree short of the love between the sexes, he would of course never have dared to say so.

There were other deviations. And Dr. Napheys declared that every "unnatural lust" recorded in Juvenal, Martial, and Petronius was practiced, not in rare instances but deliberately and habitually. He writes that he could tell of restaurants frequented by men in women's dress who indulged in indescribable lewdness. A similar observation comes from a European source. In a privately printed book defending homosexuality, John Addington Symonds quotes a correspondent in a German medical manual as declaring that when he visited the United States in 1870 he found homosexuality there more common than at home. "I was able," he adds, "to indulge my passions with less fear of punishment or persecution. . . . I discovered that I was always immediately recognized as a member of the confraternity." [12]

The increasingly cosmopolitan character of American cities encouraged more and more sophisticated vices. In the 1880's Italian *padroni* went about with bands of boys and girls who fiddled and begged in the streets; they also set up brothels in which girls of ten and twelve were the main attraction. When the crusading Reverend Parkhurst insisted on seeing something worse than ordinary houses of prostitution, his detective guide took him to the Golden Rule Pleasure Club on West Third Street. The visitors were shown into a basement divided into cubicles in each of which sat a youth with his face painted, the airs of a young girl, a high falsetto voice, and a girl's name. When the guide whispered to the Reverend Parkhurst what the boys did, the clergyman fled in horror.[13] There were similar establishments in other parts of the city.

Boy prostitutes could also be found on the streets. James Huneker, urbane critic of the arts, tells of walking up Broadway with the young novelist Stephen Crane one night in 1894 and being accosted by a boy with eyes painted purple. Crane fed the boy, and when the lad said that he needed treatment for a disease, Crane borrowed fifty dollars and gave it to him. Crane then began a novel, called *Flowers of Asphalt,* about an innocent country boy who comes to the city and turns prostitute. But when he read a part of it to an older novelist, Hamlin Garland, Garland was horrified. Crane abandoned the work.[14]

Although on the surface the proprieties were being maintained as rigidly as ever, the swing toward greater freedom was well under way. It would continue until it reached a point in our time when homosexuality would be received in some cosmopolitan circles and among youth seeking new forms of excitement as just another form of sexual expression.

20.

THE INSUPPRESSIBLE URGE

SOME students see all erotic urges as containing a principle hostile to society, with unsanctioned love forever hurling defiance at institutions and laws. The sexual passions may of course be suppressed for a time, but they surface stubbornly, and when they have been suppressed violently they sometimes surface violently. There was not a decade from 1790 to 1900 when one or more scandals of passion did not shatter the genteel patterns of American life. The details of these trespasses almost always suggest that certain otherwise respectable men and women would stop at nothing to have sexual gratification of each other. All the laws and sermons clearly influenced only outward appearances; underneath, the passions remained almost constant.

In the first years of the republic the story of tragic passion that most aroused moral fervor was that of Elizabeth Whitman. The daughter of a Hartford minister, she was related on her mother's side to Pierpont Edwards and Aaron Burr, respectively son and grandson of Jonathan Edwards, both of them brilliant men but with a reputation for licentiousness.

All that is known for certain of the Whitman affair is that in June of 1788 a woman dressed in black spent a month at the old Bell Tavern in Danvers, Massachusetts. She talked to no one. The woman fell ill and within a few weeks died. She was identified as Elizabeth Whitman and was said to have fled from her home when she found herself pregnant by her married lover. Legend and a novel, *The Coquette* (1797) by Hannah Foster, the wife of a Massachusetts clergyman, described Elizabeth as a gifted girl but a coquette with a wild nature; they said that she had turned away two worthy suitors, both clergymen, and had put her trust in a known profligate. Rumor added that the lover was Pierpont Edwards. For years the story did duty as the theme of sermons and lectures, and the novel, a pallid imitation of *Clarissa,* became one of the most popular of the age.

It did not matter that the original Elizabeth Whitman was at her death not a giddy girl but a mature woman, that she had faithfully nursed her first suitor in his last illness, that her second suitor had been subject to fits of depression or that Pierpont Edwards was at the Continental Congress in Philadelphia during most of this period.[1] Rumor preferred to have it that Elizabeth Whitman ruined her life because she put pleasure before piety, and self-indulgence before honor. Nothing was said of the character of the man who was said to have deceived her: it was her fault for having trusted him.

It would be easy to make much of the fact that many of the irreligious or morally careless men in these pages were the sons of clergymen. But the examples of Pierpont Edwards and Aaron Burr are too glaring to ignore; such men were obviously driven to seek release by the pressures of their rigid Calvinist upbringing. We cannot document Pierpont Edwards' philanderings, but many of his contemporaries who referred to him lamented that his talents as a lawyer, jurist, and defender of minority causes should have been coupled with licentiousness.

Unlike Edwards, Aaron Burr was not only too prominent to be able to conceal his amours, but a strange kind of compulsion led him to record them in his journal. Aaron's father was a strict and scholarly minister, and Aaron made an attempt to live up to the family tradition by attending divinity school. But he soon turned to the law because he had lost interest in religion and because he evidently saw no place in the ministry for a man with his passion for women. His rise to prominence in government, climaxed by his term as Vice President, was marked by amatory as well as political intrigues. Short, slight, and hardly a striking figure, it is difficult to explain his undeniable way with women except for his own consuming interest in them.

The most extraordinary evidence of his sexuality came in 1808 when, widowed, in his fifties, and sick of his disgrace after his duel with Hamilton, he went abroad. A great admirer of Mary

Wollstonecraft's theories, he had given his daughter Theodosia a superior education. The travel journal he kept for Theodosia, by then a married woman with children of her own, records various trysts, sometimes with housemaids or prostitutes, all over Europe. These entries, in a codelike, abbreviated French, at times express a kind of shame at his addiction. But even his deep-rooted contempt for hypocrisy can hardly justify his telling her exactly how much he paid for an evening with some stray woman and how well she served him.[2]

Burr's final exploit was his marriage to the dissolute Madame Jumel when he was seventy-seven and penniless and she was almost sixty and quite affluent. She proved more than a match for Burr; when he began spending her money on one of his wild schemes, she sued him for divorce, charging infidelity. Since he was almost eighty, the charge may have been exaggerated.[3]

The enemies of Aaron Burr insisted that he was an utterly profligate man, but the curious fact is that except in his sexuality he was most abstemious. Burr's career was in any event hurt far more by his political scheming than by his amorality. For a time there was, as we have seen, a spirit of tolerance in the young republic. A hundred years earlier Burr would have been pilloried; fifty years later he would have been ostracized as a reprobate. Perhaps the widest repercussion of his sexual activities was a pornographic work, *The Amorous Intrigues of Aaron Burr.*

Because Burr killed Hamilton with cold efficiency and Hamilton faced death serenely, Hamilton has appeared to be the victim of Burr's demonic envy. But Hamilton was himself a stiff-necked and arrogant man and a harsh rival. He also had his errant moments sexually. Considering how some of his crueler foes used the fact that he was born to the common-law wife of a man who later deserted his family—"the bastard brat of a Scotch peddler" was the nasty way John Adams put it—one would have expected him to be more than careful in his behavior with women. He was not. Although he was a devoted husband, he could not resist flirting with other women. And the Reynolds affair revealed that he had not stopped at flirtation.

In 1792, while Hamilton was Secretary of the Treasury, several of his enemies thought they had proof that he had profited privately from his official decisions. A shady character named James Reynolds had shown them evidence that Hamilton had paid him $1,100 for what Reynolds said was help in Hamilton's speculations. The three politicians—one of them was James Monroe—confronted Hamilton. Despite what were surely sickening misgivings, Hamilton revealed that the money had been paid to keep Reynolds silent about the affair Hamilton had been having with Mrs. Reynolds. Obviously preferring to risk his moral reputation and marital happiness rather than his political honor, he told the three men how Mrs. Reynolds had appealed to him for financial help and how he had gone to her lodgings and was soon meeting her whenever he could. Then Reynolds himself had turned up with threats and with demands for money. Hamilton had met Reynolds' demands and continued to see Mrs. Reynolds.

The three politicians decided not to make use of Hamilton's confession, but five years later a hack journalist published the entire story. The blow was stunning: when Hamilton recovered he himself made public his explanation, once again choosing moral rather than political disgrace.[4] The episode seems not to have done him much permanent harm; he emerged from the duel with Burr a martyr, and the Reynolds episode is now quite forgotten.

The late eighteenth century was a time of changing standards, and it tolerated a number of men who were as liberal morally as they were politically. It may be said, of course, that the amatory activities of Franklin, Pierpont Edwards, Burr, and Hamilton were clandestine and not a true challenge to conventional standards. It is worth noting that all four were as outspoken on political and social affairs as they were silent on the sexual code.

But there were crimes of sexuality during the first half of the nineteenth century that everyone knew about. The prevailing primness did not prevent a few of these from being as ugly and violent as those of the most dissolute era. One was the brutal murder in 1836 of Helen Jewett, "a girl of the town," in an elegant brothel run by a Roxanna Townsend. The murderer, Richard P. Robinson, apparently the girl's favorite young man, was a youth of good appearance and manners. Miss Townsend later testified that she had brought Robinson a bottle of champagne at eleven P.M. while he was in bed with Miss Jewett. Later that night, Robinson, either out of jealousy or because he feared she would reveal their affair to his society sweetheart, slew Miss Jewett with a hatchet. But he had influential friends, and, as former Mayor Philip Hone indignantly recorded in his journal, it was said that these friends secured his acquittal by bribing witnesses and jurors. Hone was even more agitated when, during the trial, he found himself surrounded by young men like Robinson who knew all the prostitutes who testified, and joked with each other throughout the proceedings. Hone's notes reveal the latitude allowed average young men of the period and challenges the schoolbook version of the young republic as a time of innocence and unsophistication.[5]

A crime that shocked New Yorkers because it also implicated some fairly respectable young people was the murder of Mary Rogers in August, 1841. The case became even more famous when in the following year, before it had been solved, Poe based one of his detective stories, "The Mystery of Marie Roget," on it. Mary Cecilia Rogers was an attractive girl of good character who was well liked by the customers of the Broadway cigar store where she was an attendant. One day her body was found in the Hudson River off Hoboken with "horrid marks" of violence on her person. Then, a year later, a confession by a suitor revealed that the girl had died while undergoing an abortion. Although Poe's story had cleverly anticipated that a former suitor was guilty of the crime, Poe showed far less interest in the human aspects of the deed than in the exercise of "ratiocination" in solving it. He ignored the agonizing plight of the girl and the dreadful role of the man who had made her pregnant and then watched her die.

Scandals in general, with their newspaper publicity, courtroom confrontations, and bitter charges, give us a glimpse of what went on behind the drawn shades of Victorian homes. To examine this evidence we must take advantage of the fact that many newspapers and magazines invaded privacy and paraded intimate details of family life with a freedom unmatched today. In a way, the Victorian seized on such morsels even more hungrily than do we who have easy access to far more candid and clinical disclosures on stage and screen and in books.

One of the first major scandals to reveal a marked sexual sophistication and no concern for sin or propriety was the

Sickles-Key affair. Compared to it, the Jewett murder was the rash act of insolent youth. The son of a New York patent attorney, Daniel Sickles was a politician constantly at the center of controversy or scandal. Something of a rake, he was known for such exploits as turning up at a session of the New York State Assembly with Fanny White, a young woman he had plucked from a Mercer Street brothel. Even when he married Teresa Bagioli, sixteen-year-old daughter of a musician of some note, it was whispered that he had seduced not only the daughter but also the mother.[6]

Elected to Congress in 1856 as a supporter of Buchanan, Sickles leased the Stockton mansion on Washington's patrician Lafayette Square and began entertaining on a grand scale. Ironically it was Sickles himself who introduced his wife to handsome, thirty-eight-year-old Philip Barton Key, son of Francis Scott Key and widower with four children. Key began to escort Mrs. Sickles to the weekly hop at Willard's Hotel whenever Sickles was busy. And Sickles was often busy, not only with politics and legal work but with other women.

The first tremor of disaster came early in 1859 when a young friend of the Sickleses, a government clerk, asserted that he had repeatedly seen Teresa and Key ride to a house outside the city. Sickles confronted Key with the charge. Key immediately challenged the friend to repeat the accusation, whereupon the youth fled to New York. Having thus allayed Sickles' suspicions, Key returned to his trysting with hardly more prudence than before. Soon Sickles received an anonymous letter informing him that Key was meeting Mrs. Sickles in a rented house on Fifteenth Street. Distraught with humiliation and rage, Sickles challenged his wife. She broke down and admitted everything. Sickles forced her to write out a groveling confession. It read in part: "I have been in a house on Fifteenth Street with Mr. Key. How many times I don't know. . . . I did what is usual for a wicked woman to do. . . . Was there on Wednesday last. . . . I undressed myself. Mr. Key undressed also. . . . I do not deny that we have had connection in that house . . . in the parlor, on the sofa. . . ."[7]

The following day Sickles called in an old friend to advise him. As they talked, Sickles suddenly saw Key waving a handkerchief at the house from the square outside. Seizing a pistol,

Sickles rushed out into the street. Shouting, "Key, you scoundrel, you have dishonored my bed—you must die!" he fired twice. Key fell, and died a few minutes later.

The shock waves that went out from Sickles' act reached the President; bumblingly, Buchanan tried to suppress the news. Some Southerners were troubled only by the fact that Key had been unarmed; gallantry apparently prescribed that Sickles should have given Key an opportunity to kill as well as cuckold him. At the trial Sickles pleaded temporary insanity—the first use of such a plea—resulting from the "defilement" of his marriage bed. The prosecution, fearing Buchanan's displeasure, made no attempt to show that Sickles had defiled that bed time and again. The trial was thus converted from a prosecution of Sickles for murder into a condemnation of Key for adultery. Sickles was triumphantly acquitted and fifteen hundred admirers gathered to congratulate him. The following day Sickles told a friend: "Of course I intended to kill him. He deserved it." [8] To the dismay of his supporters, he rejoined his wife a few months later.

For a time Sickles was ostracized. But when war came he raised a full brigade, qualifying him as a brigadier general, and he soon became known as a cocky commander. The gay dances and lavish banquets he gave during the winter encampment were the talk of Washington. But the gaiety was short-lived. At Gettysburg, Sickles lost 4,200 men in four hours and was carried from the field with a shattered leg. Later, Grant made him Minister to Spain, ignoring his record of headstrong conduct. In Spain Sickles entertained the élite of Madrid like a grandee. Since poor Teresa had died suddenly at thirty-one, he was more than ever free to pursue his amours. His most spectacular conquest was Queen Isabella of Spain, who lived in exile in Paris.

Falling out with the regime in Spain, Sickles resigned in protest. For a few years he lived in Paris. Although his wife and two children were with him, he engaged as always in intrigues and amatory adventures. He had inherited a fortune, but in time, spending and speculation wiped it out. He died penniless—but as unrepentant as ever.

It is impossible to classify Daniel Sickles. He made a mockery of many of the Alger virtues, but his fate hardly serves as an object lesson: he lived to the age of ninety-five, often in posts of honor and responsibility, and constantly enjoying sinful pleasures to the full. The Sickles-Key affair betrayed a confusion amounting to a triple standard. Sickles assumed his right to philander but felt impelled to murder a man who philandered with his wife. For Mrs. Sickles there was no punishment mainly because she was considered a subject creature too helpless to be blamed for what any man did to her.

In 1859 the nation was shocked by the Sickles-Key affair. Eleven years later the Fisk-Stokes affair was simply another scandal. Compared to Sickles, Fisk was a knave whom decent citizens deplored—as much because he was a vulgarian as because he was a libertine. But neither the law, the church, nor the opinion of the community was able to discourage him in the slightest.

Having bought Pike's Opera House, Fisk and Jay Gould rented offices in it to their Erie Railroad, redecorating it in rococo splendor. Fisk's office was a magnificent chamber with thick rugs, silken draperies, mirrors, and a marble washstand decorated with the figures of nymphs. A passageway gave Fisk direct access to the stage of the opera house and, more important, to the female members of the company. Gossip, possibly exaggerated, soon told of orgies in the Erie vice-president's office and of chorus girls who doubled as concubines.[9] Erie stockholders could now add to their catalog of grievances the unique charge that Erie office workers were surrounded by sin and distracted by debauchery.

At the same time, Fisk, keeping his wife in a mansion in Boston, installed his mistress, Josie Mansfield, in a mansion down the street from the opera house. Daughter of a California newspaperman, Helen Josephine Mansfield had a voluptuous figure, luxuriant black hair, and a soft voice. Easily seduced at an early age, she quickly learned to rely on her charms rather than her talents. After a tenuous marriage at seventeen to an actor, she turned up in New York and was soon friendly with a Miss Anne Wood, who ran an elegant bordello.

Through Miss Wood, Josie met Jim Fisk. Before long, Fisk had set her up in a four-story mansion, with servants, carriage, and coachman, and had entered with her on a life of pleasure that was the talk of the city.[10] He could never take her to the finest restaurants or hotels, but at Josie's place she and Fisk entertained some of the best-known figures in the worlds of politics and entertainment. At his Grand Opera House, Fisk concentrated on the lightest opera bouffe, simply putting on the stage what he constantly put into his life.

Then Josie began to deceive her fat lover. Her partner in the deception was Edward Stiles Stokes, a young and handsome dandy. Both his own and his wife's parents were affluent, and he shared with Fisk a Brooklyn oil refinery that was showing a profit because Erie bought its oil, but he was a reckless spender, especially at racetracks and sporting saloons.

Shortly, Josie began showing dissatisfaction with her lot as Fisk's mistress. The ruptures and reconciliations between Fisk and Josie became more and more violent. Stokes collected a $27,500 company debt and kept the money, whereupon Fisk had him arrested for embezzlement. Forced to spend a weekend in jail and deprived of his daily manicure and scented Florida water, Stokes swore vengeance. Armed with Fisk's letters to Josie, Stokes demanded $200,000 from Fisk. At the same time Josie sued Fisk for $50,000, which she claimed he owed her. The quarrel came to court, and there the whole tawdry relationship of the trio became public. It was what George Templeton Strong, respected lawyer and caustic diarist, called "a special stinkpot."

Then Fisk won several victories in court, including an indictment of Josie Mansfield and Ned Stokes on a charge of blackmail.[11] For Stokes these reverses were disastrous. He already owed $38,000 to lawyers, and now he was revealed as helping a scheming harlot cheat a bountiful lover. A vain and foolish man, Stokes drove to the new Grand Central Hotel on Broadway and shot Fisk twice as the latter started up the stairs. Fisk died the following morning.

The reaction of the city was astonishing. The newspapers had taken to ridiculing Fisk mercilessly, but the circumstances of his death evoked sympathy and sorrow. The funeral was an awesome spectacle, and one newspaper compared it with Lincoln's six years before. From the gaunt, brooding figure of the father-leader to the fat peddler turning swindler and debauchee—such was the sea-change in America's martyred heroes.

The usual explanation of Fisk's success is that he had the common touch, meaning that he entertained people, turning his frauds into farce and his outrages into jokes. But perhaps it meant mainly that he was never a hypocrite. In a time when any evidence of forbidden behavior was glossed over with cant, everyone knew that Jim Fisk had stolen millions from Erie, put Erie's offices in an opera house because he liked shows and show girls, and kept the fanciest mistress in the city. Vulgar and flashy though he might be, he was refreshing in his candor. When that pious old humbug the Wall Street speculator Daniel Drew reproved him, Fisk is reported to have replied: "No, Uncle, there isn't any hope for Jim Fisk. I'm a gone goose. . . . Some people are born to be good, other people are born to be bad. I was born to be bad. As to the World, the Flesh and the Devil, I'm on good terms with all three. If God Almighty is going to damn us men because we love the woman, then let him go ahead and do it. I'm having a good time now, and if I've got to pay for it hereafter, why . . . I'll take what's coming to me." [12]

Perhaps those who looked on him tolerantly did so because they found in him a vicarious release: he flouted the Mrs. Grundys who made them cower. Of course, a few now used his life as an object lesson. His violent death, at thirty-six, served them perfectly. Mustering all his sin-shattering eloquence, the Reverend Henry Ward Beecher cried:

> And that supreme mountbank of fortune—the astounding event of his age: that man of some smartness in business, but absolutely without moral sense, and as absolutely devoid of shame as the desert of Sahara is of grass—that this man, with one leap, should have vaulted to the very summit of power in New York, and . . . rode out to this hour in glaring and magnificent prosperity—shameless, vicious, criminal, abominable in his lusts . . . and yet in an instant, by the hand of a fellow-culprit, God's providence struck him to the ground! [13]

Although both Sickles and Fisk flourished, many respectable citizens mistrusted the former and deplored the latter. But the Reverend Henry Ward Beecher was the most famous preacher of his time, a moral guide, and, even more, an emotional force. That is why his abandonment of the old religion along with his trial for adultery make him so significant in the revolution in American standards.

His father, Lyman Beecher, was a famous Boston preacher of the old school, an exuberant character who had eleven children by two wives, including two notable preachers among his sons, and a celebrated writer, Harriet, a well-known teacher, Catharine, and a woman's rights leader, Isabella, among his daughters. He took a strong stand against drink, circuses, riding on Sunday, the theater and Unitarianism; and Henry Ward later complained that he grew up with the fear that he was trapped in a world condemned to sin and damnation. After his ordination in 1838 Henry Ward served in the little town of Indianapolis and soon acquired a reputation for glowing rhetoric, theatrical impersonations, and an uninhibited show of feeling. He also became known for his lectures to young men on such safe themes as the dangers in gambling, the theater, French novels, and licentiousness; some listeners thought his talks showed almost too intimate a knowledge of such subjects as the secret lusts of a lecher.[14]

It was hardly a surprise, therefore, when in 1847 he was asked to become the first pastor of Brooklyn's new Plymouth Church. Such was his success that within a few years New Yorkers, meaning Manhattanites, would say, "If you want to hear Henry Ward Beecher preach, take the ferry to Brooklyn and then follow the crowd."

His figure was not imposing, his hair hung somewhat thinly to his collar, his voice was not remarkable, but he had presence and an inexhaustible fluency. Scorning the "holy tones" of most preachers, he could be by turns lyrical, breezy, somber and salty, and he was the master of a soaring rapturous climax. Above all he had zest. Like Whitman and with much the same rhapsodic fervor, he hailed the prospects of the common people and the possibilities of brotherhood. Adulation surrounded him, swept over him, and drew from him gushes of love. He conjured up a "perpetual tropical luxuriance of blessed love" and he called for submission—not to God's will but to "secret chords of feeling" and "the heart's instincts." Intoxicated by his own fervor, he shouted at his listeners, "Ye are gods!" and "You are crystalline, your faces are radiant!" When they had recovered from their surprise, the prosperous citizens, ranged row on row in front of him, responded with pleasure and gratitude.

His wife, Eunice, did not age well: cold, straitlaced, her face severe, she came to be known to her Brooklyn neighbors as the griffin. Doubtless this was one reason Beecher, earning huge sums by lecturing and writing as well as preaching—not to mention testimonials for Chickering pianos, Waltham watches, and even a truss—bought paintings, gems, fast horses, a town house and country estates. Asked how he reconciled all this with the way of the meek and lowly Jesus, he declared that the belief in a relationship between poverty and sanctity was medieval. At one point he accepted an unheard-of advance of $24,000 to do a novel. But writing fiction did not come naturally to him. So he turned to worshipful Elizabeth Tilton for encouragement in his creative labors. That was the beginning of the most sensational domestic scandal that America had known.

When Theodore Tilton first came to Beecher's attention in 1854, he was a twenty-year-old reporter, tall, handsome, with long auburn hair. Beecher, charmed by his enthusiasm, had him made a general assistant on *The Independent*, a sectarian weekly. Before long, Tilton, a resourceful editor with advanced views, had sharply increased the circulation of the paper as well as his own earnings. In 1856 Beecher officiated at Tilton's marriage to Elizabeth Richards.

"Lib" Tilton was a tiny, dark-eyed, birdlike creature, more appealing than pretty. She had been a devout member of Beecher's congregation since her childhood and had taught in the Sunday school. An ardent reader of the popular novels of Charles Reade and E. D. E. N. Southworth and the poetry of Elizabeth Barrett Browning, she mixed a turbid romanticism with religious zeal.[15] In her, as in Beecher, feeling was the controlling agent. It was inevitable that sooner or later she should confuse two major outlets of emotion—the religious and the erotic.

From the first, the frankness of Tilton's admiration for Beecher was remarkable even in a time when a romantic effusiveness was common. Beecher shared the feeling. When he visited the Tilton home he found not only exciting visitors—Greeley, Whittier, Phillips, Sumner—but a heady zeal for lofty causes, and warmth. The contrast with the sterile respectability of his own home was overwhelming. "O Theodore," he confessed, "I dread to go back to my own home," and, "God might strip all other gifts from me if he would only give me a wife like Elizabeth and a home like yours." Tilton responded in kind, saying, "There is one little woman down at my house who loves you more than you can have any idea of."

Plainly the word love was used loosely here. The Tiltons were, like Beecher himself, moving away from the dark old religion of fear into the glowing new religion of love, and along the way love tended to filter into other human relationships, such as that between two men or between a man and his friend's wife.

The first indication anyone had that all was not as it should be between the Reverend Beecher and the adoring women around him at his church was a story that Henry Bowen, a founder of Plymouth Church, told Theodore Tilton in 1862. He declared that when his wife Lucy Maria, mother of his ten children, had died at the age of thirty-eight she had made a deathbed confession of her relationship to Beecher so shocking that Bowen could no longer keep it to himself. Biographers who accept Bowen's story believe he did not make it public because he feared it would ruin Plymouth Church.

When Beecher returned from a wartime trip to Europe Tilton seemed to have forgotten this story. Perhaps when he saw Beecher, now in his fifties, with a paunch and loose jowls, but still craving affection, he felt pity for him. Or perhaps he had become tolerant of other men's desires because he had begun to help himself to love wherever he found it. Whatever the reason, he and Elizabeth welcomed Beecher back into the old intimacy.

That Tilton was concerned about his wife's relations to Beecher is evident in a letter he wrote her from Iowa during a lecture tour: "Now that the *other* man has gone off lecturing . . . you can afford to come to see me. . . . You promised the *other* man to cleave to *me*, and yet you leave *me all alone* and cleave to him. 'O Frailty! Thy name is woman!'" Soon Elizabeth was protesting the innocence of her behavior:

> About eleven o'clock today, Mr. Beecher called. Now, beloved, let not even the shadow of a shadow fall on your dear heart because of this. . . . You once told me you did not believe that I gave a correct account of his visits, and you always felt that I repressed much. Sweet, do you still believe this? . . .

> It would be my supreme wish . . . to have you *always with me.* This trinity of friendship I pray for always.[16]

Her application of the sacred term "trinity" to a relationship verging on infidelity is revealing. Everything is made acceptable by being dipped in a thick syrup of sentiment.

In October, 1868, while her husband was away, Elizabeth Tilton went to hear Beecher address a great campaign rally for General Grant. The following day she hurried over to her pastor's house to tell him how glorious it had been. He was alone. The fullest account of what happened that evening came from Theodore Tilton in City Court, Brooklyn, more than six years later when he charged Beecher with debauching his wife on October 10, 1868.

This extraordinary entry appeared in Elizabeth Tilton's diary for that same day: "*A Day Memorable.*"

And later that month the following passage leaps from a sermon by Beecher:

> The man who has been wallowing in lust, the man who has been on fire in his passions, and who by God's great goodness has been brought to an hour and a moment when . . . his monstrous wickedness stands disclosed in him—that man ought not to wait so long as the drawing of his breath. Wherever he is . . . he will stand up and say, "Here I am, a sinner, and I confess my sin, and I call on God to witness my determination from this hour to turn away from it." This is the wise course, and you would think so—if it was anybody but yourself.[17]

The passage reveals how he was able to reconcile his lofty position with his undisciplined practice: he simply assumed that all men were as inwardly divided as he was.

In the spring of 1870, troubled and ill, Mrs. Tilton went away for the summer. But on the night of July 3, she returned to Brooklyn, and, according to her husband's testimony, she made—exactly as had Daniel Sickles' wife—a full confession, declaring that her friendship with Beecher had led to "sexual intimacy . . . that she had made a visit to his house . . . and that there, on the 10th of October, 1868, she had surrendered her body to him in sexual embrace . . . that she had repeated such acts at other places . . . from the Fall of 1868 to the Spring of 1870."

After days of soul-searching, Tilton decided that Elizabeth had been "trapped up in her teacher and her guide" and had followed him blindly. This decision gave him such a feeling of magnanimity as to raise him into a kind of ecstasy. All of these statements, all so overwrought, can only be understood as the emotional excesses that follow an age of repression. Under the Victorian lid, the caldron had come to a boil.

To escape from her troubles, Elizabeth went to visit friends in Ohio. From there in November, 1870, she wrote her husband:

> When, by your threats, my mother cried out to me, "Why, what have you done, Elizabeth, my child?" her worst suspicions were aroused, and I laid bare my heart then, that from my lips, and not yours, she might receive the dagger into her heart. . . . Even so, every word, look, or intimation against Mr. B. though I be in no wise brought in, is an agony beyond the piercing of myself a hundred times. . . . Once again I implore you, for your children's sake . . . that *my past* be buried—left with me and my God.

Then, on December 24 Elizabeth Tilton had a miscarriage. In a letter to a friend she said of this: "A *love-babe*, it promised, you know." [18] It was a curious comment from a woman nearly forty years old who had already borne six children, especially when she and her husband had been quarreling for months.

Trouble now broke out between Tilton and Bowen, especially over an editorial in *The Independent* that contained such statements as "marriage without love is a sin against God," and "marriage, if broken, whether broken by the body or the soul, is divorce." Bowen confronted Tilton, and, in the exchange that followed, Tilton revealed his wife's confession. Bowen at once saw an opportunity to get back at Beecher for the affair with Lucy Bowen, and without involving Lucy or himself. He burst out that Beecher must not be permitted to stay another week in his pulpit. Carried away by Bowen's indignation, Tilton wrote to Beecher: "I demand that, for reasons which you explicitly understand, you immediately cease from the ministry of Plymouth Church and that you quit the City of Brooklyn."

It was a melodramatic gesture. When Bowen delivered the letter to Beecher, Beecher's immediate response was: "Why, this man's crazy." But when he was summoned to a meeting with Tilton, and Mrs. Tilton's letter was read to him, he was staggered. He asked to see Mrs. Tilton. When Beecher entered her room, he found her—as in a painting by Holman Hunt—lying on a couch, "white as marble . . . and with her hands upon her bosom, palm to palm, as one in prayer." He asked her, he said, why she had become party to such terrible charges. With tears she said that Tilton had made her believe that if she confessed her love for Beecher, it would help Tilton confess his own alien affections.

She then gave Beecher a statement: " . . . wearied by importunities, and weakened by sickness, I gave a letter inculpating my friend, Henry Ward Beecher, under assurances that that would remove all differences between me and my husband. That letter I now revoke. . . ." This was the beginning of such a bewildering series of recantations and contradictory statements that in the end nothing Mrs. Tilton said was fully believed.

Beecher now repeatedly met with the Tiltons in an effort at complete reconciliation. At one meeting, which took place in Mrs. Tilton's bedroom, Beecher reported, "I kissed him and he kissed me, and I kissed his wife and she kissed me, and I believe they kissed each other." Perhaps Beecher hoped that such displays would make all gestures of affection between him and the Tiltons seem harmless and even silly. But then, with an unbelievable lack of discretion, Beecher and Elizabeth began to write to each other. In one of these "Clandestine Letters," Elizabeth, as emotional as ever, wrote, "Does your heart bound *towards* all as it used to? So does mine! I am myself again. I did not dare to tell you till I was sure; but the bird has sung in my heart these four weeks, and he has covenanted with me never again to leave." [19]

The illusion that their difficulties were over was soon blasted: Victoria Woodhull devoted the entire issue of November 2, 1872, of her weekly to exposing the Beecher-Tilton affair. The utterly uninhibited Woodhull gave Beecher the kiss of death when she wrote:

> The immense physical potency of Mr. Beecher, and the indomitable urgency of his great nature for the intimacy and

> embraces of the noble and cultured women about him, instead of being a bad thing as the world thinks, is one of the noblest . . . endowments of this truly great and representative man. Plymouth Church has lived and fed, and the healthy vigor of public opinion for the last quarter of a century has been strengthened from the physical amativeness of Henry Ward Beecher.[20]

Beneath the flourishes the passage contained a remarkable insight into the source of Henry Ward Beecher's influence.

When Beecher's half-sister, Isabella Beecher Hooker, demanded the truth, Beecher answered, "I tread the falsehoods into the dirt from which they spring. . . ." But he thoughtlessly added: ". . . think of the barbarity of dragging a poor dear child of a woman into this slough"; whereupon Isabella, who was an outspoken suffragist, wrote to another brother, the Reverend Thomas K. Beecher, "So far as I can see, it is he who has dragged the dear child into the slough—and left her there." [21]

Victoria Woodhull was even less charitable. Hounded from hotel to hotel, she announced, "I will make it hotter on earth for Henry Ward Beecher than hell is below!" Raking up the scandal week after week in her paper, she nearly succeeded. But Beecher remained as popular as always. He had acquired the glamour of the superior individual who lives the way others would like to live but do not dare.

Members of the Plymouth congregation now forced Tilton's expulsion, and the moderator of an "Advisory Council" of sister churches referred to Tilton as "a knave." Tilton, furious, published a reply. Hoping to avoid a civil court, Beecher decided that his own church should try him. He himself picked its six members, and his vindication was assured when his followers persuaded Elizabeth Tilton to take her place at Beecher's side. Of the adultery charge, she said pathetically to Mrs. Moulton, "For the sake of Mr. Beecher, for the sake of the influence on the world, for my own position, for my children, I think it is my duty to deny it." The one reason conspicuously omitted is that the charge was a lie. Tilton swore to the charge of "criminal seduction" and added such details as that he had once returned home unexpectedly and found his wife and Beecher locked in her bedroom.

At last Beecher himself spoke, falling automatically into those postures and appeals that had made him famous. He spoke of Elizabeth Tilton as having "thrust her affections on me, unsought." Was not his personal sacrifice warranted, he concluded, to prevent the morals of an entire community from being corrupted by "the filthy details of scandalous falsehoods?" The committee's report, read to the jubilant brethren of Plymouth Church by a professional elocutionist, described Theodore Tilton as malicious and revengeful, Elizabeth Tilton as guilty of "inordinate affection," and Henry Ward Beecher as completely innocent but just too trusting.

Tilton now instituted suit in City Court against the Reverend Beecher for willful alienation of his wife's affections. Most New York newspapers still sided with Beecher, apparently believing it more important to save "the most famous pulpit . . . since Paul preached on the Hill of Mars"—as the New York *Tribune* said—than to arrive at the truth. But the Chicago *Tribune* published a devastating analysis by Elizabeth Cady Stanton that underscored Beecher's cruelty in describing Mrs. Tilton as having thrust her affections on him. It also boldly exposed the various church-connected "rings," including the bondholders of Plymouth Church, that would do anything to protect Beecher's name.[22] And the Chicago *Times* spread out the lurid details of Beecher's affair with Lucy Maria Bowen. It smelled to high heaven; and there were still years of it to come.

After all this, the trial of Tilton *vs.* Beecher, which opened in Brooklyn on January 11, 1875, should have been anticlimactic. But it proved to be Ossa piled on Pelion—an uncensored performance of a sex drama in which a spiritual leader was revealed as a sly lecher and a devout matron as his willing victim. The trial lasted almost six months and was given more space in newspapers than any event since the Civil War. Social leaders fought for tickets, and the crowds came as though to a fair. The vaunted sanctity of Victorian private life was invaded with fiendish ingenuity and obscene curiosity.

Tilton's case was presented by only a few witnesses, principally Francis Moulton and his wife, close friends of both Beecher and Tilton. Beecher had six lawyers and almost a hundred witnesses. His own answers were often irrelevant and so flippant that the New York *Herald* declared that he presented for "scientific man a psychological problem which they must despair of solving."

Almost nine hundred times he said, "I can't recollect" or "I don't know." In many ways the most impressive witness was Emma Moulton, manifestly a woman of integrity. Telling of a meeting with Beecher in 1873, she said:

> He expressed to me his love for Elizabeth, and his great remorse and sorrow that she should ever have confessed to her husband. . . . He walked up and down the room in a very excited manner, with the tears streaming down his cheeks, and said he thought it was very hard . . . that he should be brought to this fearful end. . . . And I said, ". . . I have never heard you preach since I knew the truth that I haven't felt that I was standing by an open grave. . . . I believed in you since I was a girl, believed you were the only good man in the world. Now . . . I don't believe in anybody."

But the pastor of Plymouth Church had become an idol, the kind of public figure whose fame feeds on all publicity, good or bad. The verdict of the jurors was nine to three against Theodore Tilton. On Sunday a great throng crowded the streets around the church in the hope of seeing or hearing Beecher. But not everyone thought that the trial had been amusing. In England, George Meredith wrote: "Guilty or not, there is a sickly snuffiness about the religious fry that makes the tale of their fornications absolutely repulsive to read of. . . ." [23]

Plymouth Church nevertheless raised $100,000 to help pay Beecher's trial expense. By contrast, Theodore Tilton was financially ruined. And that fall the brethren of Plymouth Church dropped Emma Moulton from the church rolls.

No one can say why Henry Bowen was now moved to face the challenge that he had avoided since the deathbed confession of his wife fourteen years before. Perhaps he felt that Beecher was about to escape retribution forever. Going before a special Plymouth Church committee, he recalled how he had helped launch the church almost thirty years before and brought Beecher to it as its first pastor. "At last," Bowen said, "there came to my knowledge evidence of his guilt which astounded and overwhelmed me. . . . I received from a lady whom, under the circumstances, I was compelled to believe . . . full and explicit confession of adultery with Mr. Beecher." The lady, Bowen continued, had a key to Beecher's study in Plymouth Church and met with him there—until she saw another woman enter with a similar key. She never got over the shock, Bowen said, and died shortly afterward.[24] Ostensibly because Bowen had not named names, Plymouth Church responded by expelling him.

Beecher now resumed his career as lecturer. Occasionally at first there was the jeer, the coarse taunt, the audience waiting coldly. But after a while he was as popular as ever. Under the managership of Major Pond he delivered one hundred and thirty-two lectures—at from $600 to $1,000 a night—to a total of almost half a million persons.

But the embers of the scandal were not all dead. In April, 1878, Elizabeth Tilton, a decade after the event, published a letter she had written to her legal advisor:

> . . . after long months of mental anguish, I told . . . a few friends whom I bitterly deceived, that the charge brought by my husband, of adultery between myself and the Rev. Henry Ward Beecher, was true, and that the lie I had lived so well the last four years had become intolerable to me. This statement I now solemnly reaffirm. . . . I know full well the explanations that will be sought for this acknowledgement; desire to return to my husband, insanity, malice—everything save the true one—my quickened conscience, and the sense of what is due the cause of truth and justice. . . .[25]

It was the only statement she had ever made without pressure, and it had the ring of truth; but it came too late to have any effect. Tilton said nothing. Shorn of wife, causes, and spirit, he drifted to Paris. There he died, quite forgotten, in 1907.

Beecher also resumed his practice of taking sides on political and social questions. In 1884 he rejected Blaine as candidate for the Presidency but did not actively back Cleveland until the story that Cleveland had had a "natural" son startled the nation. Then, openly referring to his own ordeal, Beecher campaigned with the ardor of a man seeking vicarious vindication. He even went so far as to say to a youthful YMCA audience: "If every man in New York State tonight, who has broken the seventh commandment, voted for Cleveland, he would be elected by a 200,000 majority." He had come a long way from the *Lectures to Young Men* with its dire warnings to beware the Strange Woman![26]

On the third of March, 1887, he suffered a stroke and died a few days later. His body lay in state amid a sea of flowers, and some fifty thousand of the curious, mostly women, passed the bier.

Beecher's sexual passions were only an aspect of his dominant characteristic—what he called love and the Victorians dubbed amativeness. The trait explains not only his attraction for women, but his religion of love—not Platonic or ideal love, but personal love. This he generated in palpable waves whenever he addressed an audience, mingling amatory and religious appeals in one torrent of ardor.

But just as Beecher's powers derived from his fervor, so did his weaknesses. There was a fatal softness in him, something molten at the core. In a crisis he dissolved into tears; in his affairs with women, desire drowned out common sense. It manifested itself in all manner of minor excesses: the silly kissing, the perfervid passages in the sermons, the changes of heart on great issues. But none of these hurt him in the public eye. That he was as much the victim as the master of his emotions did not seem to matter. People may not have reverenced him, but they were fascinated and moved by him. In his excesses they found release. Henry Ward Beecher acted of his own fierce needs, but he also satisfied a deep hunger in the America of his time.

Beecher was far from typical—but neither was he unique. A career astonishingly similar to his, at least in its early phases, was that of the Reverend Isaac S. Kalloch, who is as forgotten today as Beecher is remembered. And Kalloch's career was staged, not in commercial, hybridized New York but mainly in Boston, once the hub of the Puritan world.

Like Beecher, Kalloch was the son of a prominent clergyman, his father having been a Baptist minister in Maine. A child prodigy and as great a success in his youthful preaching in Maine as Beecher was in Indianapolis, young Isaac was called in 1855 to the largest church in Boston, Tremont Temple, just as Beecher had been called to Plymouth Church. He soon became so popular that the crowds had to be turned away from his services.

A red-haired giant of a man, and handsome to boot, he was intense and fiery in the pulpit, but outside the church he was a genial, cigar-smoking youth who enjoyed a joke, a glass of whiskey, and the adoration of the ladies. If there was any difference between him and Beecher, it was that everything came easily to him. He already had a reputation as a "golden-voiced preacher" when early in 1857 he was accused of adultery. The woman, Laura Flye Steen, was, as Elizabeth Tilton was to Beecher, an old friend and the wife of a respected citizen—a prosperous Vermont merchant.

The Boston *Times* charged that the Reverend Dr. Kalloch had taken Mrs. Steen, a very attractive young woman, to a disreputable hotel in East Cambridge before and after a lecture, giving the impression that she was his wife. The *Times,* a sensational penny sheet, might have been ignored if it had not shocked the entire nation by publishing affidavits from the innkeeper and an omnibus driver claiming that they had seen Kalloch have "sexual connexion" with the lady at the hotel.

Kalloch calmly admitted that he had stopped at the hotel with Mrs. Steen to rest before the lecture and after it, but he added that both Mr. Steen and Mrs. Kalloch had known that Mrs. Steen was accompanying him. The newspaper clamor, however, was so great that Kalloch was indicted and brought to trial. At the trial the two proprietors of the hotel, the wife of one of them, and the bus driver—a very seedy crew—testified that they had peeped through a crack and seen Kalloch and the lady embrace and lie down on the floor—mercifully out of sight of the watchers—heard them utter words of love and later saw them rise and rearrange their clothes. They gave details that no newspaper today would print.

Demonstrating their confidence in Kalloch, or simply closing ranks against the common enemy, Mr. Steen and Mrs. Kalloch sat next to Kalloch in court, and Steen testified for the defense. The jury brought in a split verdict, eight voting for acquittal, thus freeing Kalloch. Evidently the sleazy character and shameless testimony of the four key witnesses against Kalloch told in his favor.[27] Many newspapers called the verdict disgraceful, but his congregation decided that he had "come out of the fire like pure gold, doubly refined" and it contributed $1,000 toward his court expenses. More than 30,000 persons tried to get into Tremont Temple the following Sunday and those who succeeded received his flowery sermon with sobs and cheers.

Fortunately for Kalloch, the panic of 1857 soon overshadowed the scandal, and piety increasing with the hard times, the reverend was able to launch revival meetings in which sinners repented in squadrons.

Now, however, Kalloch began to display the restlessness that would tear him away from career after career. No one has been able to explain this compulsion to start anew even when his affairs were prospering. Having previously visited Kansas, Kalloch made a trial sojourn in the frontier city of Leavenworth. But when the trustees of Tremont Temple offered him $5,000 a year to return, he accepted. Again his fame grew. But again scandal trailed him: the superintendent of the church revealed that female parishioners visited the reverend's study at night and that one had stayed until midnight. Again he was investigated by a church committee and again he was cleared.

But he resigned and in 1860 accepted a call to the fashionable Laight Street Baptist Church in lower Manhattan. Notwithstanding the competition of the Reverend Beecher (who deplored him) and other clerical spellbinders, Kalloch soon became known for his preaching. His aristocratic congregation was, however, too sedate for him, and early in 1864 he bid it farewell and again headed for the exhilarating turbulence of Kansas. This time "the famous Reverend Kalloch" joined a few other influential citizens in founding the town of Ottawa in the easternmost part of the state. The variety of Kalloch's involvements in the town were astonishing: he established a church, started a newspaper, founded a Baptist college, helped to organize a railroad and became its superintendent.[28]

Kalloch's activities, even the most admirable, had a tendency to end up in rumors of laxity or self-indulgence—whether it was a too easy way with women, the truth, or other people's money. Other newspaper publishers nicknamed him, in the brutal journalism of the time, the sorrel stallion, and described him as a rogue, embezzler, and lecher. Impervious to such attacks, Kalloch merely shifted his center of operations to a larger city, Lawrence. Although he dressed like a "sporting man," Isaac Kalloch at forty was a commanding figure, with broad shoulders, massive head, and clipped, curling beard. He drank heavily, gambled on his racehorses, and gave riotous parties in a stone mansion outside of Lawrence. Living so open-handedly, he was totally unprepared for the panic of 1872. In short order his farm, mansion, prize stock, and newspaper were gone, and he barely escaped bankruptcy. So in 1873 he chose a much-publicized revival meeting to make a sensational confession of sin and repentance. Although skeptics warned that he was a faker, he was promptly called back to his old pastorate in Leavenworth.

But Isaac disliked retracing his steps. Abruptly, at the height of his comeback, he went to San Francisco and persuaded prominent Baptists there to build him a huge temple and pay him $5,000 a year. To his bewildered Leavenworth followers he announced that he had a mission to convert the wicked in the coast city. But cynics claimed that he was in fact fleeing from large debts.

The Metropolitan Temple, built in 1876, was the largest Baptist church in the United States. Once more Kalloch drew such throngs that he had to repeat his sermons on the street outside the church. He was distinctly "modern" in doctrine, accepting Darwinism and questioning the infallibility of the Bible. But more and more he devoted himself to politics. Strikes, low wages, and unemployment gave rise in California to the "Sandlotters," a militant workingmen's organization. At first Kalloch denounced them as foreign incendiaries, but as they began to elect their men to office he became their champion. In no time he captured the party and was nominated for mayor.

Most newspapers, beholden to businessmen, opposed Kalloch bitterly. He ignored them until the San Francisco *Chronicle,* which the DeYoung brothers had nursed from a gossip sheet to the largest circulation on the coast, declared that he was not only still debauching virgins in his study but that his father had been equally lustful. Nettled, Kalloch answered in kind, asserting that the DeYoungs were, among other things, monsters born of a whorehouse madam. (They were despicable men, but their parents were merely middle-class Jews who had owned a variety store in Cincinnati.) The following day Charles DeYoung waited for Kalloch outside the Temple and shot him twice. For a week Kalloch's doctors claimed that he was dying, and then, on election eve, announced that he would recover. Some observers thought it a pity that both men had not managed to kill each other. But the workingmen of San Francisco voted solidly for the Reverend Kalloch.[29]

Months later Kalloch learned that Charles DeYoung—still not brought to trial—was preparing another "exposé" of him. Isaac's son Milton, a moody man who served as an assistant pastor in his father's church, did what he had long threatened: he shot and killed DeYoung. He was acquitted: Californians were accustomed to the violent settlement of quarrels and to assassins going free.

When the workingmen's party collapsed and the Democrats spurned him, Kalloch decided not to run again. For a few years he carried on as a pastor, but there was no challenge in the task. He liked the platform the church gave him, but he had no use for the doctrines and the piety. So one day in July, 1883, aged fifty-two, a bit paunchy and his beard streaked with silver, he resigned, this time saying simply that he was bored. In the few remaining years of his life he made a fortune in railroads, lumber, and large-scale farming. But he told a friend that he now had everything except fun. At his funeral there were, as he had requested, no services. He was soon so completely forgotten that in 1947 M. M. Marberry, a newspaperman, undertook a biography of him because there were no references to him in any book.

Isaac Kalloch was a lecher, gambler, drinker, demagogue, and probably an embezzler. Yet he became a famous preacher in four American cities, a college president, newspaper publisher, railroad superintendent, president of a state agricultural society, and mayor of a great city. Part of the explanation of this extraordinary record is that he was a commanding, dynamic, and gifted man, but part of it must be due to the time: in general it was the revolt against Puritan austerity and guilt; in Kansas it was the frontier with its emphasis on masculinity and rugged independence; in California it was the tolerance of violence and corruption.

Kalloch was not a weak man. In a way he was almost too richly endowed. Despite the taboos of the time and of his calling, the satisfactions he derived from indulgence were plainly greater than any pain or punishment. No experience seems to have discouraged him. No one succeeded in curbing him. All his congregations closed their ears to every charge against him.

No woman ever accused him of offending her with his advances. Why this pagan sensualist chose the ministry as his profession is in part a mystery, but clearly the reason he remained in it was that it never prevented him from enjoying all the pleasures of this world.

Sexual scandal in high places was not peculiar to the early days of the republic. Indeed, one of the most surprising episodes in the chronicles of American sexual morality is that of Grover Cleveland and his natural son. It was particularly surprising because the story exploded at the height of Cleveland's campaign for the Presidency in 1884 and because he was, nevertheless, elected.

In July of 1884, a shoddy Buffalo newspaper published what it entitled "A Terrible Tale," describing in detail Cleveland's clandestine affair with a Buffalo woman, culminating in the birth of a child. Like Hamilton in the Reynolds scandal, Cleveland responded by telling the whole truth at once: Maria Halpin had been a pretty, pleasing widow of thirty-five—Cleveland was a year older—head of the cloak department of a dry goods store in Buffalo. She spoke French and attended a fashionable church. She appears to have been intimate with several men, including Cleveland and his friend Oscar Folsom. When a child was born to her in 1874, she named it Oscar Folsom Cleveland and declared that Cleveland was its father. Although Cleveland later said that he could not be sure that he was the father, he accepted responsibility for the child because the other men in Mrs. Halpin's life were married.[30] While nursing the child, Mrs. Halpin began drinking heavily. She allowed the child to be placed in an orphan asylum. The boy was later adopted by a prominent family and disappeared from Cleveland's life. Mrs. Halpin also dropped out of sight, the only echo coming in 1895 when she wrote to Cleveland asking him for money and threatening to publish "facts" in her possession.

After the initial consternation among Cleveland's supporters, they emphasized the fact that Cleveland had taken full responsibility for his mistake and had led an otherwise blameless life. They shrewdly argued that Cleveland's single moral misstep was as nothing compared to his opponent Blaine's many political transgressions. The public apparently agreed. Cleveland's indifference to the child was attributed to his doubts as to whether he was the father. There was little sympathy for Mrs. Halpin, and she was in effect saddled with the total burden of guilt. It was assumed that she was an immoral woman but that Cleveland had gone astray only this once. None of his defenders noted that his "manly" acknowledgment had not saved Maria Halpin from utter disgrace or the baby from virtual abandonment.

Although Americans of the time would have been horrified at the excerise of *droit du seigneur,* wealth gave men privileges as well as the temerity to ignore social prohibitions. Of course we know only of those instances that became public through scandal or court trials. As he grew older, for example, Commodore Vanderbilt was known to pursue his housemaids shamelessly, and we have seen how he dallied with Tennessee Claflin and Victoria Woodhull. Probably the most dashing figure of the Civil War period in New York was Leonard K. Jerome, banker, sportsman, and man-about-town. Jerome, a tall, dark man with a huge downcurling mustache, was famous for rolling up Fifth Avenue on Sundays—shocking respectable citizens on the way to church—in a magnificent coach-and-four filled with beauties, not including his wife. Everyone knew of his lifelong affair with a society divorcee, Mrs. Fanny Ronalds. He also played mentor to ambitious young singers, even taking one into his home for a time, and the warmth with which he attended seventeen-year-old Adelina Patti on her first tour of America was common gossip.[31] His daughter Jennie, a celebrated beauty, consoled herself for an unhappy marriage to Lord Randolph Churchill—who had contracted syphilis in his youth—by taking lovers.

Although Jay Gould himself was proper to the point of shyness, especially as compared with his brazen immorality in business, two of his sons were not so inhibited. Frank Gould liked fast horses and fast women, and George Gould married a former actress and had seven children by her, but he also had three children by another actress whom he "kept" on an estate in Rye, New York.[32]

Russell Sage, the parsimonious millionaire who started as a grocer but became rich enough to finance Jay Gould, was three times brought to court by women who testified that he took sexual liberties with them. One of the women, an artist, Sophie Mattern, declared that he had visited her in her Greenwich Village studio for reasons other than business. Another, a housemaid, claimed that he was the father of her child. And the Marchioness Gregorio D'Adjuria charged that Sage had beaten her when she had refused to undress and submit to his embraces. The last two suits were thrown out of court because of the statute of limitations, but Sage never denied his guilt in either case.[33]

It would of course be dangerous to generalize about American society on the basis of the handful of instances in this chapter. This is especially true of rich or influential men such as Fisk, Vanderbilt, and Kalloch, who seem to have felt that they could defy conventional prohibitions with impunity. But it is hardly true of Elizabeth Whitman or Hamilton, certainly not of those involved in the Jewett and Rogers cases, or of Barton Key and Mrs. Sickles, or of Grover Cleveland and Mrs. Halpin. Such men as Key, Hamilton, and Beecher had, in fact, far more to lose from such behavior than the average man. Their sexual irregularities demonstrate simply that desire was greater than the fear of discovery.

It should also be evident that for every scandalous relationship that comes to light hundreds or perhaps thousands are kept successfully secret or are quietly settled before they reach the courts and the newspapers. Speaking from his knowledege as a newspaper editor, David Goodman Croly declared that for every scandal involving a clergyman and a woman of his congregation that came to light, a score were hushed up. We know from everyone who wrote about the subject and particularly about houses of assignation that it was not too difficult to carry on an affair without detection.

The chief value of our sampling is what it reveals of the attitude of the public toward moral trespass. In no instance did the men suffer disgrace as a result of charges of philandering or adultery. Even when the charges were leveled against the moral and spiritual leaders of the community, the men experienced little or no loss in followers or in popular reputation. It was not that their admirers were tolerant or broadminded; it was simply that they could not acknowledge the truth about

Beecher and Kalloch without acknowledging the self-deception and pretense of their own moral standards. Sometimes, as with Hamilton and Cleveland, they did acknowledge the irrelevance of the code by not applying it. The public seems to have realized that these men were neither immoral nor licentious, and the only way that Victorians could cope with such a contradiction was to ignore it.

21.

THE FORBIDDEN THEME

CENSORSHIP tends to whet the appetite for the sexually forbidden. One way or another, interest in sex will be satisfied. The emphasis that vice crusaders put upon sexuality is at once a result of that interest and a cause of it. That is why the Victorian era, stimulating interest by suppression, was a golden age of pornography as well as of prudery.

Putting aside for a moment such an extreme as pornography, it is easy to show that much popular fiction purveyed sexuality while advocating purity. The subject of virtue served as a justification for dealing with vice; after all, chastity must be tested by temptation and evil. In one formula of fiction, virtue triumphed over temptation and was rewarded with marriage; in another, virtue succumbed and was punished with dishonor or death. Sometimes the sexual implications were hidden—working, so to say, subliminally—or they were unconscious, and only our awareness of the disguises of suppressed desire enables us to recognize them.

The theme of such books was usually an innocent young woman faced with the threat of seduction or rape. This catered to the tastes of the women who were the main readers of fiction. The model was Richardson's *Clarissa.* In Lovelace, lust was naked and uncontrolled. "If I can have her *without* marriage," he wrote to a friend, "who can blame me for trying." It would be another century and a half before novelists would create a sexually more aggressive character. Richardson made such passion acceptable by ascribing it to a rake and by having the heroine resist it unto death—or marriage. The device was clever, veiling erotica in morality. It made *Clarissa* popular everywhere. What could be more titillating, more exciting than the way Lovelace tricked Clarissa into going off with him, kept her virtually prisoner in a house of assignation, and had her drugged so that he could rape her? Despite all its bows to purity and religion, *Clarissa* is simply a drawn-out sexual contest, with virginity as the grand prize, between a youth willing to resort to crime to enjoy it and a girl ready to die before she will yield.

Testimony to the influence of this formula can be found in half a dozen of the earliest American novels of any consequence. Although *The Power of Sympathy* (1789) by William Hill Brown, the first American novel, announces that it is "founded on truth" and was in fact based on a scandal in a socially distinguished family, the Mortons, it is only a stilted imitation of *Clarissa.* Proclaiming its purity, it is dedicated to exposing to young ladies "the fatal consequences of seduction." [1] In the very first letters—letters are the benchmark of the *Clarissa* tradition—the hero, a young Bostonian named Harrington, tells a friend that he is smitten with the charms of a young lady—she is only fifteen!—Harriot Fawcet and would like to make her his mistress. But he soon admits that he and the girl are truly in love and plan to marry.

Since this eliminates seduction from the main narrative, the author, himself a young Bostonian, introduces a series of sermonizing conversations and tales on the wages of sin. For example, precocious Harriot tells of a Mr. Martin who developed a "diabolical appetite" for his wife's sister and seduced her by setting her up in an elegant apartment. When a child resulted from this "incestuous connexion," the woman committed suicide. This doleful symposium has hardly been completed before we learn that poor Harrington cannot after all marry Harriot because she is his sister. Apparently Harrington's father had seduced a Maria Fawcet and, even after marrying another woman (adding adultery to seduction), had a child by Maria—Harriot. The author resolves this ridiculous tangle by having Harriot go mad and die of grief, and young Harrington shoot himself. This leaves only the elder Harrington to collect the wages of his sins.

The most popular early American, or Anglo-American, novel, Susannah Rowson's *Charlotte Temple* (1794; London, 1791) was also in the Clarissa tradition. It was read eagerly throughout the nineteenth century, and a librarian told me that her mother spoke of it as a daring book. It must have acquired such a reputation through its melodramatic picture of the heroine's fate. The author, who had visited America with a troupe of British actors, based her novel on a true story, that of Charlotte Stanley, but there the relationship to life ends.[2]

Accompanied by wanton Mlle. La Rue—French women were the stock wantons of fiction—fifteen-year-old Charlotte, an English girl of good family, elopes with Montraville, a British officer going overseas to fight the Americans. Montraville, unlike Lovelace, is merely thoughtless, and after establishing his adolescent mistress in a farmhouse outside of New York, he turns to a belle of New York society. Soon he is persuaded by his fellow officer, Belcour, a libertine who covets Charlotte, that Charlotte is false to him. So Montraville deserts Charlotte even though she is now pregnant. Absurdly he leaves money for Charlotte's support with Belcour, who of course keeps it. The only conceivable purpose of such twists in the plot is to increase a gullible reader's sense of outrage.

Driven from the farm as "a nasty hussy" who is bearing a "bastard," [3] Charlotte flees to the city—in a snowstorm—and seeks help from Mlle. La Rue, now the wife of rich Colonel Crayton. But she is spurned, bears her child, and dies. Driven by remorse, Montraville kills Belcour—and visits Charlotte's grave regularly forever after. Mrs. Crayton is abandoned by her husband and later dies of vice and dissipation.

What the women who read *Charlotte Temple* wanted, as the audiences of popular fiction always want, was to share vicariously another woman's transgressions, experience her sufferings—at a safe distance—and feel easy pity at her cruel fate. An even more striking example of how pious morality seized on any tale to serve its purpose, is Hannah Foster's *The Coquette*. Mrs. Foster used the fragmentary story of Elizabeth Whitman, converting that independent-minded woman into Eliza Wharton, a pleasure-loving coquette. Eliza resents "domestic confinements," rejects two clergymen as suitors, and does not heed the warnings of friends that a certain Major Sanford is "a second Lovelace." She is so infatuated with the major that even after she has heard that he has married, a friend sees her admit him to her room at night. When the friend confronts her, Eliza admits her guilt, and in the true Clarissa manner declares that she is doomed.

In case any reader has missed the full implications of Eliza's fall, Sanford tells a friend that although he prefers Eliza to his wife he would never marry her because she is "seducible." [4] This is indeed a double standard: If a man can trick and seduce an otherwise innocent woman he should not marry her; he himself remains untarnished—and free to marry any available virgin. As a kind of afterthought of the author, Major Sanford's wife leaves him and he is disgraced. Mrs. Foster knew that Pierpont Edwards, whom she believed was Elizabeth Whitman's betrayer, went quite undisgraced to his destiny. But art had to be morally just though everyone knew that reality was not.

All of Charles Brockden Brown's novels reveal, as we have seen, an interest in seducers, rapists, and their victims. In a few the interest is almost morbid. In *Wieland,* Carwin proudly tells the heroine that he is a voluptuary, and he mocks her concern over her chastity. He does not rape her—apparently because he prefers to have women yield willingly—but contents himself with her maid Judith, who is plainly willing. The title character in *Ormond* is more aggressive. Influenced by the European cult known as the Illuminati, he believes himself above man's laws; he too scorns chastity and marriage. He is Byronic long before Byron. He easily seduces accomplished and charming Helena Cleves and keeps her as his mistress until he meets the virtuous Constantia Dudley. Like all heroines in the Clarissa mold, Constantia is strongly attracted to her aggressive suitor despite his unscrupulous code. When she refuses to submit to him, he asserts that he will possess her dead or alive. In defending herself, Constantia accidentally kills him—a denouement that is pointless both as drama and morality. Like Carwin, Ormond is a Lovelace with more than a dash of Godwinism in him.

Libertines or seducible women turn up sooner or later in all of Brown's other novels—from *Edgar Huntley* to *Jane Talbot* and *Clara Howard.* How far Brown dared to go is demonstrated by *Arthur Mervyn* (1799–1800), story of an innocent youth's adventures in Philadelphia in 1793, year of the yellow fever epidemic. Young Mervyn leaves his farm home when his widowed father marries a slut. In the big city he falls in with Welbeck, an aging libertine. The city is pictured as a plague-stricken Sodom, but the youth, a kind of American Candide, maintains his faith in man even though he is repeatedly spurned, duped, and beaten.

Sexual trespasses abound. On coming from England, Welbeck had begun his career by getting his host's married sister with child and leaving her to die of shame. Mervyn finds Welbeck living with an Italian girl, Clemenza, who came to him as his ward but whom he has seduced and whom he abandons after she has borne his child. In a characteristically grotesque episode Mervyn discovers that Clemenza has been left in the home of a supposedly respectable Mrs. Villars and her three daughters, who turn out to be prostitutes.

Brown admitted that he used "puerile" Gothic elements to heighten interest;[5] and certainly his Wielands and Ormonds live by such outlandish creeds that we can hardly consider them reliable guides to the standards of the time. Often they pass, like Poe's characters, into the realm of Gothic fantasy. But we can hardly believe that this array of sexually aggressive men and erring women does not reflect at least a layer of society in which such men and women were not uncommon. But by the end of Brown's career the freedom of behavior that had marked the revolutionary 1780's and 1790's was clearly being curtailed. Disenchantment with radical extremism was followed by a retreat into respectability. For forty years there was scarcely a single American work that might have been considered unfit for an innocent young reader. Poems by Byron and Burns on forbidden themes, and "daring" novels by Charlotte Brontë, Balzac, and Sue came over from Europe, but the most admired American writers—Irving, Cooper, Bryant, Poe—produced works notable for their asexuality.

If a sexually aggressive character did appear in a novel, the reader could be sure he would turn out to be a villain, if not a fiend. In Hawthorne's first work, *Fanshawe,* a mysterious character lures the angelic heroine into a dark wood and is about to attack her when the hero frightens him off. The sexual elements here are those of a fairy tale—the golden-haired maiden led away by a foul spirit and rescued by a young knight—a rather bumbling knight, it must be said—with the villain duly tumbling off a cliff.

Similarly, the offender against moral standards in W. Gilmore Simms' first novel, *Guy Rivers: A Tale of Georgia* (1834), is a lawyer-politician who has turned outlaw and revels in his crimes. Among Rivers' sins is his seduction of gentle, trusting Ellen, who lives with her dying mother. Rivers soon abandons her, his fancy shifting to Lucy, the bright young niece of the local innkeeper. But Lucy loves another, so Rivers seizes her, and, according to the well-established formula, is interrupted just as he is about to rape her. Rivers' towering lust suggests that Simms, who came from South Carolina, had seen enough of the Southern frontier to know that outlaws, even former lawyers, had as little regard for sexual as for any other taboos. *Guy Rivers* was repeatedly reprinted, and Simms became a well-known novelist.

The point at which the morality novel of seduction or adultery became a pretext for pornography was reached in the works of George Lippard. In a number of novels, several of them huge, published between 1844 and his death ten years later at the age of thirty-two, Lippard indulged in descriptions of fornication, rape, and adultery unmatched for eroticism until the next century.

Lippard was able to gain acceptance for these massive doses of lust and crime by interlacing them with diatribes against social injustice and attacks on corrupt lawyers, merchants, bankers, ministers, and other pillars of the establishment. Just as his sexual scenes were far more lascivious than any ever published in America, so his characterizations of venality and hypocrisy in high places were more virulent, and his Gothic horrors more sensational. To provide morsels for everyone, he tossed in among his minor villains such popular scapegoats as a gorilla-like Negro and a reptilian Jewish moneylender. In fact, any attempt to classify Lippard is hopeless because his novels are such a mélange of excesses.

It was evidently this turbid mixture of emotionalism and violence that accounted for the huge success of his books, and especially his first novel, *The Quaker City; or, The Monks of Monk Hall, a Romance of Philadelphia Life, Mystery and Crime*

(1844). *The Quaker City* is said to have sold 300,000 copies in ten years. Lippard became one of the most successful writers of the period, readers waiting eagerly for the next weekly installment of his latest thriller. The arrant contradictions between Lippard's lofty statements of purpose and the indecency of his performance did not go unchallenged. But when charges of "gross sensualism" were leveled against *The Quaker City,* the publisher capitalized on them with a provocative announcement on the title page of later editions: "No American novel has ever commanded so wide-spread an interest as this work. . . . On the one hand, it has been denounced as a work of the most immoral and incendiary character; on the other, it has been elaborately praised as a painfully vivid picture of life in the Great City. . . ." Even more righteously, Lippard asserted that if a murderer deserves death by the gallows, an "assassin of chastity and maidenhood is worthy of death by the hands of any man, and in any place." It was exaggeration piled upon exaggeration, but it enabled Lippard to purvey the most lubricious scenes he could imagine. Lippard also claimed that his book was based on facts he had gathered during his "studentship in the office of an Attorney-General." [6]

The focus of *The Quaker City* is Monk Hall, outwardly a decayed mansion but actually a secret clubhouse where a group of rich Philadelphians indulges in every kind of orgy and crime. To this shrine of Gothic sexuality, a prosperous young libertine, Gus Lorrimer, lures Mary Arlington, innocent daughter of a good family, with a promise of marriage. He then proceeds to caress her until her "animal nature" is aroused. With the instinct of the true pornographer, Lippard stretches out the seduction over several chapters, periodically describing lingering kisses, the outlines of Mary's "ripening maidenhood" under her thin night robe, her throbbing pulse, and Lorrimer's hand on her heaving bosom. At last Lorrimer presses home his caresses: Mary "felt as though she was about to fall swooning on the floor . . . her bosom rose no longer quick and gaspingly, but in long pulsations that urged the full Globes in all their virgin beauty, softly and slowly into view. . . ." Then Lorrimer, "a fearful picture of incarnate LUST," takes her.

After the classic seduction of innocence comes the classic adultery: Livingstone, a merchant, learns to his horror from his junior partner that his young wife Dora is meeting her lover, his business friend Fitz-Cowles. The partner leads him to Monk Hall and into a luxurious bedchamber where he sees Fitz-Cowles asleep with Dora, his arm carelessly lying across her bare bosom.

Other such erotic tableaux, including the effect of drugs that arouse the "animal passions" of women, are interspersed with scenes of sadism. The end is a farrago of Gothic horrors punctuated by sermons entitled "Woe unto Sodom!"

Even though his experience was limited to Philadelphia and seems to have come mainly from an old-time lawyer, Lippard did not hesitate to apply *The Quaker City* formula to New York. *New York: The Upper Ten and the Lower Million* paralleled *The Quaker City* in having an innocent fifteen-year-old girl drugged, "violated," and tricked into a bogus marriage with a rich and aging lecher. Within a few months she is converted into the "Midnight Queen," presiding over a company of rich debauchees who meet for their revels in a magnificent mansion. The preface in this book seeks to justify the eroticism by a fierce assault on unearned wealth; the implication—which middle- and lower-class readers could be expected to relish—was that easily acquired riches encouraged vicious dissipation.[7] In *New York: The Upper Ten and the Lower Million,* Lippard, imitating himself, produced a caricature of a caricature.

Of the major American writers of mid-nineteenth-century America, Herman Melville alone reveals an awareness of men's capacity for aberrant sexual passions. Considering the length of whaling and other sea voyages in the 1830's and 1840's, it is hardly surprising that the only intimations of sexuality in such tales of the sea as *White Jacket, Moby Dick,* and *Billy Budd* are homosexual. But the relationships are mostly so open and innocent-seeming that readers probably did not recognize them for what they were. Only once, in *White Jacket,* a documentary of life on an American warship in the 1840's, does Melville speak of the forbidden relations that spring up among men in a ship too long at sea:

> The sins for which the cities of the plain were overthrown still linger in some of these wooden-walled Gomorrahs of the deep. More than once complaints were made at the mast in the *Neversink,* from which the deck officers would turn away with loathing. . . . There are evils in men-of-war, which . . . will

> hardly bear thinking of. The landsman who has neither read Walpole's *Mysterious Mother,* nor Sophocles's *Oedipus Tyrannus,* nor the Roman story of Count Cenci, dramatised by Shelley, let that landsman guardedly remain in his ignorance of even worse horrors than these, and forever abstain from drawing aside the veil.[8]

And yet, at the same time, the young narrator—that is, Melville himself—describes Jack Chase, "the noble captain of the top," in such rhapsodic terms that it seems plain, as the critic William Plomer says,[9] that he won Melville's "best love" as no one else ever did. It was to Chase that Melville forty-one years later dedicated *Billy Budd,* a book about another kind of manly beauty, a golden-haired, "welkin-eyed," innocent youth, a lad for whom it was evidently possible to feel an emotion far stronger than friendship. Perhaps some of the force of Billy's triangular relationship to Master-at-Arms Claggart and Captain Vere arises from the fact that in Claggart's embittered soul stifled love of the youth turned to hate while in Vere it was tragically overwhelmed by duty and obligation.

But it was in *Pierre: or The Ambiguities,* in which he turned from tales of the sea to a story of his native place and class, that Melville discloses the perverse passions that fascinated him. The relationships in *Pierre* are tantalizingly murky and confused because the sexual passion remains suppressed, making itself felt only in violent and irrational behavior.

Considered an ideal son, rich young Pierre Glendinning is in reality a victim of the age's excessive emphasis on purity. Although he is engaged to Lucy Tartan, he reveals such a loverlike attachment to his handsome, widowed mother that we foresee his difficulties in facing any normal sexual union.

When Pierre learns from a local sewing girl named Isabel, as darkly beautiful as Lucy is fair, that she is the daughter of Pierre's father by a Frenchwoman (always the immoral Frenchwoman!) just before the father's marriage, the effect on Pierre is traumatic. Stricken by guilt, Pierre decides that he must atone for his father's sin, his own life of ease, and Isabel's deprivation. To acknowledge Isabel fully but to avoid shaming his mother, he feigns marriage to Isabel and goes off to the city with her. This incredible act serves only to crush his mother, prostrate Lucy, and lead to a relationship between him and Isabel that is incestuous in all but the fact. Repeatedly, we are told, Pierre "imprinted burning kisses upon her; pressed her hand. . . . Then . . . they coiled together, and entangledly stood mute." [10] Lucy finally senses what has motivated Pierre and, swept by frustrated desire, insists on living with him and Isabel, if only as a companion. As though he must solace all who are punished for their sexuality, Pierre also gives refuge to a servant girl who has been seduced and abandoned. The youth and the women make up a household awash in ambiguous and twisted emotions.

Pierre is perhaps the only hero in American fiction whose tragic flaw is an excess of virtue. And such is the ambiguity of virtue that it is here derived from fear—fear of sexual consummation, from guilt before the fact, a Galahad-like species of Puritanism. Pierre is, in his own words, a fool of Virtue: he wants to practice on earth what is possible only in heaven. He is as much driven by a demon as is Captain Ahab, but it is the old American demon of sexual purity. The result is catastrophic: Pierre, his two loves, and his mother all die. If there is any moral in this thicket of strangled loves, it is that misguided virtue is as dangerous as evil.

In certain aspects of the novel, as in the tie between Pierre and Isabel, Melville reveals a daring grasp of the amoral force of the sexual impulse. But in other ways, as in Pierre's response to his father's transgression, he is bound by the standards of his narrow time and place. Understandably, readers did not know what to make of the book, no doubt stimulated by its stirring of buried impulses but frightened by the undertones of incest and homosexuality and the union of an aggressively pure young man and three passionate young women.

In terms of sensuality as well as sexuality, Whitman's *Leaves of Grass* was the most remarkable American book of the century. We have noted the attempts to suppress it and punish its author; next to Whitman's open exuberance and sensuality, the effort seems prissy and mean. Most Victorians must have found it impossible to cope with him at all. They understood furtive lechery and the disguised libertine, but what could be done with this relaxed, joyous, supremely benign man who opened his arms to the prostitute and made night desires, feverish caresses, the jet of sperm, the flow of woman juices, and the rank work of the body into hymns and rhapsodies. To them it seemed not only indecent but too self-revealing, too embarrassingly intimate. How could any respectable person acknowledge having even read the book? So they simply averted their gaze.

Whitman violated not one but an entire array of banned themes, and he did so in the very first edition of *Leaves of Grass,* in 1856, at the dead center of the Victorian era. He celebrated first the body in all its animalism, then the love of man and woman, and finally the love of man for man. Of the flesh and the senses he wrote: "Walt Whitman am I, a Kosmos . . ./ Turbulent, fleshy and sensual, eating, drinking and breeding," and, "Copulation is no more rank to me than death," and, "Winds whose soft-tickling genitals rub against me." [11] Of the fevers of youth he said:

> The young man that wakes deep at night, the hot hand
> seeking to repress what would master him;
> The mystic amorous night—the strange half-welcome
> pangs, visions, sweats,
> The pulse pounding through palms and trembling encircling
> fingers—the young man all color'd, red,
> ashamed, angry. . . .[12]

Of the love of woman he sang:

> I turn the bridegroom out of bed, and stay with the bride
> myself;
> I tighten her all night to my thighs and lips.[13]

and:

> Hair, bosom, hips, bend of legs, negligent falling hands,
> all diffused—mine too diffused;
> Ebb stung by the flow, and flow stung by the ebb—
> love-flesh swelling and deliciously aching;
> Limitless limpid jets of love hot and enormous, quivering
> jelly of love, white-blow and delicious juice;
> Bridegroom night of love, working surely and
> softly into the prostrate dawn. . . .[14]

and:

> Love-thoughts, love-juice, love-odor, love-yielding,
> love climbers and the climbing sap,

Arms and hands of love—lips of love—phallic thumb
of love—breasts of love—bellies press'd and glued
together with love. . . .[15]

And then revelations of the love of man for man:

Or possibly with you sailing at sea, or on the beach of the
sea, or some quiet island,
Here to put your lips upon mine I permit you,
With the comrade's long-dwelling kiss, or the new
husband's kiss,
For I am the new husband, and I am the comrade.[16]

and:

For the one I love most lay sleeping by me under the same
cover in the cool night,
In the stillness, in the autumn moonbeams, his face
was inclined toward me,
And his arm lay lightly around my breast—and that
night I was happy.[17]

As Whitman grew older, it was quite clear that he preferred young men to young women, and sometimes, as with Peter Doyle, so passionately that he had to fight against the attraction. But when John Addington Symonds, admittedly homosexual, questioned him on the Calamus poems, Whitman claimed that he was "dazed" at the "terrible" construction Symonds had put upon them, and called such inferences "damnable." [18] Once again he protested—too much perhaps—that although he had never married, he had had six children.

It became easier for the public to accept Whitman when advancing age and the sobriquet of "the Good Grey Poet" caused him to seem venerable and harmless. Teachers made the acceptance even easier by treating him chiefly as the poet of democracy and the author of such poems as the tribute to Lincoln, "O Captain! My Captain!" which could be declaimed in the most patriotic circles. The evidences of a more than brotherly affection for his fellowmen were dismissed as an excess of the spirit of camaraderie.

Although poets today can, both in language and life, be infinitely more candid than Whitman was, he still seems a uniquely bold and passionate man, one who spoke out without reckoning the cost of his reputation among proper Americans. In the struggle for uninhibited expression he was a giant. Nor can he be diminished by being treated as a creature of merely sensual and sometimes aberrant instincts. There is no more penetrating statement about censorship than the one he made to Horace Traubel: "The dirtiest book in all the world is an expurgated book."

John William De Forest, long a neglected novelist of the 1860's and 1870's, was, as a realist, one of the most interesting writers of his time. Perhaps because of six years spent abroad, his wide reading of European writers, his long service in the Union Army and his experiences in the South after the war, De Forest dealt boldly and sometimes harshly with such subjects as the power of businessmen, venal politicians, and Southern character. His treatment of love was no less candid and free of idealization. It is most impressively so in *Miss Ravenel's Conversion* (1867).

At the outbreak of war, Dr. Ravenel, a courtly South Carolina physician who had practiced in New Orleans for twenty years, takes his attractive eighteen-year-old daughter Lillie to the North because he considers Southerners corrupt and vile. In Connecticut, Lillie meets an army officer, Colonel Carter, a handsome man in his mid-thirties who comes from good Virginia stock but remains, as a West Pointer, loyal. Carter is a man of action, heavy drinker, roué; by contrast, Lillie's Northern suitor, a young lawyer named Colburne, is modest, temperate, but hopelessly inhibited by his heritage. Captured by Carter's virility and oblivious of his undisciplined nature, Lillie falls in love with him and marries him.

Delineated as frankly and fully as Carter is Lillie's Creole aunt, Mrs. Larue. An alluring young widow—once again a Frenchwoman carrying the torch of sexual liberty—she believes in taking love wherever she finds it. She admires Don Juan, she says, because there are "wise reasons" why men should pursue women. When she and Colonel Carter happen to take the same riverboat going North—after Carter's division has occupied New Orleans—she does not hesitate to entice him. "Do you not pity me?" she asks. "Thirty years old, a widow, and childless! No one to love; no right to love anyone."[19] She celebrates the *sainte passion de l'amour,* declaring, "Love always has this great defence—that nature prompts it, commands it. As for self-repression, asphyxia of the heart, Nature never prompts that." Summing her up, De Forest says: "Her vices and virtues . . . were all instinctive. . . . She was as corrupt as possible without self-reproach, and as amiable as possible without self-restraint." Carter is a willing victim. He curses himself for a villain, but he continues the liaison even after they have returned to New Orleans and his Lillie has borne a child. Later he celebrates a military victory by getting drunk with a fellow officer and two camp followers.

The portraits of Mrs. Larue and Colonel Carter are rounded out shrewdly and with understanding. They are neither bad nor good; they simply love love more than they love virtue. De Forest does not sentimentalize about purity or moralize about lust. He does, however, permit certain harsh consequences to result from the promiscuity: Lillie learns about the liaison and is heartbroken; Carter rides into his last battle knowing of Lillie's agony; and, most significant of De Forest's unromanticized view, Mrs. Larue is last seen making a handsome profit on a sale to the North of contraband cotton arranged by some of her high-placed Secessionist friends.

Outside of a few minor concessions, *Miss Ravenel's Conversion* is singularly free from the moral clichés of Victorian America. But its characterizations were subtle and serious, and young women readers, the Iron Maidens of taste, ignored it.

But De Forest was almost alone. The taboos of American fiction against the harsher realities of sexuality were not truly breached until the 1890's. By then Zola, Tolstoi, Flaubert, Maupassant, and others had shown how it must be done. Various other influences, from the growth of slums to the view that life is determined by environment, freed writers to deal with sexuality as it flourished amidst poverty and vice.

The breakthrough was made mainly by Stephen Crane. Coming from the family of a small-town New Jersey minister, he joined all those other sons of poor parsons who had rejected the remote and pallid solutions of the church. As a writer, Crane seems to have started, *ab ovo,* with an immense contempt for what he called the literature of "pink valentines" and with a conviction that even Howells and Garland were not telling anything like the whole truth about American life. All he needed as literary inspiration he got from a reading of *Madame Bovary* and Zola's *L'Assommoir.* But this was much less important than the brief period he spent as a newspaperman in New York's Bowery district, where he telescoped experience as if he knew he would die at twenty-nine and must make one year do for ten.

The result was *Maggie: A Girl of the Streets* (1893), which Crane drafted when he was twenty-one. Its story of an ignorant factory girl betrayed by a mindless young bartender, told with utter lack of sentiment and in an ironic style, challenged most of the conventions of the traditional novel of seduction. When Maggie is discarded by her boyfriend and rejected by her family, she takes to the streets and dies there.

Maggie does not abandon all the conventions of the seduction genre. The squalor and cruelty of Maggie's family are barbaric, yet there is a kind of inverted romanticism in her melodramatic downfall. How many such girls had a drunken tyrant for a mother, a near-pimp for a brother, and so feral a betrayer? No less than Richardson and his American imitators, Crane saw the woman as an innocent, pitiable victim, and the seducer as a monster. Had Maggie been aware of what she faced—as a girl from such slums might well have been—it would of course have deprived the story of much of its force.

Maggie does differ in a major respect from the tradition of *Clarissa* or of the nineteenth-century English gentleman's seduction of poor working girls. In *Maggie,* seduction has neither political nor class overtones. It is one of the triumphs of democracy that in America a rich man had no more seduction privileges and not much more sexual opportunities than a poor man. Any number of English Maggies were seduced by their peers of the London slums, but the picture given in *My Secret Life* of a well-heeled English gentleman able to seduce literally hundreds of working girls because he is of the master class is peculiarly British. If anything, well-to-do Americans bewailed the fact that so few servant girls were available and that even the few were often insufferably independent.

Altogether, *Maggie's* freedom from religious cant, its mockery of the grotesque sentimentality of its characters, and its bare, blunt style was a giant step toward the savage candor of the fiction of the 1930's. Its failure was to be expected; a few brave critics hailed it, but others called it crude and shocking.

Crane's own life reinforces our feeling that in him the respectability of Howells and James, of Lowell and Whittier, has at last been left behind. Even as a young newspaperman in New York Crane displayed a curious indifference to decorum, casually consorting with loose women. Detesting the Mrs. Grundys, he said of a gossipy woman in upstate New York who had frowned on his behavior: "No man is strong enough to attack this mummy because she is a nice woman." [20] The joke, he added, was that she was "just the grave of a stale lust and every boy in town knows it. She accepted ruin at the hands of a farmer when we were all ten or eleven. But she is a nice woman. . . ."

When New York police harassed a chorus girl and a streetwalker whom Crane was interviewing, he went into court to testify against the police and acquired a reputation for dubious associations and quixotic behavior. Mocking pretense, he questioned the Victorian assumption that every woman of the streets had been led there by some evil man. "Lots of women," he said, "are just naturally unchaste" [21]—a once-shocking statement that now seems fairly obvious. This hatred for the hypocrites along with a feeling that women were "hunted animals" may explain how he came to live for a time in a boardinghouse used by prostitutes and why most of the women in his life had either been unhappy in marriage or were harlots.

Crane's culminating gesture was his liaison, when he was twenty-five, with Cora Taylor, a woman of about thirty who managed a Jacksonville, Florida, nightclub. The club, with the surrealist name of Hotel de Dream, was not a brothel only because the "girls" did not board there. Since her husband would not divorce her, Cora lived with Crane as his common-law wife for the last four years of his life—the years of his fame as the author of *The Red Badge of Courage,* of his extravagant living and spending, and, finally, of his declining health. As improvident as Crane, dowdy, kind, ambitious, Cora was by all accounts an amiable and loyal, if not distinguished, companion. Because they would have been hounded by the police in New York, they stayed in England, where Crane's closest friend, the

American novelist and correspondent, Harold Frederic, also lived with a common-law wife.[22]

Crane's union with Cora Taylor, together with such books as *Maggie,* and rumors, quite unfounded, that he took opium and had other dreadful habits, cast over his reputation a lurid glow that caused him to be looked on askance by all proper people. But the generation of the 1920's rediscovered him, along with such other not readily classifiable artists as Whitman, Melville, and Emily Dickinson, and he has come to represent a significant step in our moral as well as our literary history.

So far we have considered only books published in the normal way and readily available to any reader. We come now to those works of a bawdy kind that were circulated privately, and to out-and-out pornography printed secretly and sold surreptitiously. The two kinds are quite different in purpose and nature. The bawdy poem or story is generally tossed off by a recognized writer as a *jeu d'esprit* or a display of lusty maleness. It is a kind of protest—albeit a rather safe one—against the forces of censorship and the spirit of gentility. It is also different from pornography in that it is more or less spontaneous, sometimes circulated only in a manuscript, and certainly not written for profit.

Several of Ben Franklin's squibs and letters were, as we have noted, of this kind. But the best-known piece of bawdy Americana is Mark Twain's *1601, or Fireside Conversation in the Time of the Tudors.* Twain later said that he had been reading widely in older English writers from Shakespeare to Pepys, with Rabelais and Margaret of Navarre thrown in for good measure, and in 1876 had decided to set down a conversation such as might have taken place at Queen Elizabeth's fireside. It was intended, he said, to show his old friend the Reverend Joseph Twichell, a Congregationalist minister from Hartford, how free the speech of noble Englishmen had once been. Clemens added that if there was "a decent or delicate word findable in it, it is because I overlooked it."

The conversationalists are a few famous writers, such as Shakespeare and Jonson, and several noblewomen, including a fifteen-year-old girl. The talk consists of random exchanges on such subjects as farting and fornication. It is as much scatological as sexual and depends heavily on the incongruity of such illustrious personages using such dirty words. Twain is here the bad boy being as naughty as he can be.

What is significant about *1601* is that Clemens' friends received it enthusiastically, one of them declaring that it would outlive *Innocents Abroad,* and another, in charge of the press at West Point, printing fifty copies on fine linen paper. The confusion of values here is bewildering: A famous writer resorts to a furtive piece of writing to give vent to his bawdy humors, and a friend solemnly wraps it in the respectability of a fine binding. Dozens of editions in many languages followed.

More like his ribald jokes or the talks he occasionally gave to men's groups was the little poem, "I thank Thee for the bull, O God . . .", that he wrote in tribute to male animals with mighty sexual organs. The introductory note is droll: "I intended it for Sunday schools, and when sung by a hundred guileless children, it produces a very pretty effect." Despite the way Samuel L. Clemens kept insisting that men must submit to moral laws, Mark Twain-Sawyer was forever exploding dirty jokes and poems. But he did it privately, among men, where the decent women he professed to adore couldn't stifle or censor him.

It is curious that another popular writer of the period who wrote naughty poems in his spare time, Eugene Field, was also a writer for boys and was in fact cherished for the homely and wholesome sentiment of his verse. Such poems as "Little Willie" and "In Imitation of Robert Herrick," which rely heavily on such body-function humor as bed-wetting and wind-breaking, are embarrassingly tame and puerile. Another book, *Only a Boy,* is attributed to Field, but it has a hero of such heroic sexual capacities as to make the attribution seem like a hoax. If Field did write *Only a Boy,* it was an almost cynical mockery of all that he stood for in the public eye.

There is no point in examining individual pornographic novels. Such works, as Steven Marcus[23] has shown, have no genuine individuality. They have only one theme, sexual activity, and only one purpose, to gratify sexual wish fantasies. To that end they generally have but two characters—a man who takes any woman he wants and can perform any number of sexual acts at any time, and a woman who is, or soon becomes, insatiably amorous. To arouse the more jaded readers, the woman may be an innocent young girl or a nun who must be seduced or debauched before she joins in the exercises. Or there may be some lurid episodes of flagellation, lesbian coupling, or sodomy. The characters have no other aspects to their lives. Nor does it matter where the action takes place. The plot is the same everywhere in the world.

What is of interest to us, then, is not the contents of such books but how popular they were. Since their readers use them to compensate for lack of more direct sexual outlets, that is, as a release for sexual energies, such works should be most in demand in a period when the more direct sexual activities have been discouraged. And so it was: From the 1830's on in both America and England—it is difficult to separate the two where these books are concerned—the publication as well as the sale of erotica flourished. In England it became a minor industry.

The first evidence of the circulation of erotica in America was the six-month jail term given in 1821 to two Massachusetts book peddlers for selling copies of *Fanny Hill* to farmers. *Fanny Hill, or the Memoirs of a Woman of Pleasure* (1748), the sexual adventures of an inexhaustibly lusty prostitute, recalls in its picaresque energy the novels of Fielding and Smollett. Part of its effect comes from its rendering of the most lascivious acts in the most orotund eighteenth-century style. *Fanny Hill* was soon popular everywhere and not least in America.

We have seen how the Reverend McDowall stunned his fellow clergymen in 1834 with a display of the obscene books and other "diabolical" objects he had collected from all over New York State. Most of these books and pictures were imported from England and France; and by 1842 there was enough of an international traffic in them to warrant a law by Congress forbidding their importation. Whereupon publishers began to produce such pornography in America. The first of these publishers, William Haynes, formerly an Irish surgeon, brought out an edition of *Fanny Hill*; it was such a success that he went on to publish more than three hundred other titles, writing a considerable number of them himself.

Most American erotica continued to be editions of European works, but obviously American titles turned up from time to time, such as *Flora Montgomerie, the Factory Girl, a Tale of the Lowell Factories, Being a Recital of the Adventures of a*

Libidinous Millionaire; The Life and Amours of Kate Percival, the Belle of Delaware; The Libertine Enchantress, or the Adventures of Lucinda Hartley; John, the Darling of the Philadelphia Ladies; and the alleged sufferings of a Canadian nun, *The Awful Disclosures of Maria Monk.* Later there was *The Secret Services of Major Lovitt,* a Civil War concoction, and a "confession" entitled *Secret History of a Votary of Pleasure.* Most of these are inferior examples of the type, shabby even among the shabby.

By the end of the Civil War the stream of pornography had become such a flood that in New York the YMCA and their man, Anthony Comstock, sprang into action: They confiscated 150,000 pounds of obscene literature and drove several dealers out of business. Comstock arrested one dealer, Conroy, three times in four years, repeatedly confiscating his stock; the third time, Conroy knifed him in the cheek. But by 1872 the trade was being carried on more openly than ever. Comstock, demonstrating to a *Tribune* reporter, arrested seven book dealers in one day and with tireless zeal hounded four publishers who, he said, had issued at least 165 erotic titles. The mailing of obscene books and pictures was prohibited by Congress in 1865 and the "Comstock Laws" followed in 1872. Thereafter for more than forty years Comstock and his lieutenants were busy confiscating everything from *The Lustful Turk* to Boccaccio, Whitman, and George Bernard Shaw. The results were always reported by weight, as though all of it was just so much soiled paper: thus in 1913 Comstock summed up his life's work with a statement that he had destroyed, among other things, 160 tons of obscene literature.

The message here is that in Victorian America pornography thrived as never before. It thrived because it was the easiest and safest, if not the most satisfactory, sexual expression for frustrated men. That it was aimed entirely at men (further differentiating it from popular fiction, which was meant chiefly for women) is clear from the fact that the main character is always a sexual Hercules who can convert even the most frigid or unwilling woman into a slave of desire and reduce her to delirious ecstasy.

Compared to the satisfactions yielded by such books, going to a brothel was dangerous, having a decent girl whenever one wanted was impossible, and masturbation was said to cause all kinds of disorders. In an age that insisted that a normal woman experienced little or no desire, what a confirmation of fantasies it was to learn how wildly passionate any woman could become! Such books were the answer to an adolescent's daydream, whether the adolescent was sixteen or sixty. What the Victorians refused to recognize was that the dreams summoned up the books, not the other way around. One need not be a psychoanalyst to realize that such books were meant chiefly for men who, far from being fierce in their lust and dangerous to society, were pathetic. They were, after all, content with a vicarious experience; lacking a woman they were satisfied by a book.

22.

PASSIONATE SOUTH AND TURBULENT WEST

TO those who think of the South as it was in plantation days, the moral and religious history of the region in its earliest period holds surprises. The pioneers of Jamestown lived under an almost Puritanical code. Church attendance was obligatory, and taxes on dress discouraged elegance. But this rigor was dictated mainly by pioneer conditions. As an affluent class emerged and the sons of Cavalier families came from England after Cromwell's Roundheads began their offensive, the entire tone of life changed. The Cavalier gentry in particular looked on extreme piety as in bad taste. The spread of plantations manned by black slaves soon gave rise to a master class disdainful of work and devoted to pleasure and sport. Among the many privileges these men assumed was that of sexual domination over slaves and servants.

From the very first, young white women who came to America as servants, and especially as indentured or bond servants, were vulnerable to sexual pressures from their masters. Alone in a strange land, it took much courage for a girl to resist a man who could make her life miserable and even sell her for the remainder of her term of bondage. The result was little chastity and a high rate of bastardy. Cruelly, girls who bore a child out of wedlock were condemned to serve an additional term to compensate their masters for the time lost in child bearing.[1] If the master was the father, the service was paid to the local church wardens. In any case, the motive of profit was added to that of lust, and only the girl suffered.

Far more widespread and corrupting was the relationship between white masters or overseers and their women slaves. Anyone acquainted with pre-Civil War plantation society knows that behind the façade of gracious living, chivalry, and hospitality—qualities that were romanticized in recollection and at best were true only of a small elite—lurked relations between white men and black women that amounted to institutionalized promiscuity. Never publicly acknowledged, it was a far more cruel and irresponsible system than Eastern forms of concubinage. Along with the forced breeding of slaves, the higher value put on light-colored slaves born of mixed parentage, and the selling of black girls into prostitution, it turned some plantations into brothels for its white men and made a mockery among the slaves of such conceptions as chastity and monogamy.

Many white men accepted the system as their divine right and justified it by what they considered their racial superiority. In this they were merely accepting the belief of seventeenth-century Englishmen that black Africans were the descendants of Noah's accursed son Ham—wild creatures only a little above the apes. Even their black color was considered God-given evidence of their benighted nature. Some states wrote this attitude into law, Louisiana declaring that "slaves could not contract matrimony" and that their sexual association was "without sanctity."

The corruption of the white man's morals often began in childhood. Frederick Law Olmsted, brilliant landscape architect responsible for many of the best parks of America's cities, wrote three richly documented books—he interviewed no less than five hundred white men—on his long journeys through the South from 1852 to 1856. In these books he told of planters who sent their sons to be educated in the North because boys could not be brought up in decency in the South.[2] The Reverend John Dixon Long, son of a Maryland slave owner, recalled that white children often heard and saw things in the slave quarters that no child should see or hear. He added that slaves often gloried in corrupting the children of their owners.[3]

It was mainly the boys who picked up licentious ways. According to Arthur Calhoun, historian of the American family, one former mayor of Huntsville, Alabama, declared that, in general, every young man in his state "became addicted to fornication at an early age." [4] Similarly, a Tennessee slave owner declared that in the slave-holding settlements of middle and southern Mississippi, where he had lived for several years, there was not a virtuous male of twenty years of age. Olmsted reported that on two occasions a planter's fourteen- and sixteen-year-old sons were supposed to share a room with him when he visited their father's plantation but that they spent both nights in the Negroes' cabins.[5]

But the full extent of the immorality of the Southern male is evident only when the grown man, having married and become a slave owner, had black women, including married slaves, gratify his desires. In the light of this behavior, the pride that such men took in the purity of their white women seems obscenely hypocritical. We are appalled by the medieval custom of *droit du seigneur* or *jus primae noctis,* yet many a Southern planter or his overseer did not wait until the eve of a slave girl's marriage to assert his claim on her body.

It was, moreover, nearly hopeless for a slave woman to deny her owner. He could punish her until she submitted, or he could sell her. In her *Journal of a Residence on a Georgian Plantation in 1838–39,* Frances Anne Kemble gives a chilling picture of what a black girl faced when she resisted. Frances, daughter of the celebrated English actor, Charles Kemble, had abandoned a successful stage career to marry Pierce Butler, who had inherited a vast Georgia cotton and rice plantation worked by seven hundred slaves. Butler preferred to live in Philadelphia, but Fanny visited the plantation for four months. She was horrified by the experience. One entry in her journal describes a slave woman named Judy who was forced by the overseer, a Mr. King, then flogged for having resisted him and finally sent off for a period of solitary exile on an island in a swamp. The woman, who had borne a son to King, declared that the swamp was so dreadful that she preferred being flogged.[6]

Other observers gave similar testimony. The Reverend Charles Elliott, an Ohio clergyman, tells of a farmer near St. Louis who took several of his slaves, including a beautiful, well-behaved quadroon girl, on board a boat headed for the New Orleans slave market. On the way, he told the quadroon that if she would submit to him, he would make her his housekeeper; otherwise he would sell her as a field slave. She submitted and in time bore him four children; he later married and sold her and her children.[7] Such a woman had no recourse whatsoever since she had no standing in a court of law.

Although Southerners used the white fear of miscegenation as a major reason for not freeing the slaves, the mixing of the races went on apace on many plantations. If a visitor had any doubt of this, it was soon dispelled, as every traveler testified, by the number of mulatto children who resembled their master or his overseer. Charles Janson, who came to America in 1793, stayed thirteen years and traveled widely, declared that it was not uncommon to see a planter waited on by a mulatto who was obviously his son.[8] Another traveler, Isaac Candler, reported in 1824 that a white man who fathered children by black women would still be received in the best society.[9] It was rarely thought monstrous that a master who begot children by a slave thereby committed them to slavery. Over and over the opponents of slavery pointed out that the best blood of Virginia flowed in the veins of mulatto slaves. After the Civil War, one Sabbath school in Jackson, Mississippi, was said to have mingled the unacknowledged sons of a governor, a senator, doctors, lawyers, ministers, planters, craftsmen, and laborers. A Louisiana planter of an old Scottish family told Olmsted that there was no "likely-looking colored girl in the state who was not the paramour of a white man," and no plantation on which "the grandchildren of the owner are not whipped in the field by his overseer." The planter spoke not out of sympathy for the whipped but out of narrow pride, adding that he could not bear the thought that his family's blood should run in the veins of slaves.[10]

But many other slave owners, motivated by greed as well as lechery, were not so proud. Slaves were wealth, so planters often bred them like cattle. Black girls were encouraged to begin bearing as early as possible. Olmsted saw an unwed fourteen-year-old who was already a mother, and Captain Marryat came upon a pregnant twelve-year-old slave girl—so light he thought she was white—near Louisville. It was even said that white men were paid the equivalent of stud fees for the children they begot upon slave women. Frederick Douglass recalled that his owner had hired a white man to sleep with a young black woman—he locked them up together at night—until she was pregnant.[11] Mulatto girls were also more profitable for sale as prostitutes for the cities, some of them bringing several thousand dollars.

In defense of Southern morality, proslavery men occasionally pointed out that there was very little public prostitution in the South and no free love or polygamy. The answer to this was given by the Reverend Long when he wrote that the South had long had its own kind of "Mormonism . . . freeloveism and spiritualwifeism" in the form of slavery. If Joseph Smith had been brought up in a slave state, Long observed, he would have had no urge whatever to found a sect that would practice polygamy. What need was there for free love, Long asked, when a million females were considered by law as without virtue or the capacity for virtue.[12]

Having licensed himself to enjoy black women freely, the white man decided that his own women were and should be paragons of virtue. The utmost modesty of behavior was required of young white girls. Dictated by men, it was a staggering bit of hypocrisy. In the end the principal victims of this expectation were the white women. As that unsparing visitor, Harriet Martineau, observed, the entire plantation system produced some women who were strong, disciplined, and able but many who were selfish, spoiled, dependent, and, it should be added, sexually unresponsive. So white men turned all the more to black women for passion and pleasure. For a white woman to have protested against being forced into her lofty and frigid role would have marked her as jealous or lascivious or both.

In the rare instance where a woman did protest, she did so in the form of an attack on the hypocrisy of the system. Miss Martineau quotes one planter's wife as describing herself as only "the chief slave of the harem"; and a sister of President Madison said: "We southern ladies are complimented with the name of wives; but we are only the mistresses of seraglios." [13] Perhaps the most scathing indictment came from Mary Boykin Chesnut, daughter of a South Carolina governor and senator and wife of a Confederate general. In her diary for 1861 she wrote:

> Under slavery we live surrounded by prostitutes, yet an abandoned woman is sent out of any decent house. Who thinks the worse of a Negro or mulatto woman for being a thing we can't name? God forgive us, but ours is a monstrous system. . . . Like the patriarchs of old, our men live all in one house with their wives and their concubines; and the mulattoes one sees in every family resemble the white children. Any lady is ready

> to tell you who is the father of all the mulatto children in everybody's household but her own. Those, she seems to think, drop from the clouds. My disgust sometimes is boiling over. . . .[14]

Some white wives reacted with spite as well as resentment, displaying a cruelty that matched that of their menfolk. Fanny Kemble tells of a black woman, Sophy, who revealed that she had been in the plantation "hospital" having a child by a white millworker named Walker while two other slave girls were having children, almost at the same time, by the omnipotent overseer, King. Soon Mrs. King came to the hospital and ordered all three slave women to be severely flogged daily for a week and then sent to the penal island in the swamp. Mrs. Butler adds: ". . . if I make you sick with these disgusting stories, I cannot help it; they are the life itself here . . . but this apparition of a female fiend in the middle of this hell . . . seems to me to surpass all the rest."[15]

Sometimes the mistress of the house would insist that a slave woman whom her husband favored should be sold. Or she would even vent her jealousy on the child as well as the mother. Olmsted reports that one slave woman killed her baby because her mistress, learning who the child's father was, treated it so cruelly. The girl was hanged. The situation of a slave caught between such a master and such a mistress is a measure of the inhumanity of the system.

Cruelty mixed with sexuality produced sadism: slave women might be whipped on their bared bodies, generally by the black slave-drivers but sometimes by white overseers. Olmsted tells of riding around a Mississippi plantation with an overseer and a fifteen-year-old youth and coming upon a slave girl cowering in the bush. When the girl would not admit to dropping out of her work gang, the overseer gave her thirty or forty hard strokes of the lash across her shoulders. When she still denied leaving the gang, he made her lie down with her clothes pulled up to her shoulders and whipped her across the loins and thighs, the girl all the while screaming, "Oh, please stop, master! oh, that's enough, master!"[16] It takes no knowledge of the Comte de Sade to know that the overseer's motives were as much sexual as they were disciplinary.

Frederick Douglass never forgot how, as a boy, he had seen his Aunt Hester stripped to the waist by her master, strung up by her wrists, and whipped until she bled.[17]

Fanny Kemble talked to a mother of several children who had been flogged while she was pregnant, causing her to miscarry. When Fanny protested against such brutality, her husband conceded that it was "disagreeable" but declared that it was necessary.[18]

We have so far considered how slavery degrades the master. The demoralizing effect on the slave was incalculable. How could a black person take chastity or marriage seriously when a master could do as he wanted with a slave girl and break up any couple at will? So marriages among slaves were often casual. Women slaves were treated almost as common property by the men. Some slaves stayed with their mates for a lifetime, but many went from bed to bed with or without benefit of a marriage ceremony. It was enough for a child to know its mother. Girls soon learned that few would honor them for chastity or fidelity and that most masters would value only their fertility. It is hardly surprising that many black women not only yielded readily to white men but used their sexual attractions to best advantage. Early in the century John Lambert noted that many mulatto girls were handsome, "fond of dress, full of vanity, and generally dispensed their favors very liberally to the whites,"[19] and Richard Hildreth wrote in 1854:

> Among the slaves, a woman . . . has no inducement to be chaste; she has many inducements the other way. Her person is her only means of purchasing favor, indulgences, presents. To be the favorite of the master or one of his sons, of the overseer, or even of a driver, is an object of desire. . . . So far from involving disgrace, it confers honor.[20]

A Negress who sought to resist a white master could expect no help even from her husband. Fanny Kemble relates how the Negro headman on her husband's plantation, a respected and "very intelligent" man, could not prevent the son of King, the overseer, from borrowing his wife and having a child by her.[21] Such acts were a devastating blow to a man's pride; they surely contributed heavily to reducing the black woman's respect for black men and to weakening Negro marital ties.

There was no limit to the white man's assertion of phallic dominance or his barbarity in backing it up. According to Olmsted, a Louisiana slaveholder who heard that a young black was becoming friendly with his favorite slave girl, "mutilated" the youth. The slaveholder was tried but was freed for lack of testimony against him. The planter who told Olmsted this story disapproved strongly of the slaveholder's act but as one might disapprove of any unseemly behavior.[22]

And woe unto the black man who showed even the slightest interest in a white woman. In *The Stranger in America* (1807), Charles Janson told of a planter who, learning that one of his slaves had "made attempts on the chastity of his white female neighbors," called in the slave and, with the help of a doctor friend, castrated the man. The doctor reported that several months later the slave stopped him and thanked him for the operation, saying that he no longer cared for any woman, white or black. The doctor felt fully rewarded for his services.[23]

Besides the relatively small number of plantation families, which were the élite of Southern society, there was the large depressed class of poor whites. They were found everywhere, but mainly in the backcountry areas such as the mountains of Tennessee, the turpentine forests of North Carolina, and the pine barrens of South Carolina. We have few intimate details of their lives, but whatever we have indicates that they were an illiterate, indolent, and dissolute breed sunk in squalor. In most areas they lived in cabins with bare log walls, "puncheon" floors, and windows without glass. Large families ate, slept, worked, and loafed in one main room. There was no privacy and little modesty; children learned the facts of sex at an early age and soon put them to use.

The Southerner's argument that the availability and loose morals of slave women helped to insure the chastity of white women simply did not apply to this class. Such a people as the "sand-hillers" of the pine barrens of the South Carolina coast were, Olmsted found, a degenerate race who placed little value on virtue. A Southern physician estimated that among these people as many children were born out of wedlock as in it. One planter declared that any white girl who worked for money would certainly be of easy virtue.[24] The degeneracy of such whites was not unrelated to the slave system, since most whites tended to scorn hard work, considering it the function of slaves.

But the sexual mores most fascinating to visitors in the South were those of New Orleans. The history of the city helps to explain its extraordinary tolerance and its hedonism. In the early days the French had sent many felons and prostitutes to the possession; by the eighteenth century it already had a reputation for lax morals—far more lax than, for example, its sister French settlement on the Mississippi, St. Louis. Concubines of Negro or Indian blood were readily available, and after a time the French nuns of the city had to establish houses for the reform or detention of harlots. The French and Spanish settlers in general took a worldly view of sexual behavior, many of them seeing no harm in a married man's having a concubine. Although the people were as law-abiding as those of other cities, gaiety was never considered sinful. In short, the contrast that it offered to, say, Anglo-Saxon Boston was complete.

Some white women doubtless made excellent mistresses, but only in New Orleans was an entire class of women trained for the purpose: the Creole quadroons and octoroons. Despite their part-Negro background, or perhaps because of it, they were considered an ideal blend for a love relationship. Generally beautiful, charming, and accomplished, they were brought up by their mothers with one aim—to become, as their mothers had been, the mistresses of white gentlemen. For them marriage to a man darker than themselves was a defeat. This also meant that a quadroon youth had to marry a girl of a darker skin; according to Harriet Martineau, women of their own color said of these men, *"Ils sont dégoutants."* [25]

A white man, whether bachelor or married, who came to New Orleans found easy escape from prudish codes and his own inhibitions. To meet an eligible mulatto he had only to attend one of the formal quadroon balls; if he met a girl he liked, he would negotiate with her mother or her aunt for her favors. Generally he set her up in a pretty house in the Ramparts district, and the association might continue for a number of years. The girl, or placée, as she was termed, would almost invariably convince herself that the lover would be hers forever; but usually he married. The longer the liaison had lasted, the more bitter was the disappointment of the quadroon—even when the house and its furnishings were turned over to her. Such a woman, Harriet Martineau reported, rarely made a second alliance. Occasionally of course the man would be disappointed in his wife—perhaps by comparison with his warm and responsive Creole sweetheart—and he would resume a relationship with his placée. If the quadroon girl and her lover had children, the pair might later marry secretly to enable the children to come into their inheritance. It was also not uncommon for a Northerner to live with a quadroon simply because he found it less expensive as well as far more agreeable than life in a boardinghouse.[26]

Other much coarser types of license also flourished in the city. In his book *Slavery Unmasked* (1856), Philo Tower, rabid abolitionist preacher, claimed that three-fifths of the dwellings in some parts of New Orleans were occupied by prostitutes and sundry kinds of mistresses. He gave lurid descriptions of streets taken over by abandoned, broken-down women, some of whom came south in the fall and like birds returned north with the spring. Since city regulations forbade streetwalkers, the doors and windows as far as the eye could see in such districts were filled with women exhibiting themselves voluptuously and gesturing obscenely.[27]

Although New Orleans was thus the most licentious old city in the land, it really practiced its own form of hypocrisy, allowing any number of unmarried couples to live together but refusing to recognize the union or its fruits. Especially cruel was its indifference to the fate of many a quadroon who had been as faithful and affectionate as any wife.

Some Southerners rationalized their abuse of slave women as no worse than the Northern use of prostitutes. Aside from the fact that one evil in no way justified the other, the Southern practice was immeasurably more vicious because it was based on force, whether or not force was used openly. By virtue of a difference in skin color between them, a man could say to a woman, "I may do with you what I please." The woman had almost no choice, and her menfolk were equally helpless: a white-skinned creature held them in thrall, and even when he was well-intentioned, personally kind, and "God-fearing," they were still his slaves, their children would be slaves, and any future master might mistreat or neglect them as he chose. Just as Southern Christians found in an Old Testament fable a religious basis for their attitudes—ignoring of course Christ's teachings—they reconciled their system with the American principles of liberty, equality, and justice by considering slaves as property, and not human at all.

The freeing of the slaves brought no great change in Southern morality or in the sexual relationships between whites and blacks. Many white men continued to look on black women as fair game, and the women still found it difficult to resist the temptations offered by white men. A bright Negro girl had small chance of advancement except as the paramour of a white man.

Captain A. T. Morgan, a young Northern war veteran, recorded in *Yazoo* (1884) his and his brother's experiences on a 930-acre plantation they rented in the Yazoo, Mississippi, area after the war.[28] He was especially disturbed to find that the aristocratic owners of the plantation, a Colonel Black and his wife, considered Negroes animals who must be kept in their place by abuse. Black girls, assuming that Morgan was Southern, kept offering themselves to him. The wife of a Negro preacher repeatedly sent him her beautiful fourteen-year-old daughter and finally chided him for not doing what the best "white gentlemen," including married men, had never hesitated to do with such a girl. The woman herself, Morgan found, was Colonel Black's favorite concubine; she was not typical but neither was she unique. Morgan's neighbor was a merchant whose wife and black concubine and his children by both women all lived cozily together. Because Captain Morgan himself married a woman of Negro descent, shaking Yazoo society to its foundations, he was able to persuade other Negro women that marriage was better than concubinage. Soon the concubines, who had been ranked according to the social position of their white lovers, began to lose prestige and make embarrassing demands of their white men.

Wherever Negroes were given more economic opportunity and a better education, their morals, at least by white standards, improved. A curious side-effect of this improvement, W. E. B. Du Bois, influential Negro sociologist, pointed out, was a sizable increase in the number of white prostitutes in the South.[29] In other words, as soon as black women were less readily available, the Southerner adopted the Northern practice. Equally unexpected was the effect on the quadroons of New Orleans. Their prestige, dependent on the fact that a white man could live with them without having to marry them, gradually waned. In general the sexual relationship between white men and black women was more and more limited to casual connections. Alfred H. Stone, a Mississippi cotton planter, asserted that "the amalgamation of the races" had slowed down sharply. "Not so long ago," he said, "it was not an uncommon thing to find an overseer or superintendent on a plantation who would have from one to half a dozen concubines. This practice has practically been done away with. The planters will not permit the overseers to do such things. . . ." [30]

Emancipation had no effect on the Southerner's pretense of being rabidly opposed to miscegenation. All Southern states continued to have laws forbidding intermarriage. Such laws simply led to an increase in clandestine relationships and permitted white men to seduce black girls without the risk of having to marry them. Courageous white men who tried to acknowledge an alliance with a Negro woman were persecuted. One man told his vigilante critics that they had their dark women secretly, but he intended to live with his openly.[31]

The ultimate effect on the Southern white man was that he tried to salve his own conscience by creating a myth of the black man as satyr and rapist. At the same time he manufactured an image of himself as the protector of womanly virtue, chivalrous knight ready to die for the honor of his lady fair. His lady fair, meanwhile, resigned herself to her sterile role: Often she not only gave up her husband to the embraces of black women, but she even turned over her children to be suckled by "black mammies." Yet the fact that black men were reputed to be lusting for her while her own men were turning to black women must have confused her mightily. A Negro sociologist, Calvin Hernton, who has studied Negro experiences with white women, believes that the white woman not infrequently ended up desiring black men even while she feared them, torn between a yearning to be taken by these men and yet dreading them.[32]

In the light of the fiendish way white men had flouted the Negro's function as a man, it is not surprising that Southerners after the war developed a guilty fear that a rebellious black man's first act of revenge would be to rape a white woman. And it is not to be wondered at that this expectation was occasionally fulfilled. Some white women—perhaps out of a subconscious wish to share the sexual variety their menfolk had enjoyed—also held this conviction. When a Negro was accused, whether justly or unjustly, of molesting a white woman, it became a practice, fostered by the Ku Klux Klan, to subject him to the mob action known as lynch law. Lynch mobs were often made up of "white trash" all too eager to vent their frustrations on some helpless scapegoat. Sometimes a combination of sadism, guilt, and fear would drive the mob to strip the victim and mutilate him. In one stroke they performed a sexual act, eliminated a sexual rival, and destroyed a bit of the evidence of their historic guilt.

Never having been permitted to develop any sense of social responsibility, many black men did not take seriously their duties as husband or father. Negroes might frown on infidelity, but they continued to look tolerantly on an unwed girl who bore a child. Many whites scoffed at the idea of blacks conforming to white standards of restraint and decorum: Captain Morgan quotes a Mississippi physician as exclaiming that laws requiring the marriage of black couples would make every "nigger wench" think she was as good as his own daughters. Black women, he declared, with the arrogant candor of the Old Nobility, had always stood between the Southern girl and "the superabundant sexual energy of ouah hot-blooded youth." Young men, he concluded, would be "driven back upon the white ladies," and this would result in prostitution like that in the North.[33]

Testimony on Negro behavior toward the end of the century reveals a kind of moral twilight illuminated here and there by rays of idealism and aspiration. On the one hand, marriage and divorce were often still casual and occasionally took place without any ceremony. A volume on Negro family life edited in 1908 by Du Bois testified that immodesty, unbridled sexuality, obscenity, and indifference to chastity prevailed. Sexual intercourse, it said, often began at puberty, and unmarried couples did not hesitate to live together openly.[34] A young Negress told Howard Odum, who studied the Southern Negro in the early

1900's: "A colored girl that keeps herself pure ain't liked socially. We just think she has had no chance."[35]

By contrast, Southern white ministers and the white presidents of Southern seminaries and normal schools testified that a large number of Negro parents, especially those of some education and means, made every effort to keep their children free of the so-called sexual vices. They said that many black women were as pure as their white counterparts. There was evidence, too, that an increasing number of black men were seeking to protect their women from degrading sexual familiarities as well as exploitation by whites and were themselves devoted husbands and fathers.

These contrasts are not difficult to explain: men and women who had been kept in barbarous bondage for centuries could hardly be expected to change their ways in a generation or two, especially when many of them still languished in poverty and still suffered from every kind of oppression and humiliation.

It is hard to believe that many Americans accepted the Romantic notion that living close to Nature fostered purity of morals and nobility of spirit. Anyone who had seen settlers in a forest clearing or on a wilderness bank knew—the Leatherstocking novels of Cooper notwithstanding—that it was struggle enough for a pioneer to keep body and soul together without having to worry about moral niceties. As the frontier moved west, travelers in Pennsylvania, Ohio, Kentucky, Tennessee, Illinois, and Missouri were surprised and sometimes shocked at the crudeness and squalor of pioneer cabins, the ragged children, the bearded, unkempt fathers, the slatternly mothers. Beyond the reach of community standards, both men and women often degenerated. Those farthest from civilization, such as the trappers and mountain men, commonly lived with Indian squaws.

The celebrated Cincinnati physician, Daniel Drake, describing life in the frontier settlements of Kentucky and Ohio around 1800 when he was a boy, recalled the prevalence of profanity, vulgarity, drunkenness, and "coarse jocularities" at house raisings and corn huskings. He also remembered the competition that the village tavern gave the village church. A forest clearing, he wrote, was far from being a Rousseauan elysium, and city people of a corresponding grade, he believed, had on the whole "more virtue and chaster manners."[36] At least in the first stages, a rough environment generally encourages a roughness in men.

But rapid as the descent into sloth and sluttishness might be in a lonely cabin, so rapid was the return to respectability as soon as the settlement became a town, as framehouses were put up along streets, and churches, schools, gardens, an inn, and a jail appeared. Before long, the more genteel families, often from New England or the Middle Atlantic States and eager to reestablish old patterns, would begin to set standards. Propriety and gentility, policed by Mrs. Grundy, would reassert themselves.

One saw the result in such a town as Hannibal, Missouri, where Sam Clemens grew up in the 1840's, in the Indiana of Edward Eggleston's *The Hoosier School-Master* (1871), in the western Missouri town in the late 1860's that E. W. Howe wrote about, and in Edgar Lee Masters' Spoon River of the 1890's and early 1900's. In his prudery, Mark Twain, writing about and for boys, could deal with murder, drunkenness, and bigotry but not with sexual immorality. Eggleston makes the townspeople of his Flat Creek uncouth, ignorant, and mean of spirit but not wicked. Howe probes more deeply. The central figure in *The Story of a Country Town* (1883), Jo Erring, destroys himself and the girl he marries through the neurotic conviction—which recurs obsessively in all of Howe's writings—that an earlier infatuation with another man sullied a woman forever. His craving for absolute purity is a fair example of the aftermath of Puritanism, which exerted its influence almost as strongly on the Middle Border as in New England. The bitter residue of Calvinism also caused the town preacher, the Reverend Westlock, to make his religion a levee against the flood of his instincts. The levee bursts, and the minister runs off with the widow Tremaine, a woman who had been a leader in attacking vice.[37] In the sense of guilt that lies behind their aggressive purity, the figures of Westlake and Mrs. Tremaine anticipate any number of characters in post-Freudian novels of small-town life. That Howe's novel is based directly on his experience is clear in his autobiography, *Plain People* (1929), where his father, the Reverend Howe, is described as having been married five times, and divorced three times, and having been ousted from his church for unseemly intimacy with a widow who is a zealous church member. Howe himself reveals a Calvinist influence not only in his compulsive concern with the purity of the woman a man marries but also in the Reverend Westlock's conviction that his passions will prove uncontrollable and that he will be damned.[38]

The most impressive evidence of how desperately the sexual passions sought release in settlements and small towns were the camp meetings. They sprang up early in the century in the Cumberland and swept periodically across the land like the waves of religious hysteria in earlier eras. The circuit riders who organized the meetings in the Middle West brought release, drama, and hope to lonely men and women struggling with an untamed environment. As intense as some pagan nature rite, the meetings were an answer to the emotional poverty of frontier life, the bleak monotony of small towns, and generations of repression.

As the great crowds gathered under the light of torches in primeval groves, buried impulses, physiological and erotic as much as spiritual, surged to the surface. The preachers lashed their listeners till they shrieked and wept, writhed and "jerked," some of them falling and thrashing about on the ground. Pent-up sexual passions were released along with the religious emotions, and there were always men, including preachers, ready to take advantage of aroused young women. A pioneer Memphis lawyer, James D. Davis, declared that those who thought a camp meeting was no place for lovemaking were very much mistaken. Referring especially to the period before 1830, he wrote:

> When the mind becomes bewildered and confused, the moral restraints give way, and the passions are quickened and less controllable. For a mile or more around a camp-meeting the woods seem alive with people; every tree or bush has its group or couple while hundreds of others in pairs are seen prowling around in search of some cosy spot.[39]

Responsible clergymen were fully aware of the dangers of the meetings. In Indiana a Methodist preacher with twenty-five years of experience told William Hepworth Dixon:

> Religious passion includes all other passions: you cannot excite one without stirring up the others. In our Church we know the evil, and we have to guard against it. . . . The young men who get up revivals are always objects of suspicion to their elders; many go wrong. . . . Far more bring scandal on the Church by their thoughtless behavior in the revivalist camps.[40]

Certain preachers, it was said, had scattered their seed as widely as their sermons. So common was the birth of babies to both married and unmarried women after some of the meetings that "camp-meeting child" became a familiar term. It was a popular saying that at camp meetings more souls were made than were saved. As we have seen, Mark Twain rejected an illustration for *Huckleberry Finn* of a "lecherous old rascal" kissing a girl at a camp meeting, and ruled out all pictures of the camp meeting as a "disgusting thing," about which illustrations were "sure to tell the truth too plainly." [41]

Camp meetings continued to be held well beyond the Civil War, but even as the religion of fear and threats gave way to a religion of accommodation and Sunday observance, the meetings left behind the abandonment to hysteria. By the 1880's, the earnest, respectable, hymn-singing evangelism of Moody and Sankey had purged revival meetings of all their erotic overtones.

The rush to California gold in 1849 and to other Western mining areas in the 1850's is commonly thought of as a primary manifestation of the get-rich-quick fever that gripped nineteenth-century America. No doubt it was that, but it was also something more—a chance to escape from the whole heritage of Puritanism, from conformity, respectability, and the long tongues of Mr. and Mrs. Grundy. That in part was why California continued to draw a stream of immigrants even after word had gone back that nuggets were not lying under every bush. That is why many who found no gold stayed on. The fact is that the Far West was for almost a decade the only area in Victorian America where men and women could do what they wanted without worrying about the opinion of their neighbors. There were no prudes in the goldfields of California or the mining camps of Colorado and Nevada, and no one missed them.

There is no need to describe once more the untrammeled freedom, turbulence, and debauchery of California in the half-dozen years after the discovery of gold at Sutter's Mill. It will not do to try to explain the explosion by saying that, like every boomtown, California attracted adventurers, rascals, and criminals; for it also attracted a remarkable number of men who left good jobs and came of good families. One pioneer reported that the loose women who established themselves in the mountain towns were wholly supported by married men who had come west without their wives. It is true that the harlots, hardy creatures, at first outnumbered the married women, but apparently the married men were not at all disturbed by this imbalance.

We have all heard how, as soon as the tent city days in San Francisco were past, the gaudiest new buildings were the saloons, gambling houses, and brothels. The gambling "hells" were lined with mirrors between which were, as travelers described them, the most "licentiously seductive pictures," including the more lascivious scenes from mythology and harem life. The better brothels were equally sumptuous.[42]

The prostitutes were of every nationality and grade. At the top were fashionable and perfumed courtesans occupying the most luxurious quarters. Among the first representatives of the French demimonde were three hundred women who were shipped over by the French government in one of its less advertised contributions to American society. These women often presided over the tables in the gambling houses, working for gamblers who also served as their pimps. Then there were the Spanish girls. Willing, languorous, with low-cut dresses over full breasts, they were a revelation to Anglo-Saxon manhood. From Chile came a group, generally good dancers, who worked in the "fandango houses." At the bottom were the Chinese whores on Telegraph Hill and near the waterfront. By 1853 San Francisco had, according to the *Christian Advocate,* forty-eight houses "kept by bawds."

One of the freshest and most candid views of the society around him was that of William Perkins, a Canadian who stayed for a time in Sonoma. He particularly liked the Spanish girls, describing them as "warm, generous and unartificial." The Frenchwomen he found fascinating in conversation but avaricious, vain, and shameless. Of the Englishwomen from Australia and sundry loose creatures from America he said: ". . . vulgar, degraded and brutish as they are in their own countries, a trip to California has not, of course, improved them." [43]

Of the most hideous prostitution of all, that of the Chinese girls in cribs and dens near the San Francisco waterfront, little was ever said. It was an abomination, and respectable people simply closed their eyes to it. According to legal contracts that the girls themselves agreed to, they were slaves for a certain term of years, with the provision that they must serve an extra week for every day of illness, including the days of the menstrual period. Traders bought them from their parents in China at any age from eight to fifteen and sold them in California, sometimes to private individuals but more often to the "trade." A few were placed in elegant parlor houses for white customers only, but the majority went into the Chinatown cribs and served all comers. Lying constantly with the dregs of a port city, they were soon diseased, and few of them lasted beyond half a dozen years. In their last days they were carried into a bare cell with only a cup of water and an oil lamp, and there they usually died before the lamp went out.

The Chinese slave whores were not a passing phase of the Gold Rush days. In the 1870's, it was estimated, there were between 1,500 and 2,000 of them in San Francisco, and even after the Oriental exclusion acts of the 1880's, when they had to be smuggled in, there were always about a thousand of them in the city. Since they first arrived in 1850 and were still available well after the 1906 earthquake, this monstrous business flourished for sixty years.[44] Not only did church missions and sensational newspaper campaigns fail to end the practice, but regular sightseeing buses took tourists to see the places where the Chinese whores served. In nineteenth-century America, the Chinese, like the Negroes and Indians, were beyond the pale, and the moral laws of white Christians were not applied to them. It is another stunning example of the compartmentalization of American morality.

That is why William Perkins hardly mentioned the Chinese prostitutes. He was busy noting the behavior of the white women pouring into Sonoma. Encouraged by the relaxed morality of the town, many of them quickly paired with men without troubling to get married. When a "good woman," the wife of an American doctor, did arrive, and proved to be not too attractive,

Perkins exclaimed: "What chance has virtue in the shape of tall, gawky, sallow, ill-dressed down easters, in rivalship with elegantly adorned, beautiful and graceful Vice!" It was too much, he added, to expect a man to prefer a "bonnetted, ugly, board-shaped . . . descendant of the puritans, to the rosy-cheeked, full-formed, sprightly and elegant Spaniard or Frenchwoman. . . ."[45]

But the good, sun-bonnetted women and the respectable families kept coming in—shock troops to the rescue of Virtue—and in time they prevailed—at least outwardly. By the end of the 1850's they had persuaded the authorities to close the fandango houses, and the first prosecution of a streetwalker in San Francisco took place in 1858. Two years later a Madame Mary Miller was charged with keeping a disreputable house and was convicted mainly because she kept it in a reputable district. Propriety began to show its prim face everywhere. When the celebrated Adah Isaacs Menken, clothed only in pink tights, rode across the stage bound to Mazeppa's back, one critic called the performance immodest, degrading, and corrupting to chastity.[46] Sarah Royce, mother of the philosopher Josiah Royce, noted that when a prominent man brought a disreputable woman to a church charity festival, a committee of gentlemen asked them to leave. Although Californians were never subjected to the Sunday blue laws that stifled Eastern towns, men no longer raised Cain on their day of leisure but turned to such genteel amusements as their women could share.

Despite this outward show of domestication and decorum, observers tell us that there was, as one Englishwoman put it, "a frightful amount of private immorality." Even women of good character tended to adopt, as Alonzo Delano said, "the morals of the country and instead of endeavouring to stem the current, float along with it." Although California divorce laws were not especially lax, the divorce rate was higher than anywhere in the states. Hinton R. Helper, who was as harsh a critic of California in his *Land of Gold* (1855) as he would be of the South and slavery in his *Irrepressible Conflict*, declared that nowhere was there so little respect for the sanctity of marriage. Even respectable women, he said, came to California only to sell their charms to the highest bidder.[47]

Sarah Royce was one of the virtuous who remained virtuous, a woman of integrity and mystical faith whom no makeshift social code could dislocate. A sensitive person, she understood fully the effect of the Gold Rush fever and described it vividly. There were some who came, she said, with the hope of "getting gold at all hazards, and if possible without work." A greater number hoped to get rich honestly by labor or legitimate business but,

> as they came to feel the force of unwonted excitement and the pressure of unexpected temptation, they too often yielded, little by little, till they found themselves standing upon a very low plane, side by side with those whose society they once would have avoided. It was very common to hear people who had started on this downward moral grade, deprecating the very acts they were committing . . . saying, "But *here* in California we have to do such things."

She goes on to describe how women accepted or even sought expensive gifts from men who had "made a strike," and then moved step by step into desertion and adultery. Two of her neighbors, both beautiful women, gave up their husbands and wrecked their homes for other men. A friend talked at first of the wife and children he had left in Illinois, but in time he ceased referring to them and finally revealed, with little sign of regret, that his wife was divorcing him.[48]

In the story of another early arrival, Mary Jane Megquier, we seem to have an example of the perilous acquiescence described by Sarah Royce. But whether it represented a true corruption and decline or an expansive response to new-found freedom is a question. Mrs. Megquier reached San Francisco with her husband, a doctor, in September, 1849, leaving her two children with relatives in her hometown in Maine. Provincial, respectable, married eighteen years, she opened a boardinghouse next to her husband's office-and-drugstore and drudged day and night. She planned to stay only until she had made "a small pile"—in two years, she hoped. At first she called California a God-forsaken place, but soon she was captured by the freedom and excitement. There were churches, she reported in her letters, but it made no difference "whether you go to church or play monte"; everyone was his own man and there was never a word about "a thing is not respectable"—a comment she detested. Soon, too, there were parties, dances, and "last and not least, so many fine-looking men" that she felt that she could stay forever.[49]

After a visit to Maine the Megquiers were back in San Francisco in 1852. When Dr. Megquier became ill two years later they again returned home together. But then they apparently separated, for in 1855 Mrs. Megquier was in San Francisco again, and she was alone. When she heard that her husband was very ill, she wrote that if he died, it would be what she had often hoped for herself rather than that she should go on living with someone "who was ever wishing me to sacrifice my health to his gratification." Her husband did die, and soon she was writing of a Mr. Johnson as the gallant who escorts her to the theater or treats her to champagne and supper. "I dread," she adds, "the thought of returning." She remained in California.[50]

Josiah Royce, born in 1855 and sharing much of his mother's idealism, felt that the true miracle of the Gold Rush was the way the community had survived all its trials by temptation. In his history of early California he wrote that

> our true pride, as we look back on those days of sturdy and sinful life, must be . . . that the moral elasticity of our people is so great . . . that a community of Americans could sin as fearfully as, in the early years, the mining community did sin, and could yet live to purify itself within so short a time, not by a revolution, but by a simple progress from social foolishness to social steadfastness.[51]

But the California in which Royce grew up was morally as well as physically very far from the town in western New York from which his parents had come. Probably owing to his mother's influence, he seems to have assumed that because California had swung back from the intoxicated extremes of 1850 it had returned to all the old values. Had he noted the persistence in San Francisco of what was known as the "Barbary Coast," perhaps the most notorious concentration of whorehouses, gambling hells, and saloons in America, he would not have been so sure that the tradition of the wilder Forty-Niners was dead and gone.

Nor did he take the measure of the attitudes and values that people like Mary Jane Megquier transmitted to the small towns of older America. The Gold Rush and the wild days in Virginia City and elsewhere were episodes in a moral rebellion, and they left their mark on all of America.

23.

THE WAGES OF PRETENSE

MRS. GRUNDY has long seemed a figure of comedy, but her emergence at the beginning of the nineteenth century makes her a significant image in our study of prudery. There have always been town gossips and common scolds, but they were treated with contempt. Not so Mrs. Grundy. Perhaps the reason for her influence is that she was part of a larger tendency—that of the social reformers. Although the reformers were more responsible and generally far more constructive than the Grundys, they all shared the conviction that they were called upon to improve their fellowmen.

The reform movement arose in this period partly to fill the gap left by the retreat of the church and partly as a result of the increasing influence of middle-class standards of behavior. Thus the temperance movement began in the early 1800's, the abolitionists first attracted attention in the 1830's, the women's rights reformers in the late 1840's, and the vice crusaders, led by Comstock, in the 1860's. But whereas the temperance groups, abolitionists, and women's rights militants met opposition, no one dared challenge the righteous judges of morality. It is a curious fact, usually overlooked, that the typical American, celebrated for his independence, submitted tamely to the expectation that he should be, or appear to be, completely pure of body and mind. Having forced his women into denying their sexuality, he sometimes paid the price of having to seek his sexual pleasures elsewhere.

Supporting this pressure for purity was the formula for success requiring a youth to be virtuous and clean-living—which meant chaste. It was not the Puritan fear of sin but the bourgeois urge to succeed that made a youth knuckle under. While he was urged to apply himself almost ruthlessly to the business of making his fortune, he was warned to keep the tightest rein on his sexual appetites.

Constantly reminded of his sinfulness, the average American was able to assert himself in every sphere except the moral one. He was proud of his right to vote and worship and settle a continent as he saw fit. But as though these activities exhausted his urge to freedom of thought and action, he was sexually proper and conforming. Americans may have behaved as they pleased in killing off beaver and buffalo, thrusting aside the Indian and the Mexican, exploiting the land and driving out competitors; but they accepted without question the dogma that sexuality was shameful and a sign of the beast. They could throw off kings and high priests, reject the principle of an inherited nobility, and move freely from class to class, but in morals they bowed—at least outwardly—to every curb and censorship. Westerners, for example, were notorious for their coarseness and profanity, and for tolerating the whores who followed them into their mining settlements and boomtowns, but when a respectable woman appeared in their midst, they made the most solemn efforts to appear respectable themselves.

There were signs that the moral prohibitions were only superficially effective. Literature was Bowdlerized by both editors and authors, but a line of popular novelists from Susannah Rowson through George Lippard to Eugène Sue and Ouida, glazing eroticism with moralizing and sentimentality, were read hungrily. The theater was deplored but was increasingly popular. Nude statues were subjected to fig leaves, but prostitution abounded, vice grew wild in San Francisco, and quadroons in New Orleans taught white Americans the art of love. On Southern plantations the white man's chivalry among white women masked his imperious lust among black women. And the slaves were free only for sexual exploitation.

There were other contradictions. Revivalist camp meetings sometimes stirred up more erotic activity than holy fervor. Abortion was an unmentionable word but an established practice. Although marriage was considered a holy bond, more and more couples resorted to divorce. While unmarried men and women were barred from any sexual experience, a married man could use his wife as he pleased, and she was expected to serve his desires even if she despised him.

For any man or woman to have an unsanctioned love affair was unthinkable, yet tens of thousands turned to Mormon polygamy, and free love experiments sprang up in a score of places. Here and there, excessive restraints provoked violent reactions. A Virginia Woodhull was perhaps born to the manner, but much more significant are the ministers' sons, such as Josiah Warren, Ezra Hervey Heywood, Stephen Pearl Andrews, Horatio Alger, and Stephen Crane, who defected or turned heretical, or who, like Pierpont Edwards, Aaron Burr, Henry Ward Beecher, and Isaac Kalloch, flagrantly flouted sexual taboos. They vividly illustrate a primary law of sexual dynamics: repression eventually breeds evasion or rebellion.

After the middle of the century, Darwinism became another source of contradiction, mostly by way of crude oversimplifications. Some found evidence in evolution that man was bound to his animal origins; but more saw proof in it that man was rising to a higher spiritual plane by repudiating such instincts.

Several writers, notably R. W. B. Lewis and Henry Nash Smith, have advanced the theory that after the decline of Puritanism America was looked upon as a new Eden in which man was, or could be, a new Adam. Support for this is found in such figures of fiction as Cooper's Leatherstocking, Hawthorne's Donatello, Melville's Pierre and Billy Budd, Mark Twain's Huck Finn and James's Daisy Miller, as well as in Thoreau at Walden Pond. It was found most of all in Whitman, who saw in America a new version of Genesis. But the average American seems to have shared this view only, or mainly, as it applied to occupying the wilderness and governing himself. In these realms he felt that he was starting afresh, quite literally in a new world, free of the political and social corruption of Europe. As an American he claimed these liberties as his birthright.

But he did not claim any comparable sexual liberties. Outwardly he showed little interest in sex. Foreign visitors early in the nineteenth century noted that American men seemed too busy making money to pay much attention to love and gallantry. Nor was there any of the easy intimacy and sexual sophistication that Henry Wikoff, Horatio Alger, and Sam Ward found in Paris, or Margaret Fuller in Italy, or that Hawthorne and James reflected in their novels of Europe. But this was not the result of an Adam-like innocence. Except possibly in young women, it was not innocence at all. It was rather a distrust, not to say a fear and suppression, of sexual emotions—in short, a residue of Puritanism. Theodore Weld and his fiancée Angelica Grimke, experiencing the stirrings of fleshly love, were a little like Adam and Eve after the Fall, but they were even more the victims of an unnatural fear—doctrinaire in origin—of their own feelings. Long before they ate of the apple, they fed on Calvinism. They may have been physically innocent, but they were theologically only too well schooled.

Fighting a rearguard action against change, the American Victorians were ostentatious in the outward observance of old taboos. By almost any standard of values pretense was their true sin. They lied, above all, to themselves. They pretended that good women were angelic and did not normally experience desire. Ignoring prostitution, foundlings, abortion, and so forth, they pretended that young men could repress libidinous desires. They refused to see that in the biological functions it is instinct that teaches us most of what we feel. Although they surely did not believe that marriages were made in heaven, they insisted that the bonds of matrimony were indissoluble and that divorce was a sin. They invented all kinds of myths about sexual physiology and kept women in ignorance about their bodies, yet when a girl became pregnant they punished her as though she alone were to blame for her plight. They told themselves that Anglo-Saxons were purer than other peoples, particularly Frenchmen and Italians, and that Negroes, Chinese, and Indians were by nature incapable of sexual virtue.

Most of all, they looked on sexuality as a vice, a necessary evil. Sexual passion in the Puritan and in the nineteenth-century view was a kind of obscene joke on mankind. It was a trial-by-pleasure that the Lord had devised in what must have been a Satanic mood. Underlying this attitude was the ascetic doctrine that self-denial is purifying and suffering is cathartic, while pleasure corrupts and weakens. Carried far enough, this made God, particularly as he is seen in Genesis, principally a source of pain and hardship, and the Devil the provider of the pleasures not simply of the body and the entire love union but of all the arts of mankind.

Back of much of Victorian morality was fear—fear of public opinion, of preachers, of one's instincts. In sexual relations before marriage the fear was of pregnancy. It has even been said that in exalting chastity the Victorians simply rationalized this fear and thus made a virtue of necessity.

Other ages besides the Victorian, especially in the Judeo-Christian tradition, have had taboos, but few have nurtured so many prejudices while denying so much evidence that their attitudes were cruel and based on distortions. We can find various explanations of the nineteenth-century use of the old Biblical arguments for repressing sexuality. But how shall we excuse the claim that it was in many ways against Nature and harmful. Nature of course takes no sides. It gives desire as much to the unmarried as the married, to the innocent as to the experienced. It cares not a whit whether a man performs a sexual act with his wife, a strange woman, another man, his daughter, or an animal. Studies have shown that for many couples copulation more than once a week and even as often as twice a day is not harmful. And masturbation as ordinarily practiced is declared to be a harmless and sometimes preferable outlet. Sexual taboos may come and go, but the instinct of desire remains. Preachers and poets have generally been aware of this—long before Freud confirmed it clinically.

Freud's analyses of the effects of frustration have popularly been interpreted, or, rather, misinterpreted as exposing its dangers and thereby endorsing a freer expression of sexuality. But this was of course not Freud's view at all. He repeatedly made clear that giving way freely to sexual impulses was neither desirable for the individual nor beneficial for society. In the individual such behavior was tantamount to living by what he called the infantile "pleasure principle." Self-control, disciplining the libido, is deemed a sign of maturity, evidence of the capacity to adjust to the "reality principle." The sublimation of sexual drives, Freud believed, was also necessary for the development of society. Civilization had been built up by sacrifices in man's gratification of his primitive impulses. The sexual energies are thereby diverted toward other ends that are "socially more valuable." Thus renunciation is, in effect, essential to progress; and self-denial is the price we pay for culture.[1]

When Freud warns us that free sexual indulgence is infantile, or that sexual satisfaction too easily obtained reduces its value, he speaks more or less from clinical experience. But when he assumes that sublimation is indispensable to establishing law and order, he seems to be submitting, as Herbert Marcuse says, to an age-old rationalization of repression. The more permissive we become, the more Victorian does Freud's view of culture and his distrust of the instincts seem. We are no longer sure that epochs of repression, such as the Victorian and the Puritan, achieve greater social enlightenment or live by loftier standards. Nor are we certain that the advances they do make owe much to the sublimation of libidinal urges.

The sacrifices made by civilized man will appear to have been worthwhile if we judge civilization by technological advances and the conquest of Nature. But when we compare the cultural achievements of, say, ancient Greece with those of Puritan or nineteenth-century America, repression seems to have produced mainly a distrust of the finest and most creative forms of expression. Early America's cultural leanness may have been partly the result of colonial immaturity. But it seems probable that the lack, for example, in American literature, painting, and music of the theme of passionate love, and of the lyricism and uninhibited feeling that mark European Romanticism was a consequence of repression and prudery.

Freud's attitude finds some support in historians—now far more rare than they were in Freud's day—who see a relationship between the achievements of a civilization and its sexual self-restraint, or, conversely, between social decline and sexual license. One such historian is Arnold Toynbee; he wrote in 1964:

> I admire the 19th century West's success in postponing the age of sexual awakening, sexual experience, and sexual infatuation far beyond the age of physical puberty. You may tell me that this was against nature; but to be human consists precisely in transcending nature—in overcoming the biological limitations that we have inherited from our prehuman ancestors.[2]

Even those who feel there is some evidence for Toynbee's view will be seriously troubled by his description of sexuality as a "biological limitation" inherited from "prehuman ancestors," or as an "infatuation" that is best postponed. And even if we allow that nineteenth-century Europe was a peak of civilization, what evidence is there that sexual repression was an important factor in its "success"?

To many of us today it appears that repression leads as often to aggressiveness and violence as to the higher forms of sublimation. Freud himself observed that among the more common kinds of sublimation was an irrational devotion to the church, the army, and the state. But he was nonetheless ready, as Norman O. Brown points out, to sacrifice much for the supposed rewards of sublimation. In the end, sublimation often appears to be scarcely more than a euphemism for repression.

But the major problem posed by sublimation, as Freud himself said, is steering a course "between the Scylla of giving the instincts free play and the Charybdis of frustrating them." [3] He spoke of the need to find a method that would do the most good and the least harm, but he admitted in *Civilization and Its Discontents* (1930) that the problem might be insoluble.[4] Critics increasingly see these doubts and ambivalences as partly the product of Freud's background; and the generality of readers are likely to continue to think of him as having alerted mankind to the dangers of repression rather than of indulgence. At the moment they seem clearly to prefer the Scylla of sexual freedom to the Charybdis of frustration.

The danger in any judgment of the morals of an earlier epoch is that we will apply the standards of our own time and place as though they were universally valid and were truly distilled from the experience of the past. But even if we recognize this danger and acknowledge that the permissiveness of our era may lead some to license or demoralization, we have come to see that any code that smothers sexuality by means of fear is doomed to cause as many problems as it solves. Excessive restriction simply goes against Nature. Man is, Montaigne said, the only animal so brutish as to consider shameful the very act that made him. So it was that in the name of purity many nineteenth-century Americans came to look on the act of love as degrading—abhorrent before marriage, and practiced after marriage only as a biological obligation. In trying to spiritualize love, they made it seem beastly. Failing in the quest for purity, they settled for prudery. The aftermath has been a revulsion that has in some respects been equally extreme.

Epilogue

SEVENTY YEARS LATER

SEXUALLY, these are the signs of the times: on a midtown corner at high noon a couple in long hair and jeans stands for a while in gentle, oblivious embrace; a dozen men and women, all well-dressed, gather in a large suburban home and, guided by a leader, undress completely, enter an outdoor pool and spend half an hour touching each other; a pair of university medical scientists, one a woman, study and photograph couples who copulate as directed; a motion picture by a noted artist-film maker shows several young women using every erotic technique, including mouth-to-penis contact, to arouse a young man made impotent by heroin; a well-known writer in a literary journal celebrates the pleasures of going to bed with a woman and a man simultaneously; a college girl describes a weekend in her dormitory bed with various boys; a woman book critic in a literary review refers to a Times Square paperback bookstore as lined with book covers of cocks and cunts; and a psychiatrist in a best-selling guide to sex warns his legions of readers against the dangers of abstinence. Each of these items is drawn from a different area of sexual expression; together they constitute a startling demonstration of the state of sexuality only seventy years after the death of Queen Victoria.

To most of us the progression from nineteenth-century prudery to the freedom of today seems to have been inevitable. It was inevitable not for any one reason but because an overwhelming variety of factors combined to make it so. Crucial was the very extremism of the Victorians. The notion that a woman's bathing suit must cover her from throat to ankles or that pants and penis were unmentionables, or that a girl's loss of virginity before marriage was worse than death grew to seem silly. It became an easy target for the deadliest weapon against any kind of humbug—ridicule. When cartoons mocking Anthony Comstock began to appear, it was the beginning of the end of Victorian prudery.

But this was merely a negative reaction. Far more important was the wide acceptance—so gradual that many were hardly aware of it—of the separation of coitus for begetting children from coitus for sexual pleasure. In accepting this distinction, Americans were at last catching up with John Humphrey Noyes, the radical Utopianist who insisted over a century ago that the "propagative" and the "amative" functions were not necessarily related and should each be used for its own ends.

Equally important was the acceptance, also gradual and still far from complete, of the idea that sexuality was not (1) a crime, or (2) a sin, or (3) an abnormal characteristic, but a private matter—indeed, a very private matter—and that it was not susceptible to official regulation unless one individual forced himself on another.

Immensely important, too, was the beginning of the liberation of woman. As women mastered higher education and penetrated the professions, as they began to vote and take part in business, it became more and more difficult for all except diehard male chauvinists to maintain that women were not the intellectual equals of men, or that they could not take care of themselves or cope with politics and government. Gone was the day when women were expected to be either clinging vines or workhorses, either dolls or slaves. When, moreover, women began to use contraceptives, the end of the double standard came in sight. Released from the threat of unwanted babies, women were ready to experience desire as fully as men. And once the population explosion was recognized as a threat and not a blessing to mankind, women's obligation to bear children and "replenish the earth" was ended forever.

The release of women's sexuality also helped to liberate man from the need to dissemble his own appetites. And when men and women learned from Freud that the repression of sexuality could lead to neuroses, inhibitions began to seem unhealthy as well as unnatural. The way was open to those who would cast off all curbs on sexuality and its pleasures.

But the radical changes in sexual attitudes in the past ten years are not to be explained in sexual terms alone. Those changes are part of a much broader challenge to all established standards and life-styles. The rebellion is not simply against the repression of sexual feelings but against the loss of all feeling in a society riddled with the dehumanizing and depersonalizing influence of technology and automation, of giant corporations and bureaucracies, of huge universities, Pentagons, and housing projects and, finally of an overpeopled environment. For some it is also a reaction to broken homes, to families forever moving from place to place, to a sense of not belonging or finding genuine affection anywhere.

The first signs of open rebellion against the old code came in the 1920's, era of "flaming youth" and "flappers." But the Depression, World War II, the escape to suburbia, and psychologists (such as Marynia F. Farnham, co-author of *Modern Woman: The Lost Sex*) who insisted that the New Woman was losing her femininity and neglecting her children and husband led women during the 1940's and 1950's away from careers and college and back to homemaking and motherhood.

First Simone de Beauvoir, then Betty Friedan, and, later, Kate Millett pinned some of the blame for this "counterrevolution" on Freud's view of women.[1] Influenced by his Victorian background and family relationships and his experience with women patients inhibited to the point of hysteria, Freud thought of women as reduced by penis envy to a kind of man *manqué*, low in libido and fated to find fulfillment only in children and a husband. This view doubtless affected the more ardent followers of Freud, but surely far more influential in luring women—and men—back to domestic security and comforts was the fifteen years of depression and war in which that generation had grown up.

The effect on sexual activity of the return of women to domestic duties is difficult to measure. Betty Friedan declared that it led many unfulfilled and bored housewives into seeking sex either vicariously in novels or directly in escapades outside of marriage. There is some support for this theory in the spectacular increase in salacious novels of the type of *Peyton Place,* which was bought and read mainly by women. And it may also be supported by Kinsey data showing that after ten or fifteen years of marriage an increasing number of wives were reporting greater sexual desire than their husbands could satisfy and were turning elsewhere for gratification.

Then, in the middle 1960's, for reasons as complex as the entire culture, came a renewed surge toward sexual liberation. A few events inspired a deep alienation: the war in Vietnam, the threat of the Bomb, the plight of black people, the assassination of charismatic public figures, the ruin of the environment. To many, both young and old, the double standard seemed to be not the one that punished the sexuality of woman while sanctioning that of man but the system that forbade the full expression of sexuality while tolerating aggressive wars, slums, and discrimination.

The rebellion, when it came, took the form of a longing, particularly among the young, to get back to more natural and simple ways of life, to primary sensations, and intimate human relations openly arrived at. That is why youth turned to communal living, to folk music and primitive rhythms, to wearing the crudest, most unfashionable clothes, to living by handicrafts, eating health foods, and, at the extreme, dropping out of all institutions—college, family, government, religions, career, marriage, morality. . . .

The changes in sexual mores have been radical—yet not truly a revolution in the sense of a firm new order taking the place of the old order—but only a welter of mutinous actions and defiant gestures, a kind of guerilla resistance. The changes have been most evident among the young because violating sexual taboos is one of the most effective ways of defying the Establishment, especially the moralists and pillars of respectability. Unlike bombing a university or a bank, defying a sexual taboo is not difficult or destructive, and it can be beautiful. It can also yield a deep relief from the sense of loneliness and alienation that besets so many young people.

Sexual activity, along with drugs, has also become, particularly for the children of the affluent, one of the last frontiers of adventure and "thrills." For some, the risks, both physical and psychological, make it that much more exciting.

The rebellion has manifested itself in countless little ways. A favorite gesture has been nudity. At rock music festivals couples have cavorted in the nude, and at protest demonstrations they have leaped naked into public fountains. In the musical play, *Hair,* nakedness was made into a powerful symbol of protest against the hypocritical concealment of the body. It was even more than that: a mind-blowing repudiation of all encumbrances, all "things." In speech, the rebellion has made the use of four-letter words and the ebullient slang of the blacks popular among both young women and young men. When they chant obscene slogans in confrontations with officialdom, they mock two inhibitions at once.

But the major prohibition that is steadily being undermined is the one against coitus before marriage. Although many still remain abstinent up to the eve of marriage, a constantly increasing group sees coitus as natural and justified if it is accompanied by some affection and a little regard for the consequences. (We must not forget that when both young women and men remain in college and graduate school until they are twenty-two or -three or -four, it is far more difficult and unnatural for them to stay chaste than it was for their predecessors a hundred or even fifty years ago.) At the most radical extreme are the hedonists or, if you prefer, the promiscuous.

The first dramatic breach of the sacred prohibition against coitus before marriage came in the Roaring Twenties. But sexual rebellion in those years might sometimes be followed by a sense of guilt and pangs of conscience. Doubtless there are some who suffer from qualms today, but the pangs are less likely to arise from moral or religious scruples than from a fear of the consequences or the desire to make a lasting attachment. To many young people and some who are not so young, morality seems irrelevant in judging a sexual act. Thus a leaflet handed to Vance Packard, author of *The Sexual Wilderness,* by an attractive coed in Los Angeles, proclaimed the right of individuals to engage in a variety of sexual acts, asserting that "Where there is no victim, every act is morally right." [2]

Where any well-bred young woman's chastity was once upon a time taken for granted, in some circles "going all the way" has become the accepted thing. And many other couples stop only short of coitus. Even those who are abstinent themselves are generally tolerant of others who go all the way. Certainly the stigma once attached to coitus becomes fainter each year. Whereas in the 1920's a young woman who had coitus before marriage was a rebel, her counterpart today may well be only a conformist.

The new freedom along with the new protections against pregnancy is perfect for the hedonists, those who believe in living only for the moment and enjoying as many sexual pleasures as often as they can. Theirs is a species of instant self-gratification encouraged by a society in which all media urge us night and day to indulge in every pleasure and luxury, and to do so without delay. For some the result has been a seeking of instant Nirvana through drugs and instant sexual fulfillment through going to bed with anyone who is available.

The question is, what is the effect of such a practice? Reports disagree. They disagree because the evidence on which they are based varies according to such factors as age, region, and class and such imponderables as love, guilt, and degree of commitment. Encouraging the completely permissive approach is the New York psychologist Albert Ellis, who sees premarital chastity as masochism, and believes that the more sexual activity a person engages in, the happier and healthier he will be.[3] But such an analyst as Rollo May finds that coupling without commitment or affection leads to the banalization of sex, to apathy and the new malaise of our society, the incapacity to relate passionately to anyone.[4] While Ellis hawks his doctrine of "assertive," go-getter sexuality and getting rid of every shred of inhibition, May declares that his patients suffer not from repression in the old sense but from too much sexual activity that has little meaning, feeling, or joy in it. Ellis and May are so far apart in their views that they appear scarcely to be talking about the same relationship. Ellis seems to be discussing a physical exercise requiring little or no commitment. May is talking about a bond—a bond of liking, respect, and concern. Ellis does not of course exclude such a tie, but he believes that it is not necessary, that one may have satisfying sex, and a great deal of it, without ties. May is saying that if there is a bond there will be just as much deeply satisfying sex, and something more. Surrounded by an ethos of uninvolvement, and unable to use the machinery of "romance," love can still find an enduring basis in what May calls "care."

Liberty also poses some smaller problems. Useful as contraceptives may be, they are still mechanical or chemical devices, and reports tell of many young women who refuse to be constantly equipped for a sexual encounter. They refuse either because it may well prove a waste of energy and spirit or because they still crave spontaneity, the unique stimulus of unpremeditated desire. Indeed, in the desperate search for the natural, for being truly carried away by emotion, a surprising number of young women have become pregnant because they have avoided taking any precautions.[5]

Rebellious as some young people may be, most of them still have need for deep and lasting unions. So far, the pleasures of permissiveness or promiscuity have not caused any significant postponement or rejection of marriage. Even though marriage may seem less and less the heavenly union it was once thought to be, it still offers the best way of overcoming human separateness, of achieving stability in a world in flux. If anything, youth's rebellion against society has made the need for an anchor and for sharing completely more pressing than ever before.

Before considering the sexual behavior of older people, we must face for a moment the disturbing challenge posed by hippies. Admittedly they are a small segment of the younger generation, and some of them are simply misfits, but out of their deep need they have created a style that throws into bold relief certain hangups in the American way of life. Tapping forgotten wells of feeling, they have experimented with living "tribally" that is, communally, and dreamed of substituting sexual love for racial prejudice, violence, and war. Many of them reject shame of the body and they caress openly. They flout censorship, ignore the proprieties, and explore every device, physical, chemical, and mystical, from hashish to Zen, for intensifying awareness and "expanding" the mind.

Their sexual insurgency is not an isolated act: it is part of a total view of life, entailing a rejection of all bourgeois virtues —prudence, discipline, cleanliness, order, a sense of obligation.

The aim is to free the individual to do whatever is in his nature to do, whether it is socially acceptable, useful, or reasonable. At its best their view is liberating and exhilarating. At its least admirable, it is anarchic, self-absorbed, and socially irresponsible, substituting, as John Hersey puts it, the cop-out for the compromise.[6] When it works, it permits its followers to escape, at least for a time, certain competitions and tensions, and, as we used to say, to loaf and invite the soul. It gives them a sense of communion with their fellows and a capacity to share their bread and wine, their drugs and sometimes their sexual partners. Like action painters and experimenters with automatic writing, they try, by sloughing off traditional forms, to give expression to the promptings of the spirit.

Aiming at sexual equality, young men and women exchange dress and hairstyles and share a four-letter-word frankness of speech and behavior. The result often is a neuterizing of the genders, reducing Romeo and Juliet to a shabby couple in tattered jeans, old sneakers, and unkempt hair. They yearn for individuality, but individuality is a rare thing; so most of them are as conformist in their clothes, manners, and talk as the most conservative members of the Establishment. And there are surely those who find sharing everything, including love, as much of a drain on individuality as is life in the conventional style.

In practice, the hippies have faced the handicap of having to live on the coattails of the society they have rejected and of attracting some fellow travelers who wanted maximum liberty and minimum responsibility. The excesses of a few of them and, even more, the profound challenge they have offered to basic assumptions of the American way of life have aroused the deepest hostility. But whether the hippie way survives as an enduring style is not important; it has already had its effect. It has made painfully clear that a segment of youth not only abhors the American system but is willing to quit it no matter at what cost. The need they have expressed for simple and unfettered human relationships may well leave a mark on the American psyche.

What of the older generation—by which I mean those who are over forty and possibly have grown children of their own.

Among these there are some who, getting from newspapers and television only the more sensational stories of "druggies" and "crazies," believe that the age is demoralized and degenerate. Many of them advocate strict controls and severe punishments. But the tide has up to recently been running against them, and they have found it hard to make themselves heard, much less heeded. The institutions that once took the responsibility for suppressing sexuality—churches, schools, government, the family—have with few exceptions lost much of their influence. The Protestant churches began making concessions long ago; the Catholic Church during the past few decades has yielded much ground, openly or tacitly, on such vital issues as celibacy, divorce, and the use of contraceptives. Many universities have let it be known that they no longer have the power and perhaps never truly had the right to regulate the lives of students, especially when many students are older than students have ever been before. Federal and local governments have repealed, relaxed, or simply not enforced many statutes against the sale of obscene materials, homosexuality, and the like. As for the family, once a most effective agent of morality, the rebellion of many adolescents against the hypocrisies of the past has led a goodly number of parents into what a West Coast theologian has called an "orgy of open-mindedness." [7] In contrast to the traditional relationship, the parents and not the children have experienced a sense of guilt. For over fifty years many enlightened older people—repudiating the strictness of their own upbringing—have encouraged youth to self-expression and self-fulfillment. The excesses have attracted more attention than the successes, but there is nevertheless little likelihood that Americans will ever go back to the old repressive extreme.

Older people hardly realize how much their own standards have changed. The change has been registered in small matters as well as large, as, for example, in accepting skirts that barely reach the thighs, or bathing suits that offer only token concealment, or both men and women living in the same college dormitories, or daughters who date at fourteen and go steady at fifteen. Menstruation and menopause are no longer taboo subjects. Venereal disease is not only discussed casually, but victims of it can get treatment without charge—despite the protests of a few relentless moralists that this takes the punishment out of promiscuity. More important is the fact that contraceptives are a commonplace and that abortion is being legalized in state after state.

No longer is there any shame attached to divorce. As far back as the 1920's it was breaking up almost one in every four families. Together with annulments, separations, and desertions, it now strikes almost one out of every two homes.[8] The side effects are considerable. Many young couples now enter matrimony with no feeling that it is "holy" or an irreversible step. A divorcée, far from being ostracized, can make a new alliance as easily as a maid. And broken homes give rise to even more sundered marriages in the next generation. Before, however, we begin to despair over the future of marriage as an institution, we should recall that young people are entering into it as steadily as ever. Almost paradoxically, the institution continues to be vigorous even as its bonds grow looser. To new generations its adaptability may make it seem that much more attractive.

Far more significant is the increasing defiance of sexual taboos within marriage. Divorce is often preceded by infidelity by one spouse or both. Even in marriages not on the verge of divorce, adultery—to the Victorians the unpardonable sexual sin, and still legally a crime in most of the United States—is widespread. The Kinsey report of 1953 showed that by the age of forty about 50 percent of all husbands and about 25 percent of all wives had engaged in coitus outside of marriage, and that 16 percent of a group of 1,100 wives had indulged in extramarital petting if not coitus. These percentages, the report showed, had been rising since 1920; and more recent studies reveal that this trend is continuing.[9]

The reasons for such assaults on an old taboo are many: unhappy marriages, the general crumbling of inhibitions, contraceptive devices, boredom, loneliness, a longing for fresh experiences and the renewal of desire. If some of these reasons seem hardly to justify jeopardizing a marriage, that may indicate the extent to which marriage is no longer held sexually sacred.

Once there was a double standard whereby a wife might overlook or forgive a husband's infidelity, but a husband would tend to consider a wife's infidelity fatal to the marriage. There is still such a dual view, but more wives forgive and forget, and fewer husbands look on a wife's transgression as disastrous. Sometimes the unfaithful husband or wife does not keep the infidelity secret from the spouse, or a husband and wife may allow each other complete sexual freedom. On occasion this may lead to such a curious practice as mate-swapping—often a sign of a husband and wife so bored with each other that they are ready for any relief no matter how desperate.

Like divorce, infidelity seems to have stretched the fabric of marriage without destroying it. Perhaps marriage will come in time to signify a union that has many uses but is not necessarily permanent, and even allows, if the partners see fit, for sexual freedom. Such freedom might end the furtiveness that often makes adultery seem degrading.

Increasingly, older people are sharing the other sexual liberties. The most revealing guides to acceptable practices are —as they have always been—the more popular sex manuals. The first popular manual to dismiss basic Victorian prohibitions, *Ideal Marriage,* by the Dutch gynecologist Theodoor H. Van de Velde, was published in 1930. Van de Velde recommended much tender foreplay to bring the woman to that blissful goal of lovemaking, an orgasm. The wide appeal of his lyrical enthusiasm for the sexual climax—the book has sold over a million copies —suggested that a host of Americans were starved for affection as well as sex. But Van de Velde still saw woman as needing to be aroused by man, and he also rejected the idea of sexual experience outside of marriage.[10]

In the light of the books by Albert Ellis, supersalesman of sex for both fun and well-being, and, even more, of such prodigious best sellers as David R. Reuben's *Everything You Always Wanted to Know About Sex . . . But Were Afraid to Ask* (1969) and *The Sensuous Woman* (1969) by "J" (Miss Joan Garrity), Van de Velde's book seems old-fashioned and a bit romantic. For the books by Dr. Reuben and Miss Garrity combine a clinical candor with an uninhibited pleasure morality. They represent the American faith in technique and "know-how."

The guiding principles of Dr. Reuben's book are chiefly physiological. As a doctor, the author is sure of one thing—

that every organ must be exercised regularly. "Use it," he proclaims, "or lose it." Where the Victorian physician warned against indulgence, the Space Age physician warns against abstinence. One has a vision of millions of readers coming away with a desperate feeling that they must copulate constantly or face atrophy. Although Dr. Reuben is a psychiatrist, his allusions to emotional or spiritual considerations are buried in a welter of information on techniques and the pleasure possibilities of cunnilingus, fellatio, masturbation, and so forth.

If Dr. Reuben is the expert who gives a medical *imprimatur* to sexual activity, Miss "J" is the amateur enthusiast. With all the zest of a mail-order ad she tells women: You too can drive a man wild sexually. Reversing the traditional roles, she is the sinner exhorting the virtuous to vice. She brings the fervor of the convert to the cause of bigger and better orgasms for all. Scorning the "ghosts of sexual guilts and bugaboos," she urges her readers to try every imaginable practice, including mutual stimulation by mouth, group sex with exchange of partners, threesomes, analingus, and a dozen varieties of masturbation. Moral considerations are easily dealt with: her friend Sue, who "had the courage to step outside the moral teachings of her family," suffered no punishment for her "supposed wickedness." Licensed by her own generosity in sharing her sex recipes, she gives the following instructions for masturbating with an electric vibrator:

> Imagine him [a lover] looking at you stretched out naked on the bed, your body open and hungry for him. Feel him caressing your breasts, running his hands down and over your abdomen, stroking the inside of your thighs, reaching higher now and gently massaging your clitoris. Let the vibrator be his hands and penis. . . . Let your fantasy man rule your mind and body. Is he thrusting deep into you while your pelvis is arching up to him, aching for him, eager to explode in the commanding ecstasy of orgasm? . . .[11]

In a society where every process is being mechanized, *The Sensuous Woman* offers a formula for ecstasy in which a machine replaces the phallus. American technology can hardly go further.

Ironically, the liberation of woman's sexuality does not lead to what feminists would consider woman's liberation. When

Miss "J" declares, "We women were designed to delight, excite and satisfy the male of the species," the apostles of Women's Lib will surely say that we have come full circle—back to woman as totally a sexual object.

Because such books plainly titillate readers and provide as much vicarious erotic experience as useful advice, they may seem to tell us more about the secret urges of readers than their actual practice. But the urge these days easily becomes father to the practice. And the complete acceptance of such books is in itself primary evidence of the revolution in American attitudes.

If we require the evidence of more serious publications, we have the works of Dr. William H. Masters and Mrs. Virginia E. Johnson, *Human Sexual Response* (1966) and *Human Sexual Inadequacy* (1970). Despite the panoply of scientific research—statistics, graphs, tests conducted in a laboratory monitored by cameras—these books have also become best sellers. Going far beyond the mere verbalizing of Dr. Reuben and Miss "J," or even the interviews used in the Kinsey reports, Masters and Johnson arranged in *Human Sexual Response* for almost seven hundred men and women of all ages to allow themselves to be studied and photographed while engaged in coitus or in masturbating.[12] When Malcolm Muggeridge, the English social critic, characterized the book as "the apogee of the sexual revolution, the ultimate expression of the cult of the orgasm,"[13] there was some justice in his charge—along with his customary anti-American bias. Far more significant than any interest in orgasms—which had in fact been stimulated by Van de Velde, a Dutchman—was the laboratory approach. It was technology that would liberate Americans from their Puritan prison. Data measured and recorded by machines would show the unhappily mated the path to sexual compatibility and orgasmic bliss. The machines demonstrated, among other things, that masturbation with a mechanical dildo gave women the most sexual pleasure. They showed, in brief, that a machine was more satisfying than a man. As it often does when applied to a human act, technology isolated the act from the rich experience of which it was an essential part. It measured everything except what Lester Kirkendall describes as the quality and consequences of an experience, ignoring one of the richest rewards of the sexual act—the pleasure that one human being can give to another. This is not to question the scientific value of the work of two dedicated scientists but its popular reception as a key to the love relationship.

As significant as the sex manuals is the attitude toward homosexuality. Where once homosexuality was so rigidly repressed that many scarcely knew of its existence, it has not only come to the surface but is increasingly tolerated and is in certain circles considered a kind of sexual connoisseurship.

The history of this development is related in part to the much broader history of masculinity. While everyone has been making much of the attack by Women's Lib on male dominance, man has been suffering an erosion of masculinity. The reasons for this are many: the passing of the part that ruggedness played among pioneers, farmers, and cowboys, and the decline of man's importance in the family, the emasculating effect—made grotesquely clear in *Portnoy's Complaint*—of the domination of boys by women and especially their mothers. Meanwhile, woman, freed to express her desires, has become sexually more demanding. Often a young man's easiest way out is to abdicate from masculinity.

The process began in earnest after World War I. Probably reflecting fears over the increase in homosexuality, the Victorians had reached a nadir of bigotry in the treatment of Oscar Wilde as a vicious criminal. The first homosexual in high places to brave criticism publicly was André Gide, early in the century, but Anglo-Saxons could dismiss him as an immoral Frenchman. Then, in the 1920's, homosexuals began to appear in American nightclubs and bars and occasionally in the streets. Radclyffe Hall's *The Well of Loneliness* (1928), dealing sympathetically and passionately with lesbianism, was banned, but, directly or indirectly it made many literate people aware that homosexual love was not a sign of degeneracy and was in some ways like heterosexual love.

In the mind of the average American, however, homosexuality continued to be associated with men who were feminine and "abnormal"; they were called "fairies," "queers," "fags," "perverts." Then in 1948 the Kinsey Report astonished the nation (although it only documented what Freud and Havelock Ellis had noted long before) by declaring that most boys engage, however briefly, in homosexual play and that a third of all American men have at least one homosexual experience.[14] It became generally known, too, that masculine-seeming men and married men virile enough to have children could practice homosexuality. Among the educated, homosexuality began to be considered a sickness rather than a moral defect and the word "pervert" gave way to "invert" or "deviant."

As more and more writers, dancers, actors, musicians, and other public figures, past and present, were identified, or boldly identified themselves,[15] as homosexuals, it became almost a sign of the liberated spirit. The claim was made that it was associated with heightened creative activity, artistic sensitivity, superior taste. The Mattachine Society, formed by homosexuals to express their viewpoint, asserted that homosexuality, far from being a sickness, was simply an orientation or propensity. Going over to the attack, they pointed out that heterosexual marriage in the United States, often marked by discontent, boredom, and infidelity, was hardly an enviable institution. Even those who had little sympathy for the practice have come around to agreeing that homosexuality or, for that matter, any sexual activity between consenting adults should not be considered a crime. In circles that pride themselves on being sociologically up-to-date the word "deviate" has been replaced by such a completely neutral term as "variant." Meanwhile, homosexuals have accepted the epithet "gay," implying a way of life more pleasure-oriented and enjoyable than heterosexuality.

Lesbianism, the other side of the coin of homosexuality, also flourishes, but it gets less attention, perhaps because, as Kate Millett points out, it offers less of a threat to masculine dominance in our society. Certainly, lesbians are almost never harassed by the law. And mannish lesbians have rarely been subjected to the kind of ridicule traditionally aimed at overly feminine homosexuals.

Lesbianism has received less attention for other reasons: The Kinsey and similar studies have shown that it is not so widespread, and it appears to be more often temporary or intermittent. It is also not so manifest; call girls, for example, commonly turn to other women for sexual pleasure even while they carry on their heterosexual activities. Unmarried women can live together, especially in cities, without provoking questions about their sexuality. Although lesbians have joined in Gay Liberation movements, they are simply not under the pressures that have made homosexuals increasingly rebellious.

Finally, straddling both domains, there is "bisexuality," the capacity to have relations with both men and women. One of the boldest champions of this third world of sexuality was the novelist Gore Vidal. In *Myra Breckinridge,* a novel of bizarre forms of sexuality, he describes "male swingers" who "assert themselves through a polymorphic sexual abandon in which the lines between the sexes dissolve, to the delight of all." Later, in a review of Dr. Reuben's book he called its view of homosexuality—as an affliction leading to misery—ignorant. Using the practice of bisexuality as evidence that homosexuality could be a matter of choice, Vidal attacked those who, like Dr. Reuben, "cannot accept the following simple fact of so many lives (certainly my own): that it is possible to have a mature sexual relationship with a woman on Monday, and a mature sexual relationship with a man on Tuesday, and perhaps on Wednesday have both together (admittedly you have to be in good condition for this)." [16] And yet it is worth noting how often novels and plays by homosexuals dealing with both homosexual and heterosexual relationships depict the latter unconvincingly or betray a dislike for women.

Bisexuality might seem indeed to be the last word in sexual liberty were it not, as critics have observed,[17] that psychiatrists see it as the kind of indeterminacy generally found in the period between the homosexual tendencies of puberty and the heterosexuality of maturity. There is even a variation of bisexuality in which the taboos against adultery as well as homosexuality are defied. In this game, two married couples exchange partners and then make a second exchange in which husbands and wives pair off. Although this practice is hardly common, the Personals columns of such an "underground" newspaper as the Los Angeles *Free Press* contains dozens of sexual invitations from "swinger couples" to others of their kind. Despite the fears of more conservative citizens, such practices have not led to Bacchanalias in the streets or, as far as anyone has reported, behind closed doors in Middle America.

If anything, they tend to make the sexual act just another social exchange, without commitment or involvement, and certainly without any of the climactic importance it once had.

Some bisexuals even assert that breaking down sex distinctions will lead to trio unions—or group marriages such as hippie communes have tried—in which no one has a fixed male or female role. Even if we dismiss these predictions as fantasies—perhaps literally pipe dreams—they do reflect a blurring of sexual distinctions.[18] We have noted the decline in masculinity. (Such manifestations as Hell's Angels, drag-racing, and the Hemingway-Mailer he-man posture are mainly *machismo*—male braggadocio.) Conversely, young women now constantly take the initiative, stealing into men's dormitories to sleep with their boyfriends, leading the way in making love even in public places such as beaches and campuses, and invading male preserves everywhere.

Some women are in fact claiming that sexual identity itself is not inborn but learned, that differences in physical capacity are the result of training, and that even motherhood is not instinctive.[19] Such claims are calculated to make the idea of man as instinctively the sexual aggressor seem to be a myth—a male myth. But anthropologists such as Lionel Tiger of Princeton insist that there are ancient and basic biochemical differences between the sexes.[20]

Meanwhile, there are those who feel that men and women can be equal yet different.[21] They believe, as Margaret Mead pointed out years ago, that each sex has valuable qualities and that it would be an inestimable loss to society to sacrifice such qualities in the effort to achieve equality. The militant Liberationist's answer has in effect been that this would mean the resignation of women to those very qualities that have allowed them to be dominated and manipulated. Thus Betty Friedan vigorously rejected Margaret Mead's glorification of the miracle of femininity and the female role while hailing Margaret Mead herself as an anthropologist who made her way in a man's world, who broke what Mrs. Mead herself called the vicious circle of a woman's role, and pioneered on the hard road to total self-realization.

To the Women's Liberation militants the possible loss of whatever desirable or attractive qualities each sex may have, or the dangers to sexuality of a kind of neuterizing of the genders, is obviously less important than the ending of women's bondage —their status as something less than total human beings.

Prostitution is not what it used to be. With the spread of sexual freedom, the old-fashioned brothel has almost disappeared and has been replaced by street-walkers and call girls. A hundred years ago women went into a "house" because they found it easier to make a living that way or because they had been seduced and abandoned or had been tricked into it, or, in the more elegant places, because they liked it.

Of course, none of these reasons explains why one woman made such a choice as against a hundred who did not. A prostitute today, psychiatrists tell us, generally comes from an unhappy home, dislikes her father, resents all men, and avenges herself by taking her customer's money and giving nothing of herself except her time. We now know that most prostitutes, far from enjoying the sexual act, despise it and commonly turn to other women for sexual affection. Notwithstanding Fanny Hill (who was, after all, invented by a man to feed the fantasies of men), many prostitutes detest themselves to the point of becoming suicidal.[22]

Our affluent society has had its effect on the motives of prostitutes. It is, for example, difficult for them to claim that no other way of making a living is open to them. Nor must a woman resort to selling herself because she has been seduced and therefore "ruined." There are, finally, many who turn to streetwalking to support heroin addiction; this becomes a vicious circle in which the prostitute sells herself to get the drugs and then takes the drugs to be able to tolerate her life.

Although American society no longer pretends that prostitution is necessary to protect respectable women, it still condones the hypocrisy whereby a prostitute who is arrested with her customer is treated as a criminal while the man goes free. Authorities agree that punishment has little effect, and arrests have fallen off sharply in recent years; but punishment remains the official response to prostitution. Despite all our supposed permissiveness, a woman is allowed to sell everything except her sexual capacities.

Except among the educated, the lowering of sexual barriers

has not had much effect on the number of prostitutes. Men still turn to prostitutes because such women are readily available, inexpensive (as compared with entertaining a girlfriend), undiscriminating, entail no responsibilities, and may consent to unorthodox practices. And if (as feminists aver) men go to prostitutes out of an urge to dominate women and command a sexual slave, it is unlikely that prostitution will ever disappear. Meanwhile, society's attitude toward it remains the chief residue of Puritanism. Lord of sexuality, man demands that woman be constantly available for his pleasure; lord of righteousness, he then condemns her as immoral and degraded.

There are signs, especially among those over thirty, of a yearning to break through the shell that isolates the individual, to establish warm, flesh-and-blood relationships with other people. This longing has led to experiments, involving millions of Americans, in what is known as sensitivity training or encounter groups. These experiments take a vast variety of forms, and although none of the better-known groups is openly sexual, many of them try to break down inhibitions against touching and caressing members of the other sex, against using forbidden words freely, against nudity in mixed company, and so forth. When conducted for individuals with personality problems, the practice suffers from the need to cope in a weekend with the complexes of a lifetime. Its proponents claim that it induces a sense of exhilaration, shared intimacy, and increased self-understanding, but critics say that it can be followed by a sudden depression and that it encourages forced emotional responses and a conformity to the group's emotional demands.[23]

Such training is probably more useful for men and women involved in personal counseling and social work where it may shake participants free of some of their moral prejudices and feelings of guilt. One organization that arranges such training, the National Sex and Drug Forum, a church-supported group managed by a minister-sociologist and a doctor, subjects small groups to a bombardment, in a luxurious setting, with erotic films, slides, and sound tracks. When the participants are sated, not to say bored, by this treatment, they are lectured in a mixture of psychology and street terms on sex as an elementary human activity that should, like eating or defecating, be considered without any moral judgments whatever.

Out of more than three hundred men and women who had participated in the program, almost all later reported that it had helped them personally and in their professional activities. The minister-sociologist who heads the sex program has said that it is the mission of the church and, by implication, of all men to "say yes to everything human." He adds: "Our work is to set people free of their hang-ups. If people want to do it and nobody is hurt by it, then God yes, do it. . . ."

Thus with the most modern forms of shock treatment is the moral revolution proclaimed. To some this will seem to be the only way to rid sexuality of the age-old incubus of morality. Or will this characteristically pragmatic American way of dealing with a delicate psychological problem desensitize rather than sensitize its subjects? The minister's affirmation is exciting, but what is meant by "saying yes to all things human"? His answer to this question, that he has faith in man, will appear to be the ultimate reaction against Calvinism.[24]

The crumbling of moral standards has become evident in a dozen other areas, and especially in the arts and entertainments. For the first time artists have almost complete freedom in the treatment of sexuality. Novelists, playwrights, painters, and film makers, let loose among a host of once-forbidden themes, are exploring them on every level, from the most sensitive evocation of love to a crude exhibitionism. As always when barriers first fall, there has been an abuse of freedom: sex is again and again exploited for all it is worth.

On stage and screen nudity has become a commonplace. (Completely outdone by art films, burlesque long ago began to seem tame and coy and eventually disappeared.) Actors and actresses are not infrequently asked to audition in the nude because they may appear on stage without clothes. *Oh! Calcutta!,* a Broadway success featured, among other scenes intended only to shock, one in which a naked couple simulated copulation. Since the actor is not aroused, the effect is, if anything, the reverse of suggestive. In another popular play the sensationalism of the relationship between a black boxing champion and his white woman was underlined by the fact that they made love in a bed in midstage. (Full copulation will surely be shown as soon as a producer can find an actor and actress physically and psychologically capable of nine public performances every week. In this, films have a distinct advantage.) By contrast, the nudity in *Hair,* a joyous celebration of sexual freedom, seemed natural and refreshing.

Each movie on a sexual theme outdoes in frankness the one that went before. Beginning in the 1940's with glimpses of a woman's face as she experienced an orgasm, films a few years ago reached the point of showing nude lovers in bed, and then, in a flood, lesbian embraces, rape, flagellation, wife exchanges, masturbation, and fellatio. But the dramatic change came with the disintegration of the old studio and star system and the rise of young, more or less independent film makers and actors who believe that films can be what they describe as open, honest, and concerned. To their best work they brought a simple candor and a feeling for the alienated that has sometimes added a new dimension to the portrayal of human relationships. Others, both young and old, have taken advantage of the new freedom to purvey sensationalism, proving only that sex can be made as boring and ugly as any other subject.

In an obvious attempt to avoid censorship, moviemakers now rate each film on its suitability for adults or children. This is really no censorship at all, for an "X" rating means only that the picture is not suitable for those under seventeen years of age; it may be pornographic or it may be genuinely worthwhile. It also serves in reverse, that is, to advertise the fact that a picture is salacious.

Meanwhile, avowedly pornographic films have emerged from the "stag parties" in which they used to be shown and now monopolize certain theaters in every city. They display every conceivable sexual act, including all the aberrations, often in close-up and sometimes in color. A billboard in front of one theater described the film as "a story of heterosexual, homosexual perversions, Lesbianism, orgy, transvestism, fetishism, narcissism, masochism, sadism, sensualism." Such films attract mostly older men; the theaters do not admit anyone under twenty-one, but, as the theater managers explain (and as those who demand official censorship refuse to realize), most young people today can get all the "live sex" they want.

A variant of these films is the live public performance of sexual acts—shades of the *tableaux vivants* of the 1840's!—put on as often as six times daily at several "exhibition halls" in midtown New York. For a fee of $5, spectators see a nude couple or a pair of lesbians copulate in a variety of ways. I include this dismal detail because the New York *Times* reported that the thirty-five men who attended one performance were mostly well-dressed, middle-aged, and somberly intent—obviously content with the most passive kind of voyeurism.

The relaxation of censorship of the printed word has been just as drastic. Every bookstore may sell any kind of book to an adult, and most public libraries make available to adult readers any number of books that would have been banned in almost every library in America as recently as thirty years ago.

Although the nearly complete collapse of censorship came in the past fifteen years, the crucial psychological breakthrough occurred in the 1920's when James Joyce's *Ulysses* revealed in one Promethean act the part sexuality plays in both the subconscious and conscious life of average men and women. Sundry works by D. H. Lawrence, Frank Harris, and, later, Henry Miller, all originally banned in the United States and thereby brought provocatively to the attention of many readers, broke down other barriers. In the past thirty years, scores of banned books, from those by the Comte de Sade to *Fanny Hill,* have been published in cheap editions. More important, every conceivable forbidden subject has been explored in every kind of printed work. Sexual relationships undreamed of by the average reader have been covered in the most intimate detail and the plainest language.

Nevertheless, *Ulysses* was banned in the United States until 1933 and writers as forthright as Hemingway were still avoiding the four-letter words as late as World War II. Now all the four- and five-letter words—most of which Chaucer and Shakespeare knew and used—appear constantly in novels and plays. Men writers may have used them first, but women writers soon took them up, at first self-consciously but after a while casually and expertly. Whereas at first such words were put into the mouths of characters in novels and plays, they now appear in poems, dictionaries and such periodicals as *Harper's, Esquire, Atlas* and *Playboy.* In *The Village Voice,* a New York weekly, the four-letter words appear so often that it is the polite words such as "copulate," "defecate," and "penis" that now seem taboo. In that otherwise severely literary journal, *The New York Review of Books,* a woman critic quoted a newspaper columnist as saying to Norman Mailer after a political campaign speech by Mailer at Sarah Lawrence College: "Norman, you gave them that high-class Harvard shit. I should go back in there and call them a bunch of dumb dike cunts." [25] Recalling the way Shakespeare used such words, one might write a sermon on the difference.

As most opponents of censorship have predicted, these banned words have already begun to lose some of their erotic or scatological force, and will, as anyone who has ever been in an army barracks or a locker-room knows, before long be drained of much of their original significance. The association with the act of sex has in addition so deeply branded "fuck" as a "dirty" word that it is commonly used, in such expressions as "all fucked-up" and "fuck you," as a general term of scorn.[26] Familiarity has bred contempt for the word—and for the act. Slang dictionaries tell us that the word has long been used in disparaging ways; but we have freely extended the abusive uses. The roots of such contempt go deep. It is easier to slough off Victorian prudery than to dispel the aura of obscenity with which sexuality has been surrounded.

The license to deal openly with the sexual act poses a new problem for writers. With the tendency of our culture to exhaust a fashion overnight, modern novelists have described the act so often and in such detail that it has become a set piece that either bores us stiff or must be read as one listens to a soprano doing a familiar aria. It has become plain that the description of passion in such a novel as *Anna Karenina,* which leaves the culmination to the reader's well-prepared imagination, has infinitely more emotional resonance than all the bedroom exercises unsparingly spelled out in the latest novel. In love affairs the sexual act will always be the same; as George Steiner says, there is only one way to copulate.[27] The abiding mystery is in the relationship, not the act.

But far more important than freedom of language or expression is the tone and nature of what is expressed. Judging from novels and plays, sexual liberty has not automatically brought sexual fulfillment. Fiction and drama of the past decade reveal that sexual love today generates a vast amount of bitterness and discontent. A novel of satisfying love, or even of a relationship not riddled with torment, is a rarity. Admittedly, writers are aware that conflict and frustration are more dramatic than the serenity of fulfillment. The activities of sexual adventurers plainly interest more readers than do those of considerate and faithful lovers. Whether in the made-to-order sensationalism of a Harold Robbins or a Jacqueline Susann or in the novels (or plays) of such writers as Baldwin, Albee, Mailer, Roth, and Oates, the love relationship is seen as a neurotic encounter between cruel or pathetic human beings. It is hard to say how much of this is a faithful picture of love in a disturbed age and how much is simply the result of the freedom of writers to record those dark areas of sexuality that have long been kept hidden.

Painters and to a lesser extent sculptors have always had a license to dwell on the sensuous, and one of their favorite ways of exploiting this privilege has been to paint or sculpture nude women. But what each artist has seen in nudes has differed greatly and has often reflected—or betrayed—the spirit of the age. Where a Greek Aphrodite was a miraculous fusion of the physical and the spiritual, where a nude by Titian was unabashedly sensual, and a "Greek Slave" by a nineteenth-century American was sexlessly marmoreal, a nude by an American artist of our time—if he does figurative painting at all—is likely to be casual, realistic, objective. Stripped of all "extraneous" associations, such as her femininity, she is little more than another piece of furniture. The fact that she is nude is of no importance.

But at the moment most American artists are not interested in the human figure, so that any urge that people may have to look at pictures on sexual themes is being satisfied by reproductions of erotic Indian temple sculpture, the "pillow books" that were traditionally given to Japanese brides, and such collections as the relentlessly intimate views of men and women in Picasso's *347*.

For those with less erotic tastes there is a vast array of mass magazines and pornographic illustrated paperbacks. Their sexual bait ranges from the often wondrously endowed "glamour girls" of *Playboy, Esquire,* and the mass picture magazines to paperback covers displaying the most explicit photographs of every form of sexual exhibitionism. Where the amorous figures on ancient Greek vases have a matchless grace and Indian temple carvings an ecstatic intensity, their American counterparts, done in color photography, are slick (in the mass magazines) or raw (in the pornographic paperbacks). Americans have of course made sensitive photographs of nude women, but these rarely appear in the mass media.

For at least fifty years the tide has been running out on government censorship. A long series of increasingly tolerant court decisions (the latest one permits consenting individuals to exchange obscene materials by mail, thus repudiating the ninety-seven-year-old Comstock Act) has brought the state to the point of allowing men to print, paint, sculpture, and photograph whatever they wish and to make the results available to anyone except minors. Implicit here is the recognition of so-called pornography as strictly a private matter.

Such a view calls into question the whole concept of obscenity and pornography as a social evil. It suggests that these concepts are rather matters of taste and individual judgment than of law or police action. It further suggests that the test of their social worth is not whether they square with some vague and arbitrary definition of what's moral or immoral but whether they injure anyone or lead to crime.

Of major importance in this connection was the report in October, 1970, of a Federal Commission on Obscenity and Pornography that there was no evidence that exposure to pornography caused crime, deliquency, sexual deviancy, or severe emotional disturbances or did damage to the morals of individuals or of the community. It recommended the elimination of all restrictions on adults who wish to obtain sexually explicit books, pictures, and films. Americans, it found, deeply value the right of each individual to decide what books he wishes to read or what pictures or films he wishes to see. The report recommended laws against the sale of pornography to young persons, against the public display of sexuality explicit pictures and the mailing of sexually explicit, unsolicited advertisements. But it deplored attempts to adjust communication to a level suitable for children.[28]

The radical-seeming conclusion of the commission did not in fact go much beyond United States Supreme Court decisions that an adult could not be denied the right to possess obscene material or to receive information and ideas "regardless of their social worth." The court has also declared that the protection of minors should be limited to statutes that do not confine adults to literature proper only for children. The court has even anticipated the doubt that obscenity incites sexual crimes. Indeed, in his concurring opinion on the *Fanny Hill* case, Supreme Court Justice William O. Douglas observed that it would be futile to try to remove "all that might possibly stimulate antisocial conduct." He pointed out that John George Haight, the British "vampire murderer," claimed he was inspired by the "voluptuous" procedure of an Anglican High Church service, and that a German rapist and murderer, Heinrich Pommerenke, testified that he had been stimulated by Cecil B. De Mille's *Ten Commandments,* particularly the scene in which women dance around the Golden Calf.[29] Both the commission and the court were evidently aware, as Kinsey had reported in 1953, that there had been no increase in the proportion of sex crimes to population.[30]

What is of the greatest significance is that a Presidential commission (obviously appointed with the expectation that it would recommend new curbs) declared, in effect, that society should no longer try to regulate the sexual interests or activities of adults. The investigations on which the majority report was based may have had their flaws, revealing, once again, how difficult it is to measure human motivation; but the objections of the minority were mainly such assertions as that the report was a license to "peddlers of smut" to destroy the moral fiber of the nation. The minority suggested, as prohibitionists always have, that the "fiber" of a nation is so delicate that it can be destroyed by pornography, that other adults are incapable of deciding for themselves what they want to read or view, and that if all sexually explicit material were banned, virtue would be served.

The implication of the majority report was that sexuality cannot be regulated by law or moral judgment. It also conveyed a sense of weariness with the tendency of prohibitionists to exaggerate the effects of obscenity. As two members of the Commission said of pornography: "We find it to be a nuisance rather than an evil. The American public apparently agrees."

Compared to many other influences[31] to which children—and adults—are constantly exposed in all media, the pornography that may fall into the hands of young people seems inconsequential. As everyone knows, there is no censorship whatever of television programs, movies, or comic books that feature and often glorify the murderous violence of men at war or the "good men" in Westerns, or the ruthlessness of international spies and romanticized gangsters—all of which children ape in their games. If we must suppress pornography, should we not also suppress all films, pictures, and books that countenance cruelty, violence, and any other activity that might inflame someone at some time to an antisocial act.

If there is any danger in the free expression of sexuality, it is not so much in pornography as in the commercialized use of sex, of which pornography is only a minor aspect. Sex—and chiefly woman as a sexual object—has become a main instrument of sales in all media. In advertisements for underwear, bathing suits, films, plays, cosmetics, and perfumes—the latter with erotic names—the sexual theme is loud and clear.[32] This is a new kind of prostitution—the use of a woman's body to sell the goods and services of an affluent society. Added to these are the movies that use performers known only for their uninhibited sexuality, novels manufactured by specialists in eroticism, and now sex manuals that sell expertise. Such a use dehumanizes not only women but all sexuality. Above all, it dissociates sexuality from all those qualities that have made it most precious: the intimacy, sympathy, and warmth of a one-to-one relationship, the sense of cherishing someone and being cherished above all other individuals, the sense of maximum commitment.

In the face of ever-increasing commercialization and mechanization, such an ideal sexual relationship may prove ever harder to achieve. But the love of the sexes is a transcending force and finds ways to fulfill itself amidst the most unpromising circumstances—in short, to build a heaven in hell's despite.

References

Background

Chapter 1 God, the Flesh, and the Puritan Way

1. Wayland Young, *Eros Denied: Sex in Western Society* (New York, Grove Press, 1964), pp. 200–2.
2. L. J. Ludovici, *The Final Inequality* (New York, W. W. Norton, 1965), pp. 52–60.
3. *The Code of 1650, being a compilation of the Earliest Laws and Orders of the General Court of Connecticut . . . in 1638–9 . . . commonly called Blue Laws* (Hartford, 1822).
4. *Bradford's History of Plymouth Plantation,* William T. Davis, ed. (New York, Scribner's, 1908), p. 364.
5. Perry Miller, *The New England Mind: The Seventeenth Century* (Cambridge, Harvard University Press, 1939), p. 472.
6. *Ibid.*, p. 472.
7. *Journal of Jasper Danckaerts,* 1679–80, B. B. James and J. F. Jameson, eds. (New York, Scribner's, 1913), entry for July 23, 1680.
8. Emil Oberholtzer, Jr., *Delinquent Souls* (New York, Columbia University Press, 1956), p. 141.
9. Quoted in Arthur A. Calhoun, *A Social History of the American Family* (New York, 1917–19), Vol. I, pp. 130–31.
10. Andrew Sinclair, *The Better Half* (New York, Harper & Row, 1965), p. 6.
11. Calhoun, *op. cit.*, Vol. I, p. 134.
12. *Ibid.*, Vol. I, p. 137.
13. Leo Markun, *Mrs. Grundy* (New York, D. Appleton & Co., 1930), p. 358.
14. *Ibid.*, quoted on p. 433.
15. *Ibid.*, pp. 445–46.
16. *The Journal of Nicholas Cresswell* (New York, Dial Press, 1924), entry for July 9, 1777, p. 249. *See also* Sinclair, *op. cit.*, p. 7.
17. Arthur Train, *Puritan's Progress* (New York, Scribner's, 1931), p. 128.

REFERENCES

Chapter 2 From Cotton Mather to Mrs. Grundy

No references.

Part 1 Prudery: The Denial of Eros

Chapter 3 The Worship of Respectability

1. Calhoun, *op. cit.*, Vol. II, p. 159.
2. Thomas Morton's *Speed the Plough.*
3. Walter S. Houghton, *The Victorian Frame of Mind* (New Haven, Yale University Press, 1957), p. 423.
4. James Fenimore Cooper, *Notions of the Americans* (Philadelphia, 1828), Vol. I, p. 105.
5. Augusta J. Evans Wilson, *St. Elmo* (New York and London, 1867), p. 394.
6. Harriet Martineau, *Society in America,* Seymour M. Lipsett, ed. (New York, Doubleday, 1962), p. 291.
7. Frederick Marryat, *A Diary in America* (New York, Alfred A. Knopf, 1962), p. 419.
8. Leslie A. Fiedler, *Love and Death in the American Novel* (New York, Dell, revised edition, 1966).
9. Francis J. Grund, *Aristocracy in America* (New York, Harper Torchbook, 1959), p. 157.
10. Marryat, *op. cit.,* pp. 431–32.
11. Martineau, *op. cit.,* p. 342.
12. Horace Bushnell, *Woman's Suffrage; the Reform Against Nature* (New York, 1869), p. 142.
13. Quoted by Lionel Stevenson in "Prude's Progress," *Virginia Quarterly Review,* Vol. 13 (1937), p. 258.

Chapter 4 Exorcising the Devils of Desire

1. William W. Sanger, *A History of Prostitution* (New York, 1859), pp. 488–89.
2. William Acton, *The Functions and Disorders of the Reproductive Organs* (4th American edition, Philadelphia, 1875), pp. 145–48.
3. William A. Alcott, *The Young Husband* (Boston, 1839), pp. 248–51.
4. Sidney Ditzion, *Marriage, Morals and Sex in America* (New York, Bookman Associates: Twayne Publishers, 1953), pp. 323–24.
5. William A. Alcott, *The Moral Philosophy of Courtship and Marriage* (Boston, 1857), p. 55.
6. Orson Squire Fowler, *Love and Parentage* (New York, 1855), p. 35.
7. Alice B. Stockham, M.D., *Tokology* (Chicago, 1894) pp. 150–60.
8. Thomas Branagan, *The Excellency of the Female Character Vindicated* (Philadelphia, 1808), p. 161.
9. *Letters of Theodore Dwight Weld, Angelica Grimké Weld and Sarah Grimké, 1822–44,* G. H. Barnes and D. L. Dumond, ed. (New York, D. Appleton-Century, 1934) II, p. 533.

10. *Ibid.*, Vol. II, p. 533.
11. *Ibid.*, Vol. II, p. 640.

Chapter 5 Forbidden Ground

1. Cited in Robert Riegel, *Young America 1830–40* (Norman, Oklahoma, University of Oklahoma Press, 1949), p. 311.
2. *Ibid.*, p. 311.
3. George H. Napheys, *The Physical Life of Woman* (Philadelphia, 1869), p. 39.
4. Edward B. Foote, *Medical Common Sense* (New York, 1864), p. 169.
5. Cited by Peter T. Cominos, "Late Victorian Sexual Respectability and the Social System," *International Review of Social History*, Vol. 8 (1963), p. 32.
6. George H. Napheys, *The Transmission of Life* (Philadelphia, 1870), p. 91.
7. Augustus K. Gardner, "Physical Decline of American Women," in *The Knickerbocker*, Vol. LV (January, 1860) p. 49.
8. John Cowan, *The Science of the New Life* (New York, 1869), pp. 110–13.
9. Peter Fryer, *The Birth Controllers* (London, Secker & Warburg, 1965), p. 117.
10. Foote, *op. cit.*, p. 338.
11. Henry N. Guernsey, *Plain Talks on Avoided Subjects* (New York, 1889), p. 105.
12. Henry Pringle, *Theodore Roosevelt* (New York, Harcourt, Brace, 1931), p. 472.
13. Henry Ward Beecher, *Lectures to Young Men* (New York, 1860), p. 205.

Chapter 6 The Word Made Clean

1. Noel Perrin, *Dr. Bowdler's Legacy* (New York, Atheneum Press, 1969), pp. 165–66.
2. *Moreau de St. Méry's American Journey, 1793–98*, trans. and ed. by Kenneth Roberts and Anna M. Roberts (New York, Doubleday, 1947), p. 287.
3. Marryat, *op. cit.*, pp. 273–74.
4. Marianne Finch, *An Englishwoman's Experience in America* (London, 1853), p. 335.
5. Frances Trollope, *Domestic Manners of the Americans* (New York, Alfred A. Knopf, 1949), p. 92.
6. Ruth E. Finley, *The Lady of Godey's: Sarah Josepha Hale* (Philadelphia, J. B. Lippincott, 1931), pp. 207–8.
7. A. J. Graves, *Woman in America* (New York, 1842), pp. 27–8.
8. Dixon Wecter, *The Saga of American Society* (New York, Scribner's, 1937), p. 316.
9. *Ibid.*, p. 316.
10. H. L. Mencken, *The American Language* (New York, Alfred A. Knopf, 1941), p. 303.
11. H. L. Mencken, *Supplement I: The American Language* (New York, Alfred A. Knopf, 1945), p. 654.
12. Mencken, *The American Language*, p. 304.

13. Allen Walker Read, "Noah Webster as a Euphemist," *Dialect Notes,* Vol. VI, Part III, p. 385.
14. *Ibid.,* p. 386.
15. *The Family Shakspere,* Thomas Bowdler, ed. (London, 1818). See title page and Preface.
16. *Gibbon's Roman History,* Thomas Bowdler, ed. (London, 1825). Introduction. See also Perrin, *op. cit.,* p. 86.

Chapter 7 Literature and the Price of Purity

1. Quoted in Houghton, *op. cit.,* p. 357.
2. Perrin, *op. cit.,* p. 5.
3. Daniel Wise, *The Young Man's Counsellor* (New York, 1850), pp. 166, 172, 174.
4. Isaac Candler, *A Summary View of America* (London, 1824), p. 74.
5. Mrs. Trollope, *op. cit.,* p. 91.
6. Harriet Beecher Stowe, *The Vindication of Lady Byron* (Boston, 1870).
7. Branagan, *op. cit.,* p. 149.
8. Cited in Frank Luther Mott, *Golden Multitudes* (New York, Macmillan, 1947), p. 105.
9. Fiedler, pp. 67–8.
10. Charles Brockden Brown, *Wieland, or The Transformation* (New York, 1798), p. 129.
11. Charles Brockden Brown, *Ormond,* Ernest Marchand, ed. (New York, American Book Co., 1937), p. 234.
12. Charles Brockden Brown, *Jane Talbot* (Philadelphia, 1887), p. 71.
13. Fiedler, *op. cit.,* pp. 212 ff.
14. R. W. B. Lewis, *The American Adam* (Chicago, The University of Chicago Press, 1955), pp. 103–4.
15. Randall Stewart, *Nathaniel Hawthorne* (New Haven, Yale University Press, 1948), p. 83.
16. Cited in Fred Lewis Pattee, *The Feminine Fifties* (Fort Washington, New York, 1940), p. 30.
17. Wise, *op. cit.,* pp. 210–18.
18. Beecher, *op. cit.,* pp. 176–78.
19. Quoted in Paul S. Boyer, *Purity in Print: Book Censorship in America* (New York, Scribner's Sons, 1969), p. 18, from a letter by William S. Walsh to Jeanette L. Gilder, February 2, 1889, in Gilder Papers XI, Schlesinger Library, Radcliffe College.
20. Justin Kaplan, *Mr. Clemens and Mark Twain* (New York, Simon & Schuster, 1966), p. 93 n.
21. Charles Butler, *The American Lady* (Philadelphia, 1849), p. 114.
22. Sanger, *op. cit.,* p. 529.
23. Ibid., p. 521.
24. Mott, *op. cit.,* pp. 110–11.
25. Gay Wilson Allen, *The Solitary Singer: A Critical Biography of Whitman* (New York, Macmillan, 1955), p. 237.

26. *Ibid.*, pp. 322, 348.
27. Edmund Clarence Stedman, *Poets of America* (Boston and New York, 1885), p. 366.
28. *Ibid.*, p. 366.
29. *Ibid.*, p. 367.
30. *The Journals of Ralph Waldo Emerson,* Robert N. Linscott, ed. (New York, The Modern Library, 1960), pp. 8 and 267.
31. *Ibid.*, p. 348.
32. *Ibid.*, p. 59.
33. *Ibid.*, p. 181.
34. *Ibid.*, pp. 111–12.
35. *Familiar Letters of Henry David Thoreau,* F. B. Sanborn, ed. (Boston, 1894). Letter to Harrison Blake, September, 1852.
36. Henry Seidel Canby, *Thoreau* (Boston, Beacon Press, 1939), pp. 261–62.
37. Joseph Wood Krutch, *Henry David Thoreau* (New York, William Sloane Associates, 1948), p. 204.
38. *Familiar Letters, op. cit.*, p. 250.
39. Mark Twain, *A Tramp Abroad* (New York, The Author's National Edition), p. 244.
40. Mark Twain, *The Innocents Abroad* (New York, The Author's National Edition), p. 138.
41. *Mark Twain's Notebook,* Albert B. Paine, ed. (New York, Harpers, 1935) p. 163. *See also* Kaplan, *op. cit.*, pp. 221–23.
42. Mark Twain, *Letters from the Earth,* Bernard De Voto, ed. (New York, Harper & Row, 1962), pp. 155–56.
43. Kaplan, *op. cit.*, p. 323.
44. *Ibid.*, p. 193.
45. Samuel Charles Webster, *Mark Twain, Business Man* (Boston, Little, Brown, 1946), p. 260.
46. Kaplan, *op. cit.*, p. 268.
47. Twain, *Letters from the Earth*, pp. 17–18.
48. *Ibid.*, pp. 38–41.
49. Mark Twain, *Mark Twain in Eruption,* Bernard De Voto, ed. (New York, Harper & Brothers, 1940), p. 315.
50. Maxwell Geismar, *Henry James and the Jacobites* (Boston, Houghton Mifflin, 1963).
51. Fiedler, *op. cit.*, p. 344.
52. *The Notebooks of Henry James,* F. O. Matthiessen and K. B. Murdock, eds. (New York, George Braziller, 1955), pp. 54–6.
53. *Ibid.*, pp. 76–7.
54. *Ibid.*, pp. 169–76.
55. A. K. Fiske, "Profligacy in Fiction," *The North American Review,* Vol. 131 (July, 1880), pp. 79–88.
56. William Dean Howells, *Criticism and Fiction* (New York, 1891), p. 128.
57. *Ibid.*, p. 152.
58. *Ibid.*, p. 160.
59. Edwin H. Cady, *The Realist at War: The Mature Years, 1885–1920, of William Dean Howells* (Syracuse, Syracuse University Press, 1958), p. 124.

REFERENCES

Chapter 8 The Theater and Other "Gates to Debauchery"

1. Barnard Hewitt, *Theatre U. S. A. 1668–1957* (New York, McGraw-Hill, 1959), p. 30.
2. *Ibid.*, p. 46.
3. St. Méry, *op. cit.*, p. 347.
4. Grund, *op. cit.*, p. 76.
5. Markun, *op. cit.*, p. 462.
6. Riegel, *op. cit.*, p. 374.
7. Sir Charles Lyell, *A Second Visit to the United States of North America* (London, 1850), Vol. I, p. 197.
8. Beecher, *op. cit.*, p. 235.
9. Reverend Rufus W. Clark, *Lectures to Young Men* (Boston, 1853), pp. 119–22.
10. Trollope, *op. cit.*, p. 92.
11. Riegel, *op. cit.*, p. 382.
12. Trollope, *op. cit.*, pp. 134–35.
13. *Ibid.*, quoted on p. 135 n.
14. Riegel, *op. cit.*, p. 382, quoting from J. W. Howe's *Reminiscences*.
15. Increase Mather, *An Arrow Against Profane and Promiscuous Dancing* (Boston, 1684), p. 1.
16. Martineau, *op. cit.*, p. 342.
17. Alexander Mackay, *The Western World* (Philadelphia, 1849), p. 141.

Chapter 9 The Shame of the Body

1. Markun, *op. cit.*, pp. 265–66.
2. Henry W. Lawrence, *The Not-Quite Puritans* (Boston, Little, Brown, 1928), p. 6.
3. Wecter, *op. cit.*, p. 301.
4. Rufus Griswold, *The Republican Court* (New York, 1855), p. 87.
5. Branagan, *op. cit.*, pp. 29–31, 33.
6. Gordon Rattray Taylor, *The Angel-Makers* (London, Heinemann, 1958), p. 261.
7. Finley, *op. cit.*, p. 134.
8. Mackay, *op. cit.*, p. 139.
9. Anthony Trollope, *North America* (New York, Alfred A. Knopf, 1951), p. 28.
10. Finley, *op. cit.*, pp. 102–5.
11. Sinclair, *op. cit.*, p. 129.

Chapter 10 Triumph of the Fig Leaf

1. Lloyd Goodrich, *Thomas Eakins: His Life and Work* (New York, Whitney Museum, 1933), pp. 55 ff.
2. Oliver W. Larkin, *Art and Life in America* (New York, Rinehart, 1949), pp. 105, 130.
3. Mrs. Trollope, *op. cit.*, p. 268.
4. Canby, *op. cit.*, pp. 337–38.
5. Markun, *op. cit.*, p. 478.

6. Larkin, *op. cit.*, p. 178.
7. Marryat, *op. cit.*, p. 272.
8. Larkin, *op. cit.*, p. 131.
9. Henry James, *William Wetmore Story* (Boston, 1903), Vol. I, p. 114.
10. Larkin, *op. cit.*, p. 180.
11. Horatio Greenough, *The Travels, Observations, and Experiences of a Yankee Stonecutter* (New York, 1852), p. 19.
12. Stewart, *op. cit.*, p. 171.
13. *The Complete Novels and Selected Tales of Nathaniel Hawthorne* (New York, The Modern Library, 1937), p. 784.
14. Stewart, *op. cit.*, p. 197.
15. Hawthorne, *op. cit.*, p. 660.
16. Stewart, *op. cit.*, p. 196.
17. Kenneth Clark, *The Nude: A Study in Ideal Form* (New York, Doubleday, Anchor edition, 1956), pp. 130–35.
18. Twain, *A Tramp Abroad*, pp. 243–45.
19. Goodrich, *op. cit.*, pp. 58–60.
20. *Ibid.*, pp. 86–89.
21. James Thomas Flexner, *Nineteenth Century American Painting* (New York, G. P. Putnam's Sons, 1970), p. 223.
22. *The Education of Henry Adams* (Boston, Houghton Mifflin, 1906), p. 385.

Chapter 11 The Pathology of Prurience: Comstock and His Kin

1. *Memoir . . . of the Late Rev. John R. M'Dowall* (New York, 1838), pp. 67, 82, 96.
2. *Ibid.*, p. 101. *See also* Robert Allerton Parker, *A Yankee Saint: John Humphrey Noyes and the Oneida Community* (New York, G. P. Putnam's Sons, 1935), pp. 69 ff.
3. J. R. McDowall, *Magdalen Facts* (New York, Privately printed, 1832).
4. *Memoir . . . of the Late Rev. John R. M'Dowall, op. cit.*, pp. 222–25.
5. *McDowall's Journal*, April, 1834. *See also* Parker, *op. cit.*, p. 72.
6. Martineau, *op. cit.*, p. 337.
7. Heywood Broun and Margaret Leech, *Anthony Comstock: Roundsman of the Lord* (New York, Albert and Charles Boni, 1927), p. 15.
8. *Ibid.*, pp. 47 ff.
9. *Ibid.*, p. 79.
10. *Ibid.*, p. 16.
11. Anthony Comstock, *Traps for the Young* (New York, 1883), p. 26.
12. Broun and Leech, *op. cit.*, pp. 155–56.
13. Comstock, *op. cit.*, p. 163.
14. Broun and Leech, *op. cit.*, pp. 172–74.
15. Comstock, *op. cit.*, p. 171.
16. Broun and Leech, *op. cit.*, p. 223.
17. *Ibid.*, p. 224.
18. David Loth, *The Erotic in Literature* (New York, Julian Messner, 1961), p. 146.
19. Broun and Leech, *op. cit.*, pp. 230–32.

20. Leon Harris, *Only to God: The Extraordinary Life of Godfrey Lowell Cabot* (New York, Atheneum, 1967), p. 333.
21. *Ibid.*, p. 292.
22. *Ibid.*, pp. 228–29.
23. *Ibid.*, p. 323.

Part 2 The Partisans of Love

Chapter 12 The Children of Reason

1. George R. Preedy, *This Shining Woman: Mary Wollstonecraft Godwin* (New York, D. Appleton-Century, 1937), pp. 31–2.
2. *Ibid.*, p. 116.
3. Ludovici, *op. cit.*, p. 179.
4. Preedy, *op. cit.*, p. 160.
5. Mary Wollstonecraft Godwin, *A Vindication of the Rights of Woman* (New York, 1890), p. 197.
6. *Ibid.*, p. 104.
7. *Ibid.*, p. 185.
8. Ralph M. Wardle, *Mary Wollstonecraft* (Lawrence, Kansas, University of Kansas Press, 1951), p. 276.
9. Ditzion, *op. cit.*, p. 41 n.
10. Sinclair, *op. cit.*, p. 56.
11. Charles Brockden Brown, *Alcuin: A Dialogue* (New York, 1798), p. 71.
12. Brown, *Jane Talbot*, pp. 70–71.
13. *Complete Poetical Works of Percy Bysshe Shelley*, George E. Woodberry, ed. (Boston, Houghton Mifflin, 1901), p. 597.
14. Newman Ivey White, *Portrait of Shelley* (New York, Alfred A. Knopf, 1945), pp. 417–19.
15. Ditzion, *op. cit.*, pp. 73–4.

Chapter 13 The Free Enquirers

1. A. J. G. Perkins and Theresa Wolfson, *Frances Wright: Free Enquirer* (New York, Harper & Brothers, 1939), p. 64.
2. *Ibid.*, pp. 89 ff.
3. *Ibid.*, p. 126.
4. *Ibid.*, p. 149.
5. *Ibid.*, p. 152.
6. *Ibid.*, pp. 170–71.
7. *Ibid.*, p. 193.
8. Mrs. Trollope, *op. cit.*, pp. 70–73.
9. Yuri Suhl, *Ernestine L. Rose* (New York, Reynal, 1959), p. 47.
10. Perkins and Wolfson, *op. cit.*, pp. 232–33, 250.
11. Ditzion, *op. cit.*, pp. 93–94.
12. Perkins and Wolfson, *op. cit.*, p. 369.
13. *Ibid.*, p. 153.
14. *Elizabeth Cady Stanton as Revealed in Her Letters, Diary and Reminiscences,*

Theodore Stanton and Harriot Stanton Blatch, ed. (New York, Harper & Brothers, 1922), Vol. II, p. 61.

Chapter 14 Love Without Fear

1. St. Méry, *op. cit.*, pp. 314–15.
2. Fryer, *op. cit.*, p. 68.
3. Ludovici, *op. cit.*, p. 204.
4. Fryer, *op. cit.*, p. 74.
5. *Ibid.*, p. 76.
6. Rowland Hill Harvey, *Robert Owen: Social Idealist* (Berkeley, University of California Press, 1949), pp. 64–66.
7. *Ibid.*, pp. 157–58.
8. *The Free Enquirer*, May 28, 1831.
9. Fryer, *op. cit.*, p. 91.
10. Robert Dale Owen, *Moral Physiology* (New York, 1841), p. 5.
11. *Ibid.*, p. 7.
12. *Ibid.*, pp. 18–19.
13. *Ibid.*, p. 44.
14. Fryer, *op. cit.*, p. 93.
15. Richard Wilson Leopold, *Robert Dale Owen* (Cambridge, Mass., Harvard University Press, 1940), p. 80.
16. Robert E. Riegel, "The American Father of Birth Control," *The New England Quarterly*, Vol. VI (1933), pp. 470 ff.
17. Charles Knowlton, *Fruits of Philosophy* (New York, 1832), pp. 18–19.
18. *Ibid.*, p. 37.
19. Fryer, *op. cit.*, p. 104.
20. *Ibid.*, pp. 105, 162.
21. Sinclair, *op. cit.*, p. 130.
22. Fryer, *op. cit.*, p. 114.
23. *Ibid.* The advertisement is reproduced facing page 61.
24. Thaddeus B. Wakeman, *In Memoriam of Edward Bliss Foote, M.D.* (New York, 1907), p. 9.
25. Edward B. Foote, *Medical Common Sense* (New York, 1864), pp. 272–75.
26. *Ibid.*, pp. 339 ff.
27. Fryer, *op. cit.*, p. 117.
28. Foote, *op. cit.*, back pages (unnumbered).
29. Fryer, *op. cit.*, p. 118.
30. Edward B. Foote, Jr., *The Radical Remedy in Social Science, or Borning Better Babies through Regulating Reproduction by Controlling Conception* (New York, 1886).

Chapter 15 Women Militant

1. Eleanor Flexner, *Century of Struggle: The Women's Rights Movement in the United States* (Cambridge, Mass., Belknap Press, Harvard University, 1966), p. 16.
2. Ludovici, *op. cit.*, p. 193.

REFERENCES

3. Mason Wade, *Margaret Fuller: Whetstone of Genius* (New York, The Viking Press), pp. 58 ff.
4. *Ibid.*, p. 80.
5. *Margaret Fuller: American Romantic. A Selection from Her Writings and Correspondence*, Perry Miller, ed. (New York, Doubleday Anchor Books, 1963), p. xviii.
6. Wade, *op. cit.*, pp. 80–81.
7. *Ibid.*, p. 88.
8. *The Writings of Margaret Fuller*, Mason Wade, ed. (New York, The Viking Press, 1941), pp. 214–15.
9. *Ibid.*, p. 199.
10. Wade, *op. cit.*, pp. 162–70.
11. Joseph Jay Diess, *The Roman Years of Margaret Fuller* (New York, Thomas Y. Crowell, 1969), pp. 68–71, 96–98.
12. Wade, *op. cit.*, pp. 280–81.
13. Robert E. Riegel, *American Feminists* (Lawrence, Kansas, The University of Kansas Press, 1963), pp. 21–22.
14. Stanton and Blatch, *op. cit.*, Vol. II, pp. 59–60.
15. *Ibid.*, Vol. I, pp. 141 ff.
16. Sinclair, *op. cit.*, p. 58.
17. Stanton and Blatch, *op. cit.*, Vol. II, pp. 82, 270.
18. Riegel, *American Feminists*, p. 57.
19. *Ibid.*, p. 58. *See also* Stanton and Blatch, *op. cit.*, Vol. II, p. 49.
20. Stanton and Blatch, *op. cit.*, Vol. II, p. 210.
21. *Ibid.*, Vol. II, p. 53.
22. *Ibid.*, Vol. II, p. 48.
23. Riegel, *American Feminists*, p. 59.
24. Stanton and Blatch, *op. cit.*, p. 41.
25. *Ibid.*, Vol. II, p. 131.
26. *Ibid.*, Vol. I, pp. 26–27, 47–49.
27. *Ibid.*, Vol. II, p. 40.
28. *The Woman's Bible*, Elizabeth Cady Stanton, Lillie Devereux Blake, Rev. Phebe A. Hansford and others, ed. (New York, 1895–1898) Part I, Preface, and p. 20.
29. Sinclair, *op. cit.*, p. 200.
30. *The Woman's Bible*, Part II, p. 113.
31. *Ibid.*, Part II, p. 114.
32. Sinclair, *op. cit.*, p. 199. *See also* Riegel, *American Feminists*, p. 61.
33. Riegel, *American Feminists*, pp. 52 ff.
34. Ludovici, *op. cit.*, pp. 151, 196.
35. Elinor Rice Hays, *Those Extraordinary Blackwells* (New York, Harcourt, Brace & World, 1967), pp. 66–70.
36. *Ibid.*, pp. 181–82.
37. *Ibid.*, p. 211.
38. Elinor Rice Hays, *Morning Star: A Biography of Lucy Stone* (Harcourt, Brace & World, 1961), p. 14.
39. *Ibid.*, p. 52.

40. Sinclair, *op. cit.*, pp. 67–68.
41. Hays, *Morning Star*, pp. 261, 95.

Chapter 16 Spiritual Brides and Earthly Lovers

1. Edward Deming Andrews, *The People Called Shakers* (New York, Dover Publications edition, 1963), pp. 6–9.
2. *Ibid.*, p. 12.
3. *Ibid.*, p. 22.
4. *Ibid.*, p. 179.
5. Charles Dickens, *American Notes* (Philadelphia, no date) The Biographical Edition, Vol. VIII, pp. 170 ff.
6. Fawn M. Brodie, *No Man Knows My History: The Life of Joseph Smith* (New York, Alfred A. Knopf, 1960), pp. 306–7.
7. Kimball Young, *Isn't One Wife Enough? The Story of Mormon Polygamy* (New York, Henry Holt, 1954), pp. 92–3.
8. *Ibid.*, p. 330.
9. Jules Remy, *A Journey to Great-Salt-Lake City* (London, 1861), Vol. II, pp. 99–104.
10. Young, *op. cit.*, p. 446.
11. *Ibid.*, p. 291.
12. *Ibid.*, p. 280.
13. *Ibid.*, p. 126.
14. *Ibid.*, p. 113.
15. *Ibid.*, p. 108.
16. *Ibid.*, pp. 183–84.
17. *Ibid.*, p. 122.
18. *Ibid.*, p. 201.
19. *Ibid.*, p. 203.
20. Markun, *op. cit.*, p. 557. *See also* M. R. Werner, *Brigham Young* (New York, Harcourt, Brace, 1925), p. 357.
21. William Hepworth Dixon, *Spiritual Wives* (London and Philadelphia, 1868), pp. 354–55.
22. John Humphrey Noyes, *History of American Socialisms* (Philadelphia, 1870), p. 539. *See also* Parker, *op. cit.*, p. 118.
23. Parker, *op. cit.*, p. 36.
24. *Ibid.*, p. 44.
25. *Ibid.*, pp. 54–55.
26. *Ibid.*, p. 64.
27. John Humphrey Noyes, *Male Continence* (Oneida, New York, 1872), pp. 7–8.
28. *Ibid.*, p. 11.
29. Dixon, *op. cit.*, pp. 289–92.
30. *Ibid.*, pp. 292 ff.
31. Parker, *op. cit.*, p. 39.
32. Dixon, *op. cit.*, p. 313.
33. *Ibid.*, pp. 335–37.

34. Noyes, *History of American Socialisms,* p. 628.
35. *Ibid.,* p. 624.
36. Parker, *op. cit.,* pp. 183–84.
37. Noyes, *Male Continence,* p. 18.
38. Parker, *op. cit.,* pp. 253 ff.
39. *Ibid.,* pp. 268–70.
40. *Ibid.,* pp. 255–56.

Chapter 17 The Extremists

1. Johann Wolfgang von Goethe, *Elective Affinities,* trans. by Elizabeth Mayer and Louise Bogan (Chicago, Henry Regnery, 1963).
2. Verne Dyson, *A Century of Brentwood* (Brentwood, Long Island, Brentwood Village Press, 1952), pp. 40 ff.
3. *Ibid.,* p. 34.
4. *Ibid.,* pp. 83–88.
5. *Ibid.,* p. 89.
6. William Baillie, *Josiah Warren: The First American Anarchist* (New York, 1906), p. 134.
7. M. Edgeworth Lazarus, *Love vs. Marriage* (New York, 1852), pp. 102, 111 ff. *See also* Ditzion, *op. cit.,* p. 330.
8. Dyson, *op. cit.,* pp. 71 ff.
9. Henry James, Horace Greeley, and Stephen Pearl Andrews, *Love, Marriage, and Divorce: A Discussion* (New York, 1889), pp. 24–33.
10. *Ibid.,* pp. 34–36, 51.
11. *Ibid.,* p. 92.
12. *Ibid.,* pp. 8–11.
13. *Ibid.,* pp. 106–10.
14. Thomas Low Nichols, M.D., *Forty Years of American Life, 1821–1861* (New York, Stackpole Sons, 1937), p. 196.
15. Philip Gleason, "From Free-Love to Catholicism: Dr. and Mrs. T. L. Nichols at Yellow Springs," *The Ohio Historical Quarterly,* Vol. 71 (October, 1961), p. 284.
16. Thomas L. Nichols, *Women, in All Ages and Nations* (New York, 1849), pp. 208–19, 229.
17. T. L. Nichols and Mary S. Gove Nichols, *Marriage* (Cincinnati, 1854), pp. 11–15.
18. *Ibid.,* pp. 99–104.
19. *Ibid.,* p. 316.
20. Gleason, *op. cit.,* pp. 285–87.
21. *Ibid.,* pp. 295 ff.
22. *Ibid.,* p. 302.
23. Bertha Monica Stearns, "Two Forgotten New England Reformers," *The New England Quarterly,* Vol. VI (1933), pp. 77–80.
24. T. L. Nichols, *Human Physiology: The Basis of Sanitary and Social Science* (London, 1872), pp. 271–74, 283, 294, 298 ff.
25. Emanie Sachs, *"The Terrible Siren: Victoria Woodhull"* (New York, Harper & Brothers, 1928), pp. 34–38.

26. *Ibid.*, pp. 49–53.
27. Johanna Johnston, *Mrs. Satan* (New York, G. P. Putnam's Sons, 1967), p. 70.
28. *Ibid.*, p. 92.
29. Sachs, *op. cit.*, pp. 96–97.
30. Johnston, *op. cit.*, pp. 128 ff.
31. *Ibid.*, p. 155.
32. *Ibid.*, pp. 205–6.
33. Sachs, *op. cit.*, pp. 238–67.
34. Johnston, *op. cit.*, pp. 255–57.
35. Ezra Hervey Heywood, *Cupid's Yokes: or, The Binding Forces of Conjugal Life* (New York, 1876), pp. 6–8.
36. *Ibid.*, pp. 16–17.
37. *Ibid.*, p. 12.
38. *Dictionary of American Biography* (New York, Scribner's Sons, 1932), Vol. VIII, pp. 609–10.
39. David Goodman Croly, *The Truth About Love* (New York, 1872), p. 10.
40. *Ibid.*, pp. 54–55.
41. *Ibid.*, pp. 57, 95, 104, 119.
42. Dixon, *op. cit.*, pp. 381–85.
43. Arnold T. Schwab, *James Gibbons Huneker: Critic of the Seven Arts* (Stanford, Calif., Stanford University Press, 1963), p. 104.
44. *Ibid.*, p. 103.
45. *Ibid.*, p. 139.

Part 3 Hidden Fires

Chapter 18 The Double Standard

1. William A. Alcott, *The Young Husband*, pp. 248–50.
2. Sinclair, *op. cit.*, p. 111.
3. Croly, *op. cit.*, p. 45.
4. Lately Thomas, *Sam Ward: King of the Lobby* (Boston, Houghton Mifflin, 1965), pp. 44–46, 52, 66.
5. Henry Wikoff, *The Reminiscences of an Idler* (New York, 1880), p. 89.
6. *Ibid.*, p. 84.
7. Richard O'Connor, *The Scandalous Mr. Bennett* (New York, Doubleday, 1962), pp. 134 ff.
8. Herbert R. Mayes, *Alger: A Biography without a Hero* (New York, Macy-Masius, 1928), pp. 82–84.
9. *Ibid.*, pp. 172 ff.
10. Eric John Dingwall, *The American Woman* (New York, Rinehart, 1957), p. 90.
11. Philip Hone, *The Diary of Philip Hone, 1828–1851*, Allan Nevins, ed. (New York, Dodd, Mead, 1927), p. 339.
12. *McDowall's Journal*, *op. cit.*, p. 98.
13. Matthew Hale Smith, *Sunshine and Shadow in New York* (Hartford, Conn., 1868), p. 371.

14. Lloyd Morris, *Incredible New York* (New York, Random House, 1951), pp. 47–49.
15. Smith, *op. cit.*, p. 631.
16. Sanger, *op. cit.*, pp. 549 ff., 569.
17. Edward W. Martin, *Behind the Scenes in Washington* (Philadelphia, Chicago, St. Louis, 1873), pp. 224, 246 ff.
18. Napheys, *The Transmission of Life*, pp. 113–14.
19. Foote, *op. cit.*, pp. 65–71.
20. William Hepworth Dixon, *New America* (Philadelphia, 1867), pp. 267–68.
21. George Ellington, *The Women of New York, or The Under-world of the Great City* (New York, 1869), p. 304.
22. David Macrae, *The Americans at Home* (London, 1871), p. 440 n.
23. Auguste Carlier, *Marriage in the United States* (Boston and New York, 1867), p. 157.
24. Ellington, *op. cit.*, p. 396. *See also* Meade Minnigerode, *The Fabulous Forties, 1840–50* (New York, G. P. Putnam's Sons, 1924), pp. 101–4.
25. Calhoun, *op. cit.*, Vol. III, p. 256.
26. Macrae, *op. cit.*, p. 440.
27. Train, *op. cit.*, p. 397.
28. Morris, *op. cit.*, pp. 216 ff.

Chapter 19 Deviations and Diversions

1. Minnigerode, *op. cit.*, pp. 141–46.
2. Markun, *op. cit.*, p. 497.
3. St. Méry, *op. cit.*, p. 286.
4. Wade, *op. cit.*, p. 90.
5. Sinclair, *op. cit.*, p. 75.
6. *Ibid.*, p. 155.
7. Charles Brockden Brown, *Ormond*, pp. 185 ff.
8. Guernsey, *op. cit.*, p. 82.
9. *Letters of Theodore Dwight Weld . . .*, *op. cit.*, p. 642.
10. Leon Edel, *Henry James*, Vol. IV, *The Treacherous Years: 1895–1901* (London, Rupert Hart-Davis, 1969), pp. 306–16.
11. George Templeton Strong, *Diary of George Templeton Strong*, Allan Nevins and Milton Halsey Thomas, eds. (New York, Macmillan, 1952), Vol. IV, p. 552.
12. John Addington Symonds, *A Problem in Modern Ethics, Being an Inquiry into the Phenomenon of Sexual Inversion* (London, 1896), p. 116 n.
13. Morris, *op. cit.*, p. 219.
14. John Berryman, *Stephen Crane* (New York, William Sloane Associates, 1950), p. 86.

Chapter 20 The Insuppressible Urge

1. Charles Knowles Bolton, *The Elizabeth Whitman Mystery* (Peabody, Mass., Peabody Historical Society, 1912), p. 75.
2. Herbert S. Parmet and Marie B. Hecht, *Aaron Burr: Portrait of an Ambitious Man* (New York, Macmillan, 1967), pp. 311 ff.

3. *Ibid.*, pp. 337–39. See also *The Private Journal of Aaron Burr,* W. K. Bixby, ed. (Rochester, N. Y., 1903), pp. 62, 81, 115, 125, 134, 137.
4. Nathan Schachner, *Alexander Hamilton* (New York, D. Appleton-Century, 1946), pp. 364–72.
5. Hone, *op. cit.*, pp. 206–14.
6. W. A. Swanberg, *Sickles the Incredible* (New York, Charles Scribner's Sons, 1956), pp. 86 ff.
7. *Ibid.*, pp. 50–51.
8. *Ibid.*, p. 67.
9. W. A. Swanberg, *Jim Fisk: The Career of an Improbable Rascal* (New York, Charles Scribner's Sons, 1959), pp. 6–8, 112–14.
10. *Ibid.*, pp. 9–10.
11. *Ibid.*, p. 269.
12. *Ibid.*, pp. 112–13.
13. *Ibid.*, pp. 280–81.
14. Paxton Hibben, *Henry Ward Beecher: An American Portrait* (New York, The Readers Club edition, 1942), pp. 91–92.
15. *Ibid.*, pp. 182–84.
16. Robert Shaplen, *Free Love and Heavenly Sinners* (New York, Alfred A. Knopf, 1954), pp. 42–43.
17. *Ibid.*, p. 57.
18. *Ibid.*, pp. 70, 73.
19. Hibben, *op. cit.*, p. 231.
20. *Ibid.*, p. 250.
21. *Ibid.*, p. 249.
22. *Ibid.*, pp. 268–70.
23. *Ibid.*, p. 281.
24. *Ibid.*, p. 285.
25. *Ibid.*, p. 292.
26. *Ibid.*, p. 307.
27. M. M. Marberry, *The Golden Voice: A Biography of Isaac Kalloch* (New York, Farrar, Straus, 1947), pp. 119–20.
28. *Ibid.*, pp. 195–216.
29. *Ibid.*, p. 276.
30. Allan Nevins, *Grover Cleveland: A Study in Courage* (New York, Dodd, Mead, 1932), pp. 162–69.
31. Anita Leslie, *The Remarkable Mr. Jerome* (New York, Henry Holt, 1934).
32. Richard O'Connor, *Gould's Millions* (New York, Doubleday, 1962), p. 312.
33. Paul Sarnoff, *Russell Sage: The Money King* (New York, Ivan Obolensky, 1965), pp. 265, 287, 288.

Chapter 21 The Forbidden Theme

1. William Hill Brown, *The Power of Sympathy: or, The Triumph of Nature* (Boston, 1789), Dedication.
2. Susannah Rowson, *Charlotte Temple: A Tale of Truth* (New York, 1794), Preface.
3. *Ibid.*, p. 161.

4. Hannah Foster, *The Coquette; or, The History of Eliza Wharton* (Boston, 1854), p. 267.
5. Charles Brockden Brown, *Arthur Mervyn*, Werner Berthoff, ed. (New York, Holt, Rinehart & Winston, 1962), p. x.
6. George Lippard, *The Quaker City; or, The Monks of Monk Hall* (Philadelphia, 1876), Preface to this edition.
7. George Lippard, *New York: The Upper Ten and the Lower Million* (Cincinnati, 1854), Preface.
8. Herman Melville, *White Jacket* (New York, Grove Press, 1952), pp. 353–54.
9. *Ibid.*, Introduction.
10. Herman Melville, *Pierre or The Ambiguities* (New York, Alfred A. Knopf, 1941), p. 215.
11. Walt Whitman, "Song of Myself," Stanza 24.
12. Walt Whitman, "Spontaneous Me."
13. Walt Whitman, "Song of Myself," Stanza 33.
14. Walt Whitman, "I Sing the Body Electric," Stanza 5.
15. Walt Whitman, "Spontaneous Me."
16. Walt Whitman, "Whoever You Are, Holding Me Now in Hand."
17. Walt Whitman, "When I Heard at the Close of Day."
18. Symonds, *op. cit.*, p. 119. See also *Eros: An Anthology of Friendship*, Alistair Sutherland and Patrick Anderson, eds. (London, Anthony Blond, 1961), pp. 290–91.
19. John William De Forest, *Miss Ravenel's Conversion from Secession to Loyalty*, Gordon S. Haight, ed. (New York, Holt, Rinehart and Winston, 1955), pp. 349–50.
20. Robert W. Stallman, *Stephen Crane* (New York, George Braziller, 1968), p. 114.
21. Berryman, *op. cit.*, p. 139.
22. *Ibid.*, p. 89.
23. Steven Marcus, *The Other Victorians: A Study of Sexuality and Pornography in Mid-Nineteenth-Century England* (New York, Basic Books, 1966).

Chapter 22 Hidden South and Turbulent West

1. Frederick Law Olmsted, *A Journey in the Seaboard Slave States* (New York, 1861), pp. 228–29.
2. *Ibid.*, p. 602.
3. John Dixon Long, *Pictures of Slavery* (Philadephia, 1857), p. 231.
4. Calhoun, *op. cit.*, Vol. II, p. 290.
5. Olmsted, Frederick Law, *The Cotton Kingdom, 1861*, Arthur M. Schlesinger, ed. (New York, Alfred A. Knopf, 1962), p. 475 n.
6. Frances Anne Kemble, *Journal of a Residence on a Georgia Plantation in 1838–1839*, John A. Scott, ed. (New York, Alfred A. Knopf, 1961), p. 238.
7. Charles Elliott, *Sinfulness of American Slavery* (Cincinnati, 1851), Vol. II, p. 66.
8. Charles W. Janson, *The Stranger in America* (London, 1807), p. 383.
9. Isaac Candler, *A Summary View of America* (London, 1824), p. 300.
10. Olmsted, *A Journey in the Seaboard Slave States*, p. 602.

References

11. Frederick Douglass, *Narrative of the Life of Frederick Douglass, an American Slave,* 1845 (Cambridge, Mass., Harvard University Press, 1960), pp. 93–94.
12. Long, *op. cit.*, pp. 261–63.
13. Martineau, *op. cit.*, p. 226, and Calhoun, *op. cit.*, Vol. II, p. 308.
14. Mary Boykin Chesnut, *A Diary from Dixie,* B. A. Williams, ed. (Boston, Houghton Mifflin, 1949), pp. 21–22.
15. Kemble, *op. cit.*, p. 269.
16. Olmsted, *A Journey in the Back Country,* p. 84.
17. Douglass, *op. cit.*, pp. 29–30.
18. Kemble, *op. cit.*, p. 161.
19. John Lambert, *Travels through Canada and the United States of America in 1806, 1807 and 1808* (London, 1814), p. 173.
20. Richard Hildreth, *Despotism in America* (Boston, 1840), pp. 165–66.
21. Kemble, *op. cit.*, pp. 249–50.
22. Olmsted, *A Journey in the Seaboard Slave States,* p. 619.
23. Janson, *op. cit.*, pp. 379–80.
24. Olmsted, *A Journey in the Seaboard Slave States,* pp. 506–7.
25. Martineau, *op. cit.*, pp. 224–25.
26. Olmsted, *The Cotton Kingdom,* p. 238.
27. Philo Tower, *Slavery Unmasked* (Rochester, 1856), pp. 335, 338–39.
28. A. T. Morgan, *Yazoo; or, On the Picket Line of Freedom in the South* (Washington, D. C., 1884), pp. 88–89, 91, 342 ff., 446.
29. W. E. B. Du Bois, "Another Study in Black," *The New Review* (1914), p. 112.
30. Calhoun, *op. cit.*, Vol. III, p. 34.
31. *Ibid.*, Vol. III, p. 33.
32. Calvin Hernton, *Sex and Racism in America* (New York, Doubleday, 1965), p. 18.
33. Morgan, *op. cit.*, p. 212.
34. *Negro American Family,* W. E. B. Du Bois, ed. (Atlanta, Ga., Atlanta University Publications, 1908), pp. 37–42.
35. Howard W. Odum, *Social and Mental Traits of the Negro* (New York, Columbia University Press, 1910), p. 175.
36. Daniel Drake, *Pioneer Life in Kentucky* (New York, Henry Schumann, 1948), pp. 183, 185–86, 189, 192.
37. E. W. Howe, *The Story of a Country Town,* Claude M. Simpson, ed. (Cambridge, Mass., Harvard University Press, 1961), pp. 34, 49–51.
38. *Ibid.*, pp. 172–75; and E. W. Howe, *Plain People* (New York, Dodd, Mead, 1929), pp. 62, 177, 173.
39. Quoted in Calhoun, *op. cit.*, Vol. II, p. 152.
40. Dixon, *New America,* pp. 344–46.
41. Webster, *op. cit.*, p. 260.
42. Elizabeth Margo, *Taming the Forty-Niner* (New York, Rinehart, 1955), pp. 33–34, 80.
43. *Ibid.*, pp. 78–82.
44. Herbert Asbury, *The Barbary Coast* (New York, Cardinal Pocketbook edition, Alfred A. Knopf, 1957), pp. 158–72.
45. Margo, *op. cit.*, p. 143.

46. *Ibid.*, pp. 229–31, 174.
47. *Ibid.*, pp. 233–35.
48. Sarah Royce, *A Frontier Lady: Recollections of the Gold Rush and Early California* (New Haven, Conn., Yale University Press, 1932), pp. 109, 115–19.
49. Mary Jane Megquier, *Apron Full of Gold: The Letters of Mary Jane Megquier from San Francisco, 1849–1856*, Robert Glass Cleland, ed. (San Marino, Cal., The Huntington Library, 1949), pp. 27, 48.
50. *Ibid.*, pp. 87, 90, and Introduction, p. VII.
51. Josiah Royce, *California from the Conquest in 1846 to the Second Vigilance Committee in San Francisco. A Study of American Character,* Robert Glass Cleland, ed. (New York, Alfred A. Knopf, 1948), pp. 375–76.

Chapter 23 The Wages of Pretense

1. Sigmund Freud, *Civilization and Its Discontents,* trans. by Joan Riviere (New York, Jonathan Cape and Harrison Smith, 1930), pp. 63, 73.
2. Arnold J. Toynbee, "Why I Dislike Western Civilization," *The New York Times Magazine*, May 10, 1964.
3. Sigmund Freud, *New Introductory Lectures on Psycho-Analysis* (New York, W. W. Norton, 1933), pp. 203–4.
4. Freud, *Civilization and Its Discontents,* p. 142.

Epilogue Seventy Years Later

1. Simone de Beauvoir, *The Second Sex,* trans. by H. M. Parshley (New York, Alfred A. Knopf, 1954), pp. 41–52, 76–80, 716; Betty Friedan, *The Feminine Mystique* (New York, W. W. Norton, 1953), Chapters 5 and 6; and Kate Millett, *Sexual Politics* (London, Rupert Hart-Davis, 1971), pp. 176–203.
2. Vance Packard, *The Sexual Wilderness* (New York, David McKay, 1968), Pocket Book edition, p. 377.
3. *See,* for example, Albert Ellis, *Sex and the Single Man* (New York, Lyle Stuart, 1963) and *The Intelligent Woman's Guide to Man-Hunting* (New York, Lyle Stuart, 1963).
4. Rollo May, *Love and Will* (New York, W. W. Norton, 1969).
5. Thomas and Alice Fleming, "What Kids Still Don't Know about Sex," *Look* (July 28, 1970), p. 60.
6. John Hersey, *Letter to the Alumni* (New York, Alfred A. Knopf, 1970), p. 141.
7. Robert E. Fitch, quoted in Packard, *op. cit.*, p. 16.
8. Packard, *op. cit.*, pp. 256–58.
9. Alfred C. Kinsey, Wardell B. Pomeroy, and Clyde E. Martin, *Sexual Behavior in the Human Male* (Philadephia and London, W. B. Saunders, 1948), pp. 417, 437.
10. Theodoor H. Van de Velde, *Ideal Marriage: Its Physiology and Technique* (New York, Covici, Friede, 1930).
11. "J," *The Sensuous Woman* (New York, Lyle Stuart, 1969), p. 44.
12. William H. Masters and Virginia E. Johnson, *Human Sexual Response* (Boston, Little, Brown, 1966), pp. 12–13.

References

13. Fred Belliveau and Lin Richter, *Understanding Human Sexual Inadequacy* (Boston, Little, Brown, 1970), p. 60.
14. Kinsey *et al., Sexual Behavior in the Human Male,* pp. 624, 628.
15. The leading article in *The New York Times Magazine,* January 17, 1971), was "What It Means to Be a Homosexual," by Merle Miller, a well-known novelist.
16. Gore Vidal, "Number One," *The New York Review of Books* (June 4, 1970).
17. Joseph Epstein, "Homo/Hetero: The Struggle for Sexual Identity," *Harper's Magazine* (September, 1970).
18. Tom Burke, "The New Homosexuality," *Esquire* (December, 1969).
19. *Sexuality and Man,* compiled and edited by Sex Information Council of the United States (New York, Charles Scribner's Sons, 1970), pp. 8–9; Millet, *op. cit.,* pp. 26–33; Betty Rollin, "Motherhood: Who Needs It?" *Look* (September 22, 1970).
20. Lionel Tiger, "Male Dominance? Yes, Alas. A Sexist Plot? No." *The New York Times Magazine* (October 25, 1970); and Jessie Barnard, *The Sex Game* (Englewood Cliffs, New Jersey, Prentice-Hall, 1968), p. 68.
21. Simone de Beauvoir, *op. cit.,* pp. 730–32.
22. Harold Greenwald, *The Elegant Prostitute* (New York, Walker, rev. ed., 1970), p. 195; Jess Stearn, *Sisters of the Night* (New York, Julian Messner, 1956), pp. 164–82; and Kinsey, *et al., Sexual Behavior in the Human Male,* pp. 603–9.
23. Bruce L. Maliver, "Encounter Groupers Up Against the Wall," *The New York Times Magazine,* January 3, 1971.
24. Phil Tracy, "The National Sex and Drug Forum," and Robert B. Miller, "Sex, Sex and Sex," *Commonweal* (November 20, 1970).
25. Margot Hentoff, "The Boys," *The New York Review of Books* (September 24, 1970).
26. For an exploration of this theme in an extreme form, see Kate Millett on Henry Miller, in *Sexual Politics,* pp. 306–9.
27. George Steiner, "Night Words," *Language and Silence* (New York, Atheneum, 1967), pp. 68–77.
28. *The Report of the Commission on Obscenity and Pornography.* As released by the Presidential Commission on September 30, 1970 (New York, Bantam Books, 1970).
29. Cited by Nat Hentoff "Where Do We Go from 'Che!' "? *The New York Times,* May 4, 1969.
30. Kinsey *et al., Sexual Behavior in the Human Female,* p. 18.
31. Susan Sontag, "The Pornographic Imagination," *Partisan Review,* Vol. 34, No. 2 (Spring, 1967), p. 212.
32. Hoffman R. Hays, *The Dangerous Sex: The Myth of Feminine Evil* (New York, G. P. Putnam's Sons, 1964), p. 284.

INDEX

INDEX

Index

INDEX

Index

INDEX

Index

Index